GRACE

GRACE

W.R. GRACE & CO.
The Formative Years
1850–1930

Lawrence A. Clayton

Jameson Books ● Ottawa, Illinois

CREDITS

Illustrations 4 and 6 courtesy of the American Museum of Natural History. Illustration 7 courtesy of the Peabody Museum of Salem. All other illustrations courtesy of W.R. Grace & Co.

Jameson Books are available at special discounts for bulk purchases, promotions, premiums, fund-raising, or educational use.

Jameson Books
722 Columbus Street
Ottawa, Illinois 61350

(815) 434-7905

Library of Congress Cataloging-in-Publication Data

Clayton, Lawrence A.
    Grace: W.R. Grace & Company, 1850-1930.
    Bibliography: p.
    Includes index.
    1. W.R. Grace & Co.—History. 2. International
business enterprises—Peru—History. 3. International
business enterprises—Latin America—History. 4. United
States—Foreign economic relations—Latin America.
5. Latin America—Foreign economic relations—United
States. I. Title.
HD9505.P4C43 1985   338.8'8885   85-14856
ISBN 0-915463-25-3

Printed in the United States of America

To

Deborah Leigh and Stephanie Leigh Clayton

Contents

Preface

This book is a history of the founding and evolution of W. R. Grace & Co., and of its role in the modernization process of Peru. It is a story of bold men who acted on a stage across the Americas, first arriving in Peru as Irish immigrants in the mid-nineteenth century and gradually building up a small mercantile firm founded in the port of Callao into the first multinational in Latin America. Not bounded by small visions, the first Graces, especially William Russell Grace, the founder of the company, also became deeply involved in American politics and inter-American diplomacy as they pursued their dreams. The story is rich and diverse, moving from the guano islands of Peru to the politics of Tammany Hall in New York. In a sense it is not simply a history of Grace in Peru, but also one of the founding of inter-American relations in all their many facets—especially commercial and diplomatic—as the United States and Latin America drew closer and more interdependent between 1850 and 1930.

The company spread its interests over several continents and became involved directly or indirectly in a myriad of activities, from banking in New York to nitrate mining on the stark and desolate north coast of Chile. Most of these activities are examined below, some in depth, some with less attention to detail and more attention to how the activities contribute to an understanding of the company, its role as an agent of inter-American relations, and as a promoter of change and development throughout Latin America. Accounting details, tables of profits and losses, and other financial matters are thus mentioned only in passing and where they supplement or illustrate main themes. W. R. Grace & Co. did not go public until the 1950s, and the internal financial dynamics of the corporation before then remain locked in the thousands of pages of accounting books that date from the era. In the main, however, we know where the investments were made and what departures and innovations they represented. The ebb and flow of monies, the issue and exchange of private stocks, the internal dynamics of those structures, and other data and analysis of that sort must

wait the patience of an accounting or business historian prepared and challenged by such an endeavor.

Today the multinational has emerged as one of the principal
brokers in the formation of world economic and political order.
But although the term is of recent vintage, the actual practices
associated with multinationals appear manifest early in the
twentieth century in the behavior of W. R. Grace & Co. Multinationals have borne a great deal of criticism as the emblems
and principal actors in the extension of capitalistic imperialism
over the past hundred years. Dependency theories defining the
relationship of the developing world to the developed world
indict the multinationals as one of the principal agents in creating and promoting an undesirable relationship. Conversely,
multinationals have been defined as the agents of modernization with all its positive connotations: better public services,
improved medical care, increased material benefits for the populations at large, and the general improvement of the well-
being of a nation and its people by the addition of capital and
technologies otherwise unavailable to the underdeveloped nations of the world. W. R. Grace & Co. represented both sides
of the emerging multinational character, and the reader will
find herein the evidence on which to make his own judgment.
What is not in doubt is the acknowledged influence of the
company in the stimulation of the modernization process not
only in Peru, but in Chile, Brazil, Costa Rica, and several other
areas where the coming of the railroads, steamships, and other
events challenged the old societies of Latin America with the
new strategies accompanying the industrial age and its demands.

Those interested in the lives of the men who made the company will find ample biographical detail in this book. I followed
the premise that the evolution of institutions (such as the company) and the elementary changes in the structure and dynamics of nations (such as the modernization of Peru) are only
comprehensible if we know the individuals and the strengths,
flaws, desires, and ambitions that formed them. Furthermore,
William Grace became a political figure of note in the 1880s and
his interest in the public affairs of the nation inevitably involved
him in the making of inter-American relations. That Grace was
twice—1880–82 and 1884–86—elected mayor of New York City
and became an unofficial adviser and consultant to American
administrations from Cleveland's to McKinley's on inter-American matters is, obviously, of interest to students of both United
States and Latin American history. Not only did Grace's company become involved directly in the War of the Pacific, but

his younger brother, Michael, helped negotiate the most important international refunding contract for an impoverished Peru after the war. William Grace also directly intervened in one of the most volatile crises between Chile and the United States in the 1890s. It would be difficult, perhaps impossible, to understand the central role that William Grace and his family played in the Chilean Balmaceda Revolution without realizing how fully Grace committed himself to the public affairs of his adopted country when he became the first foreign-born mayor of New York.

I must admit that I was attracted to the history of Grace and Peru by more than purely intellectual or academic reasons, although they would surely have been sufficient if other circumstances had not existed. I learned about Peru growing up there as a child while my father was busy working for the very company that William Grace founded. My father married a Chilean girl the year this book closes, 1930, an event which further reinforced my ties to the West Coast of Latin America. So I must admit my prejudices, although I have attempted to be as rigorous and detached as possible, given my professional training. Certain opinions and interpretations will not go unchallenged; good history, however, is not the mere recital of facts but the intelligent and forthright interpretation of those facts in the light of their times and our times.

What follows, then, is the story of a company and its role in the making of modern nations in the Americas. It is a history for those readers interested in the modernization of Peru, in the formation of inter-American relations, and in the nature and character of those men who forged a vehicle, W. R. Grace & Co., which became a household name along the West Coast of South America. Casa Grace became synonymous with American enterprise and commerce in that part of the world.

The year 1930 was selected as the terminal date for several reasons, principal among them being the fact that by 1930 the company had reached full maturity in its Latin American phase. Involved in a widely diversified range of activities from steamshipping to sugarmaking, Casa Grace was at its floodtide of involvement in Latin America. The last of the brilliant second generation of family managers passed away within a few years of 1930, and the Great Depression itself induced a retrenchment and period of very slow growth and change. Last, the modern story of Grace forms another volume and that history began precisely in 1930 with some chemical experiments in a small laboratory tucked away in a sugar plantation on the north coast of Peru. The story to 1930 is, furthermore, so full and replete that any more at this stage would have produced a manuscript of staggering size.

Any book is but the sum of the many efforts, many hopes, much work, and a great deal of serendipity. It is axiomatic but true that the author draws heavily from the goodwill of his friends and colleagues and I am delighted to be able to identify friends and to thank publicly those individuals who gave their inspiration, encouragement, time, and patience while this book was being made.

At the University of Alabama many colleagues and friends listened patiently to my endless concerns through the research and writing. Among those most constant were Ruth Kibbey, Vernon Grosse, Mary Hudson, Edward Moseley, and Helen Delpar. Linda Bell, Laila Liddy, and Sheila Rodenberry typed the final draft cheerfully, patiently, and professionally, often in spite of the excitable author's many suggestions and exhortations.

In New York City, where an important phase of the research and writing continued during 1979–80, I happily discovered a platoon of supporters, especially at W. R. Grace & Co. Among them were Chick Bloeth, Jim Roeder, Allen S. Rupley, Antonio Navarro, James P. Freeborn, Maria Campodonico, John D. J. Moore, O. V. Tracy, Richard Morris, William Copulsky, Joseph Flicek, Phillip Mougis, Joanne Henrick, Edith Neumayr, and Paul Keels. To highlight individuals is perhaps unfair, but, in this case, warranted. Richard L. Moore, Patricia Nöel Cook, and Joan D'Arcy know their roles only too well and I especially thank them for all those beautiful (and sometimes frustrating) hours, and days, and months they gave to me and the project.

Others in New York who volunteered much sought-after encouragement, advice, and help were John Duncan, Diana Habich, and Kenneth Lohf. My literary agent, James Brown, was the first to view the manuscript as a whole and his initial enthusiasm provided a rush of encouragement at precisely the right moment.

I also thank the staffs of the New York Public Library, the Municipal Archives of the City of New York, especially Mr. Idilio Gracia, the New York Historical Society, the American Museum of Natural History, and the Rare Book and Manuscript Division of the Columbia University Library for their assistance. The University of Alabama awarded me a sabbatical leave for the year 1979–80 which provided me with the vital time to write the first draft of the book, once again confirming the enduring worth of that academic tradition.

In Peru where considerable interviewing was done in January

1980, the brothers Barclay, Percy and Teodoro, were my hosts and intermediaries and their warm friendship and constant attention are not forgotten. While visiting the sugar plantation of Cartavio in the north of Peru, Ian and Dora Tait gave me the run of their home and extended a warm hospitality. Jorge Raby in Santiago was equally gracious and helpful during interviews and research in Chile.

My mother and father's long life with Casa Grace and love of South America inspired this book. One seeking the seeds of this work can find it in the lives of Maria Rosa Clayton and William Harold Clayton. My wife and daughter were dragged along in the whitewater of the whole project. To Deborah Leigh and Stephanie Leigh Clayton I have dedicated this book, a wee token for a huge sacrifice.

Atlantic
Ocean

MEXICO

Havana
CUBA
DOMINICAN
HAITI REPUBLIC
Mexico City
BRITISH
HONDURAS
Port Santo
au-Prince Domingo
GUATEMALA
HONDURAS

EL SALVADOR
Managua NICARAGUA
Caracas
San Jose
COSTA RICA Panama
PANAMA
VENEZUELA

Bogota

Buenaventura
COLOMBIA

ECUADOR Quito
Guayaquil
Iquitos
Amazon River
Para
Manaus

PERU

Cerro de Pisco
Pacific
Callao
Lima
Ocean
Cuzco
BRAZIL

Tacna La Paz

Arica
BOLIVIA
Iquique
Tocopilla
PARAGUAY
Rio de Janeiro
Antofagasta
Asuncion

CHILE
Coquimbo
ARGENTINA
URUGUAY
Valparaiso
Santiago
Buenos Aires Montevideo

LATIN AMERICA
circa 1900

Punta Arenas
Straits of
Magellan
Cape Horn

GRACE

1

The Travelers

Among the visitors to remote Peru in the 1840s was a young British naval surgeon named John Gallagher. Enchanted by the exotic country, he decided to cast his lot there on the West Coast of South America. He spent his inheritance to purchase a sugar estate near the port of Callao and settled in to increase his fortune.

But commercial success was slow in coming and the venture grew shaky, primarily because of a poor labor supply. The Indians of Peru, rooted in the high Sierras, refused to be drawn to the coast, and the prospects for success looked grim as Gallagher surveyed his largely empty estate.

Casting about for a solution, John Gallagher looked toward his ancestral homeland. Thousands of Gallagher's countrymen were then leaving Ireland, fleeing before the awful specters of starvation, disease, and death inflicted by a growing famine. Thus, the juxtaposition of Gallagher's wants and Irish needs produced a novel experiment.

Gallagher arranged with a friend in Ireland to recruit emigrants willing to renew their lives on the far coast of Peru. James Grace, minor Irish landowner, undertook to procure and provision men, women, and children to make sail for Peru and Gallagher's sugar plantation. The ship *Louisa*, 1,033 tons, sailed on the morning of April 9, 1851, with 180 passengers, dropping down the Thames from London for the long haul down and across the Atlantic on the first leg of the voyage. Among those pioneer immigrants was Grace's eldest son, William Russell Grace, nineteen years of age.[1]

One hundred one days later, her bright paint faded by the relentless tropic suns of the equatorial Atlantic and battered by cold, high seas always swirling around the Horn, the *Louisa* anchored in the roadsteads of the port of Callao, Peru, on July 20, 1851.

What the eager voyagers viewed was monumentally unprepossessing. As the anchor rattled down the hawsepipe and splashed into the harbor waters, small boats and lighters clustered about the ship ready to transport baggage and folk to shore where multihued two- or three-story adobe and cane shanties formed an irregular patchwork pattern. Another immigrant who arrived from Ireland less than two decades later recorded his feelings dolefully. "I wish to say that my heart sank within me as I thought that this was the place I had so anxiously looked forward to reaching."[2]

William too must have been beset by mixed feelings and apprehension as he looked toward a country where, as yet unknowing, he would lay the foundations of the vast commercial enterprise that would bear his name far into the twentieth century. Perhaps he caught a glimpse of an odd, ratty-looking old building distinguished from the others by its marine flavor as he stepped ashore to explore his new home. It bore the name of "Almacen de Articulos Navales de Pablo Romero" and dealt in naval stores. Appropriately enough, this ship chandlery shop was built largely from the bones of wrecks and broken-up hulks and William may have noticed that the uprights and crossbeams supporting the upper floor were the stanchions and yards of some old sailing vessel. It was now owned by Pablo Romero's son-in-law, a handsome young Scotsman from Leith named John Bryce. William would soon meet Bryce.

It was there in that small, dusty port of Callao on a chilly, damp July day south of the equator that William Russell Grace, young Irish adventurer and soon-to-blossom mercantile genius, began one of the most brilliant commercial and political careers of the nineteenth century. The company he founded would evolve into one of the first truly multinational concerns. However, his Irish companions from the *Louisa* were a good deal less successful.

The colony failed rapidly. The immigrants felt poorly paid on Gallagher's sugar plantation. They contracted malaria and dysentery and suffered miserably. The very language and culture of Peru seemed to block success and frustrate happiness. Most of them left for Australia or sailed north to the goldfields of California, certainly no nearer to Ireland, but at least lands populated largely by people of British culture, decidedly more familiar than what they encountered in Peru.

William Grace, however, discovered he liked Peru, its people, and vibrant economy based on the export of guano. Even after his father James, eldest sister Ellen, and younger brother Michael Paul returned to Ireland in 1854, William stayed. Now nineteen, he had already shipped to America once before, had worked in New York, and had then returned to Great Britain to establish his own company in Liverpool. Once again he was temporarily cutting his ties to home and family. He was the very symbol of the young man on the make in a century which itself symbolized rapid change, growth, and opportunity.

William was born in Riverstown near the Cove of Cork on the coast on May 10, 1832, while his family was on holiday. He was preceded by two sisters born to parents James and Eleanor May Russell (Ellen) in the three short years since their marriage. While William grew up on the Grace lands at Ballylinan, Queens County, more than one hundred miles removed from Riverstown, his strong attraction to the sea in later life was attributed by family members to his birthplace. Be that as it may, some natal instinct may have persisted as William grew up and learned to associate the ocean and its many moods and salt-laden winds with promises of voyages to distant lands.

His ancestors had swept into England with William the Conqueror from Normandy in the twelfth century and the first Le Gros or le Gras crossed into Ireland in the thirteenth.[3] William's more immediate eighteenth-century predecessors had evolved into firm Irish Catholic landlords with many contradictory feelings toward the English. The Graces supported the crown firmly in the multitudinous Irish rebellions over the years, but remained suspicious of the Protestant, English overlord class, descendants of those Elizabethans who had subdued the island in the sixteenth century. Being neither of the ancient Celtic, Irish stock nor of the English conquering nobility tended to breed a more flexible disposition to changing circumstances among the Graces. This asset would stand young William in good stead in the quickening world of the nineteenth century.

James Grace's estates numbered about two hundred fifty acres and provided, along with a quarry and limekiln, a comfortable existence. As was customary, only part of the land was his in fee simple; the remainder, like so much of Ireland's real estate, was held under long-term leases. James' grandfather had profitably operated a cotton mill near Ballylinan, but the rapid advances made by the English in the last century through the application of steam, the creation of factories—in short, the industrial revolution—had undercut that enterprise at Ballylinan.

Grace's immediate family was a branch of a celebrated family that had produced some notable scholars, warriors, and statesmen in Ireland. Indeed, the ancestral home, Gracefield, was located very near Ballylinan, but William, his siblings, and cousins grew up in their own more modest bailiwick, certainly a part of the extended clan, but nevertheless independent of the main line. By the time James reached Callao in 1851, another daughter and three more sons, John, Morgan Stanislaus, and Michael Paul, the baby, had been added to the family. William would draw and depend upon this large family, its cousins, and offspring for much of the talent and dedication that went into the making of the early Grace activities in Peru.

If not idyllic, William's life to age fourteen was comfortably filled with the activities and adventures of Irish country life of the 1840s. An accomplished horseman, he spent much time tracing the acres of Ballylinan, which was situated on the greatest limestone plain in Ireland and was the home of Irish horses. Because of this, he no doubt attended the quarterly horse fairs with his father in the neighboring country towns too.

Whether these fairs were surrounded by the blue mountains of county Wicklow or the bleak bogs and violet hills of the west, they were of vital economic importance to the countryman and farmer. The fair town was likely to be gray and dusty with square houses and straight roads. Such a bleak architecture and town plan were suitable and accessible for the merchandising of labor, goods, and cattle, a kind of town that suits the melancholy, though richly colored, Irish landscape just as the grim yew tree is deemed more desirable for an Irish country garden than the English rambling rose. And on fair day it was a place democratically open to all. All classes met at the same bar to debate the day's sales; sales that could affect the dealers' livelihood for the coming year.

One can speculate to what extent the stimulus of such gatherings affected young William and sharpened his inclination toward commerce and trade, just as his imagination may well have been shaped and nurtured by a Catholic Ireland's belief in the miraculous. The holy wells, the venerated stones, the thorn trees, all have magical properties and are possessed of infinite interpretation. This kind of atmosphere permeated the very lives of Irishmen and possibly helped a rather isolated and provincial youngster to think beyond the cairns and cliffs of the Irish coast.

The Irish also have an easy, almost animistic, relationship with their mountains, rivers, and seas. Rivers such as the Boyne are usually associated with Druidic goddesses. Mountains in legend are said to be fire-crested and lighted up within as palaces for the Sidhe, the faerie people. The Western sea led to Atlantis and other mythical kingdoms far beyond the misty coasts. St. Brendan himself had voyaged those storm-tossed seas and planted the faith abroad in the Dark Ages when the rest of Europe brooded and kept to itself. From such stuff is surely bred a love of boats and ships that can sail to distant and dreamed-of lands.

One can imagine young William marking his early life by the Celtic year, which begins on All Hallows Day when the Irish, ever hospitable and family-oriented, leave drink out for their dead kinsmen. This is a calendar annotated by the rush crosses of St. Bridget's Day, the Beltane fires of May Eve, and the reed pipes of the summer solstice. Events and celebrations such as these no doubt encouraged that youthful imagination to daydream and blot out the mud huts and famine walls that blighted the everyday landscape of mid-nineteenth-century Irish country life.

The poorness of Ireland was, nonetheless, inescapable, and William learned not to despise but to sympathize with those less fortunate whose fate was blamed on the English, the Protestants, sin, and, if one is to be consistent with Irish folklore, the banshees and other evil spirits that roamed the green spaces of Ireland. At midcentury those green spaces were but abysmal traps of poverty and suffering. Ireland, the Emerald Isle, was reeling under a series of agricultural failures between 1846 and 1848 that produced famine, dislocation, despair, and a massive emigration from the want and horror of the island's misery.

By 1850 Ireland had already been incorporated into the body of Great Britain for more than half a century, although it had been conquered and occupied by the English in the age of the great Elizabeth. Thus the Irish "problems" of midcentury were very much part of England's concerns.

England, however, marched to a different beat. It was pioneering the modern age at the forefront of the industrial revolution, "the most fundamental transformation of human life in the history of the world recorded in written documents."[4] While one may argue the relative significance of the industrial revolution and compare it to, let us say, man's mastery of fire, or the domestication of certain plants leading to sedentary agriculture, or the disappearance of the Roman Empire, or the emergence of Christianity (or Buddhism, or Muhammadanism), it is incontrovertible that the industrial revolution radically transformed the nature of our existence. It began in England in the seventeenth century, and by 1850 had remade the people and the land from the Elysian, farming, pastoral England of Elizabeth and William Shakespeare to the England of an angry Charles Dickens, who viewed the industrialized city life rising about him with equal portions of amazement and horror. William Grace became a principal agent for the spread of this revolution and the mixed blessings its modernizing process brought to Latin America.

At the heart of this movement was the textile industry, for it was this activity which first combined the many ingredients of the industrial revolution: technical innovations, organization, capital, skilled manpower, and raw materials. Manchester evolved into a paradigm of the industrialized city, growing tenfold in population between 1760 and 1850 and expanding rapidly around the five- and six-storied factories invented to produce effectively and efficiently the primary wares of the revolution. The power for the looms of Manchester, Lancaster, and other towns and cities came from coal-fired steam engines, themselves a breakthrough of transcending significance in the history of man's relationship to energy. The coal was found in abundance in the mines of Great Britain while cotton, especially in the first half of the nineteenth century, was easily imported from the "cotton kingdom" of the American South, then expanding into the fertile black belt of Alabama, Mississippi, and Louisiana. Between 1813 and 1850 the number of steam looms increased from 2,400 to 224,000, representing a 10,000 percent quantum leap into industrialization.[5]

If textiles launched Great Britain onto a major new trajectory, the invention and remarkably rapid development of the railroads completed the country's ascendance into the novel dimension of industrialized society. Between 1830 and 1850

England effectively built its basic railway network, completing six thousand miles that knit the country together in a revolutionary fashion. Not only was a dramatic transformation fashioned in transportation by the emergence of the railroad, but it catalyzed the iron and coal industries. This ensured the continued expansion and success of a movement based originally on the manufacture of textiles, an industry that already at mid-century had reached its limits. But by diversifying into the production of capital goods, "Britain entered the world of full industrialization . . . its economy no longer dangerously poised on the narrow platform of two or three pioneer sectors—notably textiles—but broadly based on a foundation of capital-goods production, which in turn facilitated the advance of modern technology and organization—or what passed for modern in the mid-nineteenth century—into a wide variety of industries."[6]

The human toll during the first industrial revolution was high and destructive in its overall consequences.[7] Adhering to the laissez-faire school of political economy, which proscribed any government interference in the economy, Englishmen proceeded into the industrial revolution with little foresight of the destructive capacity of the movement. In all fairness, foresight of consequences among pioneers was probably too much to expect since nothing remotely resembling the industrial revolution had ever occurred in history. The England of midcentury was dismal for the factory worker, for the dispossessed farmer, for the towns and cities that were spoiled by the factories, steam engines, and locomotives. Reforms through legislation began to appear in the early 1830s, although the reform movement proceeded fitfully through the rest of the nineteenth century.

While England moved into the industrial era, Ireland across the Irish Sea remained fastened to another, more ancient age. It possessed little coal or other minerals, had few skilled laborers and little capital, and "as a whole did not share in the immense development of British industry during the nineteenth century."[8]

The standard of life in Ireland was slipping in the nineteenth century, while in England, by contrast, it was increasing in spite of the travails of an industrializing economy. Ireland's population was eight million by 1840, an increase of three million over the head count at the end of the eighteenth century. People multiplied without a corresponding increase in cultivated land, or in the techniques of improving the yield, which consisted largely of potatoes.[9] Ironically, the potato was a native of the New World, which had been very successfully transplanted to the Old; perhaps too successfully.[10] It became a staple, indeed the prime source of nourishment for the Irish, and when it failed thousands starved.

In 1845 a blight spread from the potato crop of southern England to Ireland. It had appeared about ten years earlier in Germany and the United States, but the failure of a crop caused no unusual alarm. Blights and famines were both biblical plagues, but the collective memory of Irishmen in 1845–46 had been clouded over the years since the last famine. Very few left Ireland in late 1845 or early 1846, especially since the 1846 crop started out well.

By July, however, it became evident that that year's crop too was failing. Apprehension among the population turned to despair and panic. In the fall and winter of 1846–47 the real emigration began, Liverpool being inundated with over six thousand emigrants in January 1847 alone.[11] Added to the awful specter of starvation was disease—typhus, famine fever, and others—of epidemic dimensions. Weakened by "hunger and distress . . . the deaths from disease in the years after the famine outnumbered those of the famine years."[12]

The emigrants poured out through the ports of Ireland and England—especially Liverpool, which was better equipped to deal with multitudes—rising in the aggregate above two hundred thousand in 1849, 1850 and 1851. Between 1852 and 1861 at least another million fled their homeland.[13] Most of the Irish went to North America, especially to the United States. During the peak year of 1851, over 216,000 "emigrated to the United States, 29,000 to Canada, 1,900 to Australia. . . . The average percentage going to the United States was 76.7."[14] In only five years before 1856 (1841, 1845, 1851, 1853, and 1855) did Irish emigrants sail to places other than English-speaking lands, and in no instance did their numbers ever represent more than half of one percent of the total number of emigrants. The ones who did travel to other lands constituted the bolder and more intrepid edge of this great Irish Christian diaspora, as we shall examine below.

Of the millions of individuals caught up in this great Irish tragedy, a few decided to cast their fortunes in the remote and exotic country of Peru, then beginning its own, unique, entrance into the modern age. Caught in a crisis in one part of the Old World, these few individuals would be liberated by the opportunities opening up in the New.

When the first potato crop failed in 1845, conditions on James Grace's farms had already been deteriorating, for stone quarries closer to Dublin effectively undermined the ability of the Grace quarry to compete. James nonetheless tried to keep his workers occupied and paid during the famine. He participated in the public-works program being administered by the government, and even initiated some projects on his own property. But the expense of operating the farm in the face of the growing disaster finally convinced him to abandon the countryside for Dublin, where he found a post as a tax collector. William was enrolled in Dr. Cahill's college, a Jesuit school of some standing in the community.

The suffering of Ireland, the call of the sea, and "chafing under what William felt to be an unduly severe parental and scholastic discipline"—no doubt the Jesuit regime was strict—combined to launch the boy into a new trajectory.[15] In the spring of 1846 he left home and sailed to America, driven to rebellion by the desire for independence. Most certainly the normal dreams of a bold teenager were compounded by increasingly worse conditions in Ireland. The descriptions of starving men, women, and children with bloated stomachs, and uncomprehending, wide-eyed stares, invite equal portions of pity and horror. Escape and adventure abroad seemed especially appealing in 1846.

In New York William landed his first job with a Jew whose shop was located near Franklin Square, no doubt a first-rate introduction to the polyglot cosmopolitanism that New York already represented.[16] He experimented freely in his New York sojourn, at one time working as a cobbler's helper, another as a printer's devil. In later 1847 or early 1848 he took to the sea again, this time as a crewmember of a vessel sailing to Cuba to load sugar for Liverpool

From Cuba, where perhaps he first heard Spanish, William returned to Liverpool and thence home to Dublin. There he was welcomed with delight by his brothers and sisters. His parents were no less loving, but definitely more reserved. He bathed and was told to keep out of sight by his mother on the afternoon of his return. She wanted to prepare James for the appearance of the prodigal son. At breakfast the next morning William took his appointed and customary seat. James Grace simply ignored the presence of the young man and continued to chat as if nothing had happened.

What a homecoming! William bubbling with excitement with

stories to regale young and old alike, and father behaving like a biblical patriarch. After breakfast William finally broke down, asked forgiveness, and expressed his regret for the anxiety he had caused. Believing William to have been sufficiently chastised, James Grace then forgave his eldest son.[17] William returned to formal schooling for a short while at Belvedere College in Dublin, but his taste and talent were for business and trade. Accordingly, James Grace helped William secure a position as clerk in a countinghouse in Liverpool, and in this great port city the young man's talents found ready outlets.

Liverpool at this time was the second greatest city in England with more than a hundred fifty thousand population. It was the country's first outport, with rows of warehouses eight to ten stories high and extending for three-quarters of a mile along the waterfront. That harbor held more than eight hundred ships at a time—an interminable tangle of masts, spars, and riggings where a thousand men labored day and night to unload these voyagers from the far ends of the earth.

Chinese, Persian, Parsee, and Armenian traders in the customhouses dickered over consignments of souchong tea, rum, pikes and pistols, barroom taps, and waterproof umbrellas. There were timber from the Baltic, raw cotton from America, wine from France, Sicily, Portugal, and the Atlantic Islands, sugar and mahogany from the Caribbean, spices from the East Indies, and cod from Newfoundland. One could overhear a captain from Calcutta chartering a vessel to penetrate the Sea of Okhotsk to offer British goods to Siberian savages, or arranging a shipment of Wedgwood to St. Petersburg.

Liverpool also had its aristocratic side where merchant princes wore white cravats and evening dress coats on the Change, and well-to-do Quakers could be seen taking coffee and soberly conversing, clad in neat gray or mulberry-colored coats. There were fine residential houses, elegant Grecian buildings, and clean broad streets, and in the distance one could see the blue hills of Cheshire.

But above all, Liverpool was said to represent the England of the 1840s with its industry and enterprise. It was a premier symbol of Great Britain's wealth, consequence, and power drawn from the commercial and industrial revolutions pioneered by England. Small wonder that William was inspired to strike out on his own very soon after arriving! His new post as clerk in a countinghouse must have seemed very tame indeed. The atmosphere was alive with opportunity and profit; everyone with ambition was borrowing to launch out in new ways. And the newest way to William's eye was arranging passage for the thousands of Irish refugees of the famine, then pouring through Liverpool on their way to new lives.

He established his own company at the age of eighteen to broker passages for emigrants bound for the New World. This was a speculative business; as a broker William accepted a downpayment from the emigrants and guaranteed them a passage at a set fare, the balance being paid upon embarkation. Since the shipping company could vary the rates, the broker took his chances. That was the essence of trading and William acquired a taste for this type of enterprise, which sustained him for the rest of his life and brought him a substantial fortune. When his father arranged to take emigrants to Peru in 1851 to populate Dr. Gallagher's sugar plantation by the banks of the Rimac, William was invited to go. It looked to the young man like a good speculative investment. Second, it offered a chance to round the tempestuous, legendary Cape Horn and taste life in the far Pacific.

2

Peru

Peru in the mid-nineteenth century was an exotic land to the European and North American traveler. It was even a bit heady for native Creoles—Peruvians of pure Spanish descent—who lived in a subservient sea of Indians, blacks, mestizos, mulattos, and other castes. Almost from the very Conquest of Peru by Francisco Pizarro in the sixteenth century, the country demonstrated a quixotic nature. Not only was it a geographic oddity, a desert coast backed by a mountain chain close by with peaks soaring into the heights of eternal snows, but its native people had to a large degree proved unassimilable into the mainstream of Spanish culture introduced by Pizarro and his inheritors.

In 1850 less than one half of Peru's population of some two million spoke Spanish. They preferred Quechua or Aymara, the language of their forefathers, of the mighty Incas and of other older, sometimes cleverer civilizations that had preceded the Inca. They practiced Catholicism, but in odd syncretized fashions which often preserved the ancient rites of their ancestors better than the newer lessons of Christianity. The thin, reedy, plaintive tunes of the *quena* were in truth more characteristic of the people than the bolder, familiar—at least to Western ears—strokes of the Spanish guitar.

The great mass of Indians had risen in turbulent, violent revolts on many occasions during the colonial period. In 1779 a descendant of the last Inca emperor, Tupac Amaru II, struck at the greed and cruelty of Spanish and white masters—whiteness being synonymous with Spanishness—and triggered a movement that shook Spanish and Creole authority to its very roots.[1] It was only crushed when Tupac Amaru was captured, tried, and executed horribly in the main plaza of Cuzco three years later. The rebel was tied to four horses by his limbs and torn apart, an act committed before the eyes of his family.

The Wars of Independence of the early nineteenth century liberated Peru from Spanish sovereignty, but many argued that the master changed only venue, not color or race, Madrid having been supplanted by Lima, Spanish viceroys by Creole presidents. Indeed, politics in Peru was every bit as confusing as its polyglot people and as tricky as traversing its mountains. Between 1823 and 1850 six constitutions were proclaimed and at least thirty men had occupied the executive office. The ancient continuity of the Spanish monarchy had been forever removed by the long, embittered struggle against the mother country, but a viable substitute had not emerged. Only the caudillo, a strong man on a horse, preserved the country from seeming chaos and the centripetal nature of Peru's elementary determinants.

Slavery still existed in Peru in 1850 and the large mass of Indians continued to pay tribute, in spite of the superficially liberal and Western constitutions that proclaimed the dignity and equality of all men. But paradoxes and inconsistencies between great ideals and reality were not an exclusive Peruvian phenomenon. The United States would plunge into a terrifying Civil War in 1860, precisely to hammer out those intolerable inconsistencies between political fact and moral ideal.

Peru, however, still marched to a different drumbeat from that of the United States and the great and small nations of Europe. In the Peru of 1850 there were no railroads, and no textile or industrial mills of scale driven by steam; there existed only a thin middle class based largely on commerce and trade. Wealthy and educated Peruvians were parochial and clannish, caught between the chaotic, depressed period that followed the Wars of Independence and a new outward-seeking era just barely dawning.

A rather ironic, bittersweet nostalgia for times past—perceived to have been more prosperous, more orderly, more dependable—was noted by some travelers of the epoch.[2] Like a fairy tale, life under the viceroys was invested with some benign Camelot-like characteristics which contrasted harshly with the sad, dry, dusty exteriors presented to the traveler by Callao and Lima. One of Peru's greatest storytellers, Ricardo Palma, celebrated the viceregal days in a series of enchanting parables collectively labeled *Tradiciones Peruanas*, published in the nineteenth century. In these stories human foibles and follies were exhibited alongside noble sentiments and acts, all being played

out on a great stage populated by Spanish grandees, proud
Creoles, and the other satellite peoples of Peru. Yet somehow
all the drama and color of the City of the Kings under the
viceroys had been leached out by the debilitating Wars of Independence.

The last Spanish army in Peru surrendered in 1826 after having been besieged in Callao's great fortress of San Felipe for
over a year. While an exodus of sorts took place in the wake
of this final defeat—a defeat which in reality was only anticli-
mactic, following as it did the decisive Battle of Ayacucho,
December 9, 1824—not all the Spaniards left. Callao and Lima
remained cosmopolitan, for in the middle of the century one
could muster up colonies of not only Spaniards—in largest
number—but also Italians, Frenchmen, Englishmen, Germans,
and North Americans.

Many Europeans and Americans had been attracted to the
country, as they had to Chile, Argentina, Mexico, and Brazil,
during and after the Wars of Independence by the promise of
making quick fortunes. This was especially true of Englishmen,
who had penetrated Latin American markets even before the
formal end of the colonial period. The ports of Peru were formally opened to foreign trade in 1821, and with the consum-
mation of the independence movement in 1824, more merchants
were attracted. Yet, as D. C. M. Platt has so well established
in his enlightening and thorough study of English trade with
Latin America in the nineteenth century, the flow of Englishmen to the former possessions of Spain and America was hardly
a torrent.[3] By 1824 there were only about two hundred fifty
Englishmen in Peru, established in twenty small commercial
firms in Lima and sixteen in Arequipa. Then, after 1825, the
demand for the manufactured goods—textiles, glassware, and
the like—went slack in the small and glutted Peruvian market.
Furthermore, the generally high risks of the Latin American
trade, especially abetted by the endemic political instability that
threatened markets *and* merchants, caused a contraction in the
presence of foreigners, their goods, and their money in Peru.

During the next two decades political and social turmoil in
Peru caused widespread disruption, the breakup of ancient
patterns of existence, and even decline in the population. Lima,
the capital of the nation in every respect, actually possessed
fewer citizens in 1850 than at the end of the eighteenth century
when Spain still ruled. An unusually observant traveler in the

early 1840s, J. J. von Tschudi, recounted the travails: "Earthquakes have, at various times, buried thousands of people beneath the ruins of their own dwellings; the war of independence was attended by vast sacrifices of life; banishment and voluntary emigration have removed from Lima the families of some of the principal citizens; and epidemic diseases, the natural consequence of defective police regulations, have swept away countless multitudes of the inhabitants . . . and for several past years the number of deaths had nearly doubled that of births."[4] While traveling through Lima, von Tschudi noted that "several parts of the city are now totally uninhabited: the houses falling to decay, and the gardens lying waste."[5]

The first view most foreigners had of Peru was through the portal of Callao, which lay on the coast about six dusty miles from Lima. "It was not imposing," wrote another traveler of Callao.[6] That may have been one of the understatements of the era. More exactly, he might have described Callao as a rough and dirty town of fighting sailors, carousing mates, wanton women, soldiers, and drifters. But port cities of the world share similar natures, and Callao was not a particularly remarkable site for the average sailor off a long voyage. Yet, it did possess a curious history of catastrophes.

Callao had been reduced to rubble several times in the preceding three hundred years by monstrous earthquakes. One in 1746 overwhelmed the port in a gigantic shock and ocean wave that very nearly killed all its inhabitants. The ancient ruins of this city were allegedly visible beneath the harbor waters on a clear day, but, whether the visitor saw them or not, the melancholy possibility of seeing a dead city certainly cast a pall of sorts over Callao.

Once ashore, more familiar scenes were evident. Small commercial houses, ship chandlers' shops, taverns, and boardinghouses catering to seamen carried on business at a leisurely pace. Yankee seamen mixed with English tars and made the most of the compliant women—mostly mulattas and Negresses. One might run into acquaintances from back home, share a few drinks, smoke a good cigar, go to a dance hall, and if lucky, avoid a bone-crunching fight with others in the town. George Washington Peck observed, "I am rather inclined to think Callao a safe enough place to well disposed Americans and Englishmen. . . . I apprehend there are always shipmates enough within hearing to prevent any imposition."[7] By contrast, Lima preserved its Spanish core and imposed its accent on visitors, rather than the other way around.

★ ★ ★

Pizarro established his capital on the banks of the Rimac River in 1535. Shortly before, his warriors had toppled the mighty Inca empire, which had ruled a large space of South America stretching from the intermontane plateaus of Ecuador to the valleys and deserts of Chile. Cuzco, nestled in a high valley in the Andes, had served as the ancient capital of the Incas, but Pizarro needed to maintain seaborne intercourse with Panama and ultimately Spain. So Lima, or the City of the Kings as it was officially christened, soon became the locus of Spanish power in the South American empire.

After a long, bloody civil war among the conquistadors over the spoils of their initial victories, the crown established firm control in the middle of the century by seating a viceroy in Lima to govern the kingdoms of Peru.

The next fifty years fastened the rule of Spain securely in the New World as Philip II's reign elevated his country to its apogee in Europe as well. Stoked by the cornucopia of silver issuing from the immensely rich mines of the viceroyalty—especially from the almost legendary mountain of Potosí in Bolivia—Lima and Peru moved into the rich post-Conquest era. The wealth produced by the mines triggered trades and industries and the colony flourished in the seventeenth century.

Lima was the premier city. It housed not only the viceroy and the principal judicial and legislative body, the Audiencia, but also the See of Peru, as well as all the principal merchants and traders of the colony. Great landlords and miners built palaces in this city, which hummed as the center of intellectual and cultural life. The University of San Marcos was established even before the first viceroy brought political order to the colony. It was founded on European models and passed through most of the stages that characterized university life in Spain: some lethargic and dominated by a sterile scholasticism, and some vital during the latter stages of the Enlightenment in the eighteenth century. Celebrated poetry contests, a lively theater, balls, and other entertainment were the hallmarks of Lima, geographically remote from metropolitan Europe but certainly not a mere provincial outpost.

Over all aspects of life there was cast a mantle of religiosity, for the Roman Catholic Church permeated the warp and woof of Spanish society. The cathedral and the equally impressive churches of the various orders, such as those of St. Peter and St. Paul of the Jesuits, and of San Francisco of the Franciscans, witnessed easily to the power and grandeur of the church. The Wars of Independence produced a secular reaction to the church among the liberal patriots. Yet, even though long associated intimately and thus hatefully with the Spanish crown, the church still preserved most of its privileges and power—based on widespread property holdings—in the middle of the nineteenth century.[8]

Lima's piety fascinated travelers in this era. Peck was especially awed by the extent of ecclesiastical authority: "A great portion of Lima is occupied by churches and convents . . . some of the churches . . . are really large; often, with the monasteries and convents attached, they cover whole squares, and form cities in themselves . . . a complicated maze of buildings, where a foreigner could hardly walk along without some apprehension that he might be caught and converted unawares, in the old inquisitorial mode."[9] Certainly that was nothing more than the workings of a Protestant imagination slightly overheated by an ever present Roman Catholicism. Yet, the intense devotion of Peru's elites and masses alike stood as an interesting common denominator that would persist into the twentieth century.

Although the church presided with mystique over Lima, nothing, not even God's imprint, compared with the impression that the capital's iridescent society elicited among its observers. From the moment of the Conquest, miscegenation occurred between the victors and the vanquished in unions both illicit and blessed—mostly the former in the early years.

From these unions between conquistador and Indian came the mestizos, a race both hailed and despised with equal ardor over the course of the next four centuries. Perhaps the greatest mestizo Peru ever produced was born in this early era. Garcilaso de la Vega was the son of a first-generation conquistador and an Inca princess. After a childhood in Cuzco imbibing the lore of his Indian ancestors, he traveled to Spain as a young man to inherit his father's fame and fortune. He never returned to Peru and never collected on his legacy, but he was received well by relatives and acquaintances. He produced some of the most consequential histories of the conquest of the New World, his *Royal Commentaries of the Inca* being the magnum opus of his life. It remains a brilliant chronicle of the twin currents of Incaic and Hispanic history as they flowed ineluctably together to create the era of the Conquest. Some believe the *Royal Commentaries* to be the supreme piece of literature on that period, precisely because Garcilaso brought to bear through his maternal and paternal lines the sense of tragic balance that wav-

ered between awe of his father's deeds and admiration for his
mother's civilization. But Garcilaso's life—so unusual for he
was abundantly gifted—proved to be an aberration in the history of the colony. While other first-generation mestizos were
in some cases treated liberally and even recognized by their
fathers (imbuing them with legitimacy), the lot of the mestizos
generally evolved into one of suspicion and animosity. The
mestizos being neither fish nor fowl, the reigning Spaniards
and Creoles came to distrust and finally despise them. Their
character was said to incorporate all the worst attributes of
Spaniards and Indians. Yet the mestizo population continued
to expand, and during the Wars of Independence many distinguished themselves at arms. The president of Peru in 1850,
Ramón Castilla, was himself of mixed ancestry and certainly
typified a society in rapid flux.

The second race introduced into Peru during the Conquest
was black African slaves. Importing slaves to replace the dev-
astated native population of the Caribbean isles was perceived
very early by the Spanish as a viable means of maintaining a
working population in their American colonies. Bondsmen
were also introduced into the plantation economy of coastal
Peru in the sixteenth century. Many were already skilled arti-
sans, and they learned trades and crafts that made them particularly suited to an urban environment.[10] They too mixed with
the native Indians of Peru, the offspring of these unions being
labeled zambos, while the inevitable results of miscegenation
between the ruling whites and the black population produced
mulattos.

Further random marriages, encounters, and loose arrangements produced a veritable gallery of castes based on color,
bloodline, rank, wealth, and certain factors unique to the Hispanic world. It was critical, for example, to establish one's *lim-
pieza de sangre* ("purity of blood") to ensure that no taint of
Jewry blotched a family's lineage. When one recalls that a mil-
itant, orthodox Spain persecuted Sephardic Jews in cruel po-
groms as early as the fourteenth century, it is easy to sense the
notoriety that could befoul a family possessing a suspicious
background. Jews were not unilaterally expelled from Spain in
1492. They could convert and accept the Christian faith, an act
of apostasy that many accepted in lieu of leaving their homeland. Some, nonetheless, continued to worship their ancient
faith in secret, and these *conversos* cast a shroud of suspicion

among all the converts and their descendants in the New World as well.

The itinerant American or English or, more appropriate to this story, Irish merchant, scholar, or sailor wandering about Lima would invariably come upon the Plaza de la Inquisicion, so named after the infamous institution located on that square. In actuality, the Inquisition in Peru conducted only one *auto-de-fé* of any magnitude during its long shadowy existence as the police arm of the church. In 1634 hundreds of people were caught up in a wave of hysteria that led to the stake, but thereafter only isolated instances of the Inquisition's extirpating of heretics took place. It remained, nonetheless, a rather high-profiled censor of colonial society's morality and politics well into the eighteenth century, falling moribund only at the very end of Spanish rule. In the society of the capital in 1850 everyone was, of course, a member of the church. But the castes, blacks, and Indians equal before the eyes of God certainly were not liberated by any other egalitarian sentiment.

Although slavery ranks low on the scale of human invention, the slaves of Peru in 1850 were not debased or deprived inhumanely. The forty-eight hundred black slaves in the capital were treated exceedingly well, being "generally on much the same footing as . . . servants in Europe."[11] A slave could manumit himself, had recourse to special courts, could earn an income independent of service to his master, and was soon to be emancipated, one of the many boons during the Guano Era. Because of a peculiar set of circumstances in Peru—and throughout Latin America generally—black slavery had not reduced its unfortunate sufferers to the chattellike status of slaves of English-speaking lands.[12] They were not stigmatized automatically because of their color, an affliction peculiar to North America that was readily observed by Alexis de Tocqueville in the 1830s.

The Indian existed on another level. Although many were enslaved in the sixteenth century, the practice was eventually abolished by the crown, and Indians were nominally free men by the seventeenth. The Wars of Independence boosted their esteem and the various constitutions recognized and encouraged their participation in the progressive, democratic, individualistic society envisioned by Simón Bolívar and others of his generation.[13] Yet, in many respects, little had changed for this, the largest segment of Peruvian society since the passage of the colony to independence.

The Indian remained basically a peasant wedded by tradition and conviction to the land. Peruvian conservatives soon reimposed on the Indian the old social and economic controls—such as the rendering of a tribute—to maintain the integrity of their predominance. Long established patterns of Indian land tenure continued, based as they were on the concept of the community's ownership of the soil. These *comunidades indígenas* existed alongside the largest haciendas and plantations owned privately by the white elite, which ruled as lord over the countryside. The Indian in midcentury Peru was still a passive, somewhat enigmatic, presence on the scene rooted in his historic homelands in the high intermontane valleys of the Andes. He was considered by most of the elite to be little more than an *Indio bruto*, ignorant, docile, stubborn, and sometimes dangerous. At midcentury there were only five thousand Indians in the capital, compared with over ten thousand Negroes.

Between the blacks, the Indians, and the Creole elite stood all the issue of three centuries of miscegenation. At least twenty-two racial variations were apparent to J. J. von Tschudi, who also commented perceptively on the racist nature of the society:

> Despite the republican constitution, there prevails throughout Peru a strong pride of caste, which shows itself at every opportunity. In quarrels, for example, the fairer antagonist always taunts the darker one about his descent. By all the varieties, the white skin is envied, and no one thinks of disputing its superiority of rank. The Indian looks with abhorrence on the Negro; the latter with scorn on the Indio. The mulatto fancies himself next to the European, and thinks that the little tinge of black in his skin does not justify his being ranked lower than the mestizo, who after all is only an *Indio bruto*.[14]

It was easy to see and sense who governed Peru notwithstanding this kaleidoscopic society. Proud, arrogant, pious, generous, the adjectives easily flow and often contradict each other in grappling with the Criollo character of the time. From his Spanish forebears he inherited a tradition of dominance, which was reinforced by three centuries of rule over the great Indian masses conquered in the sixteenth century. Imperious by habit of command, he was also tempered by the countervailing currents almost always present in the Iberian character.[15]

If on the one hand he was a rabid monarchist, he was equally at ease with the Lockean principles that underscored the seditious American Revolution. He admired those liberating doctrines that leveled all men to the rank of "citizen" during the French Revolution and its contagious aftermath. No one else embodied the conflicting faces of the Criollo better than the Liberator of Peru, Simón Bolívar.

Although a Venezuelan by birth, he was hailed by the Peruvians as the champion who freed them from Spanish control. Bolívar began his intellectual life as a disciple of Jeffersonian principles. He was transported by the grandness of the logic that all men are equal and by the natural principle that sovereignty lay in the people, especially as demonstrated by the United States. Ironically, he ended his career by writing a constitution for Bolivia, his namesake, which provided for an executive elected for life and for other classic conservative constraints far removed from his earlier ideals.

Bolívar was pushed toward these decidely un-Jeffersonian views by the frustrating reality that most, if not all, of Latin America was ill prepared for the dissolution of traditional authority and its replacement with liberal institutions. That Peru was unsettled in the several decades following independence traced to a number of factors. Not the least of these was the chameleonlike Criollo nature, so often tugged apart by the contradictory forces of romanticism and reality, morality and self-interest, piety and profanity.

Whereas an examination of the Criollo mentality leads one into a morass of contradictions, more unanimity exists on the nature of the women of Peru. Women, of course, do not constitute a separate race, but one could argue persuasively that in mid-nineteenth-century Peru they certainly constituted a separate class. They merit some attention, for one runs the risk of crippling any historical effort by ignoring half of the population.[16]

The universal enchantment cast by *limeñas* over visitors to the country can be attributed to two reasons: one, the innate charm, beauty, and coquettishness of the women; two, almost all of the observers were males who had been at sea a good spell. Under the latter circumstances, the natural allure of Peruvian girls became an intoxicating experience. None other apparently was more taken than Mr. Peck, especially by the wearing of *saya* and *manto*, the latter a shawl allowing only a peek of the gentler sex's left eye: "But the eye—that single eye! It melts like a burning glass. I appeal to any traveller who has ever had to endure the full effect of it, if he did not feel the heat of it penetrate and suffuse him, so that it required all the ice of his cold mind to prevent being thawed, and resolved into a dew . . . I could feel my heart ignite and burn out like a lucifer match every time the beam lighted on me." Peck's libido moves on to figures of "tantalizing voluptuousness," and to the darker-hued girls "with shawls of gay colors, imitating the ladies, but with a more wicked witchery—with eyes that sparkle, and ways that make everything seem innocent."[17]

A more phlegmatic European, von Tschudi was nonetheless easily captured as well. "Far superior to the men, both physically and intellectually, are the women of Lima. Nature has lavishly endowed them with many of her choicest gifts . . . slender . . . small, elegantly formed feet . . . fair faces . . . large bright eyes . . . nose well formed . . . long black hair . . . falls gracefully over the bosom and shoulders . . . a captivating grace of manner and deportment . . . it will be readily admitted that the limeña is a noble specimen of female loveliness."[18]

The nation's geography also inspired von Tschudi to romantic expressionism: "When I first saw the towers of Lima gilded by the beams of the setting sun, and the chains of hills behind, rising by gradations, until in the farthest background they blended with the cloud-capped Cordilleras, I felt an inexpressible desire to advance toward these regions, that I might breathe the air of the Andes, and there behold nature under her wildest aspect."[19] Peru's geography, so varied, beautiful, and hostile, has never ceased to fascinate the country's admirers, or detractors, throughout the ages. It has been "characterized as being either too high or too low, too hot or too cold, and too wet or too dry," in what sounds like the proverbial farmer's lament.[20] Nonetheless, it does present an extraordinary combination of habitats within the confines of one moderate-sized nation.

Three distinct regions neatly separate the country.[21] A narrow belt of desert runs along the coast, broken only by rivers and streams flowing from the Andes down to the Pacific. The Andes form the spine of the country, rising to over twenty thousand feet in some areas, while the eastern slopes of these mountains give way to a tropical jungle where the headwaters of the Amazon commence their flow to the east. The jungle area makes up almost two thirds of the national territory, although in 1850, as in the distant past, it was only sparsely populated by primitive tribes.

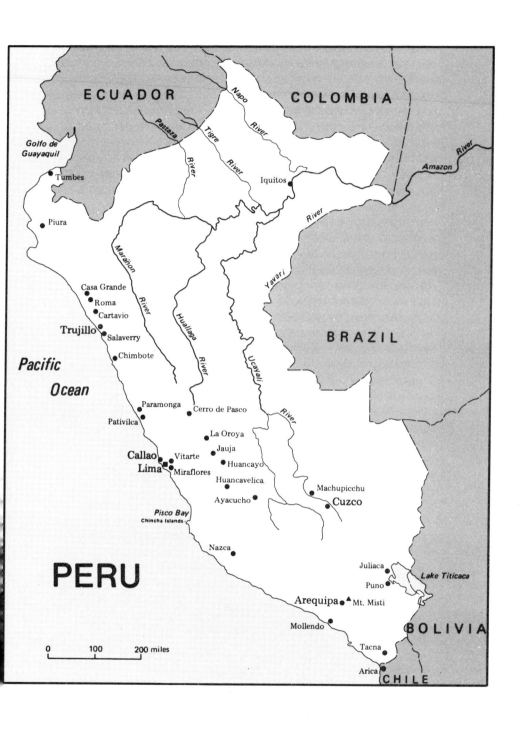

ECUADOR

COLOMBIA

Golfo de
Guayaquil

Tumbes

Piura

Casa Grande
Roma
Cartavio
Trujillo
Salaverry
Chimbote

Pacific

Ocean

Paramonga
Cerro de Pasco
Pativilca
La Oroya
Jauja
Callao   Vitarte
Lima   Miraflores   Huancayo
Huancavelica
Ayacucho   Cuzco
Machupicchu

Pisco Bay
Chincha Islands

Nazca

PERU

Juliaca
Puno   Lake Titicaca

Arequipa   Mt. Misti

Mollendo

Tacna

Arica   CHILE

BOLIVIA

Napo
River
Pastaza
Tigre
River
River
Iquitos
Amazon   River
River
Marañón
River
Huallaga
River
Yavari
Ucayali
River

BRAZIL

0   100   200 miles

The coastal area of Peru, one of the driest deserts in the world, is also the most fertile. Of the fifty-seven rivers that intersect the coast, about one third carry enough water to sustain agriculture and these valleys have always been the most productive in the country. The rivers are at their highest from January to March, coinciding with the rainy season in the mountains. All but a few of the larger ones dwindle to a trickle during the dry months, July and August. Irrigation was thus a well-developed science among the ancient inhabitants of Peru's coastal valleys, dependent as they were upon the waters of the rivers with little or no apparent rainfall. In some of the valleys there remain the ruins of ancient canals and aqueducts, testifying to this knowledge. Cotton, sugar, grapes, and assorted truck crops were grown at midcentury, forming part of the small agricultural export sector of the economy.

At midcentury the great bulk of the Peruvian Indian population still lived in the Andes, and these mountains, surpassed only by the Himalayas in altitude, have exerted a dramatic influence on Peru's historical development. There is perhaps no better single-word description of the Peruvian Andes than "diverse," although many observers are inspired to near lyrical prose in contemplating the spectacular configuration of the Sierra. David Robinson described the mountains aptly: "the Andes are one of the most complex geographical entities on the face of the earth, and, as such, anything that is said about them is either an oversimplification or an understatement; . . . the various chains that weave a complicated pattern of massive walls, divide the Sierra into large furrows, broken by long deep valleys, which provide a constant variation in relief to frustrate the traveler or delight the artist."[22]

There exist three main ranges in the north-south axis of the Andes: the Cordillera Occidental, the Cordillera Central, and the Cordillera Oriental; regional appellations serve to dismember each one these ranges into different groupings. As if grafted onto these ranges are a series of "nudos," or knots, that transverse the main chain in an east-west pattern. The "nudos are . . . centers of geographical perversity, where interrelated ranges intertwine to form an inextricable knot of residual rocks which defies man and beast alike."[23] The Nudo de Pasco in the center of the country serves to tie together briefly the north-south Cordilleras, not very far from the source of one of the greatest mineral deposits in all of Peru, Cerro de Pasco.

The variety of the mountain landscape includes volcanoes in the southern Andes, many snowcapped year round; some extensive tablelands, such as around Arequipa, which have traditionally supported large populations; major river valleys, such as the Mantaro and the Apurimac, which widen in certain areas to provide for substantial agriculture; and a spectacular scenery between these valleys and tablelands marked by sheer cliffs, jagged terrain, and seemingly impassable canyons and defiles making communication between the settled portions of the mountains difficult.

At the upper or western end of the Urubamba Valley was the heart of the Inca civilization, centered around the capital city of Cuzco. Before narrowing and twisting its way inexorably toward the jungle, the valley provides space for agricultural development. The valley narrows rapidly as one proceeds downriver from Cuzco and finally becomes a steep canyon, the river cascading and churning, tightly wedged by the constrictions of the almost sheer mountain walls. The city of Machu Pichu, only rediscovered by a scientific expedition in 1911 led by Hiram Bingham, sits astride the saddle between two mountain tops, Huayna Pichu and Machu Pichu, towering over the white capped river two thousand feet below on the floor of the canyon. Nothing is more emblematic of Andean geography than Machu Pichu, accessible only by a narrow path while clinging to ridges and veiled by mystery since the sixteenth century. But, while the dramatic mountain vistas dominated the imagination and enfolded the ancient history of Peru, it was the coastal region and, more specifically, some small islands off the desert coastline that attracted the attention of Peruvians and foreigners in 1850.

For thousands of years sea birds such as the cormorant, booby, and pelican have returned to roost on these islands after a day of feeding on the abundant sealife—especially anchovies and herring—populating the cold Humboldt Current sweeping north along the Peruvian coast. Their droppings, guano, accumulated to depths of hundreds of feet, and the fertilizing properties of guano had long been realized and exploited carefully by the ancient peoples of Peru, perhaps as far back as the first or second century.[24] On this rainless coast guano preserved a high concentration of nitrogen that ordinarily would have been leached out in a moist, rainy climate. The Incas carefully protected the birds of the islands, forbidding the extraction of guano during the mating season, for example, and they utilized the fertilizer to great advantage. Smaller amounts continued to be mined during the Spanish colonial period, although guano remained largely a Peruvian curiosity relatively unknown out-side the region. Alexander von Humboldt, the brilliant German observer who traveled through much of Latin America at the turn of the eighteenth century, did remark on the qualities of the prosaic item, but it was not until the 1840s that North American and European farmers discovered its splendid prop-erties.

The widespread use of fertilizers was only commencing in the industrializing nations of the Northern Hemisphere in this first half of the century. Yet, as populations grew and urban areas expanded, greater and greater premiums were placed on food production. That unimproved agriculture proved a dismal failure in one part of Europe, Ireland, certainly was borne out by the Great Famine.

English farmers were already fertilizing their croplands with powdered bone in the early 1840s when guano was first intro-duced. Its use grew rapidly. In 1850 almost a hundred thousand tons of guano were shipped into England alone, while the de-pleted tobacco fields of Virginia were being similarly rejuv-enated.[25] No one is quite sure who bridged the gap between these massive and rich piles of fertilizer on the Chincha Islands of Peru and the eager turnip farmers of England and tobacco producers of Virginia, but when the first commercial shipment arrived in England aboard the *Bonanza* in summer 1841 it sold out rapidly and dearly. The Guano Era had commenced, and Peru began its takeoff into the modern era.

The first two or three years of the era were marked by hectic maneuvering between entrepreneurs jockeying for position and the Peruvian government. Three contracts, the second and third canceling and superseding their predecessors, were signed by the government between November 1840 and Feb-ruary 1842. W. M. Mathew, one of the ablest students of the era, noted that "the sequence involved a progressive and very notable strengthening of the government's position."[26] In each case Francisco de Quiroz, a prominent Peruvian entrepreneur and capitalist, dominated the arrangements, which drew on capital from various firms in England, principally William Myers and Gibbs Crawley & Co.

The first contract was basically a monopoly type of agree-ment. It was soon discarded by the government, for the fee to be paid by the contractor for the privilege of exploiting the guano represented only a very small portion of the rich profits made by the sale of the first shipments of guano in Europe. A windfall profit of about twelve pounds on every six invested was being realized (the average ton of guano was selling for eighteen while the costs of production, shipping, insurance, etc., were about six), and so a second contract, dated December 8, 1841, was negotiated. This contract established the principle that the state *owned* the guano and it was not simply a business to be licensed or loosely controlled as a monopoly. This second contract provided for an advance of 287,000 pesos to the government by the contractors. This loan was secured by future government profits, the government reserving for itself 64 percent of the net receipts during the first year of its operation. These conditions represented a considerable improvement over the first contract, although by requiring large cash outlays as loans, local capitalists had to lean more heavily on English financial resources to keep the trade going.

The third major contract was signed February 19, 1842, as the trade boomed handsomely. Again, the government considerably improved its position, securing an advance of 487,000 pesos. Furthermore, the first 30 pesos per ton went straight to the government in addition to 75 percent of any profits beyond that mark.

The market for Peruvian guano slumped rather dramatically during the mid-1840s. English merchants discovered other sources of guano, principally from the South Atlantic island of Ichaboe, and until these resources were depleted exports from Peru remained low. However, by 1848 the Ichaboe guano piles were nearly exhausted and ships returned to the islands of Peru by the scores. The rich nitrogen content made the Chincha Islands guano especially valued by the farmers of Europe and North America and more than compensated for the high prices and monopoly exercised by the Peruvian government over the natural resource.

In November 1849 a new contract was signed with the Gibbs firm, providing for the extension of the consignment system, but the government pressed for greater Peruvian participation in the industry. The Gibbs contract provided that "native sons" be given preferential treatment in purveying guano.[27] However, the paucity of private capital in Peru short-circuited the best intentions of the new contract.

Then, in 1850 the government consolidated the internal debt and essentially recognized all claims made on the state since 1820. Peruvians immediately began converting old debts, bonds, and any promises that could be found (or manufactured illegally, according to some critics) into cash made available by the government. It in turn converted the internal debt into an external one to secure the cash and the net results were fourfold: a dramatic increase in the internal debt from about four million

pesos in 1850 to over twenty-three million in 1853; a concom-
itant increase in local capital; more Peruvian participation in
the trade; and a revolution in 1854 which overthrew the most
flagrantly corrupt elements in government and brought in
Ramón Castilla, a tough but honorable caudillo who imposed
a regimen of order for many years.

The changes transforming Peru at midcentury radiated from
the guano boom like the uneven rings and rivulets of earth,
pumice, and lava thrown out from the birth of a volcano. The
most obvious ones were directly related to the increase in
wealth. For example, the first modern banks were chartered in
the early 1860s (the Banco de la Providencia being the first, in
January 1863) to meet the urges of an economy stirred by the
new infusions of capital. Imports rose dramatically in the decade of the 1850s, almost doubling in the ten-year period from
1850 to 1860. The Peruvian and foreign guano consignees themselves slowly emerged as a new, energetic class in the country.
They looked to the markets of London and Baltimore for profits,
which were, in many instances, reinvested in different enterprises at home.

New wealth from guano was pumped, for example, into the
sugar industry and it dramatically boomed in the late nineteenth century. Sugar plantations had flourished during the
colonial period, cane cuttings having been introduced in the
early sixteenth century from Mexico.[28] But, like so many activities, the industry languished in the post-Independence era.
Resuscitated by fortuitous circumstances at midcentury, principally among them the increase in available capital from guano
revenues and the introduction of new sources of labor from
China, the sugar industry expanded rapidly and was producing
over a hundred thousand tons by the mid-1870s.[29]

Another rich natural fertilizer, nitrate of soda, was discovered
in abundance in the southern Peruvian province of Tarapaca
and the production of nitrates tripled from the 1830s through
the end of the 1850s. This trend certainly contributed to a more
outward-looking economy even though the politics of nitrates
eventually set off a disastrous war for Peru in 1879.[30] Changes,
too, were being induced in society by these economic forces.

Slavery, by 1850 decaying in the Western world except in
Cuba, Brazil, and the United States, was ended in 1854 and the
former slaveowners were compensated from the guano revenues accruing to the government. More important perhaps, the

contribución de indígenas, an Indian head tax or tribute surviving from the colonial period, was abolished. It had generated a large percentage of the public revenue before the Guano Era.

Both of the above measures were more than gestures but less than radical departures from the norm, for basic social structures remained intact in Peru. Yet breaking those ancient bonds—one, lifelong servitude, and the other, a palpable reminder of the Indian's defeat and humiliation at the hands of the conquistadors and their inheritors—symbolized some of the new moods of the modern age that stressed the individual and his natural rights. These liberal doctrines of the nineteenth century, really philosophical legacies from the Enlightenment, drove Ramón Castilla and others similarly minded to free the slaves and liberate the Indians from the onus of the tribute. Their efforts were supported by foreign earnings, underscoring the links between the economic and social consequences of the Guano Era.

The largest percentage of income being derived from guano, however, was not distributed widely through the country. It remained in the capital area and reinforced the primacy of Lima, especially since a great portion of the wealth was channeled into the growing military establishment and the civilian bureaucracy. A taste for European imports rapidly developed and the newly emerging commercial bourgeoisie turned to France and England not only for news of the price of guano, but also for notes on the latest fashions.

The transformation of Peru at midcentury was based on the availability of three major ingredients: natural resources, capital, and labor. While natural resources appeared as the gift of nature, and capital developed from the industrial revolution in England, labor was supplied imaginatively by immigrants transported across the immense Pacific from China. Peru, especially after the liberation of the slaves, did not have enough labor to exploit the world's growing demand for its products such as sugar, cotton, and guano.

China, on the other hand, teemed with people looking for work and a better life, and that better life was perceived to be in the Americas. That huge country was in turmoil in the nineteenth century. Its stability had been undermined by an expanding population, a demoralizing and belligerent foreign presence, and a series of internal revolutions that shook the land and displaced her people. The Opium War of the early

1840s added to the growing poverty and tenantry, which in turn were partially attributable to a population swollen by a 200 percent increase in the hundred years before 1850. That same year the Taiping Rebellion erupted and eventually engulfed most of China, adding ceaseless warfare to the misery of being poor and landless for the great majority of Chinese people. Peru, on the other hand, needed labor for the production of its expanding exports.

Not only did the black population drift away from the coastal plantations after emancipation, but Indians could not be persuaded to come down from their ancestral homes in the high Sierra. Self-reliant, reclusive, and distrustful of the white man on the coast, this great portion of the Peruvian population remained beyond the reach of entrepreneurs and their moneyed economy. Since the regular population of the coast was inadequate, Peru tried to induce European immigrants to its shores in the middle of the century. Included in this effort were the one hundred eighty Irish immigrants brought by James Grace in 1851. But, overall, these Irishmen, as well as several score German and Spanish laborers who were persuaded to try their fortune in Peru between the 1840s and 1870s, proved unable or unwilling to adapt to the different conditions. China, on the other hand, was flooded with displaced millions seeking an escape from the uncertainties of life in their homeland. Why not give them the opportunity to work in a land that needed their labor?

In 1849 a "Chinese law" was passed by the Peruvian congress to encourage the importation of Chinese coolies. A wealthy guano entrepreneur, Domingo Elias, received a small subsidy—thirty pesos per individual—from the government to import immigrants. In October 1849 the first coolies disembarked at Callao. There were seventy-nine persons in this initial consignment. Before the coolie trade ceased a quarter century later, over a hundred thousand of their fellow countrymen would be imported.[31]

The recruitment in China, the machinations at Portuguese Macao whence most were shipped, and the nine-thousand-mile voyage to Callao that often lasted four or five months exacted a high toll among the coolies. The ship *Empresa*, for example, sailed with 323 emigrants in 1852 and arrived in Callao 114 days later minus seventy-seven. Twenty-four percent had perished. The average mortality rate during the first fifteen years of the trade was between 25 and 30 percent. The notorious aspects of the trade eventually overrode all the economic arguments for its continued existence, and in 1874 the rules were radically altered and the importation of coolies all but ceased.

The coolie in midcentury Peru was put to work on the guano islands, the plantations, and the railroads. While those working on the railroads pushing into the high, cold, clear Andes were treated well, those relegated to shoveling and wheelbarreling bird droppings on the hot and humid Chincha Islands were cast into a hellish existence. Occasional winds sweeping off the Paracas Peninsula would raise great stinking dust clouds that defiled everything on or near the islands. Working ten to twelve hours a day, seven days a week, plagued by an inadequate diet, and flogged to maintain discipline, many attempted suicide by jumping into the sea or overdosing themselves with opium. Conditions began to improve in the late 1850s, especially prompted by the indignation of foreign masters and captains who easily observed the tragic existence on the islands. By the early 1870s the depletion of the guano piles, along with the end of the coolie trade, helped soften the existence of the standing army of five hundred to eight hundred men who worked the guano piles for almost twenty-five years.

The great body of Chinese immigrants, however, labored not on the guano islands or the railroads, but on the plantations of coastal Peru. Their lot was also harsh, but eminently more bearable than those assigned to the islands. They increased the basic work force of blacks, zambos, Indians, and mestizos at a time of Peru's expanding agricultural enterprises, which in some instances became entirely dependent on Chinese labor (see Chapter 11). Peru clearly benefited from the importation of these thousands of emigrants from China.

Callao and Peru generally must have fascinated young William Grace, who stepped ashore in 1851, almost contemporaneously with the first Chinese coolies arriving under decidedly more wretched conditions. A babble of languages could be heard on the waterfront, dominated by Spanish but laced with English, Italian, and other European tongues spoken by the sailors and mates off the tall ships, while the pigtailed Chinese sputtered a language alien to the Western ear as they were marched from the waterfronts to be transported to their final destinations.

William looked around, wondering what to do in this strange

country. He soon found his calling among the hurly-burly of thriving Callao.

3

Family Matters

William's instincts were sound. Soon after arriving in Peru he dissociated himself from the Irish plantation workers assembled on Dr. Gallagher's plantation and found work in a ship chandler's shop owned by John and Francis Bryce.[1]

As purveyors of naval stores, the Bryces were in a good business, for Peru at midcentury teemed with ships. Some were loading guano for the ports of North America and Europe. Others were bound for the goldfields of California, refitting and revictualing at Callao after long voyages from New York. Hundreds of New England whalers frequently called in at Callao, Paita, or Tumbez in the course of four- and five-year voyages in the Pacific. Of different nationalities, different speeds, different types, and, indeed, each unique in its construction and adaptation, all of these tall ships possessed one important common denominator: they needed naval stores—sails, pitch, tars, oakum, cordage, timbers, and the like.

Not only did William commend himself to the Bryces by his good business sense and diligent work habits, but the young Irishman also rapidly began to learn Spanish and enlarge his circle of friends among Peruvians of Callao and Lima. By 1854 he was a partner of John Bryce & Company and sometime during this period he became fluent in Spanish.

The energy flowing in Peru during the 1850s served to charge this young, ambitious Irishman. After a depression in guano exports in the late 1840s, the market recovered and Peru climbed to its apogee in earnings at the end of the 1850s. The general peace imposed on the country by the second presidency of Ramón Castilla (1854–60) helped produce political and economic stability. In keeping with this prosperous cycle William persuaded the Bryces to extend their business from Callao in two directions. First, he made a short trip north to Guayaquil in Ecuador and secured some orders in that important port city. Second, he suggested an innovation in the ship chandlery business—take the goods to the buyers rather than wait for the buyers to come to the market.

William convinced the Bryces to anchor a storeship in the roadstead at the Chincha Islands in 1856 and keep it well provisioned with a similar line of goods sold in the Callao store. This would reduce the time captains had to spend in sailing to Callao to refit and revictual before embarking on the long voyage home. It was the perfect idea for the booming times. Not only did William sell traditional products at the Chinchas, but he branched out into fresh meats, vegetables, and fruits brought out from Pisco on the nearby mainland.

The hundreds of ships that dropped anchor at the Chinchas each year to load their pungent cargo provided William with an unparalleled access to the seamen's world. While Chinese coolies and Peruvian convicts labored on the islands mining and loading guano, the captains, mates, masters, and sailors entertained themselves with dances, visits, and ship work during the three-month average layover. Wives and children quite often traveled with Yankee ship captains and added a tone of civility and gentleness that might not otherwise have prevailed at the frequent parties and teas celebrated to pass the time.

A majority of ships in the guano trade, mostly downeasters or medium clippers, were American-owned and -operated, although many flew the ensigns of England, France, Germany, or Holland. Given William's early travels to the United States, his high regard for Americans in general, and the nature of the guano trade—largely carried in American bottoms—it is not surprising that his predisposition to be friendly to, consort with, and do business with Americans was reinforced during his six-year tenure on the Chincha Island storeship.

This period also happened to coincide with the heyday of American guano imports. In 1857, for example, more than two hundred thirteen thousand tons of the fertilizer were shipped to the United States, and only two hundred five thousand went to Great Britain. Although Great Britain continued to dominate the overall commercial and financial scene in nineteenth-century Peru, the guano phenomenon was a harbinger of future trends. The United States eventually nudged aside Great Britain in Peru, World War I marking the watershed in this replacement. Meanwhile, Yankee skippers not only outnumbered their competitors at the Chinchas, but also carried a fair amount of guano to Europe—over a hundred forty ships annually sailed to Europe—while dominating the guano trade to the United States.[2]

General trade between the United States and Peru also benefited from the prosperity being induced by the guano age. Between 1851 and 1861 Peru's exports to the United States doubled in value while United States exports rose sevenfold, compared to those of the preceding decade, 1841–51. In spite of the disruptions produced by the Civil War, trade between 1861 and 1871 doubled again from the previous ten-year period. Between 1840 and 1870 the overall balance of trade favored the United States by nearly two to one.

Exports to Peru tended to vary little in their composition: coarse cottons, woolens, ready-made clothes, boots and shoes, wine and spirits, drugs and medicines, lumber, and even ice were unloaded at Peruvian ports. After guano, nitrate of soda was the major Peruvian export and by 1875 it had displaced guano. Smaller amounts of silver, wools (from Andean animals like the alpaca and the vicuña), hides, bark, sarsaparilla, tobacco, and wine and spirits made up the returning cargoes.

Whales were harpooned off the South American coast in the deep waters of the Pacific by whaling fleets from Nantucket, New Bedford, and other New England towns. Regularly calling at Peruvian ports, the fleets added to the intercourse between the countries. In 1858 over six hundred sixty American whalers were manned by some sixteen thousand seamen in the Pacific. Over a hundred fifty thousand barrels of oil were extracted from leviathan, and a million and a half tons of whalebone for corsets and other paraphernalia were carried back home. Servicing these ships in the Pacific was big business.

Whaling not only added to the coffers of Peruvians and Americans, but also inspired some of the greatest literature of the nineteenth century. Richard Henry Dana wrote *Two Years Before the Mast* and Herman Melville created *Billy Budd* and *Moby Dick*; Daniel Defoe produced the classic *Robinson Crusoe* after having heard the story of Alexander Selkirk being marooned on a tiny island far off the coast of Chile.

American historians were also discovering a drama of legendary dimensions in the Spanish Conquest of Peru. In 1847 William Hickling Prescott finished his magnificent and still unsurpassed *History of the Spanish Conquest of Peru*. Prescott's intellectual interests paralleled the commercial ties then flourishing among Americans, Peruvians, and Latin Americans in general in the 1840s and 1850s.

Working the floating market of ships off the Chincha Islands,

William Grace often passed the time with Americans in business and pleasure. Business was indeed so good that it prompted William to supplement the storeship with a small warehouse situated on the Isla Norte, the largest of the three Chincha Islands. William's commercial contacts with the United States developed rapidly during this period as well, for American captains and mates preferred to refit and replenish with American products if possible. The tendency to prefer familiar goods and services is a natural one to travelers abroad, and it reinforced William's growing familiarity with things American.

Part of Grace's routine included regular trips to Callao to visit the main Bryce shop at the corner of the Calle de la Constitución and the Calle del Muelle. There William placed new orders, completed favors promised, and kept an ear cocked for news and opportunities. On one of these short trips away from the storeship he met George Gilchrest, captain of the ship *Rochambeau* then loading guano at the Chinchas. Captain Gilchrest of Maine spoke no Spanish and was looking for the American consul in Callao. William helped him and the captain invited the young Irishman to visit the *Rochambeau* to repay the hospitality offered.[3]

A few days later William boarded the *Rochambeau* for tea. There he was introduced to the seventeen-year-old daughter of George and Mary Jane Gilchrest, Lillius, traveling with her parents.

Tea aboard ship was, as far as possible, as elegant as that of any London drawingroom or Salem garden. Under a broad awning rigged on deck, groups formed and re-formed, the men in gray and black, the ladies gliding about in tea gowns of Florentine green, China blue, elephant gray, taupe, and monsignor purple, twirling silked and tasseled parasols, and chatting softly in the accents of Maine, Massachusetts, and Virginia.

Old Spode teacups, unpacked from the straw that protected them from Atlantic storms, and Georgian silver teapots made their appearance. Linen tablecloths emerged from protective muslin coverings and were spread on trestles and planks hastily assembled by the crew. On the table Kelliher's marmalade and lemon curd tarts were joined by native mango and plantain fruit compote sprinkled with lime juice.

Often a talented member of the crew or a local maiden aunt was recruited to provide background music. Like many a downeaster carrying female passengers, the *Rochambeau* had a piano, although Captain Gilchrest's puritanical mores forbade dancing and drinking aboard his ship. The captain was sober and severe. To ensure his sobriety Gilchrest had authored and signed a temperance pledge in 1828, forswearing "any kind of strident spirits whatever." He also pledged not to "chew tobacco."[4] He enumerated the sins associated with the vices of alcohol and probably never thereafter strayed off the wagon, if indeed he had ever indulged. That pledge was taken at the ripe age of seventeen, so we may assume that William's tea host was not given to levity.

One can imagine William encountering slender young Lillius in just such a setting. What a contrast to the stern older man and his large talkative wife! No doubt the first conversation between William and Lillius, under the watchful eye of the captain, embraced acceptable subjects of discussion—books, weather, music, the voyage, certainly the exotic setting of the Chincha Islands. Friendly and forthright, Lillius listened to the serious young Irishman describe a world they both knew well—ships, men, and the sea. She had, after all, been sailing aboard her father's vessels since she was six.

She knew the clippers, downeasters, barks, brigs, and many other sailing ships of the world. Already Lillius had sailed through the Indian Ocean, the Black Sea, and numerous times across the Atlantic. She had held on tightly as a monstrous waterspout in the Indian Ocean nearly capsized her ship, watched cannonballs tear through the rigging of the *Rochambeau*'s companions while they provisioned the British during the Crimean War, and could certainly enliven any conversation on the sea's perils with her own bright memories. At sea since her childhood, she knew the rudiments of navigation from watching her father shoot the stars and study his charts in the twilight moments of dawn and dusk when navigators broke out their precious sextants and charted courses across the trackless expanses of the seas. This kind of background stood her in good stead when William later entered the shipping business. She not only became his life's companion at home, but also accompanied him on many long voyages between Europe and the American continents. He learned to respect and seek Lillius's counsel on business and political problems, and preferred her judgment to that of all others.[5]

It is easy to understand why William was attracted to a young woman like Lillius. She combined directness with a feminine softness that enchanted the young merchant. Love is one emotion impossible to analyze but easy to detect. In William, it was obvious. Not long after the party he mentioned to a friend that Lillius was the girl he was going to marry. He had already made up his mind. Now he set about convincing Lillius, and, of course, wooing the mother and father as well. That was still part of the bargain in the Victorian age.

The fact that the *Rochambeau* stayed for three months at the Chinchas—about an average layover—gave William and Lillius a great opportunity to court, although the setting was certainly unusual. The stench of the guano could be overpowering if one neared the hatches, while the hot winds coming off the Paracas Peninsula on the coast added to the occasional discomfort. The laborers digging the guano—coolies and convicts—often sought relief in suicide and Lillius recalled that the Chinese would overdose themselves with opium, "dig a grave, and lie in it. It was not uncommon to see a Chinaman lying in an open grave, still alive. When discovered, they were revived."[6]

But one learned to cope with the strange and sometimes brutal scenes of life witnessed in travels around the world. Life aboard the *Rochambeau* and its sister ships was naturally a good deal happier, although given to routine and tedium as on any ship on a long voyage. One had to be imaginative and self-reliant on such a ship and Lillius was both.

One can picture the brown-haired girl hammering brass-headed nails into her cabin walls for clothes, hanging moreen bags to store her books, putting her lantern matches and camphor to hand, arranging her embroidery and knitting yarns, checking her needlepoint designs. She became an accomplished seamstress, prompting William to lay a wager on her abilities to make a suit later in their life, so proud and sure was he of her talents.[7] She made him that suit and William won the bet, but not before Lillius had spent two or three months taking apart an old suit to model her pattern and then sewing every stitch by hand since she had no sewing machine. Lack of determination was not one of Lillius's weaknesses.

The weekly routine of meals, mending, sewing, reading, and studying one's lessons was broken by countless parties and weekly balls aboard the vessels of the guano fleet. The most predictable ceremony was the more sober Sunday service, which was presided over by Captain Gilchrest. He read a chapter of Scripture, prayed, and undoubtedly preached a little, perhaps on the virtues of temperance in alcohol and tobacco. One wonders how attentive his congregation of seamen was, longing as it was for pleasures ashore. And pleasures aplenty there were.

A large pleasure house located on the northern island (Isla Norte) of the three Chinchas catered to seamen. Rum and mulattos abounded, as did wrangling, carousing, and fighting. The balls and parties aboard ship were a different world, characterized by gentility and civility imposed by the presence of the captains' wives and daughters.

Yet staid they were not. If Captain Gilchrest was an old-fashioned moralist, other captains were by comparison tolerant and gayer. The evening balls under the tall masts and spars of the fleet were the scenes of feasting, singing, and dancing, splendid for courting. William first presented Lillius with a lovely musical jug called a silvador. Upon pouring water into one of its two necks, a soft whistling like a tropical bird issued from the other.[8] An engagement ring followed and William spared no expense. Lillius's ring sparkled with a cluster of diamonds, and her mother's—remembering the nature of courtship in the nineteenth century—glinted with a single gem. She was delighted by William's gifts which betrothed her only child to this intelligent, ambitious, and resourceful gentleman.

The *Rochambeau*, of course, finally finished taking on her cargo and made ready to set sail three months after she glided to her anchorage and brought Lillius to Peru and William Grace. They did not meet again for three years, but when they did it was in a chapel in Tennants Harbor, Maine. There they were wed on September 11, 1859, and there they began a partnership that endured down the years, years marked by travel and change, by children and wealth, excitements and tragedies, many houses, and even a mayor's mansion. But most of all by a love and mutual respect that grew through all the changes.

William brought his bride back to Peru and in early 1860 Lillius set up housekeeping at the Chincha Island storeship. Not many girls were cut from the resourceful mold that produced Lillius Grace.

William's business and personal friendships among Peruvians were extended during this period. In one instance, very soon after the Bryce storeship anchored near the guano fleet, William made a courtesy call on the civil administrator of the Pisco district and was encouraged to take on the official's young nephew as an apprentice merchant. This William did, and Manuel Llaguno became the first of many Peruvians to work with Grace over the course of the next century. Conscientious and able, Llaguno prospered with Grace and eventually became a partner in the firm. William Grace was interested in talent and diligence wherever he discovered them. Just as it made perfect sense to master Spanish in a Spanish-speaking country, it was equally practical to hire Manuel Llaguno in the country of his birth.

Coming from a large family, William also sought out his

kinfolk as business partners and juniors. English firms, especially those involved in the American trade between the mother country, North America, and the West Indian islands, had long since developed a tradition of integrating brothers, nephews, cousins, uncles, and sons into their commercial networks. It was quite natural for Grace to perpetuate this custom in his own endeavors.

One lad that Grace attracted early on to Peru was young James Lawler, a cousin born in Ireland in 1844. His family moved to New York about 1855 and on his seventeenth birthday, February 22, 1861, he went to work for William Grace on the Chincha Island storeship. His letters home from 1861 to 1865 represent a valuable record of a young man's life in that harshly exotic setting where Grace began his own career.[9]

Lawler arrived in Callao after a voyage of more than four months from New York and unhappily discovered that he had preceded the announcement of his arrival. When he presented himself to Bryce in Callao, young Lawler discovered that Bryce knew nothing about him, William Grace having forgotten to inform his older partner about the expected arrival of his nephew. After a few lost and lonely days in this strange, dusty port so removed from Ireland and New York, the error was corrected and Bryce sent James out to the Chinchas. He was received warmly by Grace and put to work on the old hulk that served as the storeship. Lawler had left behind him in New York his mother, father, five younger sisters and a brother, all of whom he loved and missed very much.

But work on the storeship kept homesickness well at arm's length. The four young men aboard the storeship—Manuel Llaguno, the bookkeeper; Michael Grace; Lawler; and Lawler's roommate, William Rook—worked from the time they rose at four-thirty or five o'clock until six at night, with the exception of from one to four, dinner and siesta time. Lawler learned the hard jobs of a sailor, including tarring, coal tarring, and slinging tackles and chains.

Grace knew that idle hands bred idle pastimes, so he kept his fellows busy, even when work had to be created. Keeping one's ship neat and sound was a traditional seaman's labor and Lawler reported coal tarring the ship all around, including the decks, chipping, and painting when business went slack. Fresh meat was one of the staples made available to the guano fleet and young Lawler, along with Michael and Rook, also carved beef.

Michael Grace arrived in 1859 or 1860 to live and work aboard the storeship with his brother and assistants. Born in 1842,

Michael first traveled to Peru at the age of nine and lived in the Callao-Lima area for three years, 1851–54, before returning to Ireland with his father at the end of the Gallagher-Grace experiment. His feelings toward Peru were formed at an early, impressionable age and they would survive for a lifetime.

Lawler liked the robust Michael, who outweighed Lawler by five pounds and possessed a stout body and strong character. Michael reciprocated the warm feelings, and was always disposed to help his younger cousin. Loyalty to family and firm was to be an essential ingredient in the success of Casa Grace, and the strong ties between these two young men give early evidence of that.

James felt compelled, as most correspondents abroad eventually do, to describe his surroundings for the folk back home:

> And now I suppose you want to know what the Chinchas look like. Imagine then, three round islands, two close together and one about three miles away, round or nearly so in form, and yellow brown in color, rising out of the sea, tall cliffs of a 100 or 150 feet high. There are two landing places on the North Island, the principal one where our store is, and the town. The other island is not much worked, only native vessels loading there now. This island is called Middle Island, as the far one is called the South Island. The ships lay to anchor in rows between the islands, the guano is taken to them in launches which they receive under the shoots. . . .

More interesting for James were the people, parties, troubles, and even an occasional sea battle to break the weary monotony of work.

Constantly getting into trouble was his cousin Tom Lawler from Australia. On September 10, 1861, Tom Lawler was discharged by William Grace, and James was sent to the store on North Island in his place. Tom Lawler had been hung over from three nights of revelry at a masquerade ball. On the last morning he lay down for a short nap after having set his helper to work cutting up the beef. Guess who showed up? William Grace was up early that morning and went ashore and caught Tom asleep. William's temper snapped. He had warned Tom once or twice before; now he discharged him immediately and loudly.

William was a forgiving man, however, especially when it came to family that irritated him, as Michael was to discover years later amid a financial crisis. In Tom Lawler's case the flash of temper was regretted and Tom forgiven. He was given back his old post, although James suspected that Lillius was the kind soul who smoothed the way for Tom in William's eyes.

Yet Tom Lawler must have been an incorrigible youth, at

least from William's perspective. In April 1862 he fired his rowdy cousin again. Maturity appears to have finally caught up with the wild Lawler in 1865, for by then he was doing very well operating a beef store in Callao. In fact, Lawler's firm developed quite nicely in the next thirty years, competing in many respects for the American trade with the Grace houses.

While masquerade balls and St. Patrick's Day celebrations occasionally relieved the monotony, a ship plowing into the storeship early in March 1862 really broke the routine. Let James describe it.

> On last Sunday there was a ship coming in and three or four captains went out to him, with one taking charge to pilot him in as is the custom here. However, they carried sail too long and miscalculated and . . . she ran into us, luckily right in the quarter near the stern carrying away Mrs. Grace's parlor which projected over the stern, carrying this completely away and the nice furniture and knick-knacks which were there. It was all swept overboard and our quarter deck rail was all smashed. Our side was smashed, there were a lot of bottles broken in the between decks. The ship listed over when she struck so that I thought she was going over for good; the fools then let go their anchor on top of us which caught in our rail and held there until she sheared off. A lot of things, canvas and things in the between decks shifted and gave us a tremendous list to starboard which was extremely dangerous for an old dried-up ship like us with our sides all open. One man and the cook was all there was on board with me. The minute she struck us, I sounded the pumps and then we straightened her up by rolling the things from one side to the other.

William Grace was on shore, probably only half watching the new arrival, perhaps measuring it for some business. From his angle, nothing seemed amiss. He was astounded to hear the crash "and saw the ship's jib boom walking off with the top of the house while chairs, tables, sofas, etc., were floating all around!" By the time William reached the smashed-up storeship, Lawler had righted the old tub and probably saved it from capsizing.

News of the Civil War occasionally reached Lawler, who answered his sister Helen's question on where he stood. James responded philosophically to the sixteen-year-old Helen. He sympathized with the South, which was provoked, but certainly not enough to warrant separation from the Union. He followed President Abraham Lincoln on slavery, perhaps having absorbed Lincoln's point of view from the few newspapers that reached him. Let the institution stand, although he was in principle against it.

Like all of us in war, James was interested in the fate of his friends and relatives caught up in the epic drama: November

9, 1861, "so John Moore had enlisted"; August 25, 1862, "the news of the war is terrible indeed though I can't help thinking McClellan is a great deal to blame in the matter. I see that the Anderson Zouaves were greatly cut up and their colonel killed at their head. I hope John Moore had escaped . . . "; October 9, 1862, "so my old friend poor Jack Moore is dead. I had expected to hear of his death . . . I liked him like a brother."

When William Grace left the storeship in 1862, he named Francis D. Stoneham to replace him. It took James some time to warm up to Stoneham, who appeared to be concerned more with trifles, such as enlarging the henhouse, than with looking out for the needs of the captains. To James, clearly the captains were more important than the chickens. While Stoneham never did learn to cultivate the captains, James eventually made his peace and managed to get along with Stoneham. Yet business declined, for Stoneham was generally disliked by the captains and everybody, and William's gregarious nature was sorely missed. The Civil War also cut into the business. American vessels were having to pay high insurance premiums and seemed to be carrying more on board to sell than they needed to buy.

The hard, lonely life on the Chinchas suited James Lawler well; yet for weaker spirits, a bottle provided consolation but spelled grief. In June 1862 Stoneham discharged Lawler's first roommate, Rook. He had taken to drinking and his books came up about six hundred dollars short. Rook had been one of William Grace's favorites, and his fall prompted James to frame the incident in larger terms. "Raise some people and you destroy them, for they cannot bear their own good fortune, and so it proved with Rook."

Lawler was still in the Chinchas when they were captured by a Spanish fleet in May 1864 in reprisal for an incident involving the murder of some Spanish nationals in the north of Peru. James reported on the movement of gunboats, the taking of prisoners, and the threats of bombardment, but he was little affected by the episode.

Late in 1864 James was promoted out of the Chinchas and to Callao. He had lived for four solid years on the storeship or its neighboring store on the barren North Island, and the green fields of the Rimac River Valley, seen from his first ride on the Callao to Lima railway, thrilled him. As always, William kept his charges busy. James worked in the Callao store all day and then returned after supper to keep his books up.

Although he had been content on the islands, moving to Callao did, of course, have its definite advantages. Lawler learned more Spanish in three months than in all the time he was at the Chinchas. Much more action surrounded him, especially with the Spanish fleet threatening to bombard Callao and a revolution in the making in July 1865. On the other hand, his $75 a month did not go as far in Callao, and he could promise to send home no more than $100 about every six months. Callao was more interesting but more expensive, even for a frugal cousin like James. Besides, there was no way of making anything extra as one could at the islands, where one had a chance to buy things on board ships and sell them for profit.

James Lawler was a good young man. He missed his large family and often wrote affectionately of them. "Tell Mother she must get Polly, Jane, and Eddy's pictures taken and send them to me, and when you kiss that young rascal Eddy for me tell him how proud I am to hear such a good account of him." He was always healthy, many such assurances going to his parents between 1861 and 1868. Yet he never saw those dearest to him again. Yellow fever struck him down late in March 1868.

Tom Lawler, the wild cousin now settled down, took up the sad duty of writing James's parents of their dear son's illness and death. James contracted the fever on the night of March 23 and he fought it for a whole week. Tom never left James's side for not only did he love and care for his cousin, but James would take his medicine only from Tom. There were always two or three, including Michael Grace and Ned Eyre, to help tend to James for he was beloved by many. "May the Lord have mercy on him. One of the roughest characters in Callao named Andrew Lawler cried like a child when he saw Jimmie die. He was such a favorite with everyone. Peruvians, Chileans, everyone in fact." Tom Lawler and Michael Grace soon also caught yellow fever, but they survived.

The bonds of love, kinship, shared hardship, and even death welded these young men together and gave them character and strength. The intangible foundations of successful lives are as important as those aspects scrutinized by accountants and economists. Perhaps more.

As a firm, John Bryce & Company was doing quite well as the century completed its first six decades. It had become the principal supplier of the Peruvian navy, for example, and these links strengthened over the years. Indeed, during the War of the Pacific, which pitted Peru and Bolivia against Chile in 1879,

William's firm was instrumental in supplying the Peruvians
with arms and munitions. By 1860 William had moved himself
well within the Peruvian-American orbit of trade and commerce, and Bryce & Co.—of which he had become a partner
in 1854—was the principal purveyor of American goods in Peru.

A new generation of Graces in Peru began with the arrival
of Alice Gertrude, born June 11, 1860, to Lillius aboard the
storeship. Before William and Lillius departed the islands in
1862, another girl, Florence Ellen, was born in September 1861.
Not only did William and Lillius leave the islands richer with
their two babies, but William had acquired a small fortune,
$180,000, as well. In 1862 they settled in a home in Callao,
where William could oversee the business with greater care.
John Bryce had by then returned to England and left his brother
Francis nominally in charge, but Francis was content to let the
more dynamic Grace brothers manage affairs.

The decade of the 1860s was as eventful for William as the
preceding ten years. By 1862 the American Civil War had settled
into a protracted struggle, and ripples of the epic clash were
noted by James Lawler in the Chinchas.

On one occasion two Yankee cruisers (or corvettes, depending upon the source) put into Callao exactly at a time when
news of the Union cause was particularly depressing. No Peruvian institution or merchant would honor the drafts which
their paymaster, a Mr. Eldridge, presented to pay off the crews
and buy supplies. Someone then sent Eldridge to Grace, who
"leaned back in his chair and said: 'I have faith in the Union
and will give you all the money you need.' "[10] That story later
helped Grace get elected mayor of New York City. Whether
embellished in the later retelling or true to the word, it rings
with consistency, given Grace's association with New York in
his boyhood, his commercial and personal contacts with Yankee
seamen and their families in his Chincha Island days, and the
influence of Lillius from the state of Maine.

Then one day in 1862, already suffering from a bout of dysentery, Grace was told he had Bright's disease (a type of kidney
ailment marked by albumin in the urine) and not very long to
live. The prescription was to leave Peru and get plenty of rest.
With Lillius and the two babies he headed for Ireland to see
his family and attend to the order of things in the light of the
doctor's lugubrious prognosis. The doctor was off by about
forty years in predicting William's death (he lived four years
into the twentieth century) and the Irish clan was certainly
happy to see William.

While home he provided for the less fortunate members of

his family and initiated an allowance for his parents. He bought a farm for his crippled brother John, a husbandman at heart. This rather dilapidated estate for which William paid thirty-eight hundred pounds was thoroughly rehabilitated by John. Not afraid to work, John would later join William and Michael in their business enterprises in the Americas.

Another brother, Morgan, had gone to remote New Zealand as an army surgeon. There he fought for many years in the wars against the primitive Maori. Good Irishman that he was, Morgan, in a nicely written memoir published at the end of the century, *A Sketch of the New Zealand War,* was highly critical of British colonial practices and sympathetic to the Maori. He also left us a note on William's character: "William was stormily successful from the cradle up . . . he conquered all difficulties with the air of an emperor, and kicked or cuffed or bluffed his way up to the top of any circle in which he moved . . . he was a fine fellow."[11] Morgan himself succeeded in Wellington after the war, setting up a prosperous medical practice while contemporaneously being elected to public office.

Of William's sisters, the eldest, Alice, married John Eyre. Their many children contributed numerous apprentices to the Grace businesses in the Americas and a new Eyre would pop up in Valparaiso or Callao or New York with regularity during the next half century. The most prominent of these was Edward Eyre, eleven years old when Uncle William and Aunt Lillius visited Ireland in 1862. He was in Callao by 1867 and later rose to the presidency of the company when William passed away in 1904. Like the literary Morgan, Edward Eyre was a bit of an egghead and the historian in the family. He added an intellectual glint to William's siblings, cousins, and nephews, no slouches themselves when it came to corresponding on the widest range of matters. Of William's two remaining sisters, Sarah and Ellen Mary, the latter proved a good balance to William's propensity for accumulating money. She helped him give it away in charitable causes or loan it to needy individuals (like immigrants on their way to America), and discovered in William a conscionable fellow who also possessed some wherewithal to do good.

While in Ireland William and Lillius suffered a tragedy that the modern age has almost eliminated in the developed countries of the world: infant mortality. Their younger baby Florence and a newborn girl both died, certainly making the children who followed dearer and more precious to a pair of parents who doted on their offspring under even normal circumstances. They left Ireland and returned to Peru in 1863, passing through

New York and the Union at the crest of its struggle to crush the Confederacy.

The tide of the war turned at Gettysburg and Vicksburg in the summer of 1863, but it was still dangerous to be at sea on a Union ship. The Confederate raider *Alabama,* for example, under its brilliant captain Raphael Semmes, sank over seventy Yankee ships in the North and South Atlantic before finally being brought to bay and defeated in a terrific engagement with the Union warship *Kearsage* in June 1864 in the English Channel.[12]

The *Alabama* was succeeded by the *Shenandoah,* also built in Great Britain. It sailed into the Pacific in late 1864 and early 1865 round the Cape of Good Hope and raised havoc with Yankee whalers, especially those in the Arctic Sea following the great sperm whales. Many of its depredations were accomplished after the formal end of the war, but slow communications doomed quite a number of whalers to the torch in those freezing northern waters. Her captain, James I. Waddell, was absolved of any deliberate postwar belligerency and eventually became master of the liner *San Francisco* on the New York to Melbourne route of the Pacific Mail Steamship Co.[13] The Pacific Mail Line was later (1915) acquired by the company that William Grace founded.

As James Lawler had noted, Yankee skippers were paying high insurance rates to be at sea risking an encounter with the *Alabama* and *Shenandoah*. These high rates and the massive recruitment of sailors for the Union navy caused serious disruptions in the American merchant marine. Indeed, all routine was disrupted by the war, and New York City was no exception. While a majority of its citizens supported the Union passionately, loud elements of its Democratic population, the famed Copperheads, were determinedly antiwar. The city itself was then, as now, an object of inspiration and awe, combining grandness and lewdness, the sacred and the profane, in crazy-quilt juxtapositions.

William and Lillius tarried in New York on their long trip back to Peru from Ireland in 1863. Lillius's father, Captain Gilchrist, had purchased a home in Brooklyn and here the Graces stayed for several weeks. But their real interests lay across the river in the city charged with emotion over the war, and sprawling rapidly northward as the wartime prosperity sparked a boomtown atmosphere. William was elected mayor of this modern phenomenon in 1880, and already in 1863 he must have been attracted inexorably to its near wondrous, dynamic nature.

The streets of New York that William traveled were made of large flat paving blocks, so uneven that one was forced to hang onto the tugstrap of his carriage on any journey. Broadway was an avenue lined with five- and six-story brownstone buildings, with windows displaying gold, silver, jewelry, bolts of silk, and brocades. At midmorning elaborately dressed women in full skirts and satin-ruched bonnets would parade their small dogs.

If it were a Sunday morning, the gambling houses and brothels on East Fourteenth Street and West Twenty-third would be shuttered and quiet. On the sidewalks demure-faced whores walked two by two to church. City bells would ring and the more upright citizens would spend an hour or two with their deity in one of the hundreds of churches dotting the skyline. After church they slowly strolled home to the Sunday roast, tipping hats and exchanging gossip along the way. Perhaps a quiet walk in a park in the early evening would round out the day.

But by late afternoon in other parts of the city, the beer gardens and concert saloons were as noisy and crowded as on any other day. Twenty years back Bleecker Street had been a fashionable neighborhood of large houses for wealthy families, but now the families had moved farther uptown and the brownstones had become boardinghouses for ballet girls and minor actresses.

The area surrounding Wall Street, where the business of the city was conducted every weekday, was composed of narrow streets with close-set buildings. Mansions of an earlier year were now converted into offices. Crowds of brokers in high silk hats, frock coats, and striped trousers gathered along with groups of very young men in derbies and frock coats with gold chains across their vests.

Wall Street was the center of the business universe. When Trinity Church's chimes struck ten o'clock, groups gathered on the sidewalks, some shouting and gesticulating, others talking quietly about high finance. New Street was filled with brokerage houses, whose rooms were small and furnished with battered armchairs and occupied by clerks on high stools. Ornate offices were suspect to the serious-minded clients who sat before the red-felt-covered desks of their brokers.

The war had caused an instability in the city and millionaires appeared and disappeared with uneasy regularity. Those who survived the crash of 1857 and the losses of the first year of the war were gratified when stocks rose 40 percent the second year. The streets were filled with former saloon owners, who sported diamond stickpins and rode in their own barouches en route to their Fifth Avenue mansions.

Along Fifth Avenue the brownstones made a steady procession beyond Thirty-fifth Street, their identical façades distinguished only by the color of their heavy draperies and curtains. Above Fifty-ninth Street squatters dwelt in a village of shacks built amid the rocks overlooking Central Park. Goats and dogs wandered about and sniffed among the garbage. Along the wharves lining the North and East Rivers, tall ships from all over the world poked their long bowsprits over gangs of men loading and unloading commerce from the seven seas.

In New York during the later years of the war, a feverish gaiety prevailed. The ballrooms of the great mansions along Fifth Avenue grew too small for the hundreds of guests that were necessary to ensure the success of an entertainment. So restaurants like Delmonico's became an innovative place to hold a ball. It was as if the deprivations and horrors of the war demanded a more lavish display to mask the grisly news from the battlefields, preserved forever by Matthew Brady and other pioneer photographers. The evening clothes, especially the women's, grew elaborate, even garish. Some hostesses wore lighted gas chandeliers as headdresses while the servants moved about clad in silver and gold livery.

William and Lillius Grace watched from the sidelines, sticking close to Captain Gilchrest's circle, marked more by sober ship captains, daily rumors of depredations by the *Alabama*, news of rising insurance rates, all focused on the movement of ships and cargoes in and out of the great port of New York. They would soon return and move more squarely into the social and political heart of the city, but, for the moment, they were only passing through. Late in 1863 William Grace and his small family returned to Peru, then on the verge of an odd, almost atavistic, rift with Spain.

Like France in Mexico, Spain was taking advantage of the internecine American Civil War to attempt to reestablish influence in her old dominions in the New World. Napoleon III's adventure in Mexico collapsed rapidly in 1866, and led eventually to the tragic execution of the erstwhile emperor Maximilian by the Mexican warrior Benito Juárez and his troops. Spain was slightly more circumspect in its approach to the American republics, but no more successful.

In 1863 two Spaniards working in northern Peru as part of an immigration project were murdered. Spain rapidly demanded indemnification and an apology. The Peruvians wavered and Spain struck.[14] James Lawler witnessed the seizure of the Chincha Islands, April 14, 1864, by a sizable Spanish fleet then conveniently in the Pacific. By late 1865 Peru and Spain were at war. Furthermore, Spain had never acknowledged Peru's independence, which had been a fact since 1824. This led many to believe—the United States especially—that the old European power was truly on the make in rather flagrant violation of the Monroe Doctrine. While these weighty matters of state were being decided, not only James Lawler but Lillius Grace inadvertently got tangled up in the act as well.

Lillius and a friend, a Miss Metcalf, had gone from Callao to the storeship to socialize with the captains and their families.[15] Just then the Spanish swooped down onto the islands. Among their captives were a hundred fifty Peruvian convict guano laborers, soon dispatched under armed guard to the mainland port of Pisco. The excitement was compounded by explosions rocking the evening as ammunition on a Spanish ship afire occasionally went off, rupturing the night air.

The next day Lillius and Miss Metcalf were escorted aboard a vessel bound for Callao by the manager of the storeship, Edwin R. Kirtley. He had succeeded Stoneham. That ship put in at Pisco to load the prisoners and their guards for transfer to Callao. In the confusion the prisoners overpowered their guards while Lillius and Miss Metcalf were quietly eating lunch. The captain of the vessel managed to signal for help and the convicts were recaptured by soldiers dispatched on a government launch. Lillius and Miss Metcalf remained sensibly locked in their cabin during the tumult on the decks above.

Upon returning to Callao the action continued, following Lillius like lightning drawn to a steeple. The Spanish fleet tarried at the Chinchas only a short while before sailing to Callao. The Spanish then prevailed upon the pusillanimous Peruvian president, Juan Antonio Pezet, in early 1865 to capitulate to their demands. Many patriotic Peruvians were outraged by this submission and Lillius was once more caught in the middle. A mob tore up part of the railroad between Callao and Lima, presumably to isolate the Spanish admiral and his staff then in Lima, and then turned on Spanish sailors in Callao. They chased one up onto the balcony of William and Lillius's residence where they killed him. The episode finally climaxed in November 1865 in a revolution that overthrew Pezet. Under Mariano Ignacio Prado, Peru repudiated Pezet's ignoble treaty and arranged a four-part alliance with Chile, Bolivia, and Ecuador to resist the Spanish aggression in the Pacific.

The allies appealed for United States intervention, but Secretary of State William Seward was reluctant to act directly.[16] Yet he followed the events closely. If another European power offered to intervene or arbitrate, then the Monroe Doctrine might have to be invoked to protect American influence in the hemisphere.

The Spanish were not idle while the United States observed. They bombarded Valparaiso, Chile, early in 1866 and then turned on the Peruvians once more, cannonading Callao on May 2. Old fort San Felipe, way outgunned, responded in kind and the noisy, smoky, battle satisfied honor before the aggressors withdrew. An armistice was finally signed in April 1871 in Washington, D.C., under the auspices of the United States. This strange, rather bloodless war was nonetheless significant for the future course of United States–Peruvian relations.

For the first time direct United States intervention had been sought in Peruvian affairs. That the United States refused to deal early in the crisis exactly as Peru and its allies wished caused some resentment, but the important precedent was set. Furthermore, the United States would become the most important peacekeeping force in the hemisphere as the Monroe Doctrine was gradually stretched and elaborated during the next century.

In 1866 William and Lillius returned to the United States and set up residence in Brooklyn. A combination of factors persuaded Grace to move his family from Peru. Dysentery once again ravaged his system and his old instinct was to return home to Ireland and recover. This he did early in 1865, having gone there from Peru before moving on to New York in 1866. The growing Peruvian conflict with Spain must have weighed in the decision as well, for not only did the Spanish seize the Chincha Islands, but they took off a large amount of guano and muddied that business temporarily by their actions.

Certainly New York itself exerted a strong appeal on Grace. After the Civil War the reunited Union emerged into a dramatic cycle of business expansion and prosperity, and New York drew Grace like a magnet. He had married an American, had developed close personal and business ties with Americans while in Peru, and he sensed the quickening, exhilarating pace of life in New York. So, after some months in Ireland and

England, William Russell Grace and his family settled in Brooklyn Heights, then quite fashionable and close to the bustling commercial district of Lower Manhattan. He rented a small office at 110 Wall Street in the ship chandler's shop of his father-in-law. Captain Gilchrest had retired from active command and located his business squarely in the center of the shipping district. It suited William well, for he liked to be close to the action.

4

Building Railroads and Fortunes

When William settled in New York, largely to trade with Peru, the American merchant marine ironically was entering a long period of decline. Steamers were gradually supplanting sailing ships and England took the lead by subsidizing her growing steam fleets, which undercut potential American competitors. Furthermore, depredations during the Civil War had caused ruinous insurance rates and many American ships had been sold foreign at considerable loss.

The United States was in reality turning away from the sea. The first transcontinental railroad was completed in 1869 and the development of the continent drew Americans inward rather than outward. Whereas the colonies and the new republic had been sea-oriented, the industrializing nation turned to the development of its own untapped resources. Coal from Pittsburgh and Birmingham, iron ore from the Great Lakes region, oil from Pennsylvania and Ohio, and other raw materials were being unearthed and burned, refined, smelted, or reduced in a host of inventive fashions to energy and capital goods. The railroads were the prime mover of this grand transition. Not only did they directly stimulate the coal and iron-steel industries with their demands, but their construction promoted major transformations in many other areas: by opening up great tracts of land for farming; by drastically reducing transportation costs; by pioneering ways of capital formation and its employment; and even by forcing the standardization of time zones.

Yet, amid this enthusiasm for the interior, New York still remained one of the great trading seaports of the world and

William's forte was trade. He moved with confidence and ambition in the commercial world and was especially knowledgeable and active in sea trade itself. Not troubled with historical hindsight, William looked to the opportunities represented by Peru, still on the crest of the guano boom and now striking up a love affair with the apotheosis of modernization, the railroad. To finance the building of railroads, however, Peru had to extricate itself from the morass of national debt and corruption created by the consignment system of marketing its most materially valuable national asset, guano.

In 1868 the government of Peru faced a projected deficit of seventeen million soles (one sol was equivalent to about one dollar) in the national budget and a growing discontent among a large segment of the politically active populace. Many had become thoroughly disenchanted with the consignment system, especially in its development since the early 1850s. Basically, the consignment system tended to foster corruption and inefficiency. Since contractors were paid a percentage of the costs of extracting and transporting the guano, they habitually inflated these costs and defrauded the government to increase their profits. They also increased the volume of their sales, rather than raise the price of guano per ton, which would have been the government's preference given the exhaustibility of the resource.[1] The effect of this ultimately was that guano was sold more cheaply than it might otherwise have been. Furthermore, abuses by the consignees—who could not be monitored closely by the government—led to fraud and eventually to the abandonment of a system originally intended to promote Peruvians over foreigners in the business.

The government was not entirely absolved of abusing the consignment system either. It came to depend more and more on the cash advances made by the consignees, and the national debt increased with some abandon as the will to reform the system consistently was outscored by the need for cash. By 1868 the abuses and the debt finally gained enough notoriety to promote a change. In Paris, on July 5, 1869, the Peruvian government sold two million tons of guano outright to the French mercantile house of Dreyfus Brothers. The Dreyfus contract fueled the Peruvian treasury with ready cash, which contributed rather to spending than to promoting capital accumulation. Three years later, in 1872, the Balta regime that had signed the contract was overthrown. Who were these powerful Frenchmen at this crossroads in Peruvian history?

Auguste Dreyfus was a grand manipulator in 1869, but like so many capitalists and entrepreneurs of the era his origins were as modest as his rise in power was dramatic.[2] Auguste came from a family of small merchants. Three of his brothers, Prospere, Jerome, and Isidore, created in Paris in 1852 a partnership called Dreyfus Brothers & Co. to trade in textiles, dyes, and miscellaneous commodities.[3] Each brother subscribed a modest amount of capital and Auguste joined the firm in 1856. He became a partner in 1858, and within a few years the ambitious and talented Auguste rose to the head of the firm. By the 1860s Auguste had settled in Lima and entered the guano trade. A shrewd businessman who studied the world market with care, he built up Dreyfus Brothers rapidly and acquired a fortune based almost exclusively on trading in guano. He knew the business well and acted with boldness in 1869, based on his strengths and the weaknesses of the Peruvian government's position.

Unlike the business that William Grace was slowly developing from New York, Auguste Dreyfus centralized and monopolized power in himself; William preferred to share the growing responsibilities with his brothers and nephews as they were integrated into the firm which expanded from Callao to New York, San Francisco, and Valparaiso in the 1870s. The opportunities for the more modest Grace business were, nonetheless, very much tied to the success of the Dreyfus contract.

The contract itself not only ended the consignment system of sales but took the production and marketing of guano out of the hands of native Peruvians. Dreyfus became the exclusive distributor of guano in the markets of Europe. In return for the two million tons it purchased from the Peruvian government, Dreyfus promised the following: to assume all debts—amounting to over sixteen million soles—the government owed the consignees for previous advances to the government; to service the foreign bonded debt, which required about five million soles annually; to pay the government an initial sum of 2.4 million soles and a monthly stipend of seven million soles for twenty months after ratification of the contract. Dreyfus would pay all these moneys from the sale of the guano and charge Peru 5 percent interest on its debts until liquidated.[4] The opponents of the contract charged that President Jose Balta and his finance minister, Nícolas de Piérola, had subverted Peru's interests to foreigners, but this disenchantment bubbled up mostly from the consignees and their supporters, now deprived of their lucrative incomes. The advantages of the contract swayed the congress and the majority of Peruvians to agree with the Balta-

Piérola program, for by consolidating the various debts of the government and stabilizing its credit, Peru could proceed to build railroads.

The desire to modernize the country with the iron horse amounted almost to a national obsession in the 1860s and 1870s. The great champion was Manuel Pardo, who became president in 1872. He exerted a profound influence on Peruvian thinkers at this crucial juncture of history. Pardo came from an old and distinguished family, had studied abroad in Spain and France as a youth, and had evolved into a dedicated liberal and apostle of the nineteenth-century vision of progress.[5]

According to biographer Jacinto Lopez, Pardo was formed spiritually and intellectually by the English, French, and American Revolutions, all of which thoroughly imbued him with a dedication to liberty, democracy, and, perhaps most important, progressive change. To Pardo the guano boom represented an unparalleled opportunity to modernize Peru by translating the unexpected riches into railroads. The guano era was but a temporary phenomenon that had to be properly turned to long-term benefits for the nation. Otherwise the boom would be but ephemeral. He was especially alarmed by the rapid increase in national expenditures without a commensurate increase in national production. What would occur when the guano was depleted? He predicted a "cataclysm," unless it was forestalled by tapping the great human and natural resources of Peru through the medium of the railroads. Not only would the railroads catalyze increases in production and commerce, but they would be endowed with an even higher mission in Peru: "to create where nothing today exists, to spawn and stimulate the elements of wealth which today are found only in a latent and embryonic state."[6] The examples were clearly drawn from the European and North American experience, and it was from those areas that Pardo also sought the capital and expertise to make the transition. Furthermore, he emphasized that Peru should guarantee as much as humanly possible two prerequisites for foreign investors: domestic political stability and protection of foreign capital. If necessary, the state itself should guarantee a foreigner's investment.

Pardo's philosophy for national development was mature and realistic for the times. As we shall explore below and in subsequent chapters, a major criticism levied at Pardo and his generation is they sold out to foreigners and alienated the national patrimony. Profits from the guano/railroad era enhanced only the small national bourgeoisie while the great mass of Peruvians remained on the margins of this first attempt at true modernization. Furthermore, this is perceived as the beginning of (or another manifestation of long-standing) dependence of the peripheral areas of the world on the rapidly industrializing European and North American sectors. But the analysis fails to perceive adequately what Peruvians of Pardo's generation sought and the means which were available. They needed railroads, and railroads could be introduced only by foreigners who had already developed the technology. The rapid translation of dwindling guano revenues into railroads was not a conscious effort to sublimate true Peruvian aspirations. If anything, it represented an honest attempt to raise aspirations and expectations in imitation of the industrializing nations to the north. If that is judged wrong, then let it be done only with historical hindsight, for Peruvians of the time did not feel the weight of foreign "oppression."

Before proceeding to the actual building of the roads, let us consider carefully one other key element in Pardo's thinking: "Who denies that the railroads are today the missionaries of civilization? Who denies that Peru urgently needs those same missionaries: without railroads today there cannot be real material progress; and without material progress there can be no moral progress among the masses because material progress increases the people's well-being and this reduces their brutishness and their misery; without the railroads civilization can proceed only very slowly."[7] That he, and others, may have bet too heavily on the railroads is probably true. But the alternative was to be content with the status quo. Pardo and like thinkers who founded the first true political party, the Civilista, in the early 1870s were unwilling to be passive and inactive. They were progressive in the context of their times and that is the way they must be judged.

The agents of this progressive modernization actively sought by Pardo's generation were international investors, foreign technicians, entrepreneurs of all stripes, persuasions, and nationalities, and the embryonic multinational corporation. William Grace was busy in New York expanding his interests and operations while in Peru the midwife of the railroads was an amazing American named Henry Meiggs.[8] He signed the first of several contracts with the government in early 1869. The Peruvian imagination, and debt, soared for the next eight years with Meiggs as he strung the narrow rails from different points on the Peruvian coast deep into the Andes, fulfilling at least one desire in Pardo's dream of a new Peru.

The first railroad in Peru had actually been built just after midcentury, in 1851, tying Lima with its port of Callao. Another link, about forty miles long, between Tacna and the port of Arica in the southern nitrate-producing region of Peru had been completed in the 1850s, but then construction ceased until the appearance of Meiggs in the late 1860s.

Although Meiggs competed with other builders for his first contracts in Peru, his reputation as an entrepreneur of unparalleled accomplishment in Chile preceded him and paved the way. He had started out rather modestly in Brooklyn in the 1840s before being drawn by gold fever to California in 1849. There he parlayed a load of lumber shipped around the Horn into a minor bonanza. Speculations in real estate became rapidly complicated by bankruptcy and he left California one step ahead of the law and his creditors. In Chile he converted his winning charm and organizational ability into railroads, living the flamboyant life of the newly rich. He not only built railroads, bribed politicians, and treated his workers with unprecedented respect, but made inroads with the ladies of Chile as well. His romantic conquests seemed only to increase his notoriety as a brilliant, accomplished rascal of monumental dimensions.

Between 1869 and 1871 Meiggs signed seven contracts with the Peruvian government to build 1,042 miles of railroad at a cost of 118,959,000 soles.[9] The Peruvian government eventually constructed over two thousand miles of railroads during this period at a cost of 185 million soles, the balance of these roads being constructed by competitors of Meiggs.[10] However, the longest and most important of the railroads were built by Meiggs. Of these, the Southern Railway from the port of Mollendo through Arequipa to Puno on Lake Titicaca was the longest, 325 miles, and the highest, over 14,000 feet, ever built in Latin America at the time. Even more spectacular was the Central Railway, originating on the coast at Callao. It penetrated the Andes as far as the mining town of Oroya and climbed even higher than the Southern, crossing one pass at more than 15,000 feet, and employed a series of switchbacks, tunnels, and bridges whose design was as singular as the technology to build them.

To finance these railroads, which were contracted at an average of £40,000 per mile, the government floated two separate bond issues in Europe in 1870 and 1872. The question arose about utilizing the guano revenues provided so conveniently by the Dreyfus contract of 1869. The answer was that increasing expenditures to support an engorged civil bureaucracy and military establishment created in the 1850s and 1860s precluded paying directly for the railroads as well. Dreyfus conveniently arranged for the loans in Europe, the first one for £12 million in 6 percent bonds selling at 82.5 and the second for an additional £15 million in 5 percent bonds selling at 77.5.[11] To service both of these debts all of the 700,000-sol monthly stipend that Dreyfus owed the government was forfeited. Further consolidation of previous debts amounted to 21.8 million soles, so that in 1872 Peru owed more than 35 million soles in external dues, which were serviced by the entire guano revenue. Annual internal expenses amounted to over 17 million soles, and only about half of that amount was being generated by taxes and customs receipts.

The improvident course of turning guano (diminishing in quantity and quality) into railroads (producing small revenue relative to capital expenditure) under these circumstances precipitated a crisis and the rise in 1871 of the Civilista party, which elected Manuel Pardo as president in 1872. But to William Grace and Michael Grace in 1869–70, the opportunities for expanding a lucrative trade between the United States and Peru based on Meiggs's undertakings were splendid business ventures. They were no more prescient than any other Peruvian bureaucrat, or American trader, or European investor captured by the mood of the times and the imagination of a Bunyanesque character like Meiggs. It was a flush time to expand business and reap profits in an undertaking—the railroads—everyone applauded.

Michael Grace was in the most proximate position to size up the Meiggs railroad contracts since he resided in Callao as the active partner in the business which itself had been reorganized to accommodate the very active Grace brothers. In July 1867 John Bryce & Co. had ceased to be and was supplanted by Bryce, Grace & Co., with John Bryce, Francis Bryce, William R. Grace, and Michael Grace all sharing equal partnerships. Michael had insisted in achieving a more commensurate position within the firm—to wit, a partnership—based on his leading role. By 1867 John Bryce had all but retired from Peru and was living in Europe most of the time, while Francis was seemingly disinterested in business affairs other than his sugar plantation and its mill.[12] Michael threatened to quit the firm and join a rival, but William, making a trip to England, persuaded John Bryce to acquiesce in Michael's demands. The result was a new partnership, with William and the two Bryces each subscribing $50,000 and Michael sharing equally in the profits as a partner with no investment but his services. The Bryces retired as active managers in the business, and each partner drew a $4,000 salary in addition to his share of the profits. During the next decade the largely passive Bryces were gradually nudged aside until the original contract signed between the partners lapsed in 1876 and the Bryces were dropped entirely, the new firm's name being Grace Brothers & Co.[13] While these internal matters proceeded, railroad fever struck Peru.

William made the first significant inroads into the Meiggs organization when he met Joseph S. Spinney, Meiggs's purchasing agent in New York. Through Spinney, whose family became good friends of William's, the Graces obtained their first contracts to provide the expanding railroad works in Peru with lumber and ties. William himself traveled north to Canada and south to the Carolinas and Georgia to purchase and arrange for shipment of the materials to Peru.

In Peru Michael and one of the Grace agents, James R. Cushier, newly arrived with a load of lumber, mingled with Meiggs and solicited more business as the railroad crews drove into the Andes. Michael's lifelong interest in Peruvian railroads dated from this period, when he became friends not only with the formidable Meiggs, but with many of his superintendents and engineers such as S. L. Crosby, who built the first leg of the Mollendo-Puno railroad as far as Arequipa. Responding to the press of business in Peru and eager to meet Meiggs and appraise him personally, William returned to the West Coast of South America in spring 1871.

William was suspicious of the extravagant Meiggs. Michael had been counseling William to be more liberal and generous in their terms of business with Meiggs. William, however, did not share his younger brother's optimism about the limitless possibilities of profits from the railroads. William's intuitions proved to be well founded. After surveying the situation and returning to New York, he ordered Michael not to sell to Meiggs unless the terms were hard cash. Michael objected and remonstrated with William: "We [in Peru] ought to know pretty well how Meiggs is situated. So long as the government is good we fear nothing and [I] cannot think of treating a man with[out] confidence who had acted so liberally toward us . . . we must make hay while the sun shines."[14]

Back in New York William dragged his feet as 1871 passed into 1872 and Michael continued to exhort his older brother from Peru. "Still you seem to think he [Meiggs] is not safe. . . . Meiggs has paid all his debts in San Francisco and has certainly acted fairly to everyone. He holds good railroad contracts and altho he has thrown money away by the shovelfuls . . . unless Peru comes to the ground we cannot see that Meiggs is going to fall."[15] Inadvertently, Michael had precisely predicted the course of Meiggs's downfall. If Peru "comes to the ground," so would Meiggs. In early 1872 the second Dreyfus bond issue to finance the railroads was moving only sluggishly in the European bond markets. William waited while Michael steamed from his brother's apparent foolish caution.

The Peruvian-Dreyfus bonds were not making much headway for a pair of reasons. One, investors were wary of such a large loan being floated so soon after the substantial one of 1870; and two, French investors in particular were making heavy contributions to pay off the indemnity demanded of France by Bismarck's new Germany at the end of the Franco-Prussian War of 1870.

William was by no means a tightfisted old woman in this affair of Meiggs, the bonds, and Peru's immediate financial future. He bet John G. Meiggs, Henry's brother in Peru, a new suit on the outcome of the bond issue and in early 1872 ordered the suit from his tailor to pay off Meiggs. However, by the middle of that year the situation had reversed as investors lost interest.[16] To instill public confidence Dreyfus itself purchased many of the bonds while others were given to Meiggs in partial payment for his services. But by May only about twenty million soles of the seventy-million bond issue had been subscribed to, and of these twenty million Dreyfus had purchased about nineteen.[17]

Michael backed off and acknowledged the possibility of real problems arising from the failure of the bond issue. He finally admitted to William that railroad fever had affected his good judgment. "I have been ambitious to show good results to the patrons of the house, and certainly have lacked experience . . . one thing is certain, your advice has made me conservative and has turned my every effort to consolidating outstanding accounts and business."[18]

Meanwhile, Peru suffered political violence in the transition from Balta's regime to Pardo's in July 1872. At the root of the disorders that shook Callao and Lima were the nation's growing fiscal crisis and the repercussions on the many sectors of society sharing in the guano and railroad boom. As the modernization process proceeded, it drew wider and wider segments of the nation into the mainstream, and the expansions and contractions of the new system naturally affected more people.

Pardo initiated a reform program which combined traditional wisdom and modern idealism: he intended to increase customs revenues; to levy new taxes on the growing nitrate-export industry in the south of Peru; to reduce expenditures on the military and civilian bureaucracy; and to expand public education to uplift the great mass of the Peruvian people. His immediate problem, however, came from the disgruntled minister of war, Col. Tomas Gutierrez. Along with his brothers Silvestre, Marceliano, and Marcelino, Colonel Gutierrez precipitated a brief but bloody revolution when he ousted Balta, who had announced he would yield peacefully to president-elect Manuel Pardo.

Pardo's overall reforms were aimed at tightening the state's financial affairs and that included downgrading the military. This Gutierrez would not tolerate. He seized and imprisoned Balta one week before Pardo's scheduled inauguration, dispersed congress, and proclaimed himself supreme chief. Lima's citizens, already well politicized by Pardo's Civilista party, were outraged, and the army garrison at Callao and the navy renounced Gutierrez's flagrant usurpation of authority. Pardo and other Civilista leaders fled to sanctuary either in foreign legations or aboard naval vessels in Callao.

That evening a jeering, pistol-happy Silvestre was shot to death in the Lima railroad station by a civilian crowd.[19] Marceliano retaliated by murdering his prisoner Balta. Tomas was captured and almost hacked to bits by a furious mob while Marceliano died leading a wild shooting spree through Callao. On the morning after this grisly scenario, the mutilated bodies of Tomas and Silvestre could be seen swinging from the towers of the cathedral in the heart of Lima.

Michael, like most others in the Lima-Callao area, was caught in the action. He took refuge with his wife and baby daughter aboard a British vessel the night that Marceliano rampaged through Callao on the way to his death. Michael's behavior was deemed "very prudent," by one of the young Grace associates then with the Callao house, Sylvan D. Hazen, for "during the night his [Michael's] house was pierced by cannon balls . . . one going clear through, destroying a bedstead."[20] Nonetheless, after this tumultuous transition to Pardo, the work on the railroads proceeded and the debt continued to increase in almost direct proportion to the decline of guano revenues.

The Dreyfus contract, never popular with many nationalistically inclined Peruvians, was terminated in 1875. A new contract with British investors, incorporated as the Peruvian Guano Company, Ltd., was concluded to sell Peruvian guano, pay an annual stipend to the government, and service the debt. But the problems of competing with Dreyfus, which still held a considerable amount of unsold guano, drove the price of the commodity down. Additionally, the great guano reserves were finally being exhausted, leaving only low-grade fertilizer, which depressed the prices even further.[21] By 1875 the government could no longer raise loans to pay for the railroads, and construction stopped.

A temporary reprieve was jury-rigged by the ever charismatic Meiggs, who induced the government to print paper money. But this expedient failed as well, and early in 1876 Peru suspended payments on its foreign debts. The Grace brothers had felt the sting of Meiggs's grandiose vision before the middle of the decade, however. In late 1872, when taking stock of transactions on the books of the Callao house, William's Irish temper flared and young Michael caught its fury.

Meiggs owed the Callao house almost $179,000, a startling revelation that snapped William's patience with his imprudent younger brother: "I would never have believed this had I not the papers before me . . . and yet besides this, coal and sleepers on the way to a goodly amount . . . if Meiggs goes you can't get clear for a loss of $250,000.00 . . . men who know Meiggs well here in California, his own agent here [Spinney] included, would not . . . trust him for $50,000.00. This I have tried to hammer into you."[22] Michael had shown good paper profits, but they were based largely on obligations from Meiggs. William grew choleric enough to suggest that if Michael demonstrated no more sense than he had recently, in spite of William's advice, "then as a friend and brother I ask you to finally let me out of the concern [the Bryce-Grace partnership] . . . as I can't see any safety in the present mode of carrying the business on."[23]

When his anger cooled, William apologized to his brother for the outburst, but not for the advice. If Bryce-Grace failed, it "would make no difference in my feelings toward you as a brother, [but] no matter what your past record has been, just make a heavy loss by Meiggs and others, use up the capital in your hands, and you will learn the bitter lesson of what it is to fail as a businessman."[24]

By summer 1873 Michael had improved on the account with Meiggs. The Pardo government meanwhile strove to keep the Meiggs enterprises solvent with cash payments. Meiggs in turn paid Michael off to keep open his dependable and absolutely necessary link with United States suppliers.[25] Bryce-Grace was by now the largest and most important merchant house in Peru doing business with the United States. In overseas trade, British merchants still controlled the overwhelming majority of business with Peru and Latin America as a whole. Yet the Graces—still very much in transition from a European to an

American cast of mind—represented the cutting edge of American enterprise.

Relations between Peru and the United States in the first half of the nineteenth century had been largely determined by the establishment and maintenance of good commercial links.[26] More than diplomats and naval officers posted to the West Coast of South America, consuls and merchants influenced the formation of ties. Americans in the Pacific appeared in large numbers in different capacities—those in the whaling industry, for example—and carried back with them not only whale oil and ambergris, but tales of the Pacific world.

The expanding American presence continued into the second half of the century, especially reinforced by the heavy volume of the guano trade and by such intense activities as railroad building. The needs and wants of this merchant and commercial community quite often determined the goals of American diplomats. For example, the negotiation of a most-favored-nation treaty between the United States and Peru and the settlement of debts owed to American merchants incurred by privations suffered during the Wars of Independence always figured high on the list of priorities of American chargés d'affaires in Lima.

In the middle of the century, Peru sent its first minister to Washington and Washington reciprocated with the upgrading of its chargé to minister status. There was a constant flow of information between consuls, merchants, and diplomats, and the Graces began to move in this circle with ease and greater influence in the 1870s. The evolution of inter-American affairs, and more specifically those related to Peru in this early period, thus became an offshoot of commercial relations between citizens of both countries. And with William Grace in New York and Michael Grace in Callao, not only were the sinews of a powerful commercial house being developed—one that would become a multinational corporation by the beginning of the twentieth century—but individuals who would profoundly influence United States policy toward Latin America were also maturing.

It was also an era of growing American interest in Latin America generally, a fact easily substantiated by the actions of Secretary of State Hamilton Fish and the United States Congress in 1870. In that one year the United States minister in Colombia signed a treaty for the construction of a canal across the Isthmus of Panama, the Dominican Republic was almost annexed to the

Union, and the Ten Years War (1868–78) by Cuban insurgents against Spanish rule stirred nationwide sentiments to recognize the rebels as legitimate belligerents.[27]

In this same spirit the Senate passed a resolution in July asking the State Department for information on the state of commercial relations between the United States and Latin America. The resolution also requested recommendations on how to compete more effectively with Great Britain, which commanded the lion's share of Latin American trade. Fish dispatched a circular letter to all ministers and consuls of the United States in Latin America to report on trade and relations in their areas.

Their replies soon began crossing the secretary's desk. In a general category, inattention or misjudgment by American manufacturers and merchants was cited as a distinct disadvantage. American prices tended to be higher at the point of shipping than those of their English and German counterparts. Insurance and commissions were apt to be higher as well; for example, they could be as high as 2.5 percent in New York versus 0.5 percent in European ports. Thick American textiles lost out to English ones, since most Latin American nations charged tariffs computed by weight. Europeans granted Latin American merchants longer credit terms than did Americans, anywhere from six to nine months as opposed to three and six by Americans. The English interest rates were frequently half of what Americans charged. European steamship companies, such as the venerable Pacific Steam Navigation Company, founded in the 1840s by an American named William Wheelright but British-controlled, provided dependable service from England to the ports of Rio, Buenos Aires, Valparaiso, Callao, and Panama. Yet, since their rates were high, they were vulnerable to cheaper sail service. This weakness would be a major card played by William Grace in gradually building up his shipping business from New York round the Horn to Peru and the West Coast. Other suggestions by American consuls and ministers on how to best, or at least match, the English were to learn the language and customs of their customers better, subsidize American steamship companies, sponsor an interoceanic canal, and encourage reciprocity treaties to lower tariff barriers. It certainly is not coincidental that the leading United States house in Peru was run by partners who spoke the Spanish tongue well, would eventually establish the first United States steamship service to the West Coast (1894), would actively sponsor an interoceanic canal (through Nicaragua) at the end of the century, and would actively seek in the 1880s and 1890s to better hemispheric relations politically and economically.

Meiggs's needs—for locomotives, cars, ties, iron, lumber, and other nuts and bolts of a railroad—were largely fulfilled from the forests and machine shops of the United States. And in this trade the Grace brothers were his major agents. United States exports to Peru more than doubled in value between 1868 and 1872 while the Meiggs projects peaked.[28] Michael snagged a big chunk of the profits on that trade, whatever William said or bemoaned of his younger brother.

In truth, it was an excellent relationship between the two brothers. William was farsighted, a gifted organizer, and a leader who was the better judge of people. Yet he possessed a short fuse, as Michael and Tom Lawler before him well knew. Michael was the impulsive, less constrained younger brother, not burdened with being the eldest and hence more responsible son in a large family that included four brothers. He was less political than William and sought his goals with less restraint, following his fortune with a more narrowly conceived vision than William's.

William had established himself firmly in New York where he settled with his family in 1866. From his small office at 110 Wall Street he chartered and operated vessels between New York and the West Coast of South America. He also participated in the shipping business as part owner of the graceful, tall-masted downeasters. Sharing ownership was an ancient means of spreading the risks in an enterprise never too far removed from the vagaries of nature. As a merchant, he also purchased goods on his own account to send to South America, or acted as the consignee for others' goods, receiving a commission for his services. His cargoes sometimes were shipped in vessels under his management or, just as often, in the holds of others whose timetable and ports of call might be more convenient. The Fabbri & Chauncey Line was often patronized by Grace since it was the only scheduled line between New York and the West Coast of South America.

Grace's interests naturally came to include shipbuilding as well as shipping, for the two were complementary. That his wife was a member of a prominent Maine shipbuilding family no doubt further influenced him in this direction. In 1867 the ship *Lillius* appeared on the registers with Grace listed as one-fourth owner, and in 1869 the barkentine *Agnes I. Grace,* named after a daughter born that year, was launched at Thomaston, Maine.[29]

Grace moved his offices twice during this period, to Sixty-two South Street (today the site of New York's re-creation of eighteenth- and nineteenth-century maritime life on the waterfront at the South Street Seaport Museum) and to Forty-seven Exchange Place, each time seeking slightly larger and more convenient quarters for the expanding business.

His growing family also needed new lodging, and in 1872 he moved Lillius and the children from Brooklyn to a three-story brownstone at 108 East Seventeenth Street in Manhattan. It was a boisterous household, frequented by old and new friends from the worlds of the sea, business, and politics. Ship captains, visiting Peruvian dignitaries, New York politicians Grace was meeting through his friendship with his old Brooklyn neighbor, Judge Calvin E. Pratt, and relatives all found a welcome at the Grace residence. People liked to be around William and Lillius and the feeling was reciprocated. It would be a great asset in 1880 when Grace emerged dramatically on the political scene as a candidate for mayor of New York.

An estate on Long Island overlooking Manhasset Bay on the Sound was purchased by Grace in 1872. He christened it Gracefield, and gradually expanded it from ninety-two to a hundred forty-four acres. He paid $30,000 for the original property, which included a large, comfortable country-style home. While definitely a merchant and quite at home at sea, the pull of the soil was strong on Grace, and he re-created much of what he remembered and admired from his ancestral homeland in Ireland. It was an instinct many were able to follow in the New World after leaving a more impoverished and unhappy home in Europe. Gracefield and a farm Grace purchased across the Sound in Connecticut were stocked with horses, ponies, cows, and sheep imported from Ireland. From Gracefield William coached two miles to the landing at Little Neck Bay to meet the commuting steamer *Sewanhaka* for Manhattan. That ferryboat would play a minor role in later getting Grace elected mayor in 1880.

Lillius and William's first son was born in 1872 and christened Joseph Spinney Peter Grace in honor of St. Peter and J. S. Spinney, Meiggs's agent in New York and William's close friend. Upon hearing of the baby's arrival, Michael quipped, "I trust he may be president of the United States and call on his uncle to look after the finance," adding in a subsequent letter that he heard William was naming his son "Joseph Spinney Peter Grace . . . if such is the case you had better turn to and increase your fortune as you will have to leave him a large fortune to sustain such a multitude of names."[30]

Michael in Peru, like William in New York, also enjoyed the

good life made affordable by the brothers' growing prosperity. He and his young wife Margarita entertained with gusto in their home, throwing one memorable party in July 1872 which drew "lots of swells . . . admiral and fleet . . . Meiggs, Bryces, Petries, Garcias and more than the house could well hold, although I made room for dancing; we had a splendid band, over 150 invited, few hid, 101 came; we had a good time but it is too much work and too costly to repeat daily."[31] During the summer months Michael and Margarita frequented the seaside resort of Chorillos, judged "very jolly, but rather too much per trip with such slow coaches and trains."[32]

In nearly all the correspondence between the brothers, candor prevailed. For example, William had sent Sylvan D. Hazen, Fabbri & Chauncey's former shipping clerk, to assist Michael with the buildup of business in Callao and he wondered how Hazen was working out.[33] Michael tried to be fair and answered that Hazen was an excellent goodhearted fellow and a good worker. However, Hazen was basically lazy, did not look into accounts and invoices, and did not make others work as Michael would have preferred. Furthermore, Hazen could not speak Spanish and was unwilling to learn.[34] Indeed, it was tough for Michael to get along with a man who did not like Spanish or Peru. Not surprisingly, Hazen lasted only a short time with the Graces, who thrived on hard work and were firmly committed to Peru. Nonetheless, Michael tried to make the best of Hazen and even reported to William on one occasion that "we pull well together and we always consult each other."[35]

No other words could have better summarized one of the essential ingredients in the growing success of Michael's and William's endeavors. Michael's optimism repeatedly surfaced in his appraisal of events with a nice feel for the language and its Irish idioms. "I don't see that one need fear much [failure of bonds; Pardo's austerity program]; . . . unless the country fails and the government is overthrown, I think things will yet turn up turnips; meantime Meiggs paid us cash so that one will I trust come out whole on all our business with him."[36]

The news Michael sent William from Peru in late 1872 was a mixture of fact and conjecture, of public and private matters. It appeared that the latest Dreyfus loans were a failure. President Pardo's economic austerity program included possible taxes on nitrates and a reduction of the army. Money was tight but Michael, ever buoyant, was optimistic.[37] In the affairs of the family, Elena Bryce was to be married to Rufino Echenique and Francis Bryce thought Rufino would make a valuable member of the firm.[38] Meanwhile, another young Grace relative—destined to become one of the major foundation stones of Casa Grace—joined the firm in 1867.

Edward Eyre arrived in Peru at the tender age of fifteen after 107 days aboard the *Nerius*. Ned Eyre joined his brother Jim, already working for Uncles William and Michael for the past three years. Both were following a familiar pattern, but whereas Jim Eyre died early, Ned lived well into his seventies and provided a major link between the generations that managed Casa Grace from 1850 to 1930.

However, young Ned's arrival at Callao was something less than grand. He had shipped before the mast and it took a good deal of "grease, hot water, soap and a nail brush" to remove "the vestiges that remained from contact with ironrust, tar, and paint." When Ned first prepared to go ashore, he donned a rather snug-fitting suit given to him by Capt. George Gilchrest and toted a small seachest, also presented to him by the good captain. It was a modest beginning, made even more so by Eyre's recollection of Callao when he first came ashore: "The sight was depressing. Nothing could have been more garish than Callao's shore front . . . and my heart sank." But tender hearts rise as fast as they sink and he was soon enveloped by his youngish Uncle Michael. Smaller than medium height, Michael had a charming smile that was cast in a rather pale face marked by grayish blue eyes and an incipient mustache.

"His welcome was kind in the extreme and I should say right here that there never was a man for whom one could work with greater goodwill."[39] Michael's nature could stir the greatest sentiments of loyalty. It could also offend mightily. Michael's career would produce wakes of both love and hate, depending upon how one viewed the charming Irishman.

The firm Ned Eyre joined in 1867 was mixed but not mixed up. Michael Grace had taken command when William departed finally for New York in 1866, and Michael was now firmly in control in Callao. Although Francis Bryce was nominally in charge, his business habits belied his interest. A well-groomed, handsome old man with closely cropped sideburns, he always carried a nice pair of gloves, John Bullish in the extreme, and was rarely seen in Callao. "Don Francisco" Bryce would pop in occasionally at the Callao store, at about eleven-thirty in the morning and be gone by three, entering and leaving through the side door. Ned never knew what Don Francisco accomplished in his visits to the Callao establishment; all the same, he was held in esteem by those who knew him and generally qualified as *un caballero distinguido.*

Michael Grace, on the other hand, arrived in the early morning and never left before six. Assisting him when young Ned came aboard were Manuel Llaguno, the bookkeeper and accountant who first joined William at the Chincha Island storeship; Juan Fernandez, salesman in charge of the counter; George Baker, cashier; William Seymour and H. Purly, runners, or men who met the incoming ships; and August Borchardt, head porter. Eyre went to work for Fernandez, a bright, intelligent, active, and resourceful fellow on whom Eyre could bestow the highest encomium of their business world: "He attended to the business of the vessels consigned to the house *promptly,* leaving no loose ends about" (italics added).

The business young Ned joined was still relatively small but highly competitive. Under the stimulus of Michael in Callao, it was constantly innovating to get the edge on rivals. It was basically a trading firm and success depended on the patronage of vessels arriving from all parts of the world, generally after long voyages, so that the need of a constant replenishment of stores was considerable.[40]

Patronage was secured in two ways: recommendation by vessels' owners, and by runners being the first to board the incoming vessels—backed by the firm's reputation, already the best among both American and British shipmasters.[41] The race to board the vessels and beat competitors was exciting. Michael decided to improve on that rudimentary tactic. He extended the system of correspondence with the owners everywhere and, in the United States, added to the list the names of the owners' agents in New York. He followed this up by starting a fortnightly shipping list, which gave the arrivals and sailings and general shipping news and was posted to the United States, Great Britain, Sweden, and Norway. Then improvements were made on the improvements. A hand printing press was secured and a little hunchback named Lyons, born in Callao but of English parents, set up the type while the junior clerks supplied the power by turning the handle. The enlarged system of correspondence and the shipping lists gave the edge to Michael, Ned Eyre, and the others running the firm in the late 1860s and early 1870s. William Grace in New York, of course, was an integral cog, adding to the business by cultivating excellent contacts. Joseph Spinney, for example, threw many of Meiggs's orders to the Graces, a decision based not only on friendship but on the growing Grace reputation for reliability and efficiency.

★   ★   ★

In 1869 a tradition ended. It was decided to close the business at the Chincha Islands because the guano beds were nearing exhaustion. In fact, it was said that from the middle island even the graveyard with the bones of the Chinamen buried there had been shipped.[42] With the closing of the storeship, its manager, John Lancaster, returned to Callao and became Eyre's immediate boss. Lancaster possessed an excellent English business education and was a "rather good fellow when sober." And there lay the source of his problems. By midday Ned was working with a drunk who was effectively finished until the next morning.[43] When Lancaster was eased out and eventually returned to England, Eyre stepped into his place, overseeing the counter business and developing a rather inflated sense of self-importance. In 1871 he was barely twenty years old. That same year William Grace came through to check on the business—especially, of course, the Meiggs contracts—and he knocked his young cousin down a notch, replacing him with Juan Fernandez. Eyre was returned to his original job, in charge of the deposits in the warehouse, and he was sore.

When Michael first informed him of William's decision, Ned decided he would quit in the face of such injustice and take a job with Meiggs. The railroad builder had noticed the young Irishman's talent and on several occasions offered him a job. But it was not that easy to shake off family loyalties. He was living with his Uncle Michael and Aunt Margarita, and it was clear that Michael had not relished implementing his older brother's orders. Coming home that day, Ned cleaned up for dinner but decided rather to boycott it than to sup in the company of Uncle William, "who was flattening me out." Margarita took Ned aside and explained it was his duty to take his medicine like a man. Not only did Margarita force Ned to take his medicine, but later on he would recall that his Aunt Lillius taught him the meaning of the term "sticktoitiveness," something most of the Grace family males seemed to lose temporarily when those famous flashes of temper consumed them. But Margarita and Lillius knew their men and boys well. They added the hardheaded rationality which often brooked the tempers and provided for a transition to the next stage, usually consisting of growth and further prosperity.

Although William's admonishment hurt, Michael helped mend Ned's feelings by promising him they would soon open an American line of general merchandise. So Eyre went back to his old job at the warehouses. Once again he had to straighten out the contents of the warehouses, tramp out after the cargo from the customhouse and beach, and tend to the odd details of the job.[44] And the new American business? Michael had been so wrapped up with Meiggs that he forgot. Eyre pressured his uncle, who finally relented and told Ned one morning to go ahead and prepare a memorandum of such American goods as could be sold to advantage. Ned was delighted with his new responsibilities.

What did Ned Eyre know about American goods? Nothing. But he did have brains and friends. He appealed to a young Italian merchant for advice and they drew up the following list:

Wooden pails—3 hoops
Wooden tubs
Corn brooms—so many in a case and sewn in a certain way
American lard—packed in a certain way
Cut nails, of determined sizes and in kegs of specified weight[45]

Eyre's list was finally polished and sent off to New York. There another sharp young man hired by William Grace filled the order. As Eyre remembered, the invoices from New York were plastered over with Charles R. Flint's comments as to the cheap prices at which the goods had been obtained, a claim that Eyre did not question; Flint was not a man to make a bad deal.[46] Charles Ranlett Flint eventually became a partner of the New York branch of the Grace houses, W. R. Grace & Co., and one of the most dynamic figures in the expansion of the business. Ned Eyre's list was eventually expanded and Casa Grace developed into the leading importer of American goods to Peru. But, aside from the Meiggs contracts, this was the beginning.

Charles Flint was born January 24, 1850, in Thomaston, Maine. His father Benjamin Flint Chapman and his uncle Isaac Flint Chapman were partners in the very successful shipbuilding firm of Flint & Chapman. They built and owned fine clippers when "an American sailing vessel could show its heels to anything afloat, and when the Yankee trade had nosed its way into every port of the world."[47] It was an old and distinguished family to which Flint belonged. Charley's ancestor Thomas Flint arrived in Massachusetts in 1642, barely a dozen years after the founding of the colony, and his grandfathers confronted the redcoats at Bunker Hill. The sea was in the blood of these New Englanders. But unlike his schoolmates, whose highest ambition was to sail the tall ships, Charles Flint dreamed of owning and operating them.[48]

His father and uncle eventually moved to New York to be closer to the center of business, so Charles went to school in Maine and Brooklyn. He graduated from Brooklyn Polytechnic in 1868 at the age of eighteen, the president of his class. Like William Grace back in 1849–50, Flint left school, searching for challenges not found in the classroom. After a two-month vacation in Maine, Flint began nosing around South Street in New York, then cluttered with the ships, cargo, and clatter of a bustling port.

Unable to land a job, he turned to self-employment, again like William and his early, enterprising participation as a broker in the immigrant trade to America. Flint printed business cards advertising his services as a dock clerk, and he received four dollars a day to measure, receive, and deliver cargoes on and off vessels. He learned the ways of dock and wharf rats and seasoned himself well by the constant vigilance needed to outwit his ingenious adversaries. Flint caught them in all sorts of tricks. While one crook casually conversed with his sidekick, his tin-lined coat would be filling full of wine from a nearby cask with a rubber siphon.[49]

Yet Charles Flint wished to be part of a firm and one of the figures he most admired was William Russell Grace. Knowing jobs would not materialize for the asking, Flint contrived a meeting with Grace aboard a ferryboat. No doubt trapped for the duration of the short voyage by this pleasant but aggressive young man, Grace agreed to hire him on Flint's terms: without a salary until he proved himself. This he soon did. He proved himself so well that when the firm of W. R. Grace & Co. was formally chartered in 1872, Charles Flint became a partner with 25 percent interest. It was later increased to 35 percent.

At that time W. R. Grace & Co. was doing a general shipping and commission business, largely with Bryce, Grace & Co. of Callao. It also was operating sailing ships to the West Coast of South America, and as a shipbroker, the firm chartered vessels to bring back Peruvian guano and nitrate of soda. To catch up because of a lack of experience, Flint worked from seven-thirty in the morning until about eleven at night, when the last Wall Street ferryboat left for its slip in front of his home on Brooklyn Heights.[50] Grace felt so confident in Flint that he left him, along with his father-in-law, George Gilchrest, in charge of the business when he traveled to Peru in spring 1871.

The diversification of the Grace houses from ship chandlers

and operators, purveyors of guano and nitrates, and railroad suppliers into a broadly based trading house took place during this period. This transition eventually provided enough resilience to weather several major crises in the coming decades. Flint's experience with the purchase of some sugar machinery in 1872 demonstrated the versatility of the firm.

The Bryces wanted a sugar mill for their estate La Estrella and Flint was asked to buy it. It was his first big venture in buying machinery. He got designs and prices from Belgium, prices from Glasgow and Liverpool, and secured a quotation from the Southwark Foundry in Philadelphia. Although its prices were the highest of all, Southwark's designs were far more progressive than the European ones, especially in saving labor.[51] He figured the American design reduced the labor force necessary by almost 60 percent. Convinced by this clinching argument, Flint contracted for the Philadelphia machine. He paid Southwark $168,000, and when sent to Peru by William in 1874, Flint visited the Bryce estate and found his machine functioning well.

The young partner was an excellent representative and trader, by his own admission liking to travel and meet people. He, Hazen, Ned Eyre, and Michael were dispatched by William up and down the West Coast and into the interiors of Ecuador, Peru, and Chile, sizing up the markets and measuring the needs. Supplying the railroads had brought Michael and his partners into contact with many remote parts of Peru. These were always carefully assessed as potential markets. One long dispatch from Flint to William discussed the following items: lard, tallow, fish, canned goods, crackers, kerosene, lamps, pails, tubs, shoe pegs, brooms, cars, tobacco, nails, cotton cloth, butter, cookstoves, condensed milk, saddles for mules, pitch, tar rope, resin, and small hardware.[52] However, as the American consuls and ministers had reported back in 1870 and 1871 to Secretary of State Hamilton Fish, English goods were tough to compete against. Flint's two long trips to South America, one in 1874 and one in 1876, took him over the land like an itinerant peddler, often confirming the English advantage in price and quality. Flint, like the U.S. diplomats and honorary consuls, made specific suggestions: put the crackers in five-pound tins; paint the broom handles; put three hoops on the buckets.

In some specific commodities, such as Oregon pine and other lumbers, the Graces were particularly successful. The people on the desert coasts of Peru and northern Chile traditionally imported woods to supplement the native materials available for construction. With the building of the railroads, the Grace partners had become the leading supplier of lumber to the West Coast, most of it imported from the Pacific Northwest. From supplying the railroads, they expanded their services into the traditional areas. In one instance Sylvan Hazen contracted to supply an entire building, a theater, for Iquique, complete with stage, scenery, curtains, dressing and waiting rooms, store and barrooms, and enough seats for twelve hundred.[53] Hazen added that any roof would do since it never rains in Iquique.

Since much of the lumber came from the West Coast of North America, it was considered advantageous to open up a branch of the business in that area. Furthermore, California also exported basic foods like potatoes, grain, flour, barley, and apples, and Michael wished to import them to South America.[54] Michael not only was thinking of expanding the California trade to include foodstuffs, but saw California also as a potential source of labor. Chinese workers by the thousands had been released upon completion of the transcontinental railroad in 1869. The presence of so many Orientals in the western United States was causing uneasiness and even riots among Americans in California. Peru, on the other hand, needed cheap labor for its expanding sugar and cotton estates. Yet Peru was on the verge of banning the coolie trade for humanitarian reasons. Michael proposed to tap the excess and apparently unwanted supply of Orientals in California to service Peru's needs. What Michael and William needed was a good representative in that state for many business reasons.

Both were thinking of their lame brother John, still in Ireland farming but with a yen to travel and improve himself like his two brothers. Michael and William plotted in a fraternal spirit and finally convinced John to sell out in Ireland and come to New York to view the prospects in America. Michael said he would like to see John established in the family business somewhere unless farming in the States interested John more and paid well, while William talked up the business end of opportunities in America.[55] John was curious about the Wild West and disposed to try business and trade. He must also have surely been sensitive to the warm wishes of his brothers. In April 1873 the firm of J. W. Grace & Co. opened in San Francisco.

The field for ambitious American merchants and entrepreneurs widened considerably in the 1870s and the Graces were often at the cutting edge of pioneering and profitable ventures. Their scope was by no means limited to the West Coast of South America, although their experiences in Peru and Chile were essential in leading them into Costa Rica and Brazil. For example, they were drawn to Central America by forces similar to those at work in modernizing Peru under the aegis of Henry Meiggs.

Costa Rica and Central America in general passed through a period of conservative dictatorial rule in the post-Independence era. Then, spurred by the growing export of coffee and the ascendancy of liberal, progressive elites to power, Costa Ricans, like their counterparts in Peru and Chile, homed in on the railroad as the vehicle to a more modern life, to increasing their wealth, and to bettering contacts with Europe and North America.[56]

Costa Rica's Tomás Guardia came to power in 1870. Ruling off and on for the next twelve years, he became the leading apostle of the railroads. He was the classic liberal dictator. Imbued with positivistic philosophy, Guardia sought, like Pardo in Peru, to bring his country rapidly into the mainstream of the Western world. With this in mind, Costa Rica contracted with Henry Meiggs to build a railroad linking the Atlantic coast with the central highlands. It was a visionary and ambitious project, given the long stretches of hot, malarial, swampy, lowlands of the east. Yet Meiggs's reputation was enough to generate not only a torrent of enthusiasm but, at least initially, adequate funds from the European bond market.

Tied up in Peru, Meiggs entrusted the project to his equally flamboyant nephew, Henry Meiggs Keith, who began work on the railroad in 1871. Already the principal supplier of the Meiggs railroads in Peru, William Grace, to no one's surprise, was appointed Henry Keith's agent in New York.

For a short while, buoyed by the Costa Rican government's initial cash advances to Henry Keith, the project looked grand, although John G. Meiggs from Peru advised Grace on several occasions to be wary of his nephew's extravagance.[57] The Grace organization supplied the railroaders with everything from excavating tools to iron, cars, and locomotives. For the work on the Atlantic coast Henry Keith introduced blacks from Jamaica; Chinese coolies were imported as well. Also associated with the project was Henry's younger brother, Minor C. Keith. Minor was destined to found one of the most important modern industries in Central America. Now, however, Minor was only slated to act as a commissary for the railroad gangs, although he rapidly expanded his scope quite as ambitiously as his brother and uncles.[58]

Minor obtained a monopoly on the importation of rum, began a sawmill near the eastern terminus of the railroad at Limon, planned to export tropical woods such as cedar, mahogany, and balsa, and also went into the rubber, sarsaparilla, tortoise shell, and banana trade.[59] Energy and ideas were never wanting among the Meiggs and Keiths. In a stroke of inspiration, Minor also imported the first banana plants from Panama to Costa Rica. While the railroad venture soon brought him and his brother to near bankruptcy before being completed, Minor eventually made a fortune in the nutritious yellow fruit, which was virtually unknown in the United States in the 1870s.[60]

The heavy cost of building the railroad finally dragged Costa Rica into deep debt and forced the small nation to default on its loans in 1876. Henry Meiggs Keith died earlier in 1875, already separated from the railroad project by the more sober Graces and elder Meiggs brothers struggling to finish the Peruvian railroads as that country also quickstepped to bankruptcy in 1876. Minor C. Keith inherited the mess left by his high-living brother, and it would be several years before the railroad project once again regained momentum.

Before he was shunted aside, however, Henry Meiggs Keith had been the ever ebullient entrepreneur, whereas William had played the role of sober pessimist. On the failure of Costa Rican bonds to sell well on the London market, Keith's remarks were, "such things are to be expected and cannot last long . . . Costa Rica is the star of the tropics." William's summation moved closer to the earth: "I am afraid they have made a regular mess of the loan in England . . . it is the Peruvian loan all over again. . . ."[61]

William, nonetheless, actively promoted the Costa Rican projects from his New York vantage point. In 1872 he entertained President Tomás Guardia on a visit to the United States, taking him out to Gracefield on one occasion and introducing Guardia to President Ulysses S. Grant on another.

When Costa Rica finally defaulted on its loans in 1876, Grace's connections with the railroad and Minor Keith were also severed. Keith persevered in the face of general disillusionment and eventually finished the railroad in 1890. His banana business grew with more success, evolving into the United Fruit Company toward the end of the century.

However, to Grace in 1876, Costa Rica was a morass of problems. He also found it hard to dissociate Minor from the behavior—irresponsible from Grace's point of view—of his late brother Henry. Besides, rapidly expanding opportunities in Peru, Chile, and Brazil consumed more and more of the Grace partners' time in the middle and late 1870s as nitrates, rubber, and sugar competed with guano and the railroads for their attention.

But, becoming part of the capitalistic world was not a gentle process. Depressions periodically shocked that world and the panic of 1873 certainly shook William and Michael, and further weakened the already shaky financial understructure of Meiggs's railroads in Peru.

Ironically, the panic was caused in part by the very success of American railroad builders. Competing fiercely, they had extended themselves too thinly in order to lay down parallel lines across the nation. Triggered by the failure of some banks in 1873, the resultant panic swept through commerce and industry with a rush of fear that brought many down in the next two years.

The Graces weathered the financial crisis, but not before some anguished moments caused largely by Michael's inability to turn credits into cash on the Bryce-Grace account in Callao.[62] William mortgaged both his home in Manhattan and his estate on Long Island to keep from going under. Remittances from Michael in Peru were insufficient, for Michael was also being drawn on heavily by a bank John Bryce founded in England. Searching out any weaknesses that could be shored up during the panic, William soon discovered that John Bryce and his General South American Co. bank had far exceeded their income, and old John Bryce himself was close to living the life of a profligate in Europe. Before the panic, when the Callao house was making a profit of 100 percent a year on capital invested, John spent recklessly. When the crunch came in 1873 and 1874, he drew heavily on Bryce-Grace in Peru. Michael was caught in the middle. His brother in New York was attempting to keep W. R. Grace & Co. solvent, while John Bryce in England continued to draw freely even as the general economy sputtered.[63] In late 1874 William took a ship to England with Lillius to see Bryce and confront the perilous situation as squarely as possible. He found a mess.

The Bryce bank had paid exorbitant dividends, had backed questionable enterprises that failed in South America, and John himself was spending up to $100,000 per year to support his lifestyle. When the troubles came, John drew on Bryce-Grace in Callao for relief, and Bryce-Grace in turn had less and less to remit to W. R. Grace & Co. in New York. William felt he was paying for John Bryce's high life and bad investments. He spent many months in Europe carefully dissociating Bryce-Grace in Peru as much as possible from the failing bank. Michael was instructed to remit only to New York and cease remittance to London. The bank's shareholders were convinced by William to make substantial personal contributions to cover losses. William sent instructions to Charles Flint in New York to do no business except on a cash basis, and to conserve funds as best as he could.

William then traveled to Peru in late 1874 to take stock of the situation there and help Michael sort out matters. Michael already was working diligently, reducing the Bryce-Grace debt to the New York house substantially. When John Bryce's bank went into voluntary liquidation in April 1875, while William was en route to New York, Bryce-Grace in Peru was clear. Next year, 1876, the partnership agreement between the Bryces and the Graces expired and was not renewed. Bryce, Grace & Co. became Grace Brothers & Co.

While William threaded his way through this thicket of financial problems that spread across three continents, Henry Meiggs made a brilliant last stand in Peru in spite of the bond disappointments, the depression of 1873, and declining health. After the failure of the 1872 bonds, the Pardo government, still committed to the completion of a national railway system, directed its efforts to keeping that great project viable.[64] If Meiggs failed, thousands would be thrown off their jobs, a major political debacle would surely occur, and the ability of the government ever to climb out of the trough of debt would be seriously compromised. Yet such was the nature of the ebullient Meiggs that even while the railroad debt was being patched over temporarily between 1873 and 1875, Meiggs launched a public works company, the Compañía de Obras Públicas y Fomento del Perú, to modernize Lima with wide boulevards, horse-drawn streetcars, gaslights, sewage and waterworks systems, and up-to-date homes for working people.[65] William H. Cilley, chief engineer on the Oroya railroad, was placed in charge of the new public works program. Cilley, from Maine, was a friend of Charles Flint's, and W. R. Grace & Co. was chosen as the United States agent for these works. William himself was still close to Meiggs. He stayed with "Don Enrique" as a house guest in early 1874 while in Peru helping Michael to finish breaking off from John Bryce's failing bank in Europe.

By mid-1875, however, it was clear to Pardo and the government that traditional sources of income had failed. Some new and perhaps even drastic measures were needed to save the nation from imminent bankruptcy.

In May the congress established an export duty upon nitrate of soda and created a government monopoly of its production and sale. It prohibited further grants of nitrate lands and authorized the government to purchase those lands then being operated by private interests. Yet a new loan based on this anticipated nitrate revenue failed to bail out the government. In August 1875 Peru was compelled to halt railroad construction. It simply was unable to pay the railway contractors for work done and materials furnished. Half a year later, in January 1876, Peru defaulted in the payment of interest upon its foreign bond issue and the construction of the railroads—already 75 percent complete—remained in abeyance. Meiggs responded to this emergency with the Promethean vitality one had come to expect from the man.

★ ★ ★

The problem was one of unrealized potential. The unfinished railroads were only producing small revenues. To achieve their full potential they had to generate considerable traffic by connecting major economic foci in the country. Callao was one. The silver and copper mines of Cerro de Pasco, high in the mountains, were another. Meiggs proposed an ambitious, multiple attack on the problem: finish the Central Railway to Oroya and extend it to Cerro de Pasco; construct a major drainage tunnel, the Rumillana, beneath the mines of Cerro de Pasco; and develop and operate the unregistered and abandoned mines of the district. Cilley reported that over a hundred fifty million ounces of silver, worth at least $70 million, were probably available in the mines in the dry zone alone. By this venture the railroads would become self-sustaining from the increased traffic, the government would derive a new source of income from taxing the export of silver and copper, Meiggs would presumably become richer and even more admired, and Peru could proceed with modernizing.

A new contract between Meiggs and the government was signed February 3, 1877, after many months of negotiations. Meiggs would be allowed to pay for the work by issuing bills—soon labeled Billetes de Meiggs—backed by government treasury bonds held by Meiggs, by two hundred thousand tons of guano turned over to Meiggs by the government to sell in the United States, and by some less firm assurances.

But this time it was not in the stars for Meiggs to rise again like the phoenix. The poor quality of guano, the failure of Peru to capitalize immediately on nitrates, and the immensity of its foreign and domestic debt were beyond his control. The strain took its ultimate toll on this Yankee Pizarro, as his fine biographer Watt Stewart styled him, on September 30, 1877.

William and Michael were not harshly affected by the suspension of the Meiggs projects. They had been disentangling themselves gradually from the web of Meiggs's financial problems since the precarious years 1874–75, and, characteristically, were investigating and acting on new opportunities and options. Nitrate of soda figured heavily in these ventures.

Like guano, nitrates were discovered to be excellent fertilizers by European and North American farmers in the nineteenth century. Nitrate of soda is made from caliche, a mineral salt located in strata of different concentrations underneath the Atacama Desert, which stretches six hundred miles from southern Peru into northern Chile.[66] Commencing with the modest export of about a thousand tons in 1830, production reached over eighty thousand tons in 1860, and continued to increase through the decade of the 1870s. A disastrous earthquake in the region of Iquique on August 13, 1868, led to scarcities and pushed prices upward, while the combatants in the Franco-Prussian War, interested in saltpeter (sodium nitrate) as a major ingredient in gunpowder, further underscored the growing dimensions of this business.

The southern Peruvian province of Tarapaca and Bolivia's only coastal territory, Antofagasta, were the richest areas in nitrates. The industry had expanded rapidly and profitably, and only in 1868 did the Peruvian government levy a small tax to help defray the costs of reconstructing from the earthquake. During the 1870s, however, the unremitting series of fiscal crises set off by the immediate expense of building the railroads combined with the worldwide depression of 1873 focused attention on this potentially lucrative source of income. Peru increased the export tax in 1873, and in 1876 it expropriated the nitrate companies in Tarapaca, hoping to maximize profits by monopolizing the industry. The ultimate ramifications of this policy—the War of the Pacific—will be discussed in Chapter 6. More immediately, William and Michael Grace were drawn to the nitrate trade as it expanded in the Peruvian economy, promising a new source of increasing business.

The brothers moved dramatically in 1878. Michael bid for the nitrate concession in the United States late that year when the American firm that had originally contracted for the concession was going bankrupt. William in New York supported Michael by traveling to London where he arranged for banking credits with Baring Brothers.[67]

Although already a naturalized citizen of the United States, William was very much the internationalist in his business dealings. He wrote to Michael that "it is more costly to do this business by credits from Baring than by securing it here, but it is much more secure, as no matter what condition the money market is in we have every assurance that we should never be called for our credit but would be allowed to renew it continuously."[68] William successfully obtained Baring Brothers backing, and with that done, the Graces secured the exclusive concession to market Peruvian nitrates in the United States for four years dating from 1879. The distribution in Europe was reserved for Baring Brothers.

While nitrates promised future earnings for the Graces, they were already plowing money into Peru's rapidly developing sugar industry in the 1870s. They owned large mortgages on three major plantations: Francis Bryce's estate near Callao; the Cartavio plantation of the Alzamora family in the northern Chicama Valley; and the Canaval's estate of Paramonga, located in the Pativilca Valley some hundred miles north of Lima. Enlargement and modernization of machinery, such as Charles Flint's purchase of a new sugar mill for the Bryces in 1872 for $168,000, rapidly increased the planters' indebtedness to the Graces. By 1874 the three plantation owners owed Bryce-Grace almost $600,000. At the end of the decade Grace acquired Cartavio in consideration of the Alzamora debt, and indeed was operating it through an *interventor* even before then.[69]

The decade of the 1870s was a major transitional period in the historical evolution of Peru. Unprecedented revenues from the guano era were channeled into the building of railroads, which eventually derailed the nation into bankruptcy. A premature vision of the railroad's power to transform the economy, and the consequent overextension of the nation's credit, forced Peru into a confrontation with Chile over control of the nitrate fields straddling their common frontier with Bolivia. A disastrous war ensued and marked a further turning point in Peruvian history.

The Graces shared in the prosperity of the guano era and diversified rapidly to take advantage of new opportunities as they arose, in trade, commerce, financing, and even agriculture. They expanded from their modest initial base at Callao and by the mid-1870s had established offices in New York and San Francisco. John Grace eventually traveled to Valparaiso and in 1881 a full branch of the firm would be established in that Chilean port. William C. Holloway, married to William's daughter Alice, ran the San Francisco office. Edward Eyre rose rapidly after the familial rift with Uncle William, and helped oversee the growing operations in Peru on a permanent basis. Michael was the floater, along with Charles Flint to a lesser extent, who moved about physically to transact business when correspondence was insufficient for the purposes of close bargaining. The business was still a family business, but one that became gradually "extended" as outsiders like Charles Flint and Manuel Llaguno were integrated as partners and as personal friends. The Llaguno association is particularly meaningful.

Llaguno originally joined William on the old storeship anchored off the Chincha Islands. William entrusted Manuel with the storeship during his periodic absences and the Peruvian eventually moved up to a partnership in Grace Brothers after 1876. When Flint & Chapman launched three downeasters in the 1870s and honored its Grace associates, the three ships were christened the *W. R. Grace*, the *M. P. Grace*, and the *Manuel Llaguno*.[70]

William and Michael were interested in acumen, thrift, adaptability, and hard work in their associates. Latin Americans would rise in the Grace organization in the succeeding century based on these principles.

Experience in Latin America, principally in but not limited to Peru, was almost a *sine qua non* for anybody working up in the Grace organization. English and Spanish were used interchangeably, and if one were slow in adopting the language of Latin America, as Sylvan Hazen appeared to be in the early 1870s, it drew a gentle but firm admonishment from the brothers. By 1875 Hazen was no longer with Bryce-Grace.

The Meiggs era left on Peru some strong imprints which transcended the immediate results of the extravagance and shortsightedness—the War of the Pacific. Many of Meiggs's engineers and technicians from the United States remained in

Peru and branched out into other businesses. Breweries, ice houses, machine shops, and similar establishments emerged as ongoing enterprises. Along with the railroads and expanding sugar estates, many of these new businesses preferred American equipment and machinery, a habit developed during the Meiggs railroad-building era.[71]

Supplying, nurturing, and growing along with these new enterprises were the Grace houses, the most prominent of the United States firms operating in Peru at the end of the Meiggs era. William Grace imparted to his siblings, nephews, and other young associates a firm feeling for Peru and Peruvians. "I like the Peruvians; I always enjoyed their society and I never looked upon them as more deceitful than [other] people . . . the English in foreign lands, I never liked; they are, in my experience, presumptuous and self-opinionated . . . .I know houses in Peru that were in my time hated as haters of Peru . . . this may be well worth bearing in mind."[72] William added, in this 1879 letter to John, then in Peru, that "if you educate your mind . . . to think kindly of the people of the country and to sympathize with them, you are received and treated as a friend."[73]

Being dynamic individuals, it was almost inevitable that the Grace brothers would soon pass beyond the simple bounds of trade and commerce. William Russell Grace moved dramatically into the mainstream of the American political scene in 1880. He became the first foreign-born mayor of New York in the Gilded Age, turning his considerable talents from making handsome profits to reformist politics. It was a major challenge, but then William enjoyed challenges.

From this new forum as a major public figure Grace would become intimately involved in the making of inter-American policies in the 1880s and 1890s. It was an era when the United States was growing even more active in the affairs of Latin America, ever more cognizant of its mission as self-appointed guardian of the Western Hemisphere. Very few, if any, of the principals in the creation of these new bonds between the Americas crossed the boundary between the private matters of business, trade, and investment on the one hand, and the public ones of diplomacy, war, and treatymaking on the other. What William Grace sought as mayor becomes part of the story of how the Graces developed as formative figures in inter-American relations in the last twenty years of the nineteenth century.

5

Mr. Mayor

THE AMERICANIZATION OF
WILLIAM RUSSELL GRACE

The call to public service that William Russell Grace answered in 1880 is perhaps unique in American politics of the Gilded Age. Not only was he foreign-born, but his business experiences were international in focus. Furthermore, he was one of the first Roman Catholics elevated to high office in the United States. He was a businessman in the age of enterprise who chose to enter politics when most of the more celebrated figures in American trade and industry—Vanderbilts, Rockefellers, Goulds, Carnegies, Fisks, and others—consistently sought their fortunes in private life with precious little service volunteered in the public orbit. Many, of course, were indirectly involved in politics, the New York State legislature, for example, being thoroughly corrupted in the 1860s and 1870s by Jay Gould. Votes could be bought for a stated amount of dollars. William Vanderbilt's notorious remark on his responsibility to the public ("The public be damned") expressed an attitude, perhaps exaggerated, commonly attributed to the great and small capitalists of the period.

With the great issue of the nation—divided or undivided—decided by the Civil War, people wished only to get on with their lives. To the west the Great Plains were pierced by the railroads, and innovations in agricultural techniques and equipment made possible the farming of this vast territory. Agricultural production in the United States doubled and tripled before the end of the century, not only revolutionizing the countryside but radicalizing the farmers. Their increased efficiency and productive energies inexorably drove down the prices of their wheat, corn, livestock, and other basic foodstuffs, and they organized into political and social bodies to preserve their interests and livelihoods. The Greenback party of the 1870s, for example, lobbied forcefully for more credit, more money, and more rights for the farmer, but their issues were sectional, not national.

In the South Reconstruction gradually tapered off as northerners grew weary of enforcing their postwar morality on the defeated Confederacy. It was enough to have preserved the sanctity of the Union in the face of the rebellious southern states and to have freed the slaves. The guarantees secured in the Thirteenth, Fourteenth, and Fifteenth amendments finally satisfied the collective conscience of the nation, and in 1877 the last of the federal troops were withdrawn from the South. What most everyone agreed were needed were more railroads, steel mills, inventions, immigrants; in short, progress, and the North was leading the country in the production of that commodity.

William wrote his brother Morgan in 1879:

> All things are booming and the flood of prosperity is overwhelming. Stocks and bonds of all kinds are way up . . . manufacturers are making money. Produces of farms are up to 20 to 80 percent. Lands, houses, etc., are improved in value & the Amr. Eagle's screams of joy are heard in all directions. We have not participated much in the grand boom of advancing prices, but have benefits flowing from this cause. We never were doing a better business than now. The Chilean Peruv. War alone mars the outlook.[1]

William was in fact becoming quite Americanized, but with an Irish twist. New York, his home since 1866, also had over two hundred thousand Irishmen—16 percent of the city's population. They were concentrated in the lower quarter of Manhattan's East Side, and by the 1870s were carrying considerable clout in New York politics.[2] Their principal vehicle for political expression was Tammany Hall, a society founded in 1789 which, ironically, was narrow-mindedly nativist in its early years. By the 1830s and 1840s, however, it had broadened its appeal to include immigrants, especially the Irish, who voted in blocs to ensure their interests.

William Marcy Tweed—Boss Tweed, as he was known—dominated city politics in a notoriously corrupt fashion through Tammany in the post–Civil War era.[3] He was succeeded in 1874 by John Kelly, who earned the sobriquet "Honest John" more because of whom he followed than from any probity in himself. Although scandal was suppressed during his regime, Honest John accumulated a fortune of half a million dollars before his retirement in 1886.[4]

Tammany Hall was but one faction of the Democratic party

in New York, although it was certainly the most celebrated. Kelly's maintenance of political control in the 1870s typified boss control in the growing metropolises of the nation. He subsidized two newspapers, the *New York Star* and the *Evening Express*, through forced subscriptions from saloon owners.[5] The leverage was provided over the saloon owners through their licenses. These could be obtained only from the Excise Commission, and the commission would issue licenses only to subscribers of Tammany's causes. All Tammany-backed candidates were assessed large sums for their nominations, sometimes as much as 25 percent of their salaries. This ensured a full central treasury to coordinate better the election of Tammany-supported candidates. Each district in New York was organized under a leader or committee, and the districts sent representatives to a higher-level organization which controlled primary and general elections. These conventions were limited to members of Tammany, and force and threats kept out dissenting elements. The apex of Tammany's activity was election day. Money and favors were distributed liberally on "Dough Day" before Tuesday's election. It was estimated that Tammany under Honest John could deliver up to sixty thousand votes. No one doubted its efficiency.

Kelly's machine could control New York City, but he faced more formidable opposition at the state level. For example, a political truce of sorts had been reached in 1874 between Kelly and the new reformist governor of New York, Samuel J. Tilden, but within two years the Democratic leaders parted ways and Kelly failed to support Tilden actively in his bid for the presidency in 1876. It could have proved a major political mistake for Kelly since Tilden won the popular vote. However, he did not win the presidency, for the electoral votes of three southern states, Florida, Louisiana, and South Carolina, were disputed and eventually given over to Tilden's Republican opponent, Rutherford B. Hayes. This represented part of the bargain to end Reconstruction and earned for Hayes a revised first name, "Rutherfraud."

During the New York gubernatorial election of 1879 Kelly again bolted from the Democratic party when Governor Lucius Robinson, Tilden's choice, was renominated. Robinson had committed *lèse-majesté* in refusing to release Boss Tweed from prison. This displeased Kelly, who decided to run himself. Thus divided, the Democrats gave the election to the Republican candidate, Alonzo Cornell. Grace stepped straight into the feuding Democratic party in 1880 and, not uncharacteristically, came out on top as mayor of New York.

★ ★ ★

What prompted his entry into politics?[6] It was probably a combination of altruism and natural interests. It was certainly not the money, for he was already a millionaire at the age of forty-seven (1879) and his various enterprises were prospering.

His very Irishness drew him toward politics, for the politics of the homeland remained volatile and much on the minds of its sons abroad. Separation from England remained a constant goal—almost a religious crusade, really—for many Irishmen, and even before the Civil War a Fenian movement promoting the separation of Ireland from Great Britain had been created in the United States.[7] Irish newspapers—no fewer than five weeklies (the *Freeman's Journal and Catholic Register, Tablet, Irish World, Irish Nation,* and *Irish American)* circulated in New York—kept the Old World issues very much alive among the immigrant population. John Devoy, of the *Irish Nation,* and Patrick Ford, creator of the *Irish World,* were committed to terrorism and violence in Ireland's struggle for independence, and the combined circulation of their newspapers reached over fifty thousand copies in the 1880s. Less radical leaders of the Irish in America, such as William Grace, supported a more gradual transition within a constitutional framework, but the burden of helping the home country was never too far from any Irishman's consciousness. The visit to New York of two Irish leaders in the struggle for independence, Charles Stewart Parnell and John Dillon, in the winter of 1879–80 drummed up enthusiasm to confront the seemingly continuous Irish crises. In this instance, not only was the independence of Ireland at issue, but crop failure raised the specter of starvation and destitution once more.

A campaign to send relief to Ireland was launched by James Gordon Bennett, the flashy publisher of the *New York Herald,* and Grace joined the effort enthusiastically. Bennett contributed $100,000 on behalf of the *Herald,* and Grace donated the services of the ship *W. R. Grace* as well as offered to pay for one quarter of her cargo to Ireland. Eventually the U.S. government donated the *Constellation* for duty in this mercy mission, but Grace continued actively in the campaign by helping to purchase, crate, label, and stow the cargo for the *Constellation* at his own expense.[8] Grace's efforts were celebrated in the pages of Bennett's *Herald* and he became a well-known public figure in early 1880. Furthermore, he was cooperating and rubbing shoulders with the like of Honest John Kelly, banker Levi P. Morton, and other major figures in public and private life in

New York. William had casually known many of these people
before 1880. John Kelly, for example, had visited the Grace
townhouse in Manhattan on several earlier occasions, perhaps
to chat about politics or mutual interests in Catholic charities.
Nonetheless, the relief compaign of 1879–80 apparently catalyzed William's decision to enter public life more actively.

In a grand fashion, he moved decisively into politics at the
top, choosing to promote a presidential aspirant in the Democratic National Convention of 1880. While his nominee and
friend, Judge Calvin E. Pratt of the New York Supreme Court,
did not win the nomination, Grace's baptism into the political
world was almost completed in summer 1880.

Because of a full business career, Grace's political profile before 1880 had been low. Intensely active in the 1870s, Grace,
his brothers, and partners had rapidly diversified the business,
faced down several major crises, and successfully parlayed a
ship chandler's shop into a growing international concern.
Grace voted for Ulysses Grant in the national election of 1872
out of respect and admiration for this military chieftain revered
by the Union, but the graft and corruption associated with
Grant's political career—especially manifested during his second term of office—turned William away from the Republicans.
On the other hand, the reformist administration of Governor
Tilden, for whom Grace voted in the 1884 election, appealed
to him. Thereafter he appeared most often in the reformist
camp of the Democratic party, although this political alignment
was not inflexible. Grace proved quite capable of shifting alliances and making compromises with Tammany and others in
local and national politics to further his ends. In 1878 Grace's
name was mentioned as a possible candidate for mayor by
several newspapers. Tammany was casting about for a neutral
political figure as a front and Grace was only one of many
individuals considered. Edward Cooper, the son of Peter
Cooper, eventually was elected for the standard two-year term,
but Grace's name would again emerge in 1880.

As noted, in the spring and summer of that year Grace injected himself into national politics by promoting his friend
Calvin Pratt for the Democratic presidential nomination.[9] The
convention was held in Cincinnati in late June and eventually
it selected Gen. Winfield Scott Hancock of Pennsylvania as its
nominee. But, for a short while William engineered an intense
campaign that came close to placing Pratt's name before the
American public as the Democratic candidate for president.

Grace's campaign was generally low-key, elevating the merits
of Pratt rather than detracting from his potential competitors.

Chief among these was Tilden. While the ex-governor really was too ill to run, he was not past keeping his enemies, especially John Kelly, off balance by allowing his name to be considered until very near the time of the convention. Grace quietly played up Pratt as a dark horse while Tilden and Kelly tilted. By the time of the convention Grace was confident that Pratt had a good chance.

Pratt had distinguished himself during the Civil War and possessed a commendable record as an independent jurist in New York. He still carried in his skull a Confederate bullet, which very nearly had killed him. The circumstances surrounding that wound would return to strike him down politically on the eve of the convention. But until then, Grace's campaign moved crisply.

He lobbied, first by mail and then personally in Cincinnati, with potential supporters throughout the nation and managed what appeared to be the classic campaign of a dark horse. The day before the convention, New York's delegates, invoking the unit rule, were pledged to Pratt. Other states, like New Hampshire and North Carolina, were ready to vote for Pratt when his candidacy was unveiled. Most of them were holding for favorite sons since no singular individual was emerging; except, of course, for the relatively obscure but popular Pratt. He seemed to be the perfect candidate. Then a rumor spread rapidly like a swirling, black thunderstorm blotting out a bright summer sun: Pratt had been baptized a Roman Catholic.

It is difficult in today's world to understand the crippling effect such a relevation had on a presidential aspirant in summer 1880. It is even more outrageous when Pratt revealed the innocent circumstances of his baptism. Wounded on the battlefield and thinking himself near death, he accepted baptism and the last rites from a close friend of his, one of the Catholic chaplains attached to a regiment under his command. The chaplain had since died, Pratt never practiced Catholicism, and the act had, indeed, been forgotten. But Pratt was forced to withdraw his name from consideration for, as Grace wrote a friend in California a few days later, "I think you will join me in saying it was wise; no matter what individuals may say or think, this country is not prepared to see a R. C. President."[10] Grace exhausted himself in the effort, writing Michael in London that "I have never passed through a more acute period of exhaustion & mental labor than I did during my stay in Cincinnati."[11] He returned to New York to rest and recuperate, but he was soon catapulted into the newspaper headlines once more, almost prophetically exposing him to wide public acclaim.

William's publicity was earned aboard the steam-powered ferry *Sewanhaka*, which plied between Manhattan and slips on the Long Island Sound. Like most high-pressure steam engines employed on ferries and riverboats of the era, there were inherent dangers in its operation, principal among these being the tendency to explode. The *Sewanhaka* engine did just that on a pleasant day late in June while loaded with over three hundred fifty commuters, including William, Lillius, and their two girls Alice and Agnes.

Amid flames and confusion, the *Sewanhaka's* captain drove his vessel toward Randall's Island to beach it. The roaring fire amidships effectively cut off the forward end from the rear of the vessel and people began jumping overboard to escape the flames driving back as the crippled boat made toward the island. In the tumult and panic, William and Lillius, who had weathered not a few crises at sea, maintained their composure. They calmed frantic passengers, helped them don the cumbersome cork lifebelts, and counseled as many as they could to wait before jumping and striking out for the island on their own. Many tried and perished in the effort. Alice became separated temporarily from her parents, adding to the anguish and uncertainty of the moment. When the ferry finally grounded, passengers on the forward end clambered down to safety on the island. Many of those on the rear with William and Lillius, still blocked by the flames and intense heat, began leaping overboard. Others were helped over the rails and into the water by the Graces. One fat lady required both William and Lillius heaving together to propel her up and over the rail. Then Lillius and William plunged in. In the water, William could hold on only to Agnes among the panicky and struggling survivors. Lillius, on the point of exhaustion, was picked up by a rescue boat, while Alice was helped out of the water by a young man.[12] The next day William and Lillius were celebrated in the New York newspapers. The *Sewanhaka* incident, tragic in that fifty people lost their lives, reinforced William Grace's name—already having achieved some prominence through his acts in the Irish relief effort—in the public as a man of conscience and courage. Grace would need both attributes in the forthcoming months as the Democrats of the city quarreled in preparing for the mayoralty election that autumn.

The Democratic party in New York was divided into two

main organizations: Tammany Hall, and those who opposed Tammany. The strongest of the latter were organized into Irving Hall. To achieve some unity in the forthcoming election, a presidential as well as local one, the two organizations agreed on the following procedure. Irving Hall would draw up a slate of names acceptable as nominees. Then Tammany—or Honest John Kelly—would select one name from those proposed.[13] Eleven names were submitted by Irving. They included leading members of the reformist, liberal movement in New York such as Peter R. Voorhis, Wheeler H. Peckham, William C. Whitney, Everett Wheeler, and Oswald Ottendorfer.[14] With little hesitation Tammany selected William Grace's name, also on the list, as an acceptable compromise candidate. This led to the charge that Irving was duped into including Grace's name, which was thought to be unacceptable to Tammany. Democrats opposed to Kelly were rankled by the boss's apparent high-handed maneuver, which placed Grace on the ballot as their nominee. The *New York Times* editorialized that Kelly accepted the nomination of Grace simply because he was the one man on the Irving Hall list who would best serve as a figurehead for the Tammany boss.[15] Whatever the case, William was now out of the trenches and on the open field. His religion drew the first fire.

The issue was joined over the possible influence of Roman Catholicism on his public school policies. It was presumed by his detractors—Republicans and Democrats—that Grace would insidiously introduce papism into the free and secular American public school system. Democrats, many of them Irish and Catholic, resented the intrusion of religion into politics generally. But Grace's political foes knew a good issue. The *Herald* envisioned the partisan hand of the Roman church in politics as leading to the virtual end of free government.[16]

Speakers in behalf of Republican candidate William S. Dowd carried the religious argument through to its ultimate absurdity. One maintained that Catholics were bound by an indefensible dogma that all education should be sectarian.[17] Grace was not without his defenders. The *Irish World* lashed back in the name of all Irish Catholics and called for unity in the face of these challenges to race and creed.[18] Treading through the middle of this sniping, Grace responded with an even temper, promising to abide by and support the prevailing American sentiments with respect to public, nonsectarian schools.[19]

Grace's nationality and, by implication, his loyalty to American ideals and the nation itself were called into question. That he was Irish-born was not the question; it was, rather, whether he had been naturalized. Naturalization papers were finally produced late in the campaign, so that Grace had a duplicate in hand by November 1. Grace had also lived a great deal of his life in South America, a fact dragged out by the Republicans as further evidence of Grace's alien nature. But this one backfired on the Republicans, for Grace had warmly supported the Union cause during the Civil War.

As previously noted, in 1862 two Union cruisers put in at Callao. Their paymaster, a Mr. Eldridge, could get no bank or institution in Peru to honor his drafts to buy coal for the empty bunkers and to pay the crews wages long overdue. The news of the Civil War in 1862 was not good for the Union cause. But Eldridge was sent to Grace and Grace's partiality for the North prompted him to help Eldridge. The old paymaster did not forget this act of confidence and conviction. When Grace's patriotism was questioned by the Republicans, Eldridge's warm recollection of Grace turned the jibe into a political plus.[20]

A few days before the election the *New York Tribune* tossed another barb at Grace. He was accused of fraud and mismanagement while acting as the Callao agent of the New York Board of Underwriters between 1865 and 1871.[21] Grace denied the charges heatedly. He had not even been in Peru for most of that period and had certainly not received an appointment as the board's agent in Callao. Grace was finally exonerated of wrongdoing by the very newspaper, the *Tribune*, that published the allegations. Its editor, Whitlaw Reid, personally examined documents presented to the newspaper by William and Michael and generously admitted to the innocence of the new mayor.[22] The rub was that this all took place after the election. When New Yorkers went to the polls on Tuesday, November 2, 1880, Grace was still fighting the charges. His initiation into the intricacies and demands of a major American political campaign while promoting his friend Judge Pratt had been wearying and somewhat disappointing. His personal campaign for mayor was bruising and tough.

When the voting was completed, William Grace won with a vote of 101,760 as against 98,715 for the Republican Dowd.[23] However, Hancock lost the presidential race to the Republican Garfield. The conclusion reached by most political observers, including Grace, was that Hancock lost the election in New York, more specifically, in New York City because of the divisive mayoralty contest.[24]

Yet, Grace was now mayor of New York. In spite of the national setback to the Democratic party, Grace moved with customary energy to take charge and produce a reformist, independent regime in keeping with campaign promises made when he accepted the Democratic nomination for the office. He was determined to promote honesty and efficiency in public service, and considered his election as the expression of the people's will, which left him free of pledges to individuals or political associations.[25] However, those very political associations and its leaders who helped elect him plagued Grace right from the beginning of his term. Even before being sworn in on January 1, 1881, he split ways with Honest John Kelly over the issue of patronage.

Outgoing Mayor Edward Cooper had the right to nominate certain members of the mayor's cabinet subject to the board of aldermen's approval. John Kelly held the post of comptroller, whose term was due to expire in December. Mayor Cooper did not intend to renominate Kelly. It was the plan of reformers on the board to oust Kelly even before Grace assumed office, for they were still suspicious of the reputed alliance between Grace and Kelly. Honest John, on the other hand, could persuade the aldermen to postpone a decision until Grace was sworn in, *if* he could induce Grace to provide him with enough patronage to satisfy the seven Republicans who sat as aldermen and held the swing votes. William refused Kelly the support, and Honest John was replaced on December 10 by the aldermen who accepted Mayor Cooper's nominee for comptroller.

The rift between Kelly and Grace widened rapidly in early January. Grace accepted one of Kelly's nominees for a minor appointment but rejected another nomination on the grounds that the person was not qualified. This was strange behavior indeed, and Kelly called for a meeting with Grace. They retired into the mayor's office alone, Kelly to explain the rules of the game, Grace to give Kelly his views on the matter. Overheard just before Kelly took grim leave from City Hall was Grace's voice declaring in loud tones that echoed through the offices: "Do not dictate to me, Mr. Kelly!"[26] Grace then turned to other matters—public education and dirty streets.

His first appointment to a vacancy on the board of education was William Wood. Grace made Wood, a Scot Presbyterian, president of the board. That somewhat allayed the fears of critics that Rome's minions would soon be directing the public schools of New York. The problem of the city's dirty streets brought Grace again into combat with Tammany and Honest John.

The street-cleaning bureau of the city traditionally was supervised by the police commissioners. Efforts by the previous mayor, Cooper, to force the police commissioners to use funds allocated for street cleaning for that precise purpose went to no avail. He removed some of the commissioners from office, but they subsequently and successfully sued for their posts. Grace went after these commissioners with gusto. They were under Tammany's wing and patently guilty of graft and malfeasance. That was wrong. The public was being defrauded. He asked them for a full reckoning of their increasing expenditures, which were not justified by the increasing deterioration of the streets. Receiving no satisfactory answer, the mayor called upon three, Joe W. Mason, Stephen B. French, and Sidney P. Nichols, to resign or prepare to stand charges in a public trial.[27]

Grace also prepared a bill for the legislature in Albany to remove the street-cleaning administration from the police department. A rousing meeting at Cooper Union won many reformers and independents to the cause. The rally was punctuated by stirring speeches such as one made by Joseph H. Choate, a Republican and future ambassador to England: "If it is true that the commissioners cannot clean out the streets, why it is at least possible that we can clean out the commissioners . . . by the grace of God—and by that other Grace whom the people of this city have chosen to execute their will—this thing shall be done."[28] A Committee of Twenty-one was formed, with Abram S. Hewitt as its chairman, to support the passage of the bill in Albany to create an independent street-cleaning department.

The battle was thus transferred to the state capital. The bill passed the senate but was upstaged by a substitute bill offered in the assembly by Kelly's supporters. It dictated that appointments to the new street-cleaning department be agreed to jointly by the mayor and the members of the board of health. These Kelly felt he could control. The Committee of Twenty-one, which soon evolved into a more permanent reformist organization, the County Democracy, raised a chorus of protests, but to no avail. The bill passed and was signed by Governor Alonzo B. Cornell, elected only two years before in 1879 on account of the rift in the Democratic party caused by Kelly's enmity for Tilden.

Grace then named James Coleman as first superintendent of the new street-cleaning department. The young man was a compromise candidate acceptable to the Kelly-controlled board of health, and under Coleman the streets began to improve in appearance. William Grace was demonstrating his grasp of the political art of compromise very well this first year. He got his street-cleaning department and then successfully reached a middle ground in arranging for its superintendent. These skills would later prove valuable when negotiating the equally tricky world of inter-American relations.

The three police commissioners Grace had fired after the public hearing constituted a more formidable barrier to reform. Their removal was subject to review by the governor and Cornell ruled against Grace's act on the somewhat flimsy technical ground that the commissioners could not in all fairness be held culpable for the City of New York's streets since the street-cleaning department was now separated from the police jurisdiction. They stayed, but Grace had removed the streets from their jurisdiction in the course of his first half year in office.

He also suppressed some of the more open and scandalous gambling establishments during this time, but this aspect of the city's life was relatively impervious to any permanent changes by Grace and the reformers.

Grace's attention was, of course, drawn to matters great and small as befits the mayor of a famed metropolis. Early on he learned that hundreds of letters and petitioners were attracted by the mayor's power, real or imagined. They ranged from disaffected municipal employees seeking redress for grievances, to citizens shocked by the "moonlight picnics" then common in the parks of New York and Brooklyn.[29] What Grace did to dissuade moonlight picnics that allegedly corrupted the morals of the younger generation is not recorded. We can hope he produced some Solomonic decision to preserve the best of innocence within the boundaries of the Victorian public's rather exaggerated sense of decency.

By virtue of its size and reputation, New York drew the attention of the world, and, naturally, so did its mayor. From Genoa, Grace, as first magistrate, received a letter in illiterate French from one Francesko Mussato. Mussato desired to come to America and open a factory for handorgans. However, being in destitute circumstances, he needed to have his fare paid and his project subsidized to realize his dream.[30] Could the mayor help?

From Barnesville, Georgia, Mayor E. J. Murphy wrote Grace and wanted to know if it was true "that five horses standing with their heads over a fence (in the city) were killed by lightning which struck the fence sixty yards away." Mayor Murphy had seen this report in the *New York Ledger* and was curious about both the veracity of the statement and the principles of science involved in this bizarre accident.[31]

C. D. Moore of Macedonia, Ohio, was interested in curing a flagging libido and wished Mayor Grace to inform him at once on the reliability and reputation of the Calverwell Medicine Co. at Forty-one Ann Street, which advertised a treatment for sexual weakness.[32]

Early in his administration Grace appointed William M. Ivins as his official secretary. The duty of answering many of these requests fell to Ivins. Given the nature and volume of requests that reached the office of the mayor of New York, one can easily surmise the breadth of the lessons in Americana learned by Grace, Ivins, and others charged with assisting the mayor in meeting his obligations, great and small. As part of the former, Grace presided over the installation of Cleopatra's Needle in Central Park in 1881. A ninety-foot obelisk presented by the khedive of Egypt to the city in 1879, it was successfully transported to America only when an enterprising American naval officer, Henry Gooringe, suggested cutting a steamer in half and rebuilding it around the obelisk.[33] During Grace's second administration, 1885–87, Ulysses S. Grant died and the task of arranging for the burial—a moment of great national sentiment—fell to Grace. His most pressing problems, however, came from the living and not the dead, and one of the liveliest then on the national scene was Jay Gould.

Gould was perhaps one of the boldest of the robber barons in an age not noted for probity among its entrepreneurs. As a reform-minded public official, Grace tangled with Gould over Gould's manipulation of the elevated railways of New York. Grace earned a quick victory in the beginning, but it proved pyrrhic. He also learned how it felt to be maneuvered by one of the great impresarios of the age.

Gould had gained control of New York's three elevated-railway companies in 1881. Not wishing to be burdened with paying back taxes, he promoted the passage of an elevated-railway exemption tax bill in the state legislature, explaining that these back taxes were excessive and the railroads had been overassessed. An earlier conference with Grace had produced nothing but intransigence by the mayor, who was determined to collect the taxes owed the city.[34] Nonetheless, Gould prevailed in Albany and the bill was rammed through the legislature.

Grace was furious and, together with his comptroller, Allan Campbell, shot off an outraged protest to Governor Cornell, calling the bill legislative robbery. It deprived the city of half a million dollars and compelled the citizens to pay for what were Gould's responsibilities.[35] Cornell was put in a bind. Public opinion swelled in support of Grace, and Cornell wished to be renominated by the Republican party to continue in the governor's mansion. He had to veto the bill. Gould, crossed by both Grace and Cornell, took his vengeance accordingly. He blocked Cornell's renomination by supplying all the "essentials" for the opposition, led by President Chester Arthur and Roscoe Conkling. A power in New York politics, Conkling was a former senator and, not incidentally, Jay Gould's lawyer.[36] Gould also opposed Grace's candidate to succeed him in the mayoralty election of 1882, but clubbed Grace more directly through W. R. Grace & Co.

Gould learned somehow that Grace had made a contract to deliver to parties in South America $800,000 worth of a particular kind of lumber, at a fair margin above the market price. When the mayor's firm came to fulfill the contract and collect the lumber, it was discovered that Gould had effectively cornered the market by buying virtually every stick of that lumber. Nevertheless, the contract had to be carried out to the letter, and, in doing this, Grace was compelled to pay $1.2 million for the lumber—a net loss of $400,000 to his firm. The mayor was not happy at the turn taken either by politics or by business.[37] To have survived Gould's animosity is perhaps the strongest testimonial to Grace's business and political wisdom, constantly being honed in the early 1880s.

Meanwhile, the death of President Garfield in September 1881 from an assassin's bullet altered the tone of national politics. Garfield's death elevated the former collector of the Port of New York, Chester A. Arthur, to the presidency, provoking one political veteran to comment, "My God, Chet Arthur the president!"[38] In an era of relatively undistinguished presidents, Chester Arthur fitted the mold, although his reputation has been improved somewhat in scholarly circles by more sympathetic studies realized nearly one hundred years after his presidency. Although the cause for reform appeared to have suffered a national setback, the momentum continued in Grace's bailiwick.

In New York the Committee of Twenty-one formally reorganized itself into the independent, reformist County Democracy, with Abram S. Hewitt as its chairman. Grace was actively involved in the County Democracy's campaign to gain the ascendancy in New York at the city and state levels. He had already decided not to run again in 1882, but naturally wished to preserve his influence and that of the reform-minded County Democracy through the elections that year. With the Republicians divided into old-line Stalwarts and liberal Half-Breeds, it looked like a good year for the Democrats. Honest John preached unity, although unity among the Democrats, no matter what the state of their rivals, was largely a chimera.

At the Democratic state convention held in September 1882 the County Democracy backed Allan Campbell, Grace's comptroller, for the gubernatorial nomination. Tammany played the field, spreading its votes among several candidates until it could judge where the strength in the convention lay. When a deadlock developed, the convention turned to the reformist mayor of Buffalo, Stephen Grover Cleveland, who had emerged as a dark horse. The Republicians nominated C. J. Folger over the incumbent Governor Cornell, still smarting from the displeasure of Gould. The divided Republicans were defeated at the polls and Cleveland, elected governor, was launched toward the presidency. The Democrats of New York City continued feuding over Grace's successor as mayor.

Kelly managed to bring all the leading factions together long enough under one roof to get his candidate, Franklin Edson, nominated for the mayoralty. Grace, predictably, balked at this choice. He felt that Edson, once in office, would prove too weak to resist the pressures of Tammany. Grace broke with the main Democratic ticket and organized a separate slate of candidates with Allan Campbell, the unsuccessful gubernatorial aspirant, as its candidate for mayor. While receiving some support from the liberal Republicans, Grace's splinter group did not unite other reform elements in the Democratic party. They stayed with Edson, and the whole Democratic ticket, including Cleveland, won the election with a handsome majority.

★ ★ ★

The newspapers of New York rendered a largely favorable verdict at the end of Grace's first term in office. Perhaps most to the point was the *Evening Post*. "It is no small praise of a public man in this city to say that he had earned the cordial hatred of Tammany Hall. This achievement alone on the part of one who, before his election, was supposed to be in close alliance with the faction, would account for the popular reaction in favor of Mayor Grace."[39] Another praised Grace's persistent and successful struggle against the corruption of the street-cleaning department, a struggle that resulted in decisive reforms.[40] Grace officially retired from public office on December 31, 1882, only to be reelected in 1884. During the interval, Tammany and John Kelly jousted with newly elected Governor Cleveland, who also discovered the problems and virtues of being Tammany Hall's enemy.

Cleveland, son of a Presbyterian minister, seemed born to combat Kelly and the Wigwam.[41] Independent, reformist, and assertive, he soon crossed swords with Tammany, vetoing several bills favoring Tammany's interests.[42]

The first bill would have reduced the fare on New York City's elevated lines. The bill was viewed by Tammany as a means to promote its popularity among the working class, which made up a large part of its constituency. Cleveland vetoed the bill since it violated a contract, even though Jay Gould happened to own the railways. Tammany charged indignantly that the governor was supporting big business at the expense of the laboring man and his traditional bulwark, the Democratic party.

Several other vetoes further alienated Tammany. A bill to reduce working hours for streetcar conductors and drivers was stopped by Cleveland's objection, as was a bill to use state funds to finance an orphanage in New York City for Catholic children. Cleveland fought Kelly over patronage and pointedly bypassed Tammany favorites when appointing harbor masters and immigration inspectors. When Cleveland sought the Democratic nomination for president at the national convention held in Chicago in July 1884, Tammany stood foursquare against Cleveland's candidacy. Tammany depicted him as antilabor and anti-Irish, even though Cleveland had earlier gained merit among many Irish Americans by providing free legal services for the Fenian prisoners, and by supporting Irish independence.

The convention in Chicago eventually nominated Cleveland on the second ballot, but not before some old-fashioned oratory stirred the emotions, if not the delegates' votes. Bourke Cockran, Tammany's leading orator, spiced the proceedings with the following: "We have been told that the mantle of Tilden has fallen upon Cleveland . . . .Gentlemen, when the mantle that fits the shoulders of a giant falls on those of a dwarf, the result is disastrous to the dwarf . . . the shoulders of Mr. Cleveland cannot uphold that ample mantle." Gen. Edward S. Bragg of Wisconsin responded for Cleveland's supporters. "They love

him [Cleveland] most for the enemies that he has made."[43]
Being Tammany's foe, as Grace had discovered, could be a
definite asset in Democratic politics.

Before the final balloting, Kelly toyed with the idea of supporting Benjamin Butler, a former governor of Massachusetts
and the detested military governor of New Orleans during the
Civil War. The possibility of Butler heading the Democratic
ticket, remote at its best moment, nonetheless prompted another political epigram that has survived as testimony to this
colorful election. A Georgia delegate summarized the feelings
of his region. Southern Democrats were willing to work har-
moniously within the mainstream of the Democratic party, but
they balked at the mention of "Beast" Butler: "We may be
willing to eat crow, but we'll be damned if we'll eat turkey
buzzard."[44]

For the Republicans the Plumed Knight of Maine, James G.
Blaine, carried the standard into the contest with Cleveland.
He was first elected to the House of Representatives from his
home state in 1862 and thereafter rose rapidly. He became
Speaker of the House in 1869 and a senator in 1876. Blaine
contended unsuccessfully for the Republican presidential nomination in 1876 and 1880, but was finally successful in 1884.
Although tainted by some shady business deals made earlier
when he was Speaker, Blaine was a strong candidate. He had
served awhile as Garfield's secretary of state in 1881 and enjoyed a nationwide reputation from having been at the center
of many domestic and international events.

Blaine's candidacy among New Yorkers was based on an
eclectic appeal. To Tammany he represented the basic alternative to Cleveland. Kelly's lukewarm support of the national
Democratic ticket, given only grudgingly in September, left
many members of Tammany free to vote for Blaine, or even
Butler, who had decided to run independently. To the Irish of
New York, regardless of party, Blaine was a proven anglophobe
who enjoyed a reputation as an English baiter and as a protector
of American rights. As a senator and as Garfield's secretary of
state, Blaine argued for a high protective tariff, pushed for
subsidies for the American merchant marine, and defended
American fishery rights off the Canadian coast. He, furthermore, irritated the English by pushing for the abrogation of the
Clayton-Bulwer Treaty of 1850. This treaty between the United
States and Great Britain provided for a joint guarantee of any
transoceanic canal that might be built across the isthmus of
Central America. The treaty was viewed by many as unneces-
sarily hampering American interests. With a Catholic mother,

a sister who was a mother superior in a convent, and as a descendant of Irish immigrants of the eighteenth century, Blaine's credentials looked good. If Cleveland was to be elected, he had to carry New York State and carry it well. To do that he needed New York City, and many traditional Democratic supporters were wavering.

William Grace emerged once more in the summer and fall of 1884 as a major force in New York politics, just when it appeared that Democratic presidential aspirations might be fulfilled for the first time since before the Civil War. The last time a Democrat was elected to the executive office was in 1858. As the campaign warmed up in September and October, it appeared to most observers that Cleveland's bid for the presidency might swing on the Irish vote in New York.[45]

While Cleveland and Blaine jousted nationally, New York's Democrats characteristically split into factions at the very moment that demanded unity. Grace supported Cleveland, and by September he was raising funds, organizing meetings, and finding speakers. At the municipal level, Grace rejected Tammany's candidate for mayor, Hugh J. Grant. Together with other independent Democrats in the County Democracy and with the more traditional Irving Hall, Grace proposed to run a slate opposing both Tammany and Republican candidate Frederick R. Gibbs.

The organizing committee of this coalition suggested Grace for mayor. He thought it over awhile and declined. They persisted and Grace finally agreed, perhaps having only played fox to foster greater enthusiasm and test his drawing power.[46] Grace's entrance into the race came late in October only a few weeks before the election. This is a somewhat wondrous phenomenon, given the extent of today's campaigns, which commence on the heels of the last election and place the national psyche on a campaign treadmill.

The effects of the New York mayoralty campaign on the outcome of the presidential race were considerable. John Kelly, of course, fought the County Democracy and its candidate, William Grace. Kelly turned Tammany's energies to meeting this old challenger and consequently his tepid support of Cleveland's campaign threatened to jeopardize the state's necessary support of its favored son in the national election. Some feared that Tammany's tacit defection would allow many traditional Democratic supporters to vote for Blaine. The Republican standard-bearer already possessed a good reputation among New York's Irish, although this would be undone with remarkable alacrity by three words uttered in New York during a toast in Blaine's behalf on election eve.

Blaine was reluctant to campaign in New York until finally induced to come late in October. Why he lagged in campaigning in the swing state is not exactly known, although he was weary from a heavy schedule in other states and probably felt that New York would fall in line without direct need of his presence. Nonetheless he came, and one of the first events he attended was a rally for him on October 29 offered by a group of Protestant ministers.

The main speaker was delayed at a wedding in Philadelphia and the group chose a substitute, Rev. Samuel Burchard, to produce some appropriate remarks.[47] The Reverend Mr. Burchard rose to the occasion. Inspired by the power of his own rhetoric, Burchard denounced the Democrats as the party of "rum, Romanism, and rebellion." The remark passed almost unheeded and unnoted, save for one reporter, who jotted it down. Within a few hours it was being repeated at Democratic headquarters and was soon released by the Associated Press. The *New York World* was the first to publish it the next day.[48] The Democrats were delighted by the effect of Burchard's phrasemaking. Blaine tried to defuse the bomb, but it had already exploded. One Cleveland supporter noted that if anything would elect Cleveland, those words would do it, and predicted a stampede of the alienated back to Cleveland.[49] There was. Of the more than one million votes cast in New York in the national election of 1884, Cleveland won by the very slender margin of 1,149. But he won. Grace succeeded in his bid as well, defeating Tammany's candidate Grant by slightly less than ten thousand votes, and drubbing the Republican, Gibbs, who only drew half as many votes as either Grace or Grant.

"Rum, Romanism, and rebellion" probably did more to break the Blaine campaign than any other single utterance in this election, which turned heavily on personalities rather than issues. At one point during the campaign Cleveland's fathering of an illegitimate child was dragged out by the Republicans and celebrated by the doggerel "Pa, Pa, where's my Pa,/Gone to the White House, ha, ha, ha." That was matched in philosophical content by "Blaine, Blaine, James G. Blaine,/The monumental liar from the state of Maine." Nonetheless, beneath the political limericks, Cleveland's victory signaled the national approval of a reform leader virtually untouched by the scandals and rot diffused through politics in the post–Civil War era.

Grace's candidacy in New York was closely allied to Cleveland's cause and the ex-mayor's campaign was a crucial ingredient in forming the Cleveland victory. It was generally conceded that Grace helped swing the many Democrats who were disenchanted and troubled by Cleveland's candidacy back into the majority camp. They viewed Grace as a champion of reform and honesty, and transferred their loyalties from him to Cleveland. One major historian concluded that the election of 1884 was perhaps the most confused in American history, with Republicans fighting each other, Tammany sulking, and the Irish divided as well.[50] In the final analysis, however, while "rum, Romanism, and rebellion" did indeed throw Blaine's ranks into confusion, William Grace's candidacy and active support of Cleveland made their change of political commitment away from Blaine at the midnight hour much easier. Cleveland might have been a Protestant and not thought of as a great friend of the workingman, but Grace was Catholic and a champion of the public commonwealth.

Once the euphoria of victory passed, Grace once again moved to take charge as mayor and, as was the wont of city politics, was soon trading shots with Tammany over patronage and power in the city.

The specific issue was over appointments of major city officials whose tenure was about to expire in December. The outgoing mayor, in this instance Franklin Edson, could opt to let his successor appoint new officials, or he could push through his own choices at the very end of his term.[51] Edson, like others before him, including Grace in 1882, chose to preempt the incoming mayor. He nominated two Tammany selections to the office of commissioner of public works and that of corporation counsel to replace those named by Grace in 1882, Hubert O. Thompson and G. H. Lacombe, respectively.

The appointments were subject to the approval of the board of aldermen. Here Grace joined the lists. Unable to hold the line with aldermen susceptible to Kelly's inducements, Grace and his supporters sought a court injunction to block the board from doing business and thus meeting to confirm Edson's nominations. Tammany undid this attempt, but Grace's supporters, including a young Republican assemblyman named Theodore Roosevelt, obtained another injunction aimed directly at Mayor Edson.

But the Tammany tiger finally got the upper hand on Grace with respect to the commissioner of public works.[52] Ignoring the injunction, Edson sent a new nomination, that of Rollin M. Squire, to the aldermen for approval. They confirmed the mayor's choice and Squire, a virtual unknown, was sworn in at 10:30 P.M. at the very end of Edson's term.

At midnight New Year's Eve, Edson departed his office. The burly president of the board of aldermen, a saloonkeeper from the Fourth Ward named William F. Kirk, then stepped into the office and was sworn in as mayor by a Tammany judge. The city charter provided for the president of the board to officiate as mayor in the absence of the elected executive. Grace was slated to be sworn in at noon of January 1, so Kirk technically was within the law. Kirk then nominated Edson's brother-in-law, E. T. Wood, as corporation counsel. There was no need for confirmation by the board of aldermen since an act of the state legislature went into effect at midnight removing that requirement. However, Grace's people were ready. The keeper of the mayor's seal refused to relinquish his charge while a blockade engineered by the incumbent Lacombe physically kept Wood out of the corporation counsel's office. At noon Kirk abandoned the mayor's office and Grace took the oath, receiving a parade of well wishers for the next four hours. He reappointed Lacombe as corporation counsel but had to accept Squire as the legally appointed public-works commissioner. Politics has often been labeled the art of compromise, and Grace had well mastered the necessity of demonstrating hardness or resiliency as the occasion warranted.

Grace became a noted fixture in the American political scene during his second term as mayor of New York. It would be a considerable asset to his company's future expansion, and especially as Grace became more influential in the development of inter-American relations. He presided over such national events as the burial of Ulysses S. Grant, helped plan for the erection of his monument (not finished until 1897), and fought numerous skirmishes on the local front with celebrated figures like Joseph Pulitzer, publisher of the *New York World* and the pioneer of yellow journalism.

Among the mayor's appointments to public office was Grace Dodge, the first woman named to the board of education. She initiated industrial education in the public schools and later helped to found Teachers College of Columbia University. He promoted others in office largely on merit, and liberally used his new powers to remove officials without the approval of the governor.[53] The four members of the board of tax assessors were relieved of their offices and replaced by Grace's people, and His Honor continued to maintain a suspicious watch on his new commissioner of public works, Rollin Squire. It was well that he did. After prolonged investigation, Squire was revealed as little more than the tool of a powerful contractor in the city, Maurice B. Flynn, who had originally advanced Squire's name to his friend Mayor Edson.

Flynn had suborned Squire in the coarsest sort of way. The following letter, when discovered, ignited a scandal of modest dimensions that nonetheless proved embarrassing to everyone concerned. The letter, dated December 26, 1886, read:

> Maurice B. Flynn, Esq.
> Dear Sir:
> In consideration of your securing not less than four County Democracy Aldermen who shall vote for my confirmation as Commissioner of Public Works . . . I hereby agree to place my resignation as commissioner in your hands . . . and, further, to make no appointments in said office without your approval, and to make such removals therein as you may suggest and request, and to transact the business of said office as you may direct. Very truly yours,
>
> Signed
> Rollin M. Squire[54]

William Ivins, Grace's private secretary during his first term as mayor and now his city chamberlain, smoked out the letter and produced Flynn's admission to its authenticity.[55] Hubert O. Thompson, former commissioner of public works, was implicated as a close accomplice of Flynn's in recruiting the pandering Squire. That both Flynn and Thompson were staunch members of the County Democracy embarrassed not only Grace, who had originally named Thompson to his office at the end of his first term in 1882, but the reformist Democrats as well.

Grace already had set in motion a separate investigation of Squire's financial handling of his office when the letter surfaced. The mayor formally charged Squire and, after an emotional meeting, removed him from office. Meanwhile, the County Democracy expelled Flynn and would have followed suit with Thompson, who—perhaps providentially—died two days before the public divulgence of the letter and its contents.

As was commonly known, Ulysses S. Grant had been a notoriously naive businessman and was badly served in his later life by a series of swindlers. One of these had been Ferdinand Ward, and Grace became ensnared during his second term in another minor scandal because of Ward's dealings.

Ward and one of Grant's sons had become partners in a larcenous brokerage firm in the early 1880s. They traded on the general's reputation and contracted large loans, made invisible investments, and fraudulently dragged the Marine Bank into a morass of debt and eventual dissolution. Grace had an account at the bank and had also loaned Ward money.

Ward landed in jail to face a grand jury investigation in late

1885. From behind bars he hurled charges in many directions, most of them picked up by Pulitzer's *World* and given ample publicity. With respect to Grace, the *World* charged that the mayor had shared in the profits of Ward's "rascalities" while both contributed to wrecking the Marine Bank.[56] Grace promptly sued Pulitzer for libel and fifty thousand dollars in damages.

While Grace fought to keep himself clear of Ward's mudslinging, one of Grace's subordinates, E. H. Tobey, a clerk at W. R. Grace & Co., was indicted along with Ward and two others. Ward was tried and sent back to prison, but when Tobey was called later in 1886 he did not appear, having been sent to Peru on W. R. Grace & Co. business. Grace contended during the grand jury proceedings that Tobey had "gone it all alone," but the residue of impropriety by one of his employees rubbed off on his reputation as well.[57] The suit against Pulitzer did not materialize and Ward's accusations against Grace were never substantiated, somewhat ameliorating the damage from the allegations made by Ward and the *World*.

Grace declined to run for mayor in 1886. The War of the Pacific (1879–83) between Peru, Bolivia, and Chile prostrated Peru before the conquering Chileans and W. R. Grace & Co.'s fortunes had been closely allied to the Peruvian cause. Not only did his business need him at this crucial juncture, but the County Democracy, with Grace's full support, nominated Abram S. Hewitt for mayor.

Hewitt's reputation as a staunch supporter of honest reform convinced Grace that his philosophy would be well tended if Hewitt won the election. Contesting Hewitt were Henry George, the famous author of *Progress and Poverty*, and the Republican Theodore Roosevelt. George's book had been published in 1879 and the author had become the champion of the laboring classes and the scourge of unfettered capitalism, which he proposed to harness with a single sweeping tax on property. Tammany felt threatened by both Roosevelt and George. The full-throttled, almost maniacal, toothy Roosevelt was certainly beyond Tammany's control, whereas George threatened Tammany's sway over the laboring classes. So Honest John joined the County Democracy to support Hewitt, who was elected by a comfortable margin over both George and Roosevelt. Grace retired from public office on December 31, 1886, with a national reputation that kept him involved in public affairs for the rest of his life, although he was never again elected or named to public office.

6

War of the Pacific

Like the Civil War in the United States, the War of the Pacific proved to be a fundamental event in the transition of Peru into the modern age. The American Civil War ended the putative sovereignty of the states over the national constitution and triggered an avalanche of growth and development in its wake that created the basis of a modern American industrial nation. On the West Coast of South America Chile went to war with neighbors Bolivia and Peru in 1879. This War of the Pacific, not settled by treaty until 1883, established Chile as a major power on the South American continent and humiliated both Peru and Bolivia. From the ashes of its defeat Peru, torn by internal turmoil as well as prostrated by Chilean invaders, developed a new survivors' manual for the modern world. The Grace businesses, so closely identified with Peru, inevitably were drawn into the vortex of war, and even before, into the long train of historical imperatives and events that led to the war.

The subject of historical causation is perhaps at no other time more controversial than when events seem to tumble appallingly into place on the road to war. The coming of World War I seems now to have been an ineluctable catastrophe ordained by the nature of the great powers. Could it have been avoided? To maintain that it could is to subscribe to the theory that great men can alter the course of history. To acknowledge its inevitability is to accept a grander design than the cumulative efforts of mere men. This design may be divine or secular, depending upon one's philosophy. Karl Marx described the historical process as quite predictable, based on an understanding of class antagonisms and of the gradual transition of societies through different economic stages, beginning with the most primitive organizations of men to a sophisticated capitalist era. Marxian analysis thus has the comforting ring of inevitability. Nonetheless, it is flawed in a crucial respect, for it fails to take into account the liberty that men preserve to behave irrationally and outside the strictures of their economic conditions.

The War of the Pacific was caused by both men and events, and one is never altogether sure whether it was the events that impelled the men or the men who made the events. A certain amount of greed, nationalism, patriotism, fear, and bravado went into its making, but it could not have occurred without the precise confluence of all the ingredients of this witch's brew. Its occurrence was tragic, but nonetheless indicative of the vices and virtues accompanying Peru's transition into the modern period.

On the simplest level, the war was caused by competition between Chile, Bolivia, and Peru for the guano and nitrate riches discovered on the sterile Atacama Desert, shared by all three countries. But the value of this wealth was not evident until the middle of the nineteenth century. Even before then, however, the Atacama region had been disputed between Chile, Peru, and Bolivia.

The Atacama was first crossed by Diego Almagro in 1537 on his way to attempt the conquest of Chile. Almagro's rude experience with its dry, forbidding climate and nature stamped it as a place to avoid. During the colonial period the port of Arica in the northern half was developed to load silver carried down by mule trains from the mines high in Bolivia, while a few other small towns nestled along the river oases crossing the desert were also settled. But the value of the Atacama remained low, except perhaps as an example of an extreme of nature. As a result, the borders between the various provinces under Spanish rule were poorly delineated.

By 1776 the old viceroyalty of Peru that once had sprawled over all of Spanish South America was divided into three viceroyalties: Peru, New Granada, and La Plata. Each covered an area larger than any one nation's modern configuration, but administrative divisions within each viceroyalty already tended to follow recognizable modern frontiers. Chile, for example, was governed by a captain general responsible to the viceroy of Peru, while Upper Peru (roughly, modern Bolivia) was a separate entity responsible to the viceroy of La Plata with headquarters in Buenos Aires.

The breakup of the old viceroyalty of Peru left some lingering resentment among the Creoles of Peru, especially when Bolivia

Chinese coolie laborer on a Peruvian sugar plantation, circa 1860s. One of over a hundred thousand Chinese immigrants to Peru who arrived between 1849-1873 to labor in the cotton and sugar fields scattered along the coast of Peru, and who supplied the principal work force on the Chincha Islands digging guano. The man pictured at left was chained and shackled to prevent escape, an extreme form of punishment meted out only to the most chronic rebels.

The ruins of La Fortaleza, located in the Pativilca Valley very near Hacienda Paramonga. La Fortaleza was built by the great coastal kingdom of the Chimu who were ultimately conquered by the Incas. Typically, modern agricultural industry was situated in the midst of precious reminders of the great Peruvian antiquarian past. La Fortaleza today is one of the best preserved of the precolonial fortresses of Peru.

The Cathedral of Lima. An impressive structure built in the colonial period, it was rather squat and massive, so constructed to survive the earthquakes of the region. The Cathedral represented the dominant role of the Roman Catholic faith in Peru. The Roman Catholicism of the Graces made them more compatible with the country and its culture than other foreigners whose Protestantism clashed with the ruling elite.

Guano cutting on the Chincha Islands, showing thickness of the ancient beds, circa 1860. Coolie laborers are hewing at the immense pile of guano.

Guano vessels at anchor, North Chincha Island in the background. The view was taken from Central Island.

Guano fleet of Chincha Islands, Circa 1860.

Bryce, *Grace Storeship, circa 1850s, early 1860s, anchored off the Chincha Islands, Peru. Innovation by William Russell Grace to better service the guano fleets.*

Lillius Grace, circa 1860s.

William Grace, circa 1860s.

This is the storefront, circa 1866, of the firm that young William Russell Grace joined in 1854. Figure with right hand thumb in waistcoat is George Baker, cashier. 4th figure on Baker's left, with broad-brimmed white hat is Manuel Llaguno, bookkeeper. Llaguno was first hired by William Grace to work on the Chincha Island Storeship. Michael Grace's room and balcony are over the store. Note the bollards in foreground and the sailor's dress on some individuals.

▼

Callao, circa 1860s. It was to this leading port that most of the ships of the guano fleet went to revictual and refit and it was here that William Russell Grace first landed as a young man of nineteen in 1851. It was a rough city, but vital and dynamic at midcentury, and the Graces' first prosperity was closely tied to its fortunes.

Part of the guano fleet, 1860. These ships were the ones worked by William Russell Grace as he rose in the John Bryce concern.

Edward Eyre came over from Ireland in 1867 at the age of fifteen to work in Callao with his uncles Michael and William Grace. Eyre's presence was an example of the strong family ties in the early company's development. He was preceded and followed by dozens of relatives into the firm. Eyre eventually rose to the presidency and always retained a strong attachment to Peru.

W. R. Grace, *graceful downeaster launched from the shipyards of Flint & Chapman, Bath, Maine, in 1873. She measured 1893 tons and was operated by W. R. Grace & Co. for many years on the New York to California run, making twelve trips around the Horn in this trade, her fastest recorded time being 115 days. She wrecked in September, 1889, near Lewes, Delaware, bound in for Philadelphia from Le Havre, the victim of a terrific hurricane.*

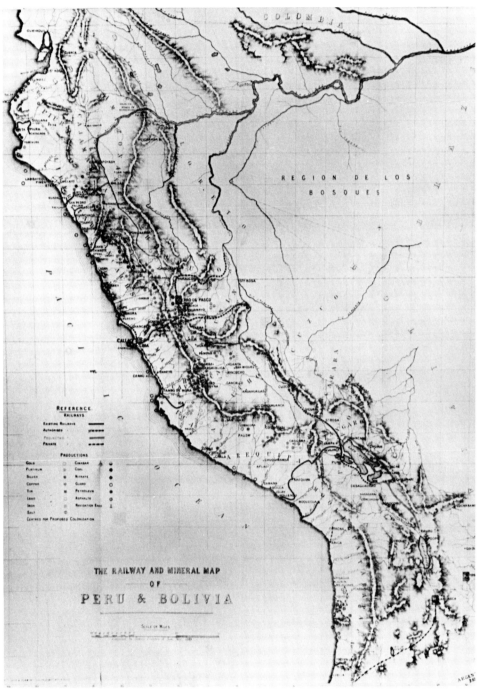

Railway and Mineral map of Peru and Bolivia, 1889. This map shows the controversial Peruvian railroad system at the very peak of negotiations leading to the Grace Contract of 1890. The Contract entrusted the railroads to the British Peruvian Corporation in return for forgiving the immense foreign debt of Peru. Michael Grace was instrumental in negotiating the contract.

Michael P. Grace, William R. Grace's youngest, most flamboyant brother, who worked with William all his life in Latin America, the United States, and Europe. A brilliant financier, Michael was also a dynamic promoter of many of the businesses that launched the company in the nineteenth century.

One of Michael Grace's first residences in Callao. He took the upper story of the building on the right when he got married January 16, 1869. Later Grace turned it over to Edward Eyre when he married April 21, 1877.

The same building almost forty years later, showing a decided improvement: streetlights; trees, sidewalks and a general air of prosperity.

India house, headquarters of W. R. Grace & Co. from 1885-1913. Located on Hanover Square, India House today is a national historic monument, occupying a site in the city associated with the earliest Dutch merchants of New Amsterdam.

William Russell Grace, founder of W. R. Grace & Co. and mayor of New York, 1880-1882, 1884-1886.

John W. Grace, lame brother of William R. Grace, who came over to America in the early 1870s to work with his brothers William and Michael in the expanding business of W. R. Grace & Co. John founded a partnership in San Francisco and then later managed the Grace houses in Valparaiso and Callao.

Desamparados Railroad Station, Lima, 1908. The main station on the Central Railroad linking the coast with the central Sierra. Less than thirty years earlier, this same scene might have taken place with Peruvian soldiers waiting to board trains for the short trip to Callao on their way to defend the southern provinces of Peru from the attacking Chileans during the War of the Pacific.

Miguel Grau, Peruvian hero of the naval Battle of Iquique. His modern, heavily armed monitor Huascar *battered the Chilean frigate* Esmeralda *into a sinking hulk, thereby breaking the Chilean naval blockade of Iquique and rallying the morale of the Peruvian nation during the early stages of the War of the Pacific.*

Peruvian monitor Huascar. *Commanded brilliantly by Miguel Grau, the* Huascar *ranged up and down the Peruvian and Chilean coasts for most of 1879, foiling Chilean attempts to establish complete control of the sea with her more powerful navy. The Chileans finally caught up with* Huascar *in October, 1879, and captured her in a terrific engagement during which Grau lost his life.*

The valiant captain, Arturo Prat, and crew of the Chilean frigate Esmeralda *created a legend by their heroic actions in the Battle of Iquique. Sunk by the more powerful Peruvian monitor* Huascar, *Prat nonetheless ennobled himself by dying in a supreme act of courage. It stirred national sentiment among the Chilean people and kindled a powerful determination to crush Peru.*

Naval Battle of Iquique, 21 April, 1879. The Peruvian monitor Huascar *is backing off after the last and fatal ramming of the Chilean frigate* Esmeralda, *going down by the bow. The battle marked one of the high points in the Peruvian Navy's performance during the War of the Pacific, but, ironically, Chile was emotionally charged by the valiant actions of her officers and sailors martyred on the decks of the* Esmeralda.

was stripped from Lima and given to Buenos Aires to govern when the viceroyalty of La Plata was created in 1776. In the post-Independence era the Atacama region— roughly six hundred miles in length—was divided among the three countries of Bolivia, Peru, and Chile, although Bolivia had to assent to Peru's possession of Arica, the most natural outlet to the sea from the Altiplano, or high plateau, of Bolivia. In the 1830s Bolivia and Peru joined in a confederation which Chile objected to; a war ensued and Chile defeated the Peru-Bolivia confederation, advancing its claimed border northward from the 25° to the 23° parallel. Peaceful adjustments ensued in 1857 and 1866 and Chile's claim receded to the 24° parallel. Bolivia's Pacific coastline nonetheless shrank because of Chilean aggressiveness, and part of Bolivia's coastal province of Antofagasta remained in dispute.

Complications in the Bolivian-Chilean dispute grew increasingly strident in the second half of the century because of the new value placed on the guano- and nitrate-rich Atacama.[1] Chilean and English capital predominated in the exploitation of the mines on both sides of the border, while travelers noted the overwhelming presence of Chilean laborers and English managers in the Atacama.[2] Bolivia feared the encroachment of Chileans, who naturally carried their national loyalties with them into Bolivia's coastal province with its capital at Antofagasta.

Spain's adventuring in the Pacific in 1865–66 prompted a temporary alliance between Chile, Bolivia, and Peru in the face of the common enemy. In 1866 Bolivia and Chile agreed essentially to rule cooperatively over the disputed region between the 23° and 25° parallels. The principal provisions mandated that they share customs receipts from the export of guano and other minerals from the region while all other exports would be duty-free. Chilean products could be imported duty-free through Mejillones, which would also possess the sole customhouse. That same year some Chilean miners discovered a very valuable nitrate field on the coast near Antofagasta and a company, the Compañía de Salitres de Antofagasta (later expanded to Compañía de Salitres y Ferrocarril de Antofagasta), was formed to exploit this rich zone.

It was a flush time for miners and investors, and succeeding developments generally bore out their optimism. Guano deposits at Mejillones were thought to be very rich, and silver mines at Caracoles in the interior of the province of Antofagasta also drew Chilean capital and labor.[3] Over \$14 million was invested in, and more than five thousand individuals attracted to, Caracoles by 1872. A not dissimilar movement of Americans into the Mexican province of Texas had occurred in the 1820s and 1830s. They, too, rapidly populated and made prosperous a region only lightly controlled and utilized by a different nation, and the result was war. Yet, in the Pacific, a further complicating factor existed—Peru.

As far as back as the colonial period Peru and Chile had been rivals in certain areas of commerce, especially since Peruvian shippers and shipowners virtually monopolized trade in the Pacific. Chilean wheat farmers, copper miners, and others would have preferred greater control over the movement and pricing of their goods throughout the viceroyalty of Peru. But until the end of the Spanish dominion, Lima, the seat of the viceroyalty, and its merchants and governors continued to hold sway.

During the Wars of Independence, Chile was radicalized and became independent half a dozen years before Peru was liberated by the armies of José de San Martín and Simón Bolívar in the early 1820s. The initiative in West Coast affairs began to slip from Peru, which remained conservative and loyal to the Spanish monarchy well after the independence movement liberated virtually all of South America from Spanish control. Furthermore, Peru's political and military leaders had been notoriously fickle in their loyalties throughout the long wars. That Chilean and Argentinian troops marching under San Martín, as well as Chilean ships commanded by the fighting admiral Lord Cochrane, fought in Peru's liberation movement set a precedent of sorts for the Chileans: that of actively promoting self-interests by intervention in the affairs of Bolivia and Peru.

This policy was especially reinforced in the mid-1830s when Chile went to war with both Peru and Bolivia. Under an erratic but brilliant leader named Andres Santa Cruz, Chile's two rivals united in a confederation that directly threatened the balance of power on the continent and certainly was perceived as against Chile's best interests.[4] After decisively defeating a combined Peruvian-Bolivian army under Santa Cruz at Yungay in early 1839, the Chileans broke up the confederation. They began to view themselves more and more as crucial powerbrokers on the southern half of the continent, an area referred to as the southern cone. Chile gained further leverage by the middle of the nineteenth century because of its rising commercial prosperity and continued political stability. Not only were its miners and investors making profitable incursions in the Antofagasta region, but Chile was more actively pushing its border disputes with the Argentinians, especially over the crucial Straits of Magellan.

Ironically, the demands of the war with Spain in the late 1860s, a war which temporarily allied Chile, Bolivia, and Peru (and Ecuador), also precipitated a naval arms race between Peru and Chile that added to the friction between the two countries in the 1870s.

In 1864 and 1866 Peru ordered two ironclad warships from shipyards in Great Britain. The *Independencia* was a rammed frigate and carried a powerful battery for the times, although all muzzle loaders. The second warship, the monitor *Huascar*, would achieve immortality during the War of the Pacific, and was a splendid example of the most modern naval design.

It was built by Laird Brothers in Birkenhead in 1865 and christened *Huascar* in honor of one of the last Inca emperors to rule before the Spanish conquest of the sixteenth century. It displaced eleven hundred thirty tons and was iron-hulled throughout with thick four-and-one-half-inch armor. To pierce its foes the warship carried a six-foot ram attached to its prow, and a watertight bulkhead immediately behind the ram protected *Huascar* from the shock of collisions. It measured two hundred feet in length, was thirty-five feet wide at its waist, and drew about twelve feet. A twelve-hundred-horsepower steam engine driving a screw propeller was its prime means of propulsion, again in keeping with latest designs. It could make eleven knots top speed and carried a crew of two hundred. When first launched in 1866, it was equipped with a two-masted brigantine rig. The sails were scrapped by the Peruvians when *Huascar* entered service in the Pacific, but certainly were emblematic of an era in transition from sail to steam.

The warship's firepower was impressive. It mounted two Armstrong ten-inch-caliber guns, each capable of firing a three-hundred-pound projectile from its housing in a rotating turret protected by five and a half inches of armor. Supplementing the main armament were two smaller forty-pound cannons, and to spray the enemy's deck, a deadly Gatling gun was located in a small protected crow's nest atop the mainmast.[5]

The Peruvian government also decided to take advantage of surplus materials left idle by the end of the Civil War in the United States, and Jose Antonio García y García was dispatched north in 1866 to buy two monitors in his capacity as an envoy extraordinary.[6] Once in the United States, García turned to

William Grace for assistance in outfitting and getting the vessels ready for sea. This was certainly a familiar routine to Grace, who, after all, had cut his teeth in the ship chandlery business in Peru.

Grace also helped García recruit the crews for the two monitors, and to purchase two auxiliary steamers as escorts for the long voyage to Peru. It took almost two years to refit, equip, man, and in every respect prepare the small squadron. When all was ready the two steamers departed New York to join the monitors, rechristened the *Atahualpa* and *Manco Capac*, off the mouth of the Mississippi. William's father-in-law, George Gilchrest, commanded one of the steamers, the *Marañon*. The trip from New York to Peru tried everyone's patience and endurance.

The *Reyes*, the other steamer accompanying the *Marañon*, was first driven by a gale off New Jersey into Delaware for repairs. After arriving off the coast of Louisiana, Captain Gilchrest discovered his boiler was ruined by inferior coal and a drunken engineer. When the crew was informed that it would have to serve two years in the Peruvian navy, it abandoned the ship. In a storm off Cuba one of the monitors lost control and proved the worth of its ram by accidentally lancing the *Reyes*, sending it down with the loss of seven men. The *Marañon*, *Atahualpa*, and *Manco Capac* arrived at Callao in fall 1869 after eight months of adventurous voyaging that testified to the dangers of steam navigation in this era.[7]

Peru obtained naval advantage over Chile with the acquisition of the *Independencia,* the *Huascar*, and the two monitors, *Atahualpa* and *Manco Capac*. However, Chile was spurred on to seek naval parity and ultimately superiority. It ordered two powerful ironclads, the *Almirante Cochrane* and *Blanco Encalada*, built in English shipyards. Delivered in the mid-1870s, they were superior in armor and firepower to the comparable Peruvian vessels. Moreover, the officers and men of the Chilean navy received much better training than their counterparts in Peru.[8]

While the naval race proceeded, the rapid expansion of Chilean investments and activity in the Atacama continued to foster suspicions and enmity among the Peruvians and Bolivians. A Peruvian naval show of force in 1871 off the coast of Mejillones had provided the immediate excuse for the Chileans to order the *Almirante Cochrane* and *Blanco Encalada* from England. A naval race was thus overlaid on an old commercial and political rivalry. Furthermore, the strong currents of a New World economy which put a premium on such items as guano and nitrates rounded out the complicated dimensions of the prelude to this war.

Two treaties, one concluded in 1873 and the other in 1874, tended to harden the differences between the future combatants. The first, concluded between Bolivia and Peru in 1873, has been described as a "secret" treaty or a "defensive alliance" aimed against Chile. In fact, it was neither a secret treaty nor a defensive alliance. Chileans rapidly learned of its provisions and it simply provided for consultation between Peru and Bolivia before any boundary changes might be made.[9] While Chileans were suspicious of the treaty, they had been no less ingenuous earlier when tempting Bolivia to yield in its claims to Antofagasta by offering it the possibility of acquiring Peru's port of Arica.

The second agreement was reached between Chile and Bolivia in 1874 and it was largely an attempt to improve the treaty of 1866, which provided for the joint administration of Antofagasta. Bolivia promised to refrain for the next fifteen years from imposing any new taxes on the Chilean-owned and -operated Compañía de Salitres y Ferrocarril de Antofagasta.[10] This agreement between Bolivia and Chile soon foundered on Peru's fiscal problems, further emphasizing the interlocking factors at large in the the mid-1870s.

It will be recalled that by 1875 Henry Meiggs's railroad building had dragged Peru down deeply into debt. Guano revenues no longer sufficed to keep the various projects going and the issuance of new bonds, such as in 1870 and 1872, would have produced precious few, if any, buyers in the European bond markets. In desperation, paper money was issued and a large public-works project undertaken to modernize Lima and presumably stimulate the economy, but these were only stopgap measures.

Nonetheless, the increasing value of the nitrate industry in Peru's southern province of Tarapaca provided a toehold of hope. Exports of nitrate rose in value from £1,471,000 to £3,615,000 between 1870 and 1875 and the decision to nationalize the industry was taken in 1875. The owners were paid off in special nitrate bonds, although most of them were kept on to manage their works.[11] By 1878 the majority of owners had been bought out by the government and the industry was organized into the Nitrate Company of Peru.[12] It was precisely at this juncture that Michael Grace obtained the concession for the exclusive distribution of Peruvian nitrate of soda in the United States. It was quite a business coup, but the timing was inauspicious. The deal, supported by Baring Brothers credits, was closed in January 1879. In less than six months Chile, Bolivia, and Peru were at war.[13]

The immediate cause was a ten-centavo tax levied by the Bolivians on each hundred pounds of nitrates exported through the port of Antofagasta. To be successful in its nitrate industry, Peru had to ensure that Bolivian and Chilean exports did not undersell its own commodity. The Peruvians were able to persuade the Bolivians to levy this new ten-cent tax, which was promptly rejected by Chile as a violation of the Sucre Treaty of 1874. The Chileans contended that the treaty guaranteed them exemption from any duties for a period of fifteen years. Hence, the duty constituted a unilateral violation of the treaty, and the Chilean Compañía de Salitres y Ferrocarril de Antofagasta refused to pay the tax.[14] The Chilean government supported the company and declared that any attempt to collect the tax would be answered by "revindication" of the province of Antofagasta by Chile. The issue was bandied back and forth for most of 1877. Then, in early 1879 the Bolivians seized the company's property with the intention of selling at public auction. Chile landed troops at Antofagasta on February 14, 1879, and Bolivia declared war on Chile a month later. Peru sided with its old ally and Chile thus declared war on Peru April 3. The war put the Graces into a quandary, for they did business in all three countries, although their principal loyalties were to Peru.

The predicament of Charles Flint best exemplified the dilemma. By spring 1879 Flint had been serving as the Chilean consul in New York for three years. He was, additionally, directing the Chilean legation in the absence of the chargé d'affaires.[15] Flint knew Chile from earlier travels, had drummed up business for Grace in Valparaiso, and was a charming and talented person. It was only natural to serve Chile in other respects as well, such as being its consul in New York. Flint also knew Peru well, and was a partner of W. R. Grace & Co., very definitely known as a Peruvian house. When the war erupted, "I was, in a way, on both sides."[16]

When Peru called on William Grace and his firm for assistance in obtaining arms and munitions, Flint promptly severed his official diplomatic ties by cabling his resignation to Santiago.

But in the hectic interval between the act of turning over all the papers of the legation and consulate to a Chilean who happened to be in New York, and helping William with the acquisition of war materials for Peru, Flint was caught in the middle. "In taking prompt measures to secure munitions many telegrams had to be sent; and before I could turn over the papers of the Chilean consulate, I received a letter from one of the employees of the telegraph company, in which he offered, for a consideration, to disclose to the Chilean consul certain of Charles R. Flint's activities in connection with obtaining munitions for Peru. He little suspected that he was offering to let my left hand know what my right hand was doing."[17]

Grace was traveling in Great Britain during the tense months immediately preceding the declarations of war. He arrived home only a few days before Chile's declaration of April 3 and trenchantly observed that "the bombshell exploded as it always does in such cases—when least expected."[18]

Michael in Peru had already alerted Flint in New York to be prepared to fill orders for munitions and arms, and Flint moved with speed to acquire rifles and munitions. He also acted with imagination on the second major problem associated with supplying Peru with materials: how to transport the munitions across neutral Colombia (then in possession of the Isthmus of Panama).

The long voyage around Cape Horn was deemed too dangerous, for the Chileans would surely intercept anything that had to traverse their long coastline. Flint made some preliminary inquiries and ascertained that Colombia would be quite neutral although not aggressively so.[19] The problem was to disguise the munitions adequately so as not to violate Colombian sensibilities. Flint decided to try his imagination on a consignment of ten Pratt and Whitney dirigible torpedoes destined for Peru. He lost a good bit of sleep until he discovered that oilcloth, framed in the ordinary way, weighed just about the same as a layer or two of oilcloth with a torpedo inside.[20] Conveniently, Peru bought a lot of oilcloth in those days and soon ten torpedoes were on their way to Peru comfortably nestled in the center of ten cases of oilcloth and shipped in company with many more cases of oilcloth that did not have torpedoes inside.[21] A thousand rifles carrying the labels "agricultural machinery" were also dispatched in those hectic spring months of 1879, while cartridges embedded in lard barrels went to load the rifles.

Meanwhile, Peru and Chile were fighting for command of the sea, deemed imperative for eventual success, given the nature of the long barren coastline shared by Chile, Bolivia, and Peru. If troops and armies were to be moved effectively—as they had during the Wars of Independence—the challenges at sea had to be eliminated. Chile had already gained a foothold in Antofagasta, while Peru managed to bolster defenses in her adjoining province of Tarapaca. The Chilean navy then mounted a blockade of Iquique, which led to the first major naval engagement.[22]

The Peruvian monitor *Huascar*, under the command of Miguel Grau, and the ironclad *Independencia*, commanded by Capt. J. G. Moore, were ordered from Callao to reinforce Arica and to proceed to Iquique to lift the blockade. Meanwhile, the Chilean High Fleet under the command of Juan Williams Rebolledo sortied from Iquique en route north to Callao. Admiral Williams carried with him the most powerful Chilean warships, the *Blanco Encalada* and the *Almirante Cochrane*, having left the smaller, more vulnerable frigate *Esmeralda* and corvette *Covadonga* to maintain the blockade of Iquique. The Chilean fleet passed the *Huascar* and *Independencia* on the high seas May 19. Thirty-one miles separated them and neither saw the other. On May 20 the *Huascar* and *Independencia* steamed out of Arica's roadstead early in the morning, headed south for Iquique. With the main Chilean battle fleet on its way to Callao, nothing stood between Grau and the port of Iquique but the *Esmeralda* and *Covadonga*.

The morning of May 21 was wreathed in a heavy fog. The *Covadonga* was plying slowly back and forth on patrol. At about six-thirty the sun started to bake off the fog and a young seaman on lookout spied the smoke on the horizon.

"Smoke to the north! Smoke to the north!" he cried from his lookout station, alerting the officer of the deck for the moment they all had been anticipating. Capt. Carlos Condell was on deck in a flash, binoculars pasted to his eyes as he searched through the lifting fog. By now most of the officers and crew were topside, stomachs knotting in anticipation.

"Who are they?"

"It's the *Huascar*, and the *Independencia*, sir. I've served aboard them both." Condell listened as one of the old English sailors spoke softly at his elbow. He kept his eyes fixed on the smoke smudge now growing more distinct.[23] Condell estimated the distance at about six miles, and closing.

"Hoist a signal to the *Esmeralda*. 'Smoke to the north.' "

Aboard the *Esmeralda* Arturo Prat had already been up for

hours. By nature a quiet and contemplative man, Captain Prat had only the year before been awarded his lawyer's degree from the University of Chile, far exceeding the career goals of the average naval officer. The young captain waited for the signal from *Covadonga* to be officially noted by the signalman and then brought to himself. Prat had already read the flags. The sun was growing warmer as the Peruvian fleet neared. There was still plenty of time to take care of business and crew.

"Signal the *Covadonga* to 'come alongside to talk.' " As the *Covadonga* neared, Captain Prat ordered the transport *Lamar* to weigh anchor and escape to the south. The *Esmeralda* and *Covadonga* would make their stand alone. Were they ready?

As the *Covadonga* neared, Prat signaled again.

"Reinforce your charges." Both ships now swarmed with sailors making ready for battle. Bulkheads were knocked down, guns run out, the decks cleared for action. Far down in the bowels of the ships the surgeon and his assistants prepared for the grisly work of tending the wounded and dying. Once more Prat signaled.

"Have your men eaten?" There was always time for breakfast. Why die on an empty stomach?

In the space of a few minutes *Covadonga* reached hailing distance and Prat gave Condell his last orders. They would place themselves between the Peruvian ships and the shoreline of Iquique, and get in as close as possible to the beach. The heavier Peruvian vessels would have to shoot carefully to avoid piling shells into the city, now coming alive with hundreds of people hurrying down to the water's edge to watch the naval battle unfolding before them.

The time to part was rapidly approaching as the smoke smudges of the early dawn materialized into the low-slung, heavily gunned *Huascar*. Perhaps thinking of the immortal Horatio Nelson, Prat issued his last order to the *Covadonga*, "Let each man do his duty."

The laconic Condell responded, "All right," and ordered the *Covadonga* into the wake of the *Esmeralda*.

Aboard the *Huascar*, Grau and his navigator were up before dawn as the Peruvian fleet drew near to Iquique. What would they find? His orders were to lift the blockade. The Peruvian public had been clamoring for action and although President Mariano Prado wished to wait and get the fleet up to snuff, the pressure was too great. For his part, Grau was happy to be at sea and on the prowl. The deck trembled rhythmically under his feet as the *Huascar* drove through the calm night sea toward the Iquique coastline. Keeping station by his side was the *Independencia*.

As the fog lifted Grau and the officers on deck made out the forms of the *Esmeralda* and *Covadonga* maneuvering close to each other. Transports or men-of-war? Where were the *Cochrane,* the *Blanco Encalada*? If what he saw through his telescope was true, the day promised to be good to the *Huascar* and the Peruvian cause. Below decks the engineers were securing everything possible as the word filtered down into their oily, gloomy world of pounding pistons and rackety steam fittings—prepare for action. Stokers, stripped to the waist, complained and cursed faithfully about the bad air and heat, all the while working themselves up for the moment of combat.

"Sir, they are the *Esmeralda* and *Covadonga*," an officer said to Grau.

"There don't seem to be any others around, eh, Mr. Aguirre?" Grau asked rhetorically of his executive officer, Elias Aguirre. Both were firmly attached like barnacles to the heavy steel wall of the conning tower just aft of the *Huascar*'s main battery.

"Mr. Navigator, make for the *Esmeralda*. We should be within range in about fifteen minutes I'd say." Grau shot his orders out crisply. It was 8:15 A.M. "Call the crew together, Mr. Aguirre."

The crew hustled up the ladders and gathered as quickly as possible on the open fantail deck. The captain stood one level above them, grasping a rail and leaning slightly forward.

"Men of the *Huascar*! The hour to punish the enemies of our homeland has arrived! And I expect you know how we will do it, harvesting new laurels and new glories worthy of shining alongside those of Junín, Ayacucho, Abtao, and the Second of May. Viva Peru!"

"Viva Peru!" thrice bellowed the hoarse chorus. The voices carried across the waters like a volley to the *Independencia*, sending shivers up Captain Moore's spine.

On the *Huascar* Grau ordered battle pennants hoisted and sounded general quarters. Beyond the *Esmeralda* he could now make out the teeming citizenry of Iquique gathered on the beaches and bluffs, waving and in an apparently uproarious mood. What Grau could not hear, but what he could easily guess from the situation, were hundreds of voices not only echoing his harangue to the crew, "Viva Peru! Viva Peru!" but also crying, "Ahora si! Ahora si!" ("Now! Now!") What sweet revenge was soon to fall on the hated Chileans!

Prat on the *Esmeralda* was acting well, Grau thought as his ship closed range rapidly. It was now 8:30. I can't shoot straight into him, not with the shoreline just beyond swarming with patriotic Peruvians. Let's start with a grenade.

The first one lobbed by the *Huascar* splashed in between the *Esmeralda* and the *Covadonga*, exploding into a harmless but spectacular geyser of foam and water just as Prat issued his last immortal words to his crew, fully prepared to die for their country beneath the ten-inch Armstrong rifles of the powerful enemy. "Boys, the fight is unequal; our flag has never been struck before the enemy. And I don't expect us to be the first! As long as I live this flag will wave, and I assure you, if I die, my officers will know how to do their duty! Viva Chile!"

"Viva Chile!" Prat's valiant crew responded, throwing hats into the air as the first grenade exploded, sounding the overture of the battle.

Prat maneuvered the *Esmeralda* as close inshore as possible and waited for the inevitable charge of the *Huascar*. Grau could not bring his main battery directly to bear on the *Esmeralda* but the *Covadonga* was susceptible. It was slowly moving south and was not protected by a vulnerable city behind it.

The *Huascar*'s turret slowly and ominously rotated, bringing the Armstrong guns to bear on the *Covadonga*.

"Stand by! Fire!" The mouth of the cannons erupted in black smoke as the blast literally shook the *Huascar* and deafened those officers and men on the conning tower. Grau watched intently through his glasses. A miss. The projectiles fell harmlessly a few hundred yards short of the *Covadonaga*, now moving more rapidly south.

Once again the *Huascar*'s main battery roared, spitting out fire and smoke. Everyone in the tower pressed palms to ears as tightly as possible, but the blast still pierced through painfully. In the *Huascar*'s turret, eardrums split open and the blood flowed freely down cheeks and necks. The lot of the gunners. No one wavered or wiped. They listened for the report of the last salvo, already manhandling the next projectile into the great guns amid a world of sweat and blood, marked only by the punctuation of orders and the roar of their guns.

The second salvo tore through the flimsy hull of the *Covadonga*, instantly killing surgeon Videla and three others, leaving a trail of blood and mangled debris. But the *Covadonga* was not Grau's prey. He turned the *Huascar* more directly back to the *Esmeralda* and dispatched the *Independencia* to intercept the *Covadonga*. As these two combatants steamed southward toward Punta Gruesa in their deadly waterborne ballet, the *Huascar* closed within five or six hundred meters of the *Esmeralda*.

With one side facing the hostile city and the other awaiting the onslaught of the *Huascar*, the *Esmeralda* was all but doomed. Never mind. Dressed out with all its pennants and battle flags as if preparing for some gala fiesta, Prat's ship unloosed a salvo from its small forties as the *Huascar* neared. The boom and smoke and cordite smell from the guns felt good. *If we have to go down, it will be fighting.*

The monitor's turret again flashed and sent two deadly three-hundred-pound projectiles in the *Esmeralda*'s direction. But they passed harmlessly overhead with a deadly whistle and caromed in the hills beyond the city.

"Captain, let's get in a few meters more!" the gunnery officer shouted to Grau standing almost next to him. Everyone was half deaf from the cannonades.

"Can't do it, sir. Torpedoes are strung out all around her."

"Do the best you can," Grau answered. Just then a volley was let loose by the *Esmeralda*. Grau remained stock still, eyes fixed on the small frustrating opponent across the water. Nobody on the conning tower ducked as one or two of the small shells pounded into the five-inch armor of the monitor leaving barely a dent.

Ashore the early morning excitement had worn thin among the thousands of onlookers. Colonel Benavides in command of the Peruvian forces ashore was more perceptive than the civilians, who expected a quick and exciting killing. He sensed Grau's problem and ordered a battery of nine-inch cannon rolled down to the water's edge. The artillerymen manhandled the pieces into position with grunts and heaves. *Esmeralda* was the target.

"Load!" shouted the officer in charge of the battery.

"Fire!" The gun carriages recoiled as the barrels exploded into action. Adjustments were rapidly made after the first miss. The second and third salvos took more deadly effect, blazing through the top deck of the small Chilean corvette. Three men were blasted in the first instance; three more as the Peruvian gunners ashore zeroed in on their target.

The plucky Chileans answered in kind. Lt. Francisco Sanchez directed the *Esmeralda*'s fire ashore while Ignacio Serrano kept up a staccato of shooting toward the *Huascar*. It was now near eleven o'clock. The Peruvian battery ashore was slowly battering the *Esmeralda* into pieces. With one boiler shattered and able to make only two or three knots, the *Esmeralda* pulled away from the hellish spot and made its way painfully toward the north.

Amazed but exasperated by the *Esmeralda*'s continuing resistance, Grau prepared to ram. It was 11:30. The battle was now over three hours old. It had to be concluded.

"Mr. Aguirre, pass the word along. We are going to ram."

From his post on the bow of the shattered *Esmeralda* Lt. Luis Uribe, Prat's second in command, saw the monitor begin its turn, aiming its deadly underwater prow toward the *Esmeralda*.

"Captain! Captain! They're going to ram!" Uribe cried out almost in a hysterical pitch.

Prat nodded and calmly ordered the *Esmeralda*'s helmsman to turn toward the monitor and present a smaller target. Now for the end, Prat thought; God give me the courage to endure.

As the vessels closed rapidly, Grau's engineers and stokers below decks dropped everything and slipped wrists through the leather handholds nailed to the bulkheads. Only thus could they avoid being hurled, with perhaps fatal results, against the steaming boilers and interior surfaces.

"Stand by to blast her with the Armstrongs as soon as we collide," Grau ordered his gunners, frustrated most of the morning. Now they would get their chance.

Rifle fire from the *Esmeralda* pinged off the decks and armored sides of the *Huascar* in the last moments of the charge. The few cannon it could bring to bear added their blast to the cacophony of noise and smoke. Then the ten-inch Armstrongs roared at point-blank range and the effect was devastating. Forty or fifty Chilean sailors became fragments of human beings. The ram struck home, sending a groan and violent shudder through both vessels. Grau and his crew held on tightly as the *Huascar* finally ground to a halt.

Prat drew his sword. "Board her, boys!" he shouted into the din and confusion, leaping onto the deck of the *Huascar*. Save for one, Sgt. Juan de Dios Aldea, nobody heard or saw the brave captain hurl himself onto the steel plates of the monitor.

Prat and Aldea were almost immediately picked off by marksmen on the *Huascar*, some shooting from the conning tower, others from the crow's nest. Prat dropped to one knee just a few feet short of the conning tower, struggling against his wound, fighting off unconsciousness. One of the *Huascar*'s sailors leaped out of the main turret, flushed by the battle, and slew the Chilean captain instantly with his pistol.

The *Huascar* backed off the stricken corvette and prepared to ram a second time. The scene was repeated, the *Esmeralda* now dead in the water from the devastating blow to its machinery by the first ramming. As the *Huascar* crunched once more into the corvette, Lieutenant Serrano leaped aboard the monitor in imitation of his fallen leader, followed by ten or twelve sailors armed with rifles and machetes. One of the *Huascar*'s lieutenants, Jorge Velarde, was caught in the midst of the boarding party, which landed like a swarm of bees on the ship. They cut

Velarde down before falling to the *Huascar's* sharpshooters and machine gunners.

Once again the *Huascar* pulled free of the smashed and bloody Chilean ship, now listing heavily and littered with human and material wreckage. Miraculously, it still floated and flew its colors. It would not surrender. The *Huascar* pulled back far enough to get a good run for a third time. Twenty minutes elapsed between the second ramming and the last attack. At 12:10 P.M. the two ships again collided before the thousands of onlookers, now silenced by the awful battle nearing its end. The last ramming fatally pierced the heroic *Esmeralda* and it went down by the bow. The Chilean flag slowly disappeared beneath the water, still waving bravely through the acrid, smoky hell surrounding both ships.

The *Huascar* launched its boats to pick up survivors, fifty-four out of a crew of two hundred. One man, Lieutenant Velarde, lost his life on board the monitor.

To the south of Iquique the *Covadonga* had been desperately trying to stay ahead of the powerful *Independencia*. Four sharpshooters on the Chilean corvette peppered the *Independencia's* only bow piece, while Captain Condell hugged the shoreline. If the two-thousand-ton *Independencia* followed the four-hundred-twelve-ton *Covadonga's* wake into shallow water, there might be a resolution to this uneven battle.

As they rounded Punta Gruesa, Condell felt his keel scrape the top of a nasty reef, finally gliding over unharmed.

"Now we've got 'em!" Condell exclaimed. "Come about, hard to starboard," he snapped at the helmsman and the *Covadonga* slowly turned to the right.

Somewhat perplexed by the maneuver, but now given a clear shot, the *Independencia* prepared to ram the Chilean apparently turning to fight. A sickening crunch as the large Peruvian ironclad plowed into the reef and destroyed her keel ended the infuriating chase for Captain Moore and the Peruvians. Exuberant, Condell in the *Covadonga* crossed the grounded ironclad's bow twice and raked her with *Covadonga's* small battery before turning north to succor the *Esmeralda*. But Prat and his valiant vessel had already been martyred by the *Huascar* and Condell turned south when the *Huascar* appeared, steaming down along the shore, alone, searching for the *Covadonga*. The Battle of Iquique was over. The naval blockade of the port was lifted, but at what a price! Peru now had only one capital vessel, the *Huascar*, to oppose the newer, heavily armed *Cochrane* and *Blanco Encalada*.

From April through September 1879 Grau made brilliant use

of the *Huascar*. He caught up with the *Covadonga* at Antofagasta and shot it up before returning to Iquique and capturing the *Cousina*. Grau then turned on the *Magallanes*, but was forced to beat a retreat when the more powerful, but slower, *Cochrane* arrived on the scene. Grau, however, continued his raids, at one time capturing the troop transport *Rimac* with an entire battalion of Chilean cavalry aboard. Promoted to admiral, Grau rapidly rose in the esteem of his nation. In October Grau would follow Prat to the grave in an act of valor equal to the heroic Chilean's sacrifice, but in the meantime, he raised havoc with Chile's war plans.

The Peruvians knew that the inherent balance of naval power in the Pacific still was heavily weighted toward Chile with the *Cochrane* and *Blanco Encalada* at large. The two Civil War–age monitors that Captain Gilchrest had shepherded into the Pacific for Peru in 1869 were by now immobilized by boilers deteriorated almost beyond repair. But inventions and innovations in naval warfare were proceeding rapidly in the second half of the nineteenth century. The Civil War especially had stimulated the inventiveness of Americans.

The famed encounter between the Union *Monitor* and the Confederate *Merrimac* (in truth renamed the *Virginia*, but remembered more popularly by the former name) ushered in the age of ironclads and turret guns. They revolutionized naval warfare by effectively eliminating the wooden ship and its fixed artillery as the naval standard. The addition of steam further underscored the radical departure from traditional warfare at sea.

Unable to match the strength of the Union surface fleets whose blockades—implementing the Anaconda strategy—were slowly choking off the southern lines of supply to the world, Confederate officers and inventors themselves produced a series of makeshift ironclads and submersibles to try and offset the Union advantage in resources and industrial production. The first working submarines were built, mines (a term used interchangeably with torpedoes in the language of the times) were improved, and other gadgetry were developed to rupture the blockade and try and prevent Union attacks on southern ports—attacks like the one Adm. David Farragut launched on Mobile in 1864. When informed of the torpedoes and mines protecting the narrow harbor channel his fleet had to thread, Farragut was prompted to make the remark forever immortalized in naval lore, "Damn the torpedoes, full speed ahead." Farragut carried the day, for ultimately the resources of the South could not match those of the North. The few submarines and torpedoes produced by the Confederacy were over-whelmed by scores of Union monitors and ironclads pouring out of the shipyards of the industrialized North. While some Union warships were sunk or severely damaged by the intrepid southern submariners and torpedo experts, these successes were often accomplished at cost of their own vessels and lives.

The North also, of course, produced notable technological advances. The Union, furthermore, possessed the materials to implement many of its inventors' ideas. A young engineer named John Louis Lay devised the spar torpedo, which was no more than a charge mounted on the end of a long pole or spar. Using a small steam launch, Lay and a crew that included Lt. William B. Cushing attacked the Confederate ironclad *Albermarle* one evening on the Roanoke River. They successfully planted the charge and sank the *Albermarle*. The daring raid with this primitive device, however, cost them the loss of their launch and the lives of their entire crew, with the exception of Lay and Cushing, who almost miraculously survived.[24] Experimentation continued after the Civil War, and by 1879 the techniques and ideas first developed during the war had been considerably improved.

Lay himself evolved the concept of the modern torpedo and actually developed a working model which could be launched from afloat or from shore. It had a range of about one mile and was controlled by two wires, one for direction and one for detonating the charge.

The new technology that could be introduced in the War of the Pacific was considerable, and it also represented a good proving ground for inventors. The availability of this new weaponry was not lost on the participants and their agents, especially to William Grace and Charles Flint in the United States. Their partiality to the Peruvian cause led them to promote actively the acquisition and dispatch of those inventions to Peru.

The most promising weapon was the torpedo, and there were several competing designs and alternatives to choose from. The U.S. Torpedo Company had a weapon similar in type to Lay's, except its was guided by one wire. Flint even persuaded John Ericsson, the inventor of the original *Monitor*, to try his hand in designing torpedoes.[25]

When the war commenced between Chile and Peru on April 3, Flint and Grace were already studying and assessing the best torpedo designs. The U.S. Navy maintained a torpedo testing

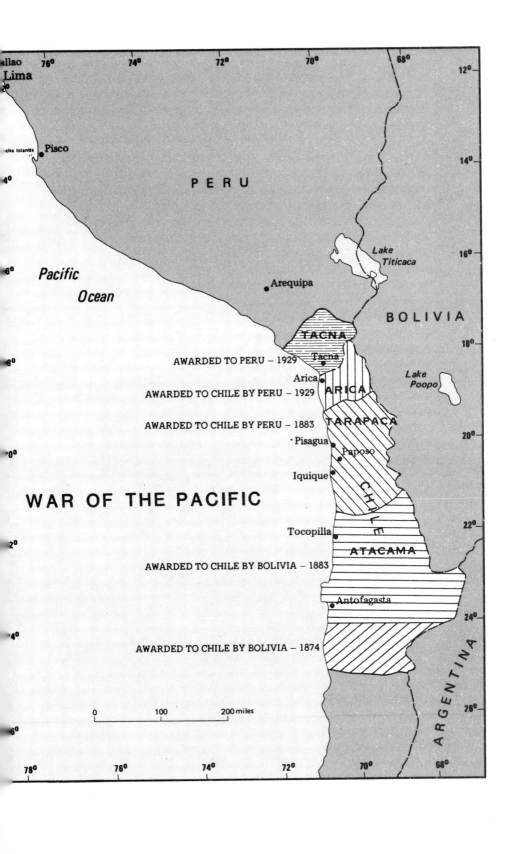

station at Newport, Rhode Island, where they also tested the best designs for torpedo boats to launch the weapons. Both Lay and the U.S. Torpedo Company built special boats for the task, although navy officers tended to favor a different design by Nat Herreshoff. Not only did Herreshoff, a shipbuilder from Bristol, Rhode Island, design good torpedo boats, he also subsequently designed five successful defenders of the famed America's Cup yachting contest.[26]

Within a week after the declaration of war, Grace had several torpedo boats and torpedoes built by both Lay and the U.S. Torpedo Company on the high seas to Peru. The leader of the Lay team, W. W. Rowley, took the pseudonym of H. J. Patchen to protect himself in the passage across Panama, made difficult not only by Colombia's neutrality but by Chileans and friends of Chile in the area.[27]

The Herreshoff boat had also attracted Grace's attention. It was a fast, quiet boat, and on Long Island Sound William participated in one test that convinced him of its appropriateness. He ordered one for $18,500 and prepared to send it to Peru. The problem was the craft's length. It was fifty feet long and difficult, if not impossible, to disguise. He thus shipped it to Panama with no attempt at concealment, and billed it to the Compañía Cargadora del Peru, a guano dealer in Callao.[28] The fastest carrier then operating on the West Coast, the Pacific Steam Navigation Company (PSNC), was controlled by English sympathetic to the Chilean cause. They refused passage to the steam launch, quite rightly suspicious of its ultimate function. Yet, when the Peruvian government made a generous offer to purchase two PSNC steamers, the company accepted and the Herreshoff boat and five others eventually reached Callao.

How did the torpedoes and boats perform in the war? Unevenly is perhaps the kindest description. An attempt was made in April in Callao to torpedo a small Chilean ship then in the harbor. The torpedo was launched and controlled by one of Lay's men, Stephen Chester, from the decks of the *Huascar.* Something went wrong, as is the wont of new and untried weapons, and the torpedo circled and headed back for the *Huascar.* The prized Peruvian monitor had to scramble to avoid being blasted by its own torpedo.

In their search for able and experienced technicians to man the boats and their torpedoes, Grace and Flint turned to Union and Confederate veterans. One agreed to sink the *Almirante*

Cochrane and *Blanco Encalada* for the fee of one million dollars. This struck William as a bit steep.

In the course of recruiting, Flint discovered a Confederate veteran named Read who had been in the torpedo service on the Mississippi. He agreed to go to Peru or anywhere.[29] Read, an 1860 graduate of Annapolis, not only was an experienced torpedo expert, but had demonstrated exemplary bravery during the Civil War. In one instance he boldly sailed a captured Union schooner into the harbor of Portland, Maine, and took out a revenue cutter within sight and sound of thousands of Yankees. Read also served with the Colombian navy after the Civil War, spoke Spanish, and knew South American ways.[30]

Flint took Read to Bristol, Rhode Island, where he helped test the Herreshoff boats on Narragansett Bay. Read agreed to go to Peru and sailed on August 20 with an engineer, John H. Smith. As Flint noted with satisfaction, Read followed "their [torpedo boats'] tests in Narragansett Bay, he followed them across the Isthmus, and he followed them into war."[31] However, getting into the war proved to be not a simple task.

The Peruvian navy commissioned Read a commander and he rapidly devised a plan to launch a surprise attack on the *Cochrane* and the *Blanco Encalada*, both then in Valparaiso undergoing repairs. If successful, Read would receive a substantial amount of prize money, and this rankled Peruvian naval officers. Several offered to lead the attack for nothing, as did a one-legged army colonel. Their problem was not patriotism, but inexperience; as one American on the scene observed colloquially, none of them "knew a torpedo from a Chinese stinkpot."[32]

Yet, Stephen Chester's snafu with the *Huascar*, almost sinking that powerful monitor with its own torpedo, had done nothing in particular to reinforce Peruvian confidence in the cocky American torpedo experts. They represented three distinct concerns—Herreshoff boat people, the Lay Company, and the U.S. Torpedo Company—and they bickered with one another as well as with the Peruvians. Read and his engineer Smith, for example, were ridiculed as blockheads by Ford Snyder of the U.S. Torpedo Company team. Smith asserted that he had been a chief engineer in the U.S. Navy, but Snyder snorted that Smith was a dilapidated old Scotsman who never came nearer to being a chief in the navy than Sitting Bull did to being president.[33]

But before Read or any of the others were able to launch their attacks on the Chilean ironclads, the *Huascar* was finally brought to bay.

The *Huascar* and the smaller *Union* had sailed on September 30, 1879, for the south when they met with *Blanco Encalada* and other Chilean warships on October 8 off the coast of Angamos.[34] Grau turned southwest to avoid battle with the more powerful *Blanco Encalada* and escaped momentarily. A change of course to the north, however, brought him into contact with the *Cochrane* and two smaller Chilean ships, the *O'Higgins* and *Loa*. Grau detached the *Union* to seek safety and then attempted to make a run for it. The *Cochrane* was now in range, however, and Grau prepared for battle in this first historic engagement of ironclad warships on the high seas. He turned the *Huascar* to ram the Chilean. The maneuver failed and the *Cochrane* brought its powerful battery to bear, first destroying the bridge on the *Huascar*, and killing both Grau and the next two officers in line of command. Another accurate blast destroyed the *Huascar*'s main battery. With the steering gear already in shambles and no firepower, *Huascar*'s fourth officer, now in command, ordered her scuttled to prevent capture. Chilean boarders arrived in time to keep her afloat and took her as a prize back to port.

Grau was martyred no less than Arturo Prat earlier in the war, but the effect of the loss of the *Huascar* proved irreparable for the Peruvian cause. American diplomatic representatives in the two capitals made much the same observation on hearing the news. From Santiago, Thomas A. Osborne wrote that "the capture of the famous turreted monitor *Huascar* by the Chilean navy has produced here the most unbounded enthusiasm. . . . This naval victory leaves Chile undisputed master of the seas"; and from Lima, Isaac P. Christiancy commented that "the loss of this single vessel changes the whole aspect of the war . . . which has consisted almost entirely of the achievement of this . . . vessel and the efforts of the Chileans to take her, and gives the Chileans full control of the sea."[35]

The meaning of the *Huascar-Cochrane* engagement far transcended the boundaries of the war between Peru and Chile. The United States still had not transformed its fleet from wood to iron in the post–Civil War doldrums affecting the military establishment. On the other hand, France and England had already moved well along the path to modernizing their fleets. The naval engagements of the War of the Pacific, especially the historic one between the *Huascar* and the *Cochrane*, shook naval strategists and Washington politicians out of their dated patterns of thinking. Yet, while the modernization of the American fleet was prompted in no small part from the lessons being learned off the coast of Peru and Chile, Peruvians benefited little from the loss of the *Huascar* and its heroic commander.

Torpedoman Read was still anxious to apply his skills, especially in view of the disaster suffered by the Peruvian navy. He proposed to repair one of the old Civil War–age monitors Peru possessed and put to sea in it. He would launch his torpedoes from its decks, but the chief engineer of the Peruvian navy vetoed the suggestion as too risky and impractical, given the dilapidated state of the monitor's steam engine. Read eventually lost interest in the cause and returned home when told that prize money would not be awarded under any circumstances. Snyder of the U. S. Torpedo Company did manage to go south, but his efforts caused the powerful Chilean navy few problems. Peru's coastline thus lay open to invasion, deprived as the country was of its capital ships and unable to depend upon the disputatious torpedo experts for results.

Late in 1879 Chilean forces moved with decision on Peru's southern provinces of Tacna, Arica, and Tarapaca. They landed at Pisagua and other points on the coast and conquered the area in a campaign that lasted until July 1880. Long-range artillery manufactured by Krupp in Germany, control of the sea, and a soldiery better trained and armed than the more numerous Bolivian and Peruvian conscripts provided the ingredients of victory, although the Peruvians and Bolivians fought valiantly for their cause. For example, in the final desperate defense of the citadel overlooking the sea at Arica, Coronel Francisco Bolognesi realized the end of the struggle against the Chileans was at hand. Facing ignominious capture, he wrapped himself in the flag and leaped from the cliff to his death.[36] But acts of individual valor could not overcome the superior arms and collective élan of the Chilean armies.

After the fall of Pisagua and the loss of all Tarapaca, the Peruvian government began to lose the confidence of the people, especially under the progressive military pounding of the Chilean armies. It began with the resignation of President Mariano Prado in December 1879. Under the pressure of defeat—for President/General Prado had been commanding the reeling Peruvian armies in Tarapaca for many of the preceding months—he left the country, ostensibly on a fundraising and arms-buying expedition to North America and Europe. He was replaced by the Civilista party's old foe, Nícolas de Piérola, who continued to fight with vigor if not success.

Attempts to purchase ships, arms and munitions abroad, especially in Europe, were frequently frustrated by very able

Chilean diplomats who worked ambiguous neutrality laws to advantage. William Grace was able on occasion to help the Peruvians circumvent the effects of such obstructions. Through his friendship with Baring Brothers in London, Grace arranged for the purchase of Krupp and Armstrong guns for the Peruvian armies, even though Baring Brothers was the financial agent for Chile as well.[37] While a majority of British commercial and mercantile interests favored the Chilean cause, such large and prestigious firms as Baring Brothers and the Pacific Steam Navigation Company were not averse to dealing with both Peru and Chile during the course of the hostilities. Yet the problem of sympathies and sides plagued most of the noncombatants and neutrals caught in this sanguinary struggle along the Pacific.

Late in December 1879, after the Chileans captured the nitrate-rich province of Tarapaca, William Grace had to face the likely possibility that Chile might not only win the war but eventually bring the entire nitrate business under its control.[38] How to deal with such a possibility "once peace is concluded" formed one aspect of the problem. It was compounded in the case of Grace and others by their very sympathies for Peru, sympathies which conflicted with their good business sense. If Chile were to win the war—already the likely conclusion by the end of 1879—Grace would have to deal with a victor from the disadvantage of having backed the loser. Grace was not alone in the dilemma, for it was not an easy war in which to remain neutral.

American diplomats who were supposed to remain neutral almost to a man aligned themselves with the nations where they were stationed. This severely crimped the efforts of United States diplomacy to negotiate a truce or peace among the belligerents.[39] The progress of the war during 1880 made it even more difficult to remain neutral or nonpartisan.

After the capture of Tarapaca, Arica, and Tacna, Chilean warhawks gained the ascendancy in the high councils of government. Before peace could be settled, they demanded not only the cession of Tarapaca, but that of Arica and Tacna as well, plus the payment of a large indemnity as reparation. Peruvians unequivocally refused these terms and the Chileans moved to soften the Peruvian will to resist.

Iquique was settled permanently and incorporated for all practical purposes into the Chilean national territory. Then an Irish soldier of fortune in the service of Chile, Gen. Patrick Lynch, launched a series of raids along the northern Peruvian coast. The object was twofold: plunder, and destruction of the

war spirit of Peru. General Sherman had marched through the
Confederacy in 1864 and 1865 with much the same goal, justifying the plaguelike advance of his armies with the observation that "war is hell." Lynch destroyed cotton and sugar
plantations, burned public structures, killed livestock, set
Chinese coolies free from their bondage, and left turmoil in his
wake. He collected tributes and ransoms from those willing
and able to meet his demands for sparing their properties.
Foreign property was generally respected by Lynch, enabling
many Peruvians to protect their property by transferring it to
foreign ownership before the arrival of the Chileans.[40]

The inherent social tensions in Peruvian society, largely between the ruling white Creole minority and the great mass of
Indians, blacks, mestizos, mulattos, and Chinese, erupted under the liberating impact of the war into violence and class
struggles. In the north many members of the lower classes
joined the Chileans in looting and pillaging, often betraying
the identities of landlords and wealthy merchants to the Chileans in retribution for the oppression, real or perceived, of past
years and centuries.

Among those on the scene was the very perceptive owner
of Cayalti, a sugar-producing hacienda on the north coast near
Chiclayo. Antero Aspillaga feared as early as June 1880 that
internal disorder would plunge Peru into far deeper social and
racial troubles than those caused by an invading army. The
uprising of the Paris Commune of 1871 came to Aspillaga's
mind as civil disorder followed in the wake of the Chileans.[41]
After Lynch's army pillaged Chiclayo, Peruvians joined the
enemy in looting and gladly revealed the names of property
owners and other Peruvians of the privileged class to Lynch
and his commanders.[42] It was not a happy time, and American
attempts to facilitate a truce were muddled by the political transition then taking place in the United States, for 1880 was an
election year.

Nonetheless, the United States arranged a meeting in October 1880 between the representatives of Peru, Bolivia, and
Chile aboard the USS *Lackawanna*, present at Arica.[43] The United
States had two goals as it attempted to reconcile the warring
nations. One was to prevent a European-sponsored peace that
might upstage the Americans in their role as arbitrators of the
Western Hemisphere and thereby dilute the strength of the
Monroe Doctrine. Second, like most of the other neutral nations, the United States sought to end the war for humanitarian,
political, and economic reasons. Politically, the United States
saw the hand of England at work in Chile and thus tended to

align itself with Peru, while economically, it wished to protect the lives and save the property of its citizens in the war zones. But the *Lackawanna* conference came to no avail, and Chilean forces prepared to advance on Lima and attack the capital. As their army of twenty-five thousand marched and leapfrogged north along the coast toward Lima, the elections in the United States lifted James A. Garfield to the presidency and William Grace to the mayoralty of New York.

Garfield was inaugurated in March 1881 and he appointed James G. Blaine as his secretary of state. By then the Chileans had captured Lima (Battle of Miraflores, January 15, 1881), and the Peruvian situation was even more desperate than at the end of 1880. Although Blaine has traditionally been credited with forging the foreign policy of the United States between March and September 1881, when Garfield died from an assassin's bullet, Garfield himself had long been interested in promoting closer ties with Latin America.

As early as 1872 Garfield, as a member of Congress, addressed the imbalance in trade between the United States, England, and Latin America, an imbalance heavily favoring the English. Garfield asked why the United States provided only a tenth of Brazil's imports while buying half its exports. Why did Brazil buy from England and not America?[44] Garfield rightly adduced that economic and political influence followed on the heels of commercial success, and as such he promoted increasing ties between the United States and Latin America.

Thus, although Secretary of State Blaine was more active than his chief in the field of inter-American affairs, he found a willing executive who had formulated some of his own ideas on the subject years before the election of 1880. Blaine lobbied for the rapid intercession of the United States in Latin American disputes to prevent conflicts and encourage peace. He also attempted to impose a doctrine of immutable borders in his foreign policy, hoping to prevent further wars attributable to conflicts born on the frontiers.[45] While this doctrine very obviously was inspired in part by his knowledge of the origins of the War of the Pacific, he was nonetheless convinced that the English were ultimately behind Chilean aggression, commenting that "it is a complete mistake to see this as a Chilean war against Peru. It is a British war against Peru using Chile as its instrument."[46] That allegation was never proven, although it afforded Blaine a good handle with which to beat the English during domestic political campaigns. In fact, England was not particularly interested in promoting a Chilean war of conquest. Blaine, however, preferred the image of an aggressive England, for the United States defense of Peruvian rights and sovereignty could be cast onto the larger stage of Atlantic politics more familiar to American audiences.

American attempts to help negotiate a peace in 1881 were made increasingly difficult after the capture of Lima by the Chileans. The Battle of Miraflores cracked Peruvian confidence and society even further, and emboldened the Chileans to push for stiff peace terms.

★ ★ ★

The final push into the capital took place January 13–17 and, as in most of the successful Chilean campaigns, combined control of the sea with military operations. The Peruvian army of about thirty thousand was officered largely by members of the ruling caste of Creoles, while its ranks were filled by mestizos, mulattos, cholos, blacks, and Indians. Little sense of patriotism or nationalism existed among these Indian and cholo conscripts. Nothing else better illustrates this point than the following story recounted by Heraclio Bonilla.

> After the battles of San Juan and Miraflores which led to the occupation of Lima by the Chileans, Patricio Lynch, commander in chief of the Chileans, visited one of the hospitals in the city in the company of the French admiral Du Petit Thouars. Lynch was trying to explain to the Frenchman the reasons for the Peruvian defeat. He approached two wounded Peruvians, and after some expressions of sympathy, he put the following question, separately to each one: "And why did you take part in the battle?" "I fought for don Nícolas [Piérola]," answered one; and the other: "I for don Miguel [Iglesias]." Lynch put the same question to two Chilean casualties, who both appeared surprised as they answered: "For my fatherland, sir." Lynch turned to Du Petit Thouars with the remark: "That is why we won. These fought for their country, the others for don So-and-so."[47]

Whether true or apocryphal, the story rings consistent with the great amount of evidence depicting the Indians of Peru—who made up the majority of conscripts in the army—as basically unassimilated into the small modernizing segment of Peruvian society located largely on the coast. It was these very Indians whom Manuel Pardo had earlier attempted to reach with the railroad as the great civilizer and tool for progress. Whatever the veracity of Lynch's observation, or the merits of Pardo's goal, Peru's stratified society certainly throttled its ability to wage war well. The details of the capture and subsequent Chilean occupation of Lima added to the trials of Peru.

After the defeat of the Peruvian defenders at Miraflores, discipline in the Peruvian army broke down. This in itself is not unusual. Defeated armies reeling back from battlefields often are transmogrified into notorious hordes, pillaging and looting as they stream away from the victors. The demoralized Peruvian army behaved no differently, except for one local variation: they turned on the large population of Chinese shopkeepers and petty merchants as easy targets. The night of January 16 was particularly terrifying. An English eyewitness recalled that gunfire began to be heard in all directions and fires to break out as night fell. The mobs roving through the streets looted Chinese-owned shops with special license and brutality, murdering sixty or seventy Chinese in the process.[48] Foreign legations and warships in Callao became improvised havens for hundreds, even thousands, of neutrals and noncombatants. John Grace and Ned Eyre, then representing the company in Peru, took refuge aboard such a ship. Earlier, Manuel Llaguno had been transferred by William Grace to New York to protect him and his family from possible reprisals by the Chileans.[49]

Elements of the Chilean army entered Lima on January 17 as Piérola escaped into the rugged mountainous interior to continue the fight. The next few months were the most nightmarish for Peru. The old political order continued to break up under the blows of defeat, and Piérola was stripped of his office in February and replaced by a Civilista lawyer named Francisco García Calderon, who had the approval of the Chileans. Lima was sacked during these months with a thoroughness not soon forgotten by the Peruvians. Simple pillage and robbery accompanying the immediate occupation of Lima yielded to more systematic looting of the capital and country at large. Books and rare manuscripts from the National Library and Archive, animals from the zoo, and parts of the Southern Railway built by Meiggs ten years earlier were packed or crated and shipped back to Chile.*

Chile demanded a harsh peace: all of Tarapaca, Arica, and Tacna, and an indemnity to boot. Chile threatened to make separate arrangements with Bolivia, giving it access to the sea through Peru's port of Arica. From the mountains Piérola and Gen. Andres Cáceres continued to resist, making the discussion of peace terms difficult. Even President García Calderon refused to countenance the cession of all three southern provinces. His display of patriotism was rewarded by exile to Santiago.

---

*A distinguished Chilean historian once told this author—in a matter-of-fact manner—that any historian of Peru interested in the colonial and pre-1879 period must in all seriousness consult the national archive in Santiago, which received most of the celebrated manuscript booty.

Meanwhile, Cáceres continued his fight in the mountains with an army, the Montoneros, largely recruited from among the Indians, while the Chileans eventually approved of Gen. Miguel de Iglesias as president in late 1882. It was with Iglesias's government that the Treaty of Ancón, bringing official hostilities to a close between Peru and Chile, was signed on October 23, 1883. Through all these tragic proceedings, especially from the moment Lima was captured in January 1881 to the signing of the peace treaty, foreign interests, especially those of England, France, and the United States, were deeply involved at both the public and private levels.

Diplomats and consuls were motivated by a combination of humanitarian sensibilities and economic determinants to intercede often during the war. One must recall that nineteenth-century man continued to believe that certain humane principles of civilization obtained even in war. While these sensibilities were gradually being destroyed by the machines of modern warfare, one still tried to protect women, children and neutrals from the perils of combat.

In many instances, consuls and ministers of the United States and European powers intervened to ameliorate the brutal conditions of war. After one heavy bombardment of Iquique, neutral representatives admonished the Chilean admiral, prompting this gentleman to promise to give notice before the next attack.[50] During Patrick Lynch's raids along the northern coast, American consuls frequently injected themselves into the process and helped to bargain for terms and ransoms.[51]

On the other hand, the economic motive for intervention was best represented by the views of Isaac Christiancy, the United States minister to Peru in 1881. Christiancy wrote Secretary of State Blaine that a complete Chilean victory would mean the ascendancy of "English over American influence on this coast [and the United States] should intervene in compelling a settlement of peace on reasonable terms."[52] Christiancy went so far as to suggest establishing a United States protectorate over Peru if Chile persisted in its expansionist, inflexible course. Blaine had already recalled Christiancy even before the minister made that impractical suggestion, but the secretary was also quite determined to maintain Peru's territorial integrity. Christiancy's successor, Gen. Stephen A. Hurlbut, arrived in Peru early in August 1881 and soon became a leading champion of the Peruvian cause.

Blaine's vision of the United States role in hemispheric affairs was ample and ranged far beyond the confines of trying to settle the War of the Pacific. In November 1881 he issued a call for the convocation of a pan-American conference the next year in Washington to organize a permanent organization to arbitrate disputes and to promote stability in the region. Blaine hoped that the net effect would be to foster trade between the Americas and increase American influence in an area often neglected by the United States.[53] Although this general plan did not fructify until 1889, when the First International American Congress was finally convened, Blaine and Garfield were promoting a political idea already being expressed commercially and economically by individuals such as Henry Meiggs and the Grace brothers.

William Grace, it will be recalled, began his first term as mayor of New York in January 1881, precisely the month when the fortunes of Peru in the war turned worst with the loss of Lima to the Chileans. Michael was in charge of much of the Grace operations for the next two years while William discharged his duties as mayor.

Michael was faced with the unenviable chore of piloting the Grace fortunes through a period of intense instability while the three warring nations tried to agree on how to end the war, fix debts and indemnities, and make territorial changes. Michael's goals were twofold: one, preserve the Grace interests in Peru as best as possible, and that meant preserving Peru's integrity as best as possible from the demands of the Chileans; and second, actively pursue business opportunities in Chile, where Grace had already been trading since the 1870s.

The extent and specific nature of Grace's assistance to Peru were known to only a few individuals, but Chileans for the most part recognized that Grace was a "Peruvian house" whose sympathies lay with, and whose resources doubtless had been utilized to help, Peru. Thus there existed a natural coolness to the Graces in Chile. Nonetheless, Grace deemed it prudent to establish the best possible relationship with the victors in the interests of maintaining a viable presence on the whole West Coast of the Americas, and on October 19, 1881, Grace & Co. was organized in Valparaiso. It began with a capital of £36,000, £6,000 of which was contributed by each of the following partners: Noel West, living in Valparaiso and named the new manager; John W. Grace and Edward Eyre, in Lima; and William R. Grace, Michael P. Grace, and Charles Flint, in New York. West had been with the Pacific Steam Navigation Company and was an Englishman well thought of by the Chileans.

Michael's efforts to protect Grace in Peru were closely tied in with Blaine's schemes to preserve the territorial integrity of Peru, and to guard foreign investments—particularly in the nitrate industry—in Peruvian territory under Chilean occupation. Blaine thought the best means to achieve this end was to form an international company to manage the Peruvian guano and nitrate deposits then under Chilean control. This company, formed by Levi P. Morton, the United States minister in Paris, was called the Compagnie Financiere et Commerciale du Pacifique and represented Peruvian bondholders throughout Europe.[54] Blaine's plan was to have the Compagnie Pacifique manage the Peruvian guano and nitrate fields, pay Chile an appropriate indemnity, and thus maintain the national boundaries of Peru intact. Grace's firm would be a stockholder in the firm and hold the exclusive right to distribute Peruvian nitrates and guano in the West Indies and North America.

The Chileans peremptorily rejected the plan. They had conquered Tarapaca, Arica, and Tacna and were not about to yield what had been won in blood to an international firm concocted by Americans in Paris and Washington.

Michael sensed the resolute Chilean feelings, although he hoped Blaine's initiatives would dissuade Chile from taking all it had conquered. His assessment, nonetheless, was, "I am satisfied that the U. S. gov't will not use force. I consider Tarapaca lost to Peru for ever and that the Paris gentlemen are chasing a phantom."[55]

Meanwhile, Minister Hurlbut in Lima led the Peruvians to believe that intervention by the United States against the intransigent Chileans was quite possible. Negotiations, later repudiated by Washington, even took place between Hurlbut and the García Calderon government, which agreed to the establishment of an American naval base at the spacious port of Chimbote on the northern coast of Peru. In December 1881 Blaine once again put pressure on the Chileans to submit to American mediation on favorable terms to Peru: that is, no cession of territory and the guarantee of neutral property rights in those territories now controlled by Chile. Blaine's messenger was William Trescot, whom Blaine sent to Chile with sharply worded instructions. Twice President Arthur read (or scanned, perhaps) and then signed these instructions before Trescot sailed in December. Arthur had succeeded to the presidency after Garfield died in September. In December Arthur removed Blaine and replaced him with Frederick T. Frelinghuysen, and by the time Trescot reached Santiago in January or February 1882, Arthur and Frelinghuysen had backed away from Blaine's strong stand. Trescot's orders were essentially nullified and Trescot himself was mortified to learn that the Chileans had known of the change in his orders fully two weeks before he himself heard of their modifications.[56]

What happened in the transition from Garfield to Arthur? The best answer is politics. Arthur was a member of the Republican party's unreformed Stalwart faction, which dominated the GOP in the post–Civil War years. Garfield represented a more progressive, liberal wing of the party. The result was that a continued and consistent United States policy in the mediation of the War of the Pacific was sacrificed to domestic politics.[57] In his partisan zeal Arthur decided to grind some old axes against the Half-Breed Garfield and appointees like Blaine. Dismissing the secretary of state was one swipe. Publishing much of Blaine's correspondence with his ministers in Chile and Peru in 1882 was another.

That the domestic squabbles between a factionalized Republican party should so profoundly affect the international scene is regrettable but true. It is even more reprehensible within the context of the following assessment: "In the long view of history, the noisy struggle between Stalwarts and Half-Breeds may appear to have all the meaning—or, better, lack of meaning—of the conflicts between Byzantine Greens and Whites or Florentine Guelphs and Ghibellines . . . and yet it took the center of the American political state for several years, and served as the excuse for the assassination by a disgruntled office seeker, Charles Guiteau, who declared on shooting the president that 'I am a Stalwart, now Arthur is president.' "[58]

Michael became disgusted with the American political scene as the threads Blaine had been weaving were rapidly unraveled. An interview with President Arthur late in 1881 left Michael flat, and he wrote Noel West in January that *"Am. Intervention is all a humbug . . . Uncle Sam has backed down."* To Ned Eyre in Lima Michael expressed himself with even greater vehemence. The United States will be thoroughly hated on the West Coast, will be jeered and laughed at by all the foreign legations, will be made fun of by the Chilean press, and will be thoroughly despised by the Peruvian people, who will blame them to a very great extent for the present trouble. What galled Michael even more was the invocation of the Monroe Doctrine by the United States to block European attempts to mediate in 1880–81, promising Peru that the United States would arrange matters itself. After raising the hopes of the government and people of Peru, the United States then abruptly withdrew and left Peru open to the mercies of a victorious army.[59]

Perhaps Michael was overstating the ability of the United States, or England, or France to dictate to Chile. Chile would not budge on Tarapaca, as Trescot recalled for John Grace in Lima on the way home from his frustrated mission to Chile. The foreign minister, Jorge Balmaceda, refused to discuss the matter of Tarapaca with Trescot, and bluntly stated that Tarapaca was now irrevocably Chilean territory and that if the United States wanted Tarapaca for Peru, then it must fight for it.[60] This alternative was certainly not included in Trescot's orders, which, in any case, had been effectively repudiated by the time he arrived in Chile.

Once the United States position became clear, Chile proceeded to push for a final settlement on *its* terms. A new Peruvian government under Miguel Iglesias was gradually strengthened by the Chileans still occupying Peru, and in October 1883 a preliminary treaty was agreed to.

In the mountains Andres Cáceres kept up a lively guerrilla warfare against the foe with his *montoneros*, but that war developed strong racial overtones in 1882 and 1883. Bands of Indian guerrillas would raid and attack the homes and haciendas of whites and *mistis* (mestizos) just as often as the camps and armies of Chileans trying to eliminate resistance. The War of the Pacific had released some powerful social forces. A Chilean commander was stunned by what he saw in November 1883: "All the Indians of Huanta and Huancayo are in revolt. The few with whom we could make contact declared that their objective was not to fight the Chileans or the Peruvian peace party, but the entire white race."[61] The specter of social rebellion was not confined to the highlands. In some of the more populous coastal valleys, blacks massacred Chinese and whites indiscriminately in the war's disorderly wake.[62] As the Chilean army withdrew gradually from Peru, scattered violence flared up and directly threatened the interests of the propertied class. Accommodation and agreement with the Chileans—no matter how onerous the terms with respect to the national patrimony—seemed to be the only way of preserving the interests of those who still ruled Peru.

The negotiations ultimately leading to the Treaty of Ancón were born of powerful external and internal forces that combined unfelicitously for Peru in 1883. On the one hand, the United States was no longer actively and threateningly pressing for Peruvian interests. United States diplomacy had failed, and its vagaries and inconsistencies had alienated the very nation Blaine had sought to help.[63] On the other hand, the internal turmoil caused by the war's social disruptions was crying for resolution.

Not only were segments of the general populace rebelling against traditional patterns of authority, but the ruling class of Peru was truncated by the war. A survey made in 1870 was repeated in 1894, and it revealed that of eighteen millionaires discovered in 1870, none remained in 1894; 11,587 individuals had been classed as rich in 1870, whereas only 1,725 were listed as such in 1894; the well-off numbered 22,148 in 1870 and only 2,000 in 1894; laborers had decreased from 1,236,000 to 345,000; and, finally, beggars had swelled from 0 to 500,000.[64] However crude a scan this may be, Peru by 1883 and 1884 had lost more than territory from the war; the Treaty of Ancón signed on October 23, 1883, represented the end of formal hostilities under trying circumstances.

The treaty was formally ratified on March 18, 1884. It was a treaty complicated by two major considerations: one, Bolivia's defeat and aspirations also had to be considered in any final settlement of territories along the Pacific coast; and two, the immense Peruvian foreign debt was secured by large guano and nitrate deposits in territories Chile had conquered and would probably keep. The Bolivians wanted guarantees of access to the sea, while Peru's creditors, mostly English bond-holders, wanted guarantees that Chile would acknowledge and honor a large percentage of the Peruvian debt hypothecated by deposits of guano and nitrates in the rich province of Tarapaca. That Tarapaca would be irreversibly annexed by Chile was no longer a subject for real debate by the time the treaty was negotiated. The treaty provided for the unconditional transfer of Tarapaca and Antofagasta to Chile; the former was Peruvian territory, and the latter was the mineral-rich desert province disputed between Chile and Bolivia for over half a century.

However, the Tacna-Arica area north of Tarapaca was so wedded to the Peruvian sense of national territory that the Chileans were forced to make some concessions for the sake of the peace. They would, of course, have preferred outright annexation, but Peru, even under the presidency of Miguel

Iglesias, adamantly resisted the unconditional loss of Tacna-Arica. The solution agreed to in the end was to allow Chile to continue its occupation of Tacna-Arica for a period of ten years, at which time a plebiscite would determine permanent ownership. Whoever lost the vote would receive ten million silver pesos in compensation.[65]

As for the immense Peruvian debt, the problem remained unsolved. The Chileans denied responsibility for any portion of it that might have been secured by the guano and nitrates of Tarapaca, although they did authorize the sale of a million tons of guano from the Lobos Islands, half of which would go to creditors holding a lien on Peruvian guano.[66] For the great bulk of the debt, over $250 million, the bondholders would have to deal with the Peruvian government. To a nation beaten down and battered so thoroughly by war, this financial cross weighed even more heavily than it might have under better circumstances. At precisely this point Michael Grace slogged into the morass of debt and despondency to defend his interests and those of Peru, still very much bound together.

7

The Grace
Contract

There are several different threads to the story that culminated in 1890 with a contract popularly known as the Grace Contract in Peru (alternatively called the Tyler-Aranibar and Aspillaga-Donoughmore Contract after various principals in the case). Basically, Michael Grace helped Peru renegotiate its huge external debt by turning over to English bondholders various assets of the nation, principal among them the railroads, both finished and unfinished. The debt was forgiven in return for these cessions and Peru's credit abroad was reestablished. Chile, Peru, the bondholders, William Grace, Her Majesty's Foreign Office, the American presidency, the legacy of Henry Meiggs, and other tangible and intangible powers were all orchestrated by Michael between 1885 and 1890 into a complicated agreement—the Grace Contract. It lifted from Peru a huge burden inherited from before the War of the Pacific, and made even heavier by the losses from that war.

Peru's postwar problems were complex, each bearing on and influencing the resolution of the others. The cessation of hostilities with the Treaty of Ancón only seemed to raise the nonmilitary problems into sharper relief. Morale had been seriously shaken by the Chilean victory, and postwar leaders had to contend with a people shell-shocked and unsure of their ability to withstand another such confrontation if it should ever occur. Racial violence had erupted during the course of the war's later campaigns, emphasizing the problems of a mixed society still, in many respects, highly unintegrated. The budding railway network of the country had been damaged and, in some cases, literally uprooted and taken off as war reparations or booty.

Large portions of the nation's sugar and cotton plantations had been burned and sacked. And the immense loans of 1869, 1870, and 1872, on which Peru had defaulted in 1876, loomed as a dark cloud over any recovery program the nation may have wished to launch.[1]

The security for these loans—guano and nitrate deposits—had been largely hypothecated to English bondholders, who blocked attempts by Peruvians after the war to generate new sources of revenue in the European money market. Complicating the problem of the Peruvian debt to the bondholders (about $260 million) was the stark fact that the territory which contained the richest and most promising guano and nitrate deposits now belonged to Chile by virtue of the Treaty of Ancón. The province of Tarapaca had been irrevocably annexed to the Chilean nation, and Chileans were basically unwilling to allow their newly acquired riches to be siphoned off to pay a Peruvian debt to European bondholders. Or, as Jorge Basadre, Peru's most distinguished and balanced modern historian, phrased the problem: "Was Peru obliged to pay her external debt, especially after the treaty of peace had transferred to Chile the territory containing the most important deposits of guano?"[2]

Without settling this immense debt, Peru simply could not begin to recover from the ravages of the war. Its internal sources of income had been drastically reduced by the war's effects, and its external sources—potential European investors—blocked any new loans until the old debts were settled. Only one major potential source of revenue existed in Peru in this period, the unfinished railroads. Into this quagmire of conflicting claims and international enmities plunged Michael P. Grace, looking out for himself and still committed to Peru, two principles he found perfectly compatible.

The origins of the Peruvian debt, of course, lay in the halcyon days of Henry Meiggs's railroad-building efforts. Peru had defaulted on its debt in 1876 and construction of the railroads had ceased until a new contract was signed with Henry Meiggs on February 3, 1877. That contract was important for several reasons. It not only got work on the railroads started once more, but also reintroduced some old goals. Meiggs was to finish the railroad to Chicla and then extend it to Cerro de Pasco, the rich silver-mining district. At Cerro, an old project that had lain dormant since 1861 was revived and made part of the contract. A drainage tunnel, called the Rumillana, was to be constructed to rehabilitate the mining district and bring it back into fruitful production. Furthermore, Meiggs was given the right to develop and operate unregistered and abandoned mines in the district in order to promote the restoration of general prosperity to the area.

Meiggs initiated the renewed project but the struggle to cope with all his problems finally overwhelmed him on September 30, 1877. His will provided for the creation of an executive board to carry on his business. The board formed the Oroya Railroad and Cerro de Pasco Mining Company and continued with attempts to fulfill its obligations under the contract of February 3, 1877. Before Meiggs died he had already pushed the railroad from Anchi to Chicla and made definite plans for the drainage tunnel. By 1881, when work on the railroad, tunnel, and mines ceased because of the war, a part of the tunnel—about two hundred forty meters of a total length of twenty-seven hundred—had been completed by Meiggs's heirs (the Oroya Railroad and the Cerro de Pasco Mining Company), and a reduction plant for the treatment of ores from the Cerro de Pasco mines had been installed in the district.[3]

Following the interruptions of the war, the next major change with relation to the Central Railway and the mines of Cerro de Pasco introduced Michael directly into the picture. On January 20, 1885, the Oroya Railroad and Cerro de Pasco Mining Company sold to Grace all of their franchises, rights, privileges, and obligations, lock, stock, and barrel, with relation to the railroad, the tunnel, and their properties and leases at Cerro de Pasco. Michael then signed a contract with the Peruvian government, dated February 27, 1885, agreeing to extend the line from Chicla to Oroya within four years, and from Oroya to Cerro de Pasco within seven years, and to finish the Rumillana Tunnel within two years after opening the railroad to public traffic between Oroya and Cerro de Pasco. Grace also acquired various rights and properties at Cerro de Pasco. The transfer was full and complete and left Michael in possession of the Meiggs legacy. How did this happen?

With the departure of Henry Meiggs from the scene, his heirs were left in a leadership vacuum. Although they were able to operate the completed parts of the railroad profitably, some of Meiggs's old engineers, especially William H. Cilley, former chief engineer of the Central Railway, wanted a stronger hand. They wanted someone to take charge and realize Henry Meiggs's grand vision of extending the network to Cerro de Pasco and thus fulfill their old chief's dream.

Cilley approached the Graces, William and Michael, in New

York early in 1883 and suggested they acquire controlling interest in the Meiggs company. Cilley himself owned shares in the company and thought he could induce others, such as John G. Meiggs, to sell enough of theirs to give the Graces controlling interest.[4] William was reluctant. He foresaw a long, slow, laborious process of recovery for Peru that he compared to the tortuous Reconstruction of the American South. Furthermore, William likened the possibility of striking it rich from the Cerro de Pasco mines to chances of finding the buried treasure of the "late lamented Captain Kidd."[5] Yet Michael was not to be denied.

Setting aside forty thousand dollars for the effort, Michael Grace and Cilley first tried secretly to get control of the Meiggs company. When this failed, Grace traveled to London in 1884 and made an open proposal to a son-in-law of Meiggs, Alexander Robertson. As an executor of Meiggs's estate, Robertson was empowered to act with authority and he favored the Grace-Cilley overture. By late 1884 Michael held 37.5 percent of the stock in the railroad and mines, while Cilley held another 37.5 percent, and Robertson the balance.[6] Early in January 1885 Michael acquired full control of the railroad, the tunnel, and the Cerro de Pasco mining properties. This included not only all the rights of the company but all of its obligations toward the government as well.[7]

Michael became a naturalized citizen of the United States on June 19, 1882, and his acquisition of the Meiggs rights and properties naturally attracted the attention of the United States minister in Lima, Charles Buck.[8] The entrance of Michael Grace onto the scene was reported back to Washington with satisfaction by Buck, who believed the Graces could complete the great works abandoned by Meiggs and heirs. Buck would make many enemies as minister between 1885 and 1890, including both the Graces and the Peruvian government, so one can appreciate the agile posture that Michael had to assume in the various negotiations between American citizens and a Peruvian government that came to consider Buck as virtually persona non grata.[9]

Even though Michael and William Grace were both naturalized United States citizens by 1885, they retained strong ties, financial and political, to Great Britain, and moved back and forth across the Atlantic with ease as they dealt with the financial and political loci of power in both worlds. Added to this was their long experience with Peru, giving them additional insights into a third country culturally and physically different from the North Atlantic world. It is within this international context that we can consider Michael Grace's acquisition and early improvement of the railroad and the mines of Cerro de Pasco. It is also within this cosmopolitan context that we note the emergence of the multinational character of W. R. Grace & Co.

To generate capital to fulfill his contract of 1885 Michael turned to the American money market rather than to England, as had been traditionally the case. The flow of capital in the nineteenth century had been largely from east to west, for the great natural resources of America were frequently exploitable only with large injections of British capital. Andrew Carnegie, for example, made many of his early millions not by producing steel but by producing British capital on frequent trips to his home country for that purpose. Yet, the development of finance capitalism was an essential stage in the growth of the American industrial state, and Michael's ability to tap this source demonstrated the growing maturity of the American strain of capitalism.

On June 28, 1886, a syndicate was organized in New York to develop the mines. Known as the Cerro de Pasco Syndicate, it brought together as investors "a number of men of high standing in the community, possessed of ample means, and [with] the ability and resources necessary to carry out the enterprise that the syndicate [had] undertaken."[10] Ten participants in this first syndicate, each contributing $10,000, were the three sons-in-law of the late William H. Vanderbilt, Arthur Twombley, W. Seward Webb, and W. D. Sloane; John J. Mackay of the Comstock lode; Secretary of Treasury William C. Whitney; Robert Payne of Standard Oil; Frederick Billings of Northern Pacific; Henry B. Hyde of Equitable Life; Joseph W. Drexel of Drexel, Morgan & Co.; William R. Grace himself.[11] Once the syndicate was formed, Michael employed and sent a commission of mining engineers to Peru to investigate thoroughly the Cerro de Pasco region at a cost of £22,000 sterling. Michael continued to operate the railroad, made necessary repairs and replacements, and prepared generally for the extension of the railway and the construction of the drainage tunnel.[12] Meanwhile, the bondholders in England were pursuing their interests, which, like Michael Grace's, were inextricably linked to Peru's financial problems and promises.

When Peru defaulted on its debt in 1876 the bondholders formed a committee specifically entrusted to manage their interests.[13] They hoped to salvage some of their investments through the sale of Peruvian guano, so the Peruvian Guano Company was organized in England in June 1876. But the bondholders were dissatisfied with the meager results and appealed to the Foreign Office for assistance. By this time, not only was Peruvian guano declining in quality as the richest reserves were depleted, but the fertilizer market was being challenged by nitrate of soda as well.

The bondholders' appeal to the Foreign Office introduced a new element into the affair. Lord Salisbury, the foreign secretary, went against the prevailing rule established by Lord Palmerston's circular of 1848, which maintained that the British government was not interested in bondholders' disputes. Exceptions had been provided for in Palmerston's circular, and Salisbury invoked these to side actively with the bondholders, maintaining that in the Peruvian case, "a misapplication of property specifically hypothecated to the creditors" had occurred.[14] Before the Foreign Office could circulate a memorandum to other powers protesting this violation of property, the Peruvian government under President Prado offered to pay the bondholders £300,000 annually from its own guano revenues. Prado's action was prompted by Salisbury's personal interest in the matter and with the knowledge that England and France would soon make their protests official. Then the War of the Pacific shattered the scene.

The conquest of Tarapaca by Chilean armies completely clouded the picture of the Peruvian debt to the bondholders, for the principal remaining guano deposits were located precisely in that province. Furthermore, in late 1879 the Peruvian government acknowledged that £4 million due the Dreyfus firm was also hypothecated on Peru's remaining guano reserves. This was at a time when Peru was desperately trying to raise funds abroad for arms and munitions and it was willing to make these contradictory wartime promises.

★ ★ ★

The loans of 1869, 1870, and 1872 had been hypothecated not only on guano, but on the unfinished railroads, so the bondholders' committee quite naturally viewed the railroads as a supplementary means of satisfying its claims. Nícolas de Piérola's government acknowledged this position when it implicitly recognized the bondholders' lien on the railroads by issuing a decree on January 7, 1880, granting the bondholders ownership of all the national railroads.[15] By this drastic measure Peru hoped not only to improve its credit to enable it to purchase war materials abroad, but also to place the ownership of the railroads into foreign hands and forestall Chilean damage to and disruption of the lines.[16] The bondholders never availed themselves of the decree. Instead, they turned to Chile for compensation from the captured guano resources of Tarapaca.

In 1882 the bondholders' committee arranged an agreement with Chile to divide evenly the revenues generated from the export of guano from former Peruvian territories. This understanding between the bondholders and the government of Chile was formally recognized in the Treaty of Ancón, signed in October 1883. Certain clauses of the treaty allowed the sale of one million tons of guano, 50 percent of the proceeds to go to Chile and 50 percent to the creditors of Peru whose loans had been secured by the guano.[17] Thereafter, guano sales would be equally divided, but only from those deposits then currently known or being worked, until the guano was exhausted or the debt paid. Chile claimed exclusive rights to any new deposits, be they guano, nitrates, or otherwise. Furthermore, aside from clauses in the treaty specifying compensation for the creditors, Chile did not recognize any further claims on its new territories, whatever their origin ("el expresado gobierno de Chile no reconoce creditos de ninguna clase que afecten a los nuevos territorios que adquiere por el presente tratado, cualquiera que sea su naturalezy procedencia").[18]

The bondholders' committee had sought satisfaction only from the Chileans through 1885, feeling that Peru, beaten and dismembered, could offer little redress.[19] When John Meiggs approached the bondholders with the proposal that they take over the lines, he was rebuffed. The bondholders were uninterested in investing further in Peru. A subsequent suggestion by Meiggs to hand over all the railroads of Peru to the bondholders, with generous concessions tacked on, was also brushed aside by the committee in late 1885.[20]

However, during the course of that year Michael Grace rather dramatically appeared on their horizon, not only as the new operator of the Central Railway and the owner of the Rumillana Tunnel and mining concessions at Cerro de Pasco, but also as a strong supporter of Peru. On July 6, 1886, the bondholders' committee formally authorized Grace to negotiate a settlement with the Peruvian government, giving him full power of attorney to represent the bondholders before the government.[21] The intrusion of Michael Grace into this increasingly difficult and important phase of developments for Peru, Chile, and the English bondholders, involving the governments of Great Britain, France, and the United States as well, bespoke a powerful personality with clear aspirations and goals.

It was precisely these aspirations and goals that led to the signing of the Grace Contract of 1890 and that have created so much controversy over the years. In a word, what motivated Michael Grace? The answer—complicated like Grace's character—is basically twofold: he was genuinely committed to helping Peru restore its credit and prosperity; and he wished to make a profit.

One of the first obstacles Michael overcame was at home. William was reluctant to commit so much of his time and money to a cause he deemed hopeless. Michael faced his brother down with some persuasive reasoning:

> You had an ambition to become mayor of New York. It was a proper one and . . . it gratified both yourself and friends. You were willing to suffer pecuniary loss. . . . I never said a word except to encourage you. . . . Now, I have an ambition to consummate one of the most daring and splendid financial achievements. . . . I have the ambition, and I think it is an honorable one, to be known . . . as the man who negotiated with the creditors of a nation, reestablished their debt on a paying basis, and freed a Republic from a millstone that was hanging about its neck and preventing it from taking its place among the nations of the earth. Of course, if this undertaking of mine succeeds there will be great pecuniary profits both for me and for the firm of W. R. Grace & Co. which has such great interest in the development and prosperity of Peru.[22]

William was finally convinced and asked Michael what he thought the venture might cost. In the range of a quarter of a million dollars, Michael replied. William agreed to subscribe a portion of that cost, and asked only that Michael yield in his efforts once the total sum had been spent.[23]

In a later incident, Michael turned his considerable charm and powers of persuasion on a good friend and ally of his in Peru, Aurelio Denegri. The arrangements for renegotiating the debt were then in an extremely fragile stage and nearly collapsing, made so by a new threat of the Peruvian government to nationalize *all* railroads. Michael's exhortation brilliantly summarized his view of Peru's future, a future that promised abundant capital and prosperity once the debt was settled. It also perfectly capsuled the progressive, liberal creed of the era, one that today is associated with the diffusionist theory of historical development as opposed to the dependency school:

> You, as a statesman and a merchant know well that Peru requires, as every country on the face of the earth does, to inspire confidence at home and abroad, to succeed. We offer Peru the means of inspiring this confidence by disposing with one stroke of the pen, of her foreign

debt, introducing immediately as a consequence, foreign capital, commencing at once the extension of the railroads, establishing important banks through the country and through the means of syndicates, developing her mining resources. . . . The fact is, that *all my whole views and efforts are centered upon re-establishing the credit of the country* thereby introducing capital to properly extend and repair the railroad system, to establish a banking system if it can be done to the advantage of the country and the investors, to the introduction of foreign capital for the development of mines and agricultural properties and the increase of commerce; thus increasing the fiscal rent and enabling the government to exist, meeting its obligations, as they mature; the development of the different enterprises offering means for everyone who wished to work, thus consolidating internal peace; and, if, as I think, these developments can only be turned into a mining fever the country will be rapidly populated and daily growth will consolidate the stability of the government; and your mining properties as mine, your agricultural properties as mine, your numerous outstandings as those of every man who has numerous floating credits, your commerce as that of every other citizen and foreigner will daily become more valuable; and as the country grows, there is no reason that we should not all grow in prosperity and wealth.[24] [Italics added.]

Michael Grace's plan was to place himself between the bondholders and the Peruvian government and negotiate an agreement with which both sides could live. The bondholders wanted proper compensation for their investment and Peru desired to settle with honor and dignity. The focus was, of course, on the railroads. By early 1885 Grace had placed himself squarely astride the most important one, the Central Railway. He also had obtained concessions to the ultimate terminus, the mines of Cerro de Pasco and the promise they held for the reinvigoration of the country's economy.

Grace first made contact with the bondholders in April 1885 in Santiago. There a lawyer representing the bondholders, C. L. Smyles, was negotiating with the Chileans, as well as seeking their opinion on how much Peru could be forced to yield in settlement of the debt. Michael talked with Smyles several times in Santiago. From there Michael sailed home, stopping at Lima briefly to consult with President Iglesias. Grace arrived in New York in May and put his impressions and suggestions to paper in a long letter to the bondholders' committee. In a separate note to Ned Eyre, then in charge of the Grace house in Lima, Michael instructed his younger nephew to entertain Smyles well on his arrival in Peru, and to see that Smyles met all the various principals, including President Iglesias. The president was asked to listen to Smyles but make no commitments or rejoinders until a Peruvian commissioner was named to London. The commissioner should be directed to consult closely with Grace.[25]

In the letter to the bondholders dated May 18, 1885, Michael laid out the situation frankly. Grace began by noting that bondholders were not regarded very highly in Peru since they had been considerably sympathetic to Chile during the war. Furthermore, by negotiating with Chile between 1880 and 1885 before turning to Peru, the bondholders' committee had tacitly acknowledged Chilean responsibility for the debt and relieved Peru of some of the burden.

Having made those preliminary remarks, Grace then described Peru's assets that could possibly be relinquished to the bondholders. The old resource, guano, was listed, with Michael's optimistic (and largely unfounded) opinion that perhaps new fields would be discovered which could be used in some fashion to satisfy the bondholders. Next came the railroads, which had produced more promises than revenues to date. All were in need of repairs and some were uncompleted; these expenses would be heavy. Nonetheless, the railroads still constituted the greatest promise and, besides, had already been hypothecated to the bondholders. A fifty-year lease on the railroads granted by the Peruvian government was suggested as a possible measure. Nitrates were another possibility, especially, of course, undiscovered fields. Royalties on the export of nitrates might be collected by the bondholders for a time.

Grace's key proposal, however, was to insist that any agreement between the bondholders and Peru should relieve Peru of the entire debt; a final arrangement could come only "in exchange for an absolute quittal of all claims of its foreign creditors."[26] Michael offered to broker the negotiations between the bondholders and Peru. This offer was essentially accepted by mid-1886, and it was as intermediary that Michael traveled between Lima, New York, and London for the next four years seeking the common ground.

The immediate problem Grace faced in 1885 was how to deal with the chaotic military-political situation in Peru. If the bondholders' committee tended to be stiff and somewhat stubborn, negotiating with Peru was even more difficult. President Iglesias was unable to subdue the old warrior Andres Cáceres, who had never yielded to the hated Chileans, and now waged guerrilla warfare against the Iglesias regime from the mountains. Iglesias bore the stigma of having signed the hated Treaty of Ancón, making the Cáceres revolution even more popular. By late 1885 Cáceres held a large part of the country and for a time was in possession of much of the Central Railway, suspending traffic and throttling commerce.[27] Cáceres' campaign was further aggravating a country already in a postwar depression.

During 1885 general business was largely paralyzed, much rolling stock and bridges on the railroads were destroyed by the combatants, and Cerro de Pasco was itself finally captured by Cáceres' troops.

Michael urged Iglesias to suppress the revolution vigorously and restore order rapidly. Grace was frustrated by the apparent lack of understanding in Peru of the relationship between political stability and foreign capitalists. When one is asked to invest, "the answer is always: 'but just think, sir, the history of Peru shows that this country has never known real peace since independence. . . . Just think of its present state.' ''[28]

When the year ended, Michael was back in the United States, in bed with a hip broken when he was thrown from a horse. From New Jersey he followed the notices from Peru. Cáceres gradually consolidated his position in the highlands and then descended on Lima with his army. At the end of the year Iglesias acknowledged defeat and a provisional government of ministers was organized. In June 1886 the popular General Cáceres was elected the constitutional president. Cáceres proved as cantankerous as the bondholders' committee was stubborn during the next four years of negotiations, testing everyone's patience to the limits, but certainly none other's more than Michael Grace's.

During the second half of 1885 and the first half of 1886 Michael negotiated with the bondholders' committee in London through A. R. Robertson, one of Henry Meiggs's sons-in-law. The bondholders pressed for many advantages and, at the time, Michael agreed to most, some of which were outlandish. They included complete control of the Mollendo customhouse for a number of years, the concession of the railroads forever, and amazingly generous land and colonization rights along Peru's tributaries to the Amazon. [29]

Meanwhile Michael instructed Ned Eyre (in Lima) through the course of 1886 to keep after Cáceres; try and convince the president of the absolute necessity of reaching accommodation with the bondholders on the premise that "everything she [Peru] gives away will come back to her tenfold in future prosperity."[30] The old general remained obdurate, telling Eyre that since the Chileans now owned the guano and nitrate wealth of Peru, let the bondholders deal with them.

Grace seemed to be wedged between a rock and a hard place, but, like his brother, he was a born negotiator. Besides, his interests in the Central Railway, in the Rumillana Tunnel project, and in the revitalization of the Cerro de Pasco mines were at stake. If Peru continued to languish, so did his business properties. A large percentage of his investments were tied up in Peru and that fact alone made him perhaps one of the most interested participants in the negotiations. That he could understand the commercial mentality of the bondholders as well as the fiercely national pride of Cáceres was probably his greatest strength.

The bondholders' committee had finally worked up a formal proposal by May 1886 and asked Michael Grace to serve as its agent in the negotiations with Peru. At the heart of the proposal were the railroads. These the bondholders proposed to take over, providing Peru with guarantees to extend and complete certain portions.[31] They also wished to receive concessions to coal mines along the Chimbote line in the north of Peru, to the ancient mercury mines of Huancavelica, and to any unclaimed oilfields in the far north.[32] The bondholders furthermore envisioned establishing eight colonies in the jungles of Peru east of the Andes. A monopoly on all guano exports was also part of the package. Everything would be conceded on a seventy-five-year basis, and until they had a return of £700,000 a year, they would collect the customs duties at the Southern Railway port of Mollendo to make up this sum. After the return on the bonds had reached 5 percent, however, the government would have a 25 percent participation in the profits.[33]

Even Michael blanched at the above demands. He told the bondholders he would travel to Lima only with wide discretionary powers to amend the bondholders' proposal in Peru's interests. One portion of the bondholders' proposal, however, did meet with Michael's approval since it held the Chileans equally responsible for the debt: "The Peruvian bondholders claim that it is inequitable and unjust for the Chilean government to seize by right of conquest a large and valuable part of the security hypothecated to them without giving some adequate satisfaction to the bondholders."[34] Strong Chilean objections to this position would prove to be among the chief impediments to ratification of the Grace Contract.

President Cáceres stood in the path of successful negotiations even more immediately than the Chileans, and Ned Eyre's attempts to soften the old general's position had been frustrating. Eyre interviewed Cáceres at the presidential palace early in July and laid before him plans for the recovery of the nation. Michael Grace's growing interest in the Cerro de Pasco mines and contracts to extend the Central Railway to the mines were but one aspect. Eyre told Cáceres that the bondholders themselves "have manifested their desire of bringing capital & immigration & from creditors to become a source of wealth to the country."[35]

Eyre's arguments drew little more than a shrug from the president, who showed not the slightest enthusiasm.[36] Cáceres' general response was "como los vamos a dar nuestros ferro carriles que nos cuestan tan caro?" ("How are we going to give them our railroads which cost us so dearly?")[37] Luis Bryce, then minister of finance, supported Cáceres and reiterated the commonly held opinion that Chile should be the responsible party since it had seized the territories upon whose riches the debts were mortgaged. Bryce was the son of John Bryce and probably no friend of the Graces. At this point Michael took a steamer for Peru.

Although Lord Donoughmore, an Irish nobleman of some charm, had been named as the bondholders' official representative, he was little more than a figurehead. The real negotiator was Michael Grace. He wrote the bondholders in July: "His Lordship [Donoughmore] must be given to understand that we are the men commissioned to handle the situation & that matters will be put before him for his signature."[38]

Grace arrived in Lima late in August just as the minister of finance was delivering a gloomy report to the Peruvian congress on the state of the economy. Trade was in a great depression, and showed little promise of improving.[39] All of Peru's major exports—sugar, cotton, wool, and minerals—had dropped in volume of production, while world prices had also declined from the previous decade. Revenues from customs receipts were not matching government expenditures, and new taxes could not be collected in a country in disarray from war and revolution. The railroads, on which so many millions had been spent, were producing paltry revenues or none at all. In his address Luis Bryce specifically cited the Mollendo road "which cost the state so many millions [and] has not produced a single centavo for the Treasury since the day the contractor delivered the work to the government."[40] All attempts to raise money in Europe to extend and operate the railroads had been blocked by the bondholders, who would continue to do so until they reached a satisfactory settlement with Peru. Peru and the bondholders had to deal with each other, no matter how distasteful the chore. To complete the railroads, the government needed the bondholders, and to settle debts outstanding, the bondholders had to accept ownership of the railways.[41] To bridge this gap was Michael Grace's intention.

The proposals that Grace conveyed from the bondholders immediately provoked a running controversy in public as well as private circles. The most promising statement during these preliminary discussions came from a presidential commission of three distinguished Peruvians, Aurelio Denegri, Francisco Rosas, and Francisco García Calderon. They were interested not so much in the exact value of the debt that would be forgiven by the bondholders, as in the industrial and commercial opportunities that would open for Peru if an agreement with the bondholders were reached. To them, any concessions made by Peru would constitute a form of investment, and, furthermore, European colonization and immigration would be stimulated as well.[42] They were particularly committed to the value of European immigration, which was ranked higher than railways and capital as a means of making progress and modernizing the state.[43]

Newspapers editorialized on the negotiations under way in late 1886 and the following aligned themselves in favor of an agreement: *La Opinión Nacional; El Buen Público; El Comercio; El Nacional; La Nación;* and *El Callao.* On the other hand, *El Sol* opposed the negotiations, whereas *La Epoca* was founded early in 1887 by Adan Melgar precisely to block Grace and the bondholders.[44]

Leading the opposition against the formula that Michael brought with him—now being popularly referred to as the Grace Contract—was José María Quimper, who published a pamphlet late in the year outlining his objections. In *Las propuestas de los tenedores de bonos* (The bondholders' proposals), Quimper lashed out at the bondholders' proposals. Chile was accused of being behind the settlement, adding a sinister element to the negotiations; the English wanted to plant a beachhead in Peru, similar to the East Indies Company which controlled large portions of Asia; the resources of Tarapaca (that is, Chile) should be employed to service the debt; the arrangements suggested by the bondholders for the railroads and mines infringed on the sovereignty of Peru; they were illegal; they should be repudiated; Peru would be absorbed by Grace or those who held the contract; the bondholders and Grace were simply interested in getting a firm hold in anticipation of the completion of the Panama Canal; and finally, "la proyectaba colonización no era sino una farsa, pues el tiempo de los milagros habia pasado"—"the projected colonization project was but a farce since the age of miracles had long ago passed."[45]

The debate over immigration, then being championed as a panacea of sorts for countries in need of a more progressive, modern populace, was particularly strident. Immigrants from Europe were just then swelling the population of American countries, principally the United States, but millions were disembarking at the ports of Argentina, Brazil, and Chile as well.

Domingo Sarmiento, one of the greatest Argentine presidents and thinkers, was widely quoted for his pithy summary of the benefits of immigration, "To populate is to civilize." Prominent Latin American positivists who led an influential progressive movement based on the philosophy of Auguste Comte encouraged immigration as a means toward modernization and progress.

Peruvians had earlier tried to induce Europeans to come settle in their country, and Irish, Spanish, and German colonies had at one time been attempted. The results, however, had been lackluster. Now the champions of the Grace Contract were once again heralding the rejuvenating promise of immigration. But Quimper and others found the arguments specious. Their pessimism proved right in the long run, for no great wave of European immigrants leavened, "whitened," or "civilized" Peru with their Old World work habits, blood, or capacity for industrialized labor. But the subject of immigration stirred the imaginations and fired debate within the context of the bondholders' proposals. The trials of modernizing a nation were long and arduous, questions along the way being raised about basic goals and means and consequences. The Graces stood foursquare in the corner of opening Peru to the world to receive those energies flowing especially from Europe and North America. Michael's endeavors were aimed precisely at realizing these ambitious goals.

On December 14, 1886, Michael presented a revised set of proposals which modified some of the original bondholders' demands. The usufruct of the railroads was reduced from seventy-five years to sixty-six years, and other financial commitments by Peru to the bondholders were trimmed as well. Early next year, on January 27, Aranibar, the new minister of finance, issued a ruling favorable to the second Grace proposal. His successor as fiscal interino de la nacíon (interim attorney general), Manuel Atanasio Fuentes, opposed the new contract. Fuentes claimed not only that Michael Grace lacked the power to negotiate such agreements, but also that the promises inherent in the bondholders' proposal were simply chimeras:

> Said contract proposed colossal enterprises which in our poverty have lulled and rocked us with sweet visions in our dreams. Here is a position all debtors would certainly favor: a creditor's representative who not only gives his debtors generous terms, but work and bread as well. We must be wary of dealing with those not born in this land with regard

to Peruvian matters and contracts. Sad but wise experience counsels
us to keep an eye open, or as the gallego said: wide eyes, big ears, and
barefoot.

On the other hand, the Council of Ministers (Consejo de
Ministros) issued a statement, unanimously agreed to, on February 19, 1887, strongly supporting the revised Grace proposals, although suggesting further reductions in Peru's liability
to the bondholders. This statement was signed by President
Cáceres and sent to congress. It argued persuasively for the
agreement in four major areas: one, the necessity of reestab-
lishing not only the external but internal credit of the nation
to release economic forces, to get the currency moving again,
and to create new and more powerful fiscal resources; two, the
necessity of completing the construction of the railroads and
repairing and returning to regular service those in a lamentable
state of deterioration; three, the importance of studying and
then exploiting the riches of the principal mining centers; and
four, the utility of creating new centers of population to facilitate
and stimulate immigration further.[46]

Although the bondholders' position and that of the Peruvian
government were approaching a confluence, Grace did not feel
he held adequate authority to agree to some of the major modifications suggested by Peru. Aranibar was thus appointed as
a special commissioner to travel to London and negotiate a
settlement directly with the bondholders. He and Michael took
ship late in February 1887. This moved the negotiations into
the second major stage, one even more convoluted than the
first.

In London Michael found the bondholders as difficult to deal
with as Cáceres had been in Peru. The press was almost unanimously against the proposed contract, the large houses were
timid, the stock exchange was much opposed, and at times
Michael almost despaired of success.[47] But the Aranibar mission
did succeed, producing an agreement between Peru and the
bondholders which was signed May 26, 1887. This Grace-
Aranibar Contract was amended and debated heavily in Peru
before ratification, but its provisions formed the basis for the
final agreement.

The principal clauses concerned the railroads, additional
compensation for the bondholders, and a statement about Chilean responsibility. The railroads were to be ceded for sixty-six
years, while the bondholders would also "have the right to take
some £120,000 annually from the customs revenues of Mollendo
and Paita to guarantee the service of the debentures they would
issue to finance the completion of the railroads."[48] Part of the

pact was to put the roads into good working order and to complete the unfinished portions. The bondholders were also to receive the right to establish a bank in Lima as well as receive large land grants in eastern Peru to help foment immigration. A corporation, to be known as the Peruvian Corporation, was to be established specifically to implement the provisions of the contract.

The most important concession made by the bondholders was cancellation of half the debt. The other half they hoped to collect from Chile, declaring that they would continue to hold the other 50 percent of the bonds "to collect from whom it may concern but without Peru bearing any further responsibility."[49] President Cáceres presented the proposed contract to congress in July 1887. Then the debate erupted once again, only this time it was complicated by the official Chilean reaction to the Grace Contract: Santiago was unequivocally opposed.

The basis for the Chilean opposition lay in the Treaty of Ancón, which relieved Chile of any responsibility for Peru's debts with those exceptions noted in articles four, seven, and eight. These all referred to the extraction and sale of known guano deposits.[50] Chile also harped on the potential violation of Peruvian sovereignty if the bondholders were allowed actually to take over the collection of customs at Mollendo and Paita. President José Manuel Balmaceda of Chile added that the land grants for colonization in eastern Peru additionally violated Peru's sovereignty.[51] The Chileans wondered publicly how the British government would react if the Peruvians failed to live up to these obligations to British citizens (the bondholders), and Santiago implied that these vast concessions made by Peru were clearly dangerous precedents for other nations of Latin America. But the Chileans were fishing for something more tangible than Peru's sovereignty and honor. They wished to take advantage of Peru's problem to complete the acquisition of the provinces of Tacna and Arica.

Chile proposed to pay Peru ten million pesos for Tacna and Arica and end that problem. The Peruvians could apply the ten million to paying off part of their debt to the bondholders and thus relieve the pressure London was putting on Chile on behalf of the bondholders.[52] According to the provisions of the Treaty of Ancón, a plebiscite would be held in 1893 in Tacna and Arica to decide their fate. The loser would pay the winner ten million pesos, and Chile figured that Peru simply did not have that sum to pay *in the event* Tacna and Arica were to vote for reintegration with Peru.

If the bondholders *and* the British government could be

swung behind the idea of the ten-million-peso transfer, then Chile calculated Peru would have to fall in line. With this in mind, the Chilean foreign minister, Augusto Matte, made a secret proposal to the British minister in Santiago, Hugh Fraser, in April 1888. The proposal was incorporated into the Matte-Fraser protocol. The protocol listed the Chilean objections to the Grace Contract, and Matte "suggested that Great Britain inform the bondholders of Santiago's 10-million-peso offer to Peru and of the obvious fact that Peru might transfer that sum to its creditors."[53] In May Matte visited Peru and made the same suggestions. Then, in June 1888 the Foreign Office in London spoiled the scheme by rejecting interference in any proposal that envisioned the transfer of Peruvian territory.

From the moment that Aranibar arrived back in Peru with the contract it was evident that Chilean opposition would be strong. The declarations made by Chile were not taken lightly by Peruvians, only very recently humbled by Chilean arms. Chile could perhaps force Peru to pay the Chilean half of the debt if the contract retained the responsibility clause that Chileans found so objectionable.

In Lima Cáceres was alarmed to the point of considering withdrawing the contract.[54] Michael exhorted Cáceres to resist the Chileans, who feared Peru's recovery from the war. They wished to keep Peru, a larger and potentially more prosperous nation, perpetually hobbled to preserve their dominance in the region.[55] It was imperative for Michael to instill resolve in the face of this strong Chilean opposition. Meanwhile, European creditors were also attacking the contract.

Bondholders' committees in France, Belgium, and Holland threatened to continue holding Peru responsible for its debts even if the Grace Contract was passed. In Peru, others holding administrative rights over railways since the death of Henry Meiggs threatened to lobby in congress against the contract if the English bondholders did not deal with them fairly.[56] They need not have worried, for Cáceres withdrew the Grace-Aranibar Contract from consideration by congress in September 1887. Michael attempted unsuccessfully to bring direct pressure to bear on Peru through the British minister in Lima, Sir Charles Mansfield.[57] But Cáceres backed off; not so the bondholders, who now went after the Chileans with gusto.

The bondholders' committee in London, frustrated by the apparently successful Chilean interdiction of the Grace Contract, tried to coax the Chileans into compensating the bondholders directly. They met several times with the Chilean minister early in 1888 in London and asked not only for "the proceeds from the export of guano under the 1882 decree [but also] a portion of the proceeds from the customs at Tarapaca, a concession that Chile could not countenance."[58] Increasingly irritated by Chilean intransigence, a member of the bondholders' committee took matters into his own hands and blocked a quotation of a new Chilean loan from appearing on the stock exchange. That act precipitated the rupture of negotiations between Colonel North, representing the bondholders' committee, and the Chilean minister.

The British Foreign Office tried to steer a neutral path through these complicated negotiations in 1887 and 1888. The undersecretary, Sir Julian Pauncefote, was a close friend of the earl of Donoughmore, giving the bondholders some leverage in that area.[59] Ever aware of precedent and past policy, the Foreign Office nonetheless attempted to remain noninvolved, but the bondholders' lobby finally produced action. Early in February 1888 a stock exchange committee was persuaded to smooth the path for further negotiations by allowing a quotation for the Chilean loan blocked earlier.[60]

The bondholders also succeeded in persuading Pauncefote that the situation was extremely urgent, as a memo of Pauncefote's, dated February 11, clearly indicates: "The annexed letters [of Donoughmore and G. A. Ollard] show that the Grace Contract is in great peril of being wrested from the bondholders by American syndicates and others. This would be deplorable as it would destroy the last chance of the settlement of the question and take out of English hands concessions (especially ones on the Pacific seaboard) which it is most important to keep under British management."[61] The British minister in Chile was then instructed to open discussions with the Chilean foreign minister as soon as possible. This led to the Matte-Fraser protocol of April 1888, which proved unacceptable to both Great Britain and Peru.

Meanwhile, Peru had decided in September 1887 to nationalize its major railroads. That act pushed the complicated international and financial negotiations closer to complete confusion, to the despair of almost all parties. The United States interceded on behalf of its citizens affected by this turn of events, adding the influence of the ascending American power to the debate over the Peruvian debt.

The initiative to take over the principal railroads came from an increasingly restive and frustrated Peruvian congress. The object was to increase Peru's bargaining power, for by taking possession of the railroads certain members of congress hoped to force the bondholders into a final settlement, especially since it appeared that Chile was manipulating the scenario much to its satisfaction as matters stood in September 1887. So the Peruvian Chamber of Deputies, with Cáceres showing only lukewarm support, passed a law late in September 1887 ordering the president to take possession of the Southern Railway. It ran from Mollendo on the coast to Lake Titicaca, and provided the principal outlet for Bolivia to the sea. At the time, Southern was being operated by John L. Thorndike, a member of the old Meiggs team. Within a short time the Chamber of Deputies also ordered the seizure of the Northern, or Salaverry, Railway system, which was operated by E. C. DuBois, another former member of the Meiggs organization.

The next railroad threatened by the Chamber of Deputies was Michael Grace's Central, or Oroya, Railway. This threat prompted the Grace brothers into action. As the leading United States house in Peru with interests in railroads, mines, sugar plantations, and, of course, general commerce, they promptly petitioned the United States Department of State to intervene on their behalf and on the behalf of all United States citizens—Thorndike and DuBois—so threatened. On September 29, 1887, William Ivins, the Grace representative in Washington and William Russell's former chamberlain while mayor, asked Secretary of State Thomas F. Bayard to intervene and prevent the proposed nationalization of the railways. Not only would it prejudice Michael Grace's interests, but United States trade and commerce would be seriously harmed if Grace's contracts were abrogated.[62]

By December both the Southern and Northern railway systems had been ordered taken by congress in spite of the remonstrances of the United States. This triggered another forceful representation by the Graces to Secretary Bayard. William not only contended that the seizures were illegal, but also ventured a criticism more commonly heard in the twentieth century with respect to public versus private management of industries: "Again, the Peruvian government well knows that if the roads should be taken by them and fall into the hands of government administrators, the result would be that within a few years they would not only not be extended, but the probability is that they would not be in existence."[63] William also knew that Cáceres was not in accord with the congressional activists demanding nationalization, and he passed this opinion on to Bayard for transmittal to the United States minister in Peru at that time, Charles Buck.

Peru's domestic political problems only clouded the scene further. A series of cabinet crises had afflicted the Cáceres government since its inauguration to the point that an editorial in *El Comercio* declared in October 1887, "in effect we find that a third of Cáceres' presidency has passed, and during this time the government has been able to do nothing, as the different ministries that have conducted public business have been peaceful only in the intervals between one legislature and the next."[64] Peru's leaders were very much divided on this complicated issue of the contract and their divisions had produced little accord. The opposition to the contract was centered in the Chamber of Deputies, while the major support lay in the Senate and with Cáceres himself. Cáceres and his cabinet were reluctant to implement the railroad seizures authorized by congress as contrary to the interest of the contract. Yet, unless they obeyed congress, the cabinet would fall again and keep Cáceres stymied.[65] It made for a sticky political impasse.

The year 1888 was crucial not only for the resolution of the railroad dispute between Thorndike, DuBois, Grace, and the Peruvian government, but also for the continued debate and emendation of the Grace Contract. In early February the government took forcible possession of the Northern Railway, operated by DuBois, in spite of the protests of the United States minister Buck. Michael Grace made a direct appeal to President Cleveland in a private interview. He forecast further confiscation and violation of American property and rights if no intercession was made on behalf of DuBois.

Peru's nationalizing spirit also threatened to upset the already trying negotiations between the bondholders and the government over the Grace Contract, and Michael cooperated closely with the bondholders in London to induce the Foreign Office to pressure Peru to leave the railroads alone.[66] Michael predicted, however, that the Foreign Office would not intervene in Peru, for no British subjects or property was as yet directly affected.[67]

While Michael and William lobbied forcefully in Washington on behalf of Thorndike, DuBois, and their own interests, they also kept up the pressure in Peru. Michael wrote a long letter in late February 1888 to Aurelio Denegri, a supporter of the Grace Contract and a leading member of congress, hammering away in behalf of the contract and arguing against the seizure of the railroads. Grace tied the two issues together persuasively and logically:

You know how difficult it has been to carry this system of financial

regeneration [the Grace Contract] to its present point. You know how
difficult it was to get men in Lima to join you, Doctor Rosas, Doctor
Aranibar, and García Calderon and others in showing the public that
this project was really the only one by which the credit of Peru could
be redeemed . . . but I contend that taking forcible possession of the
roads held by Mr. Thorndike, Mr. DuBois and Mr. Watson [another of
the old Meiggs team]—whether the government be justified or not—is
a mistake. It gives another pretext to the many enemies of the country
to expound their theory that the country is unstable and unsafe to
invest capital in.[68]

Michael was not as allergic as William to the principle of
government control over the railroads, and he was certainly
willing to negotiate the issue. If the matter were to be referred
to the courts or if the government would deal directly with the
different concessionaires, he could envision some workable solution to the impasse developing from outright seizure.[69] Michael's approach during the entire protracted proceedings was
to seek the middle ground, some compromise to which all parties would be willing to accede, even if not completely satisfied
with the final product. That, indeed, constitutes the art of mediation.

Invariably the press sniffed out a good story and Michael was
forced to give some interviews when he would rather have not.
Private talks and public announcements are often at odds during the course of delicate negotiations, and Michael advised
Ned Eyre, who was doing his best to keep the lines of communication open in Lima, to sort out the most "advisable" of
newspaper clippings Michael was sending him from the United
States for release to friendly papers in Lima.[70] Grace had learned
the lesson well—news made public in one country was not
necessarily the best news to release in another. As one fanned
a sense of indignation in Washington to pressure Peru, one
could be pushing equally hard for a more conciliatory approach
privately.[71]

However much Michael wished to come to an agreement
with the Peruvian government over the Grace Contract and the
new issue of the railroads, he knew that Chile had to be dealt
with first. Grace was so sure of continued Chilean obstruction
that he decided to travel to London himself in March 1888 to
find out how far the British government would go in the whole
business of breaking the Chilean objections to the Grace Contract.[72] Furthermore, Grace suspected that Chile was behind
Bolivian investments in the Southern Railway. Thorndike had
accepted Bolivian capital in a partnership to operate the Mollendo-Puno road at a time when Bolivia still entertained active
hopes of obtaining a corridor to the sea.[73] Michael thought Chile

hoped to satisfy Bolivia by carving this corridor out of Peru. Writing in late February 1888 to J. A. Miro Quesada, Peru's minister in London, Michael said, "I am already convinced by what has happened & is happening that Chile's political ambition is to dismember Peru of its southern department, giving it to Bolivia."[74] But Michael fell ill before he could sail to help his representative, G. A. Ollard, and the bondholders in England. William took the baton and traveled in his stead.

William parleyed and lobbied in England for more active intervention by the Foreign Office and combined his efforts with those of the bondholders themselves. Pauncefote finally was prompted to instruct the British chargé in Santiago, Fraser, to negotiate with Chile. This he did and the result was the Matte-Fraser protocols. They proved unacceptable to England, for the protocols were premised on the permanent incorporation of Tacna and Arica into the Chilean national territory without the plebiscite. Chile also still adhered firmly to those provisions of the Treaty of Ancón which released it from any responsibility to Peru's debtors not expressly provided for in the treaty. While Chile continued to balk and resist British attempts to modify its position, Michael and William, who returned to the United States in May, were trying to cope with the Peruvian seizure of the railroads.

By June 1888 both the Northern system and Thorndike's Southern Railway had been taken. Peru sent a special envoy, Felix Cipriano Coronel Zegarra, to Washington in June to present its case, and for the next several months the Graces or their representatives labored intimately with Zegarra, Secretary of State Bayard, and President Cleveland to resolve the new crisis.

The point man for dealing with Zegarra was W. M. Ivins, posted more or less permanently in Washington during the summer of 1888. Ivins was an experienced negotiator who knew the value of friendship in achieving ends. When Zegarra arrived in New York, Ivins was there to meet him at dockside and get him settled in personally since William Grace was out of town. Ivins tended to Zegarra for five days in New York and then accompanied the Peruvian to Washington.[75] The object was not only to cultivate Zegarra's goodwill but also to establish his confidence in the Graces.

Ivins tutored Zegarra on Bayard's personality and the most effective way to commend himself to Bayard. Privately, Ivins reported to his boss that "I am sure that he thinks we have his personal interest at heart and . . . that we will try to make [of his] mission [a success] the results of which he need not be ashamed of."[76] Ivins measured Zegarra carefully in the light of

the forthcoming negotiations: "Zegarra is a free trader and a
believer in hard money and on these points he will have a
natural means of making himself appreciated by Mr. Bayard
somewhat better than most people from his part of the world
could do. Furthermore, he is affable, not given to flattery, very
quiet in his manner, and I think can easily win Mr. Bayard's
goodwill."[77]

Ivins consulted with Bayard often during summer 1888, arguing the case not only for the Graces, but for DuBois, Thorndike, and other lesser concessionaires with an interest in the
Zegarra mission. One of Ivins' first goals was to transfer the
formal hearing of the case from Lima to Washington. Ivins
insisted upon this point since the Graces distrusted the judgment of the United States minister to Peru, Buck, and the issues
were of such importance as to merit the secretary of state's
attention.[78]

That argument did not persuade Bayard, so Ivins charged
Buck specifically with favoring Thorndike's case to the prejudice of the Grace and DuBois interests. Buck was not only living
in Thorndike's home in Chorillos, a suburb in Lima, but was
believed by the Peruvians to be Thorndike's agent. Furthermore, Thorndike was reputed to have made common cause
with the Bolivians and there was a strong antinational feeling
against him politically, whereas there was nothing of the kind
against the Graces.[79] After meeting with Zegarra later in the
month and recognizing the extent of his authority to argue the
Peruvian case, Bayard agreed to transfer the case to Washington. Certainly Ivins' arguments helped score this initial point
as well.

Bayard, like Her Majesty's foreign secretary, was in no rush
to jump into a private affair whose principals he felt were simply
paying the penalty of bad investments. If that were the case,
the United States government, like the British, did not wish to
intercede. So he questioned Ivins closely on the background of
American investments in Peru. He wanted to find out whether
the Graces had made their investments in the railroads with a
knowledge that Peru had an unstable government and was
likely at any time to violate its obligations with contracting
parties. Ivins knew that Bayard was arguing that anyone who
entered into contractual relations with Peru did it with his eyes
open and deserved only commiseration but not assistance. Ivins
showed Bayard that the origins of the business in all three cases
ran back to a time when Peru was in high credit, and he dwelt
particularly upon the fact that Cilley was one of the original
engineers and parties in interest with Meiggs.[80]

Bayard also had to sort out the merits of the different claims, especially in view of the fact that Zegarra insisted on treating the DuBois and Grace cases separately from the Thorndike issue. In this instance Ivins concurred with Zegarra, whereas Thorndike wished to have all the cases consolidated into one. Thorndike was challenging two rather powerful forces in Peru: one, the very administration of the country represented by Zegarra; and, two, the Graces. At this juncture the Grace fortunes were still closely allied to Peru on two issues Peruvians and the Graces considered of profound importance: the successful completion of the Grace Contract, and the preservation of Peruvian territorial integrity. Thorndike represented an anti-Peruvian element and the Graces—through Zegarra—attacked him with a logic that appealed directly to Peruvian national sensibilities. Zegarra possessed imperative instructions from his government not to relinquish Thorndike's railroad unless compelled to do so by the application of force by the United States government.[81] Before conceding this point, Peru would fight. Why? Precisely because Thorndike was tainted by his Chilean-Bolivian connections.

Peru would rather resist the United States than surrender its position on Thorndike's case, because to do so would have been equivalent to an absolute surrender to the Chilean-Bolivian policy. That Thorndike was in active conspiracy with Chile and Bolivia was clear to the Graces and to Peru. The possible loss of more national territory was patently unacceptable to Peru, and the Graces played their patriotic card with good effect.[82]

The Grace opposition to Thorndike was not entirely born of altruistic sentiments. Some old business grievances now could also be settled. Making common cause with Zegarra might enable the Graces "to repay the latter [Thorndike] for some of his bad offices in the recent past, because I am satisfied that unless he [Thorndike] can get us to go behind him strongly with the Secretary of State, he will stand very little chance, and if we can get Zegarra to agree with us on satisfactory terms, both for ourselves and DuBois, we can leave Thorndike to his fate and punish him for his past bad faith not only to us but to Peru."[83] Thorndike arrived in New York late in June to protect his interests. He took a few pot shots at Michael and was answered by a Grace cannonade.

Thorndike felt Michael Grace would be unable to consummate the Grace Contract in London unless Thorndike was included in the deal. Ivins and his boss, William Grace, promptly disabused Thorndike of that notion: "His talk with me yesterday and meeting with W. R. Grace today has certainly shaken him in this belief, not only because we have told him about the financial part of it, but because he, after his [expletive deleted] with us, really entertains no hope of speedily regaining possession of his road through the intervention of our gov't."[84] Nonetheless, the Graces were willing to make common cause with Thorndike before the State Department, since their problems—the seizure or threatened seizure of private property—bound them as unwilling allies.

Bayard now had to size up Zegarra's unflinching position on the Southern system. Was it a bluff? If it was, it was a winning game, for Bayard and the United States were unwilling to use force to coerce Peru.[85]

As the summer proceeded, it became apparent to Ivins that Bayard's position on intervention was unalterable, especially in view of the custom of the United States government not to resort to force on behalf of individuals where there were disputed questions of fact, and even then not until an arbitration had been refused by the offending party.[86]

Following the complex business, political, and diplomatic juggling that summer is somewhat akin to keeping track of a three-ring circus in full performance. While Ivins was busy in Washington, Michael returned to London to prod the bondholders. Aside from the railroad affair, Ivins was also in the thick of William and Michael's battle over control of the booming rubber business in Brazil. Politically, another election year had rolled around and Ivins was preparing for a vigorous campaign.[87] William was on the stump for Cleveland, then waging a battle against David Hill, the incumbent Democratic governor of New York with presidential aspirations. Last, Ivins was assisting Bayard on a fisheries treaty under consideration. It was Ivins' strategy to help the administration wherever possible in order "to commend myself from every possible point of view even though I do so at the cost of blood and gray matter."[88] Four years of political service on the firing line in New York with William Grace had honed Ivins well for lobbying before the Department of State and the Cleveland administration. A good leader is best measured by the capability and achievement of his subordinates. Applying that criterion, William and Michael Grace were very successful leaders, especially when one places such men as Ivins, Edward Eyre, and Charles Flint on the scales. Ivins would be tested well that summer of 1888.

In early July it became apparent that the Peruvian government intended to seize the Central Railway in addition to the Southern and Northern systems already under its control. This brought the Graces directly into the fray, if it were possible to be involved any more deeply than they were.

On Saturday, July 7, during the quiet noon hour, Ivins received an urgent wire from Ned Eyre in Lima advising him that the Peruvian government had cabled Zegarra for his views before it seized the Oroya or Central Railway.[89] The message stunned Ivins once more into action, and he immediately abandoned New York for Washington that afternoon. It also revealed that Zegarra's communications had somehow been compromised by Eyre, who supplied Ivins with Zegarra's instructions from Lima.[90]

Eyre's wire was forwarded to Michael in London, who showed profound disgust at the situation and said that if the Oroya should be seized, he would abandon his whole project and leave Peru to its own resources.[91] He had already been tempted to such a course several times in the preceding three years, but one gets the feeling that Michael was in this fray to the end. His Irish temper could be triggered by such news, but his tenacity and persistence in the face of incredibly complex obstacles almost always overrode his immediate, and often visceral, reactions.

By Sunday morning Ivins was discussing the current situation at length with Zegarra in Washington. He soon learned that Zegarra was quite as irritated as the Graces by the news that the Oroya road might be seized. As Ivins tried to impress upon the quiet Peruvian envoy that the seizure of the Oroya would paralyze the negotiations in London and force the United States to act (Ivins' turn to bluff a bit), Zegarra blew up and told Ivins he agreed completely with the imbecility of seizing the Oroya at this point: "He told me again with much heat and earnestness that if they all made fools of themselves and rushed headlong to the devil he was determined that it should never be laid at his door."[92] In fact, Zegarra had already telegraphed Lima three times since he had arrived in Washington in June urging the government not to seize the Oroya.

Ivins by now had Bayard convinced that Michael Grace's interests were more than merely pecuniary and commercial; they, instead, involved a settlement of major international issues if negotiated to a successful conclusion. For the first time Ivins succeeded in making Bayard see and admit that the success of Grace's plans involved the whole future of Peru. A proper settlement would not only relieve him of many annoying disputes, but also demonstrate the willingness and ability of the United States to help Peru out of its difficulties.[93]

Once persuaded of the transcending value of settling these issues, Bayard was more at ease in informing Zegarra that the United States would intervene and attempt to arbitrate the disputes. The secretary of state asked the Peruvian envoy to instruct his government to return the DuBois and Thorndike properties to the status quo ante and to refrain absolutely from any further seizures or aggressions pending the discussion of the points in controversy.[94]

The United States had now taken a stand—although still opposed to active intervention—and this seemingly gave Ivins and the Graces further leverage. The appointment of a joint commission to arbitrate was the next step toward resolution of the problem. Actually, as both Bayard and Ivins knew well, the United States could do little beyond cajoling Peru with words in an effort to reach an honorable solution. Force was out of the question, as Bayard clearly recognized. "The thing that staggers Mr. Bayard most, in case the worst comes to the worst, is the futility of attempting to coerce so weak and puny a state as Peru, as he fears it would only result in a long and ultimately fruitless occupation of the country and would on no account restore the values of the railroad properties," which was, after all, the goal of the exercise.[95] Zegarra was clearly playing his strength—the very weakness of Peru—quite well. He delayed an answer to Secretary Bayard's suggestion for a return to status quo ante before negotiations could proceed. By then, September 1888, the spotlight once again focused on Lima.

While Zegarra, Ivins, and Bayard sparred in Washington through the slow, hot month of August, events were proceeding rapidly in London and Lima toward renegotiation of the original Grace-Aranibar Contract signed in May 1887. If an overall agreement were reached by the bondholders and Peru, then the question of the seized railroads would fall into place. In late August Michael Grace returned to Peru with Lord Donoughmore, and Eyre cabled Ivins that "the crisis has passed," by which Ivins understood Eyre "to refer both literally to the cabinet and metaphorically to the Oroya Railroad."[96]

In Lima, Donoughmore and Michael Grace negotiated directly with the minister of hacienda, Antero Aspillaga, and they worked rapidly through September and part of October toward a new agreement that would take into account all of the events and factors that had cropped up since May 1887. The opposition in Peru to the original Grace-Aranibar Contract still had to be overcome, but the bondholders' reduced demands helped smooth the way. The rights to the oilfields in the north were dropped as well as the bondholders' plan to install their own customs officials at Mollendo to collect duties. As noted, the railroad concession was reduced from seventy-five to sixty-six years and some other terms were made more favorable to Peru.[97] The crisis over the seizure of the railroads was left in temporary abeyance, for it was recognized that if the new contract was ratified, the railroad concessionaires, such as Dubois, Thorndike, and Grace, would deal directly with the corporation—the Peruvian Corporation—slated to succeed the bondholders and carry out the terms of the contract.

The threat to the Oroya actually never was realized. Charles Watson, the main contractor of the Southern Railway and another of the old Meiggs team, attributed this to a twenty-thousand-peso loan that Michael Grace made to the Peruvian government in July 1888.[98] Since Watson was no friend of the Graces, the association of the loan with the government's failure to seize the Oroya Railway stands only as an allegation. In the same period, 1887–88, the Lima Chamber of Commerce was created and among its founding members was Edward Eyre. One of the first acts of the chamber was to provide loans for the government, and the Grace brothers were, of course, among several who became creditors of the government.[99]

With some of the bondholders' demands moderated and the railroad issue temporarily shelved, the way was cleared for a new contract. The Aspillaga-Donoughmore Contract, or the Grace Contract, was signed on October 25, 1888. When submitted to congress, that body predictably balked.

A secret protocol—soon known by everybody—stipulated that the contract would not go into effect until approved by Chile. Since the contract absolved Peru of all its indebtedness, the bondholders obviously would have to turn to Chile to collect on the remainder of what they believed their just dues. Chile protested vigorously to Peru in late 1888 and gave those who opposed the contract a further weapon. "How can we accept the contract, when Chile is opposed and we have no means to resist," one senator was quoted in private.[100] The government then withdrew the protocol and resubmitted the contract to congress, appealing also to the British Foreign Office to intercede against Chilean meddling in the internal affairs of Peru.[101]

This time the Foreign Office did not hedge. It fired off a

rebuke for Chile's unwarranted intrusion into the affairs of a sovereign nation's relations with British subjects (read bond-holders).[102] England's strong pro-Chilean sympathies were being sorely tried by Chile's intransigence on this issue. Mean-while, the French government remonstrated with the English on behalf of its own Peruvian creditors, largely Dreyfus, who were unhappy with the Grace Contract.[103]

The situation in Lima at the turn of the year was raucous. Congress voted five times on the contract between November 1888 and February 1889, with fewer than seven of the eighty-three members of the Chamber of Deputies changing their votes.[104] Early in December a public rally held by supporters of the contract turned sour when detractors gained the upper hand. Epithets and threats—"down Cáceres . . . death to for-eigners . . . attack Grace's house"—rang through the night.[105] After a Christmas recess, the debate was renewed in January and February.

Still leading the resistance in congress was José María Quim-per, who had opposed the contract since its proposal by Michael Grace in 1886. Quimper's tactics would have warmed the heart of any southern filibusterer in the United States Senate. In one instance he spoke for two entire days, consuming most of the time reserved for that special session of the congress. Not bash-ful, Quimper later published his words from the two-day mar-athon in a 257-page tome.[106]

The supporters of the contract finally got a motion for closure passed early in February, whereupon thirty members of the Chamber of Deputies stormed out of the assembly in high dud-geon. Without a quorum, congress adjourned February 14, 1889, seemingly no nearer ratifying the contract than in 1887. Donoughmore packed his bags and started back for England, recalled by the bondholders' committee to save on expenses. But Michael Grace, as was his wont, dug in and helped contrive a new tactic that eventually brought congress back together for an affirmation of the contract.

In April 1889 Cáceres, now thoroughly disgusted by the de-laying tactics in congress, determined to finish this matter which he deemed crucial to Peru's future. He named Pedro de Sola as prime minister, and Sola, who was also Michael's law-yer, advised the remaining members of congress to invoke, very simply, majority rule. The dissenters were declared neg-ligent in the performance of their congressional duties and, furthermore, were held to have obstructed the majority will of the congress. Their offices were vacated and new elections were promptly held. These elections returned, as was expected, mostly procontract members of congress, including Antero Aspillaga, now a deputy from Chiclayo and the former minister of hacienda, and Aurelio Denegri, a deputy from Lima and ex-president of the chamber.[107]

Several extraordinary sessions of congress were called in the wake of this election. The Chamber of Deputies approved the contract on July 26, 1889, after more debate and several further modifications. It was then sent to the Senate, which ratified it on October 25, 1889.[108] Included in the contract was the key clause forgiving Peru all debts contracted in 1869, 1870, and 1872; they were, it added, irrevocably and absolutely laid to rest and could not be raised in the future for whatever cause or motive.[109] The cancellation of the debt was one battle that Michael Grace had waged with unswerving allegiance to Peru. A commitment to Peru on this issue, of course, meant that Chile would be the offended party, and Chile was indeed offended.

Before the contract was signed formally by the president of Peru, Chile rattled its saber, asserting that the contract transparently violated the terms of the Treaty of Ancón. The bondholders wanted a "Chilean payment of £4 million in order to relieve itself of obligations incurred as a result of its acquisition of Peruvian territory."[110] This was a liability specifically denied in the treaty.

William and Michael were perfectly aware that the accord was only as good as Chile's acquiescence, so William worked hard in New York for much of 1889 and into 1890 to persuade Chileans and their friends to yield and compromise. William entertained the Chilean minister to the United States at his home Gracefield, and later spoke at length, and convincingly, with Augusto Matte, the brother of the Chilean foreign minister. Matte was traveling through New York on his way to England and William was able to convince Matte that the contract was a good one for Chile.[111]

William's basic argument was that a healthy and contented Peru was a better neighbor than a vindictive one still smarting from defeat, a situation aggravated by continuing Chilean opposition to its recovery. Peru, although defeated and going through a trying time, was already rearming and regaining some of its military strength, and was certainly not a totally vanquished nation. Furthermore, Chile's amazing successes in the past ten years had antagonized Argentina and Brazil, its

natural competitors for influence in the southern cone of the
continent.

It was precisely at this juncture that Brazil overthrew its old
monarchy and established a republican form of government.
The revolution of November 1889 helped clear the path for
closer relations with republican Argentina, which in turn "des-
ignated December 8 as a national holiday for celebration of the
advent of the Republic of the United States of Brazil."[112] Not
only were celebrations in order; Brazil and Argentina rapidly
moved to patch up old disputes, prompting Chile to improve
its relations with Peru and England to balance the new Argen-
tine-Brazilian understanding.[113]

England, however, was in no mood to comfort Chile since
Chile had rebuffed the contract and left English property hold-
ers—the bondholders—once again in limbo. A stiff note from
the Foreign Office to Santiago late in November 1889 advised
that continued interference with the contract was simply un-
warrantable. At the same time Whitehall backed up Peru and
recommended that the contract be ratified immediately.[114]

In early January 1890 Chile reached a decision to come to
terms. Not only was the rapprochement between Argentina
and Brazil a clear threat to Chile's new position as a great power
on the continent; but, if England was to remain a strong sym-
pathizer, its bondholders must be satisfied. Chile's financial
situation was good and it could afford to settle the debts. Furthermore, President Balmaceda, just approaching a constitutional crisis with a rebellious parliament, was anxious to clear
the air with respect to Peru and the bondholders.[115] On January
8, 1890, a convention was signed between Chile and Peru in
Santiago.

Chile agreed to pay the bondholders about £2.25 million in
cash, bonds, or benefits. This satisfied the English creditors,
who in return relieved Chile of its obligations related to the
debt.

In explaining the settlement to the Chilean congress, the
foreign minister admitted that his country had relinquished
resources that were its legal property, but argued that "this act
has infused new life into the organism of a neighbor nation and
friend which found itself utterly prostrate, and has completely
removed the possibility that its creditors might press a claim
against us which, although it would lack a strict juridical basis,
might have created a dangerous situation."[116]

The Grace Contract was now in place, and by April 1890 the Peruvian Corporation was in operation. Peru passed into a new era. The only major controversy that remained was largely academic, but the Grace Contract and its implications touched off almost as much dissension among scholars as its making did among the businessmen, bondholders, diplomats, and politicians who negotiated the tortuous route.

For a balanced assessment, we have borrowed from the findings and interpretations of the late Jorge Basadre, Peru's greatest historian of the national period. Basadre felt that the Grace Contract represented the best arrangement under bad circumstances: the railroads were in a state of deterioration; the bondholders were blocking Peru's access to moneys abroad; the Chileans were in opposition; the English Foreign Office waxed hot and cold; and so forth. The contract broke this impasse and by the very nature of its solution invited foreign capital into the country. In one sense, it was a liberating, progressive act that enabled Peru to draw freely again upon the capitalists of Europe and North America. According to the Marxist, dependency point of view, those very ties reinforced colonialism and thus were a step backward.[117] Between the extreme views, Basadre's opinion stands out for its balance:

> That unique alliance predicted between Peru and her creditors to make the country flourish dramatically did not develop. Nor did the pessimistic vision of the contract's more furious and hotheaded adversaries come to pass, a vision which had predicted the perpetual fettering of Peru hand and foot to preserve foreign interests; or, as Carlos Lisson wrote in his *Sociologia del Peru*, Peru did not fall into the hands of the cruelest and most profane masters, the usurers. In sum, the past was liquidated and the country, thinking herself free of her overwhelming foreign debt, confronted the future in pursuit of reconstruction.[118]

That the contract had been personally profitable for Michael Grace and the other concessionaires was undoubtedly true. Charles Watson received £82,000 in cash and £375,000 in stock in the Peruvian Corporation, and Thorndike received £50,000 in cash and £100,000 in Peruvian Corporation stock, as well as the construction contract for the extension of the Southern Railway. Michael Grace received £150,000 in cash plus a 3 percent commission on the shares, bonds, or cash distributed among the bondholders for his service as the bondholders' agent.[119] Additionally, Grace was granted the contract, whose estimated worth was about £100,000, to extend the Oroya Railroad.[120] Taken together, Grace earned between a half million and a million dollars, if one counts future profits from the contract to extend the Oroya Railroad.

★ ★ ★

The Grace Contract represented a good trade for all parties under trying circumstances. If Michael Grace made a healthy profit, Peru was in turn liberated from a financial millstone. That the private interests of Michael Grace were not incompatible with the public welfare of Peru was the premise that Grace operated on for those five challenging years. The Grace role in the modernization of Peru was clearly related in this business which freed Peru of one of the yokes of the process itself—massive debt. The debt was accrued as Peru discovered the modern markets for its guano and nitrates and committed itself with a near religious fervor to the railroads as one of the principal vehicles to the progressive world. As the Graces pursued their legitimate business interests across the Americas and across the Atlantic, they acted as one of the principal conduits for the flow of moneys and technologies into Peru. Michael Grace's contract was but one act in this complicated play.

No less important was the Graces' increasing influence in the making of inter-American relations, with special emphasis on Peru. From the War of the Pacific to Michael's successful conclusion of the contract, the Graces strove to maintain a strong and independent Peru in the face of a near disaster during and immediately after the War of the Pacific. The Graces helped identify Peru's aspirations with those of the United States, then trying to reduce the predominant commercial and diplomatic weight of England in the Southern Hemisphere. That Chilean destinies were perceived to be closely tied to English commercial interests furthered the Peruvian orientation of the Graces and the United States government. It was not an unequivocal commitment, nor one made with disregard for present and future good relations with Chile. Yet, English commercial dominance in Latin America was coming under scrutiny and being challenged by American entrepreneurs and traders in this era, and no other "American" house of trade possessed such a strong and competitive stance against the English. That the Graces were originally Irish, of course, lent some fuel to their anti-English sentiments.

While Michael ranged far and wide in the late 1880s, William kept the focus on business. A main part of that business continued to be ocean transportation. Steam was rapidly supplanting sail throughout the world and Michael and William's dependence upon fast steamers to get them around three continents deeply impressed them. While winding up the negotiations for the Grace Contract, they were also deciding to go into steam. It would be a major move, for it would strengthen the backbone of their business and tie them even more closely, if possible, to the West Coast of South America, even as the company was developing to stature as a major United States concern.

8

From Windjammers to Steamers

THE EXPANDING BASIS OF A BUSINESS EMPIRE

Ask the average man on the street if he has ever heard of W. R. Grace & Co. and you will more than likely receive a politely negative nod. Then rephrase the question and mention the Grace Line and chances are the response may be, "Oh, the old shipping company; sure, I've heard of it." Perhaps even the time for that recognition has passed, since Grace Line ceased to exist in 1969 when it was sold to a Greek shipping tycoon. Sold twice more since then, the old Santa fleet has all but disappeared from the sea and must be slowly fading from memory as well.

Shipping was always at the heart of the business empire that the Graces created across the Americas, and William's love for the sea and trade and commerce certainly must be credited with imparting this dedication to things maritime.

From rather modest beginnings as ship chandlers in the 1860s, the Graces moved through part ownership, full ownership, and finally to the establishment of a line, the Merchants Line, serving the Americas. They bought their first steamships in the early 1890s and pioneered steamship operations between New York and the West Coast of South America. By World War I, Grace was operating the most important and extensive shipping services between the Americas. It brought the company into contact with virtually all of Latin America, and it is no mere coincidence that during this period, roughly from the 1860s to the end of World War I, the Graces invested widely in disparate parts of the continents—from rubber in the Amazon to nitrates in Chile—which were served by their ships.

The twin bases for the Grace enterprises remained Peru and the United States, and it was from the latter that William Grace directed actively his company's maritime endeavors. From his first office in New York at 110 Wall Street, Grace began chartering some ships and buying shares in others, two timeworn ways of participating in sea trade.

The premise of part ownership was basically to spread the risks in a business peculiarly prone to the elements. Part ownership and insurance provided two cushions needed to survive the sea's disasters, which invariably struck if one was in the business long enough. Conversely, profits were also spread, but it was a good way for men of smaller means to participate directly in an ancient business. Besides, if a captain or master owned part of a ship, he was more likely to look after its welfare. If he owned part of its cargo as well, his attitude toward meeting timetables and the most efficient operation of the ship was improved further.

As early as 1867 William Grace was registered as a partial proprietor of ships; a quarter of the *Lillius* belonged to him that year. In 1869 he purchased the *Gladiator* and renamed her *Lilly Grace*; he also owned one sixteenth of the newly launched *Agnes I. Grace,* named after his youngest daughter by the ship's builders at Thomaston, Maine.[1] Grace also chartered vessels for service between the Americas, not only to carry his own goods but also for others on commission (see Chapter 4).

Chartering was an open venture, one that required skill, a good knowledge of the markets, and, perhaps most important, the willingness to take some risks. William Grace possessed all three.[2] Ships normally possessed a cargo capacity of a thousand tons or less in those days, but cargo was frequently so scarce that the charter contract almost always had to cover the privilege of making two, three, or more ports. The charterer usually had twenty-five to thirty "lay days" for loading. If not assured of a full load, the charterer would purchase and ship unsold merchandise in order to fill up or complete the cargo. This was perhaps one of the most speculative portions of the business.

The charters, or shipowners, were usually paid a lump-sum

price for the voyage, in which bargain the shipowner and the charterer each haggled for the best advantage. It was always a gamble for the charterer, especially if his full cargo (still being contracted) could not be accommodated by the ship's peculiar construction. If the vessel's hatches were too small or it did not have bow and stern ports to accommodate the loading of timbers (of which Grace sent a great deal in the early 1870s for Meiggs's railroad construction in Peru), the charterer had to secure the alterations from the shipowner. Each individual charter thus required much negotiation.[3] Whether the charterer struck a bargain or suffered a serious loss depended on his judgment. The full charter price was invariably payable upon termination of the voyage, although an advanced sum in pounds sterling was required by the owner, for the dollar was unrecognized in foreign trade.[4]

American vessels were preferred, but few of suitable size were available. Grace and others thus chartered vessels flying many different flags, including those of England, Norway, and Germany. The trip from New York around the Horn to Valparaiso often ran to about a hundred days, and the uncertainties of weather, cargo, crew (subject to disappearing in foreign ports), and competition added to the risks. But Grace produced more black ink than red in the ledgers, especially in the late 1860s and early 1870s as the Peruvian railroad boom neared its peak.

The small quarters of 110 Wall Street eventually proved too cramped, and in 1870 William Grace moved his offices to 62 South Street, as close to the tall ships as he could get. Within a year, these quarters were vacated and new rooms were taken at 47 Exchange Place, still very much in the center of New York's old shipping district.[5] W. R. Grace & Co. would stay at that address for ten years as the business expanded.

Variety and diversification were constants in the Grace formula for success. William always sought hard-working persons, with good connections if possible, whose familial or other backgrounds might enhance the ongoing Grace business or promote a penetration into complementary sectors. The attachment of Charles Flint to the firm in 1869 fulfilled all the criteria. Flint proved to be a most energetic and successful young partner. He brought with him a splendid talent for selling and persuading people, and he added another tie to New England shipbuilders, who were supplying some of the ships going into the foundations of the Grace maritime enterprises. William had already formed one attachment to the Maine shipbuilding and shipping community through his father-in-law, George Gilchrest. With the addition of Flint to the partnership, the ties to New England shipbuilders were strengthened.

Flint's seafaring lineage was long and distinguished. His father and uncle, Deacon Benjamin Flint Chapman and Isaac Flint Chapman, were partners in one of the most successful shipbuilding and operating firms in the nineteenth century, Flint & Chapman.[6] Partnerships were still the most common form of business associations and they usually reflected close family as well as business ties. William Grace's various "houses" in New York, Callao, and San Francisco were all organized as partnerships, and all bore a strong family resemblance.

However, Flint & Chapman must have been the closest partnership of any nineteenth-century firm. It was an absolute partnership; all the property was held jointly and no individual accounts were kept, even for household expenses.[7] At Thomaston, Maine, the partners built identical houses on adjoining lots. When they moved to Brooklyn in 1858, they rented two adjacent brick houses on Fort Greene Place. When they ceased being renters, they purchased identical adjoining brownstones on Oxford Street. Last, they bought two lots in Brooklyn Heights with the intention of building identical residences. But one was a corner lot, stalling the act temporarily. However, during the Civil War they joined with another Thomaston friend in New York, Edward O'Brion, and bought an entire side of Montague Terrace, thus enabling Chapman and Flint each to have a corner. One contract was signed for decorating and furnishing the two houses, and purchases of supplies were made day to day from the same shopkeepers. Few partners were closer than Messrs. Flint and Chapman.

Although the Grace brothers and cousins never aspired to any such degree of intimacy, they did prefer to enter into partnerships with blood relatives, or, failing that, with relatives by marriage, followed by close acquaintances. When Charles Flint became a partner in W. R. Grace & Co. in 1872, it was no accident that relationships between the Graces and Flint & Chapman became even more cordial. That same year W. R. Grace & Co. took over the New York agency of Flint & Chapman vessels from J. W. Finell & Co.

Within the next decade three graceful downeasters launched from Flint & Chapman's shipyards in Bath, Maine, bore the names of their new friends and business colleagues. The *W. R. Grace*, a ship of 1,893 tons, was launched in 1873; the *M. P.*

Grace, 1,928 tons, and the *Manual Llaguno*, 1,732 tons, followed in 1875 and 1879 respectively.[8] Another of the Flint & Chapman downeasters launched in 1876 bore the name *Santa Clara*, giving credence to the notion that Grace Line's later practice of naming its steamships after saints came from this early association between William Grace and the Chapman brothers.

The *W. R. Grace* and *M. P. Grace* served most of their careers on the New York–San Francisco run. They were never owned by the Graces, a fact in itself not unusual, since it was common to name ships in those days after friends and relatives. The *W. R. Grace* made twelve trips from New York around the Horn to California and its fastest time was a respectable 115 days. In September 1889, bound in for Philadelphia from Le Havre, France, it was caught in a hurricane and wrecked near Lewes, Delaware. All hands were saved, including the captain's pet dog.

The *M.P. Grace* was a faster ship than the *W. R. Grace*. It made its first run from New York to San Francisco under the command of Capt. Robert P. Wilbur in 102½ days. It also outlasted the *W. R. Grace*, carrying lumber until 1906 from Puget Sound to the East Coast. That year new owners sold the *M. P. Grace* as a barge and it foundered off Shennecok Light near the northern entrance to Chesapeake Bay.[9]

The alliance between the Graces and Chapmans extended to the West Coast as well. When John Grace set up the San Francisco house, Capt. James W. Chapman became one of the partners. He remained a partner until 1880, when he ventured out on his own.[10]

Success in owning and chartering ships in the 1870s led to the natural ambition of establishing a formal line, which entailed maintaining scheduled service over a regular route. This William Grace did in 1882 when the Merchants Line was founded.[11] It paralleled the only other line, that of Fabbri & Chauncey, then operating between New York and the West Coast. Grace rapidly drove Fabbri & Chauncey out of business by cutting rates, first on the Chile run and then on the extension of the line to Peru. Once Grace got the lion's share of the business, Fabbri & Chauncey was bought out by Merchants Line and the rates were raised once again to their normal level.[12]

Business expanded so well for W. R. Grace & Co. in the late 1870s and early 1880s that another office move was necessitated in 1882. This time the firm occupied the vacated offices of the Standard Oil Company at 192 Pearl Street.

In the wake of the Standard move, some pieces of office furniture were left behind to be disposed of. Among them was a six-by-five-foot flat desk, which had been made especially for John D. Rockefeller. The asking price was two hundred dollars. William sent a young office boy, Maurice Bouvier, to the new Standard Oil headquarters at 26 Broadway with a hundred-dollar offer. Rockefeller generously reduced his asking price by fifteen dollars. Grace increased his by the same amount. The final price was one hundred fifty dollars. The incident provides some insight into the nature of these men, already millionaires, who never forgot their habits of frugality nor their keenness for driving a good, hard bargain.

In 1885 William Grace moved his company again, this time to a lovely three-story building on One Hanover Square, which today survives as India House. Originally, India House was built in 1837 by Richard A. Carman, probably as a storehouse. Hanover Square itself had long been associated with commerce in the city of New York, existing as early as the seventeenth century when the water's edge lapped up to its Dutch slips and wharves. The house that Richard Carman built became the Hanover Bank about 1851 and was later acquired by one of its tenants, a tobacco importer named Robert L. Maitland. In 1870 the cotton exchange moved in and traded there until 1885 when W. R. Grace & Co. took over the building.

The size of India House, three ample stories, helped to accommodate a growing concern, especially active in the mid-1880s because of Grace's investment in one of Latin America's booming exports of the latter nineteenth century, rubber. The rubber business extended Grace beyond Peru, but the business eventually went flat.

No other product better symbolizes the "boom and bust" cycle of certain Latin American economies than the rubber phenomenon.[13] Until the middle of the nineteenth century, rubber was used largely by the primitive Indians of the Amazon basin for waterproofing canoes or for playthings. The Portuguese settlers of the colonial period employed rubber occasionally in making boots, and in the 1820s small amounts of rubber were exported to Europe to impregnate textiles such as raincoats. Still, rubber remained a rather exotic substance until Charles Goodyear patented the vulcanization process in 1844 and made rubber commercially viable.

Rubber is derived from the natural latex of certain tropical trees and shrubs, the most important being the *Hevea brasiliensis*. Vulcanization made the use of rubber practical in the developing fields of railway mechanicals and general engineering, and as insulation in the growing electrical industries. Like guano and nitrates, the industrialization and modernization of the Western world stimulated a dramatic rise in the production of rubber.

Exports from the Amazon basin rose from thirty-one tons in 1827 to almost fifteen hundred tons in 1850. This was doubled by 1867. Thirteen years later over eight thousand tons were being exported annually. Production again doubled between 1880 and 1890 as demand increased in the electrical and engineering industries. By the turn of the century, the rubber boom was in full swing, catalyzed by the bicycle craze and the growing automobile industry, both dependent on pneumatic tires.

The Amazon was transformed by the process, just as surely as rubber in its finished form was facilitating the transformation of Europe and North America. The cities of Belem, Para, and Manaus in Brazil and Iquitos in Peru exploded with an influx of immigrants, entrepreneurs, merchants, and hangers-on, all interested in exploiting the boom. Manaus, located nearly a thousand miles up the tropical Amazon, became the richest and most modern city in all Brazil, sporting an opera house, Paris fashions, electric lighting, and trams.

Thousands of immigrants, especially from the impoverished, drought-plagued Brazilian state of Ceara, poured into the Amazon basin to work as *seringueiros* ("latex gatherers") in the jungles where the wild rubber trees grew. The loneliness of the jungle, disease, and hunger took a terrifying toll on the *seringueiros*. They gathered the latex from irregularly spaced *Hevea* trees in the dense jungle and brought it to gathering points on the river where the crude rubber balls were transferred to company agents in exchange for credit. From there the rubber was floated downriver to the major export centers, such as Para, and thence shipped to the markets of Europe and North America. It was a lucrative business for the transporters, owners, and lessees of rubber-producing lands, and certainly for the merchants and entrepreneurs in the cities. It was only natural for William Grace to be attracted to the rubber business. It was one of the booming enterprises in nineteenth-century Latin America and, like railroad building in Peru and Costa Rica and the guano and nitrate booms in Peru and Chile, promised much to those swift and sharp enough to get a part of the trade.

By the early 1880s Grace had established two merchant houses in Brazil, one in Para and the other in Manaus. He owned 80 percent of Sears & Co. in Para and 70 percent of Scott & Co. in Manaus, both rubber buyers and exporters. Richard

F. Sears was his man in Para and J. Alvin Scott his counterpart in Manaus. Both companies were making handsome profits in the early 1880s and both young partners were treated like members of the Grace family, as was the wont of William, who earlier had taken in Charles Flint in the same fashion.[14] When in New York, Scott and Sears, oft with their families, stayed at the Grace home, enjoying the warm hospitality of William and Lillius. Charles Flint enjoyed the same familiarity. Furthermore, Flint was the active partner of W. R. Grace & Co. in the rubber business. Indeed, he would later in his life achieve perhaps his greatest fame by founding a corporation of some renown, the United States Rubber Company.

In every Grace business at least one of the partners was expected to be well versed in a Latin American commodity, whether guano, nitrates, rubber, sugar, or any other item bought, produced, or exported by the Graces. In this case Charles Flint learned the rubber business well by making several trips to the Amazon in the mid-1880s, while he and William Grace jointly cultivated the rubber market in the United States. The price of rubber in the United States rose and dipped according to the general economic scene and it called on the best business instincts of Grace and Flint. For example, the price of "fine para" had been pegged at $1.08 per pound in 1883, but by August 1884 it had dropped to $0.50 per pound.[15] W. R. Grace & Co., however, was short three hundred thousand pounds when the market temporarily collapsed and it weathered the short crisis without a great loss. Because of the market's instability Grace and Flint proposed that the leading manufacturers in the United States join in a consortium to stabilize the business.

Combining forces to reduce the ravages of fierce competition was, of course, becoming a common practice among American entrepreneurs of the era. The actual accomplishment of such arrangements—by the oil, and steel, and meatpacking industries, for example—created immense monopolies and trusts. These, at the turn of the century, were attacked by Progressives, who condemned the apparent suffocation of free enterprise and competition and the arrangement of so much power in the hands of so few people. Certainly the most notable of the trust-busters was Theodore Roosevelt, who campaigned to break up the trusts and took great glee in following up on his promises during his terms as president, 1901–08. Yet the trusts or combinations foundered as often from the intense competitiveness of the participants as from Progressive reformers in government. In 1885, however, the Grace-Flint idea seemed sound to the rubber manufacturers and the following agreed to the formation of a syndicate to regulate the market: Boston Rubber Shoe Co. (E. S. Converse), L. Candee & Co. (H. L. Hotchkiss), the East Hampton Rubber Thread Co. (E. T. Sawyer), the New Jersey Rubber Shoe Co. (Christopher Meyer), the National Rubber Co. (A. O. Bourne), and the Woonsocket Rubber Co. (Joseph Banigan).[16]

Meanwhile, the price of rubber rose in late 1885 and prosperity infused the rubber barons with optimism again. Business was so good that William Grace decided in late 1885 to create a separate corporation, the New York Trading Co., to handle the Grace rubber trade. Charles Flint retired from W. R. Grace & Co. with the intention of becoming president of the new company. Grace paid Flint a quarter of a million dollars for his share of the partnership in W. R. Grace & Co., not a bad sum for the young man who had talked William Grace into hiring him fifteen years before without a salary to prove his worth. He certainly had accomplished the latter. The New York Trading Co. also absorbed two of its rivals, Earle Brothers of New York and George A. Alden & Co. of Boston, and a manufacturer, the Woonsocket Rubber Co. of Rhode Island, to reduce possible competition.[17]

Then a spat between the Graces and Flint blew up into a full-fledged fight. Perhaps Flint's reputation as the "father of trusts" best symbolizes the underlying differences that inexorably drove the two partners apart.

Flint was a supreme organizer and consolidator. In a lively memoir written later in life, he explained that trusts and industrial consolidations were the "most essential factors in economic development," although freely admitting that "cooperation in merchandising and industrial production tended to what would now [1923] be judged in restraint of trade."[18] William Grace was not particularly interested in cornering any one market, but in having a good share of a good business.

Flint's desire to employ the New York Trading Co. as the vehicle to consolidate the growing rubber business under one umbrella struck Grace as "Napoleonic" and immensely "speculative."[19] He forced Flint to accept a position as treasurer of the new company while Michael was made vice president and George Alden became president. Sharp words and flashing tempers were brandished in the "heated and acrimonious discussion" leading to Flint's subordination, only further souring the relationship between the old partners.[20] Before the end of the decade, Flint bested the Graces in a bitter battle that raged contemporaneously with Michael's efforts to renegotiate the Peruvian debt.

The battlefield eventually was littered with bruised egos, lost opportunities, and broken subordinates. Richard Sears, for example, was but one pawn in this struggle. Flint thought little of Sears, while Grace considered his man in Para very capable, and he assured Sears that Flint's attempts to take over the Sears firm in Para would be resisted. By mid-1886 Grace was already thinking of withdrawing altogether from the New York Trading Co. when another Flint act contributed to the growing rift.

Cables laid between the continents had recently helped to transform communications in the business world. In 1878–79 the Mexican Telegraph Co. and the Central and South American Telegraph Co. were established by James A. Scrymser with the backing of J. P. Morgan and other New York investors, including William and Michael Grace.[21] The Grace brothers were included among Scrymser's board of directors. Active and successful traders, they especially were aware of the value of rapid and sure communications.

In 1881 Scrymser's company linked Galveston, Texas, with Mexico City, and the next year the line was extended to Lima. Then, on January 29, 1887, Grace Brothers, Lima, received the exclusive concession to build and operate a submarine telegraph cable between Lima and Santiago.[22] This line was completed by 1890. The establishment of these cable services between the American continents ensured rapid communications without having to route messages through Europe—largely Lisbon and London—which already possessed cable service to South America.

The Graces' reliance on this revolutionary new form of communications was characteristic of their pioneering business practices between the Americas. Extensive cable books, codes, and other paraphernalia preserved from the period in the Grace Papers (in the Rare Book and Manuscript Collection at Columbia University) testify to the above.

When Charles Flint persuaded the Grace cable clerk to scramble the codes employed in the cable traffic, William Grace quickly smelled a rat and fired the clerk. He went to work for Flint, adding the proverbial insult to the injury and confirming Flint's complicity in the matter. William and Michael were determined to crush Flint and to "force them [the Flint group] to wind up."[23]

The Graces wanted either to buy out the Flint interests in the New York Trading Co. or to sell all of their shares in the same company, hoping either way to precipitate a crisis in the Flint coalition, which by now included George Alden, the president of the company. But Charles Flint was a master tactician who thought coolly and acted well under pressure. Although the Graces prevailed at this stage and the New York Trading Co. was broken up in the summer of 1886, the battle was only joined, not won. William was also trying at this time to undermine Flint with the major buyers and manufacturers in the United States.

He held long conversations with E. S. Converse of Boston, then the largest user of rubber in the country, and suggested that a new syndicate be created to purchase rubber around the world for producers such as Converse's Boston Rubber Shoe Co. Grace's scope included Brazil, Central America, and Africa. With a capitalization of over a million dollars and a business projected at seven million, Grace was thinking along the lines of Flint's grand vision, perhaps contagious in a prospering economy.[24] All of the major manufacturers would be included in the new corporation and Charles Flint would, of course, be left out in the cold. So much for the plan.

To promote this new corporation, William sent Michael on a trip through New York and New England. To follow Michael, Flint sent a private detective.[25] Charley Flint followed close by. On Michael's heels at one moment, Flint was ahead of him at another, countering the efforts of Converse and William Grace to line up manufacturers behind the proposed new corporation. Joseph Banigan of the Woonsocket Rubber Co., H. L. Hotchkiss of L. Candee & Co., and others were by Flint talked out of participating in any proposed new corporation.

Meanwhile, Sears in Brazil was being undermined and discredited by Flint, who supported Sears's competitors and disparaged his credit and business reputation.[26] As New York sank into the muggy months of August and September, Grace's and Sears's errors in buying long on rubber were compounded by Flint's shrewd manipulation of the market and the manufacturers. Grace cautioned Sears in Para to ease up on his purchases. It was becoming increasingly difficult to sell at a profit, and even at a price that covered costs.

Flint and his allies, growing in number, kept undermining Grace's attempt to firm up the corporation. While Converse stood by Grace with certainty, the others were more easily wooed by Flint with his stories of Sears's inefficiency and Grace's neglect of the rubber business, which Flint described as a "mere sideshow" to the main Grace interests.[27] By the time Grace was able to arrange a meeting of the principal manufacturers in Boston on September 29, the proposed common front no longer existed. Converse backed Grace and urged the four other men present to do the same, but there was no unanimity.

Grace, in truth, was overextended. He and Sears were grossly overstocked, and when prices broke in October Grace wrote Sears in Para that "it is a bitter pill to have $800,000 of rubber on hand with a falling market and nobody buying. . . . You can scarcely understand how the Flint-Earle-Alden people have sought to work hell here & it is unfortunate we gave them such a chance by getting so big a stock on hand."[28] Furthermore, Grace could hardly give the rubber business his undivided attention, for he was still serving as mayor. Michael was entering a crucial stage in the negotiations between the bondholders and Peru, while Williams Ivins, William's chamberlain and personal secretary, could shoulder only so much responsibility.

By December 1886 Flint's victory was complete. The losses suffered by Grace and Sears were the heaviest in all their business experience, but William was philosophical in the face of these reverses. "We know you loaded us up; . . . we know too, we could have, instead of advising you, peremptorily stopped your buying, but we . . . trusted altogether too much to the promises of the big manufacturers."[29] Grace took the blame and tried to prepare for a recovery in the year 1887. He advised Sears that while the business front was dismal, the domestic side, as far as he could influence it, was being taken care of: "Your wife lately spent a few days with us; my wife enjoyed her company very much. I took them to the theater twice & altogether I hope she had a good time."[30]

Expectations for the Graces and Sears picked up in early 1887, but Flint had done his homework well. His New York Commercial Co. enjoyed a very prosperous year, selling over two million pounds of rubber on a rising market, and he gradually shoved the Graces out of the scene. The Sears Commercial Co., on the other hand, did no better in 1888, or in 1889, when Ivins was sent on an inspection trip to Para. He reported that Sears was an exhausted man and near collapse from insomnia, and that the formerly prosperous trade in merchandise business along the Brazilian coast had gone the same way as rubber—down. Then Ivins quit and joined Charley Flint. William Grace, engrossed in the making of the Grace Contract, no longer had any stomach for rubber along the Amazon. The Sears Commercial Co. was liquidated and Sears himself, a broken man, was offered a respectable position with W. R. Grace & Co.[31]

In 1890 the great boom in Brazilian rubber began, spurred throughout the decade by the rise of the bicycle craze in the United States with its demand for rubber tires, and followed by the invention of the automobile.[32] In 1892 Flint put together perhaps his most famous "combination," the United States Rubber Company. By then, and even before, William and Michael Grace had cut their cables from the scene along the Amazon. Their interests and talents flowed in many different channels during the dynamic 1880s. Certainly one of the most interesting was a real canal a Frenchman named Ferdinand de Lesseps was trying to dig through the Isthmus of Panama.

The dream of cutting a path between the seas to link the Atlantic and the Pacific was almost as old as the discovery of the narrow isthmus itself in the sixteenth century by Vasco Núñez de Balboa. However, the engineering problems were of such monumental dimensions that little advance was made on the idea until the nineteenth century, when inventions like steam shovels and dredges provided men with the means to manipulate nature on a grand scale. The first application of steam technology to Panama was actually not in the building of a canal, but in the completion of a railroad in 1855.[33] Steamers operating in the service of the Pacific Mail Steamship Co. linked the two coasts of the Americas, making regular runs down to Panama where passengers, mail, and cargo could be transshipped on the railroad.

Yet the railroad was only an improvement, albeit a good one, on the old system, replacing the mule with the locomotive. A canal would be the ideal solution and Lesseps was the visionary who first attempted to dig a canal with the possibility of success.

Lesseps had completed the Suez Canal in 1869. On the basis of this world-heralded engineering triumph he promoted an endeavor of even greater magnitude, the attempt to dig the Panama Canal.[34] He formed a company, the Panama Canal Co., which was rapidly oversubscribed by patriotic Frenchmen of great and small fortunes alike, and began the task in 1881.

Naturally enough, the concept and task of building a canal attracted the attention of the Graces. They were, after all, among the principal promoters of trade and navigation between the Americas and an isthmian canal would immeasurably improve and shorten communications between the East Coast of North America with the West Coast of South America. William Grace was not entirely convinced of the soundness of digging the canal across the steamy, malarial Colombian province of Panama, and at the end of the century he would lead a syndicate to build a canal across the rival route in Nicaragua. Yet, in the early 1880s when the dirt was flying at Panama, there was business to be done there.

The enormous effort of Lesseps and the Panama Canal Co. demanded a wide assortment of auxiliary services to support the actual digging. Lumber, for example, was needed for railroad ties, housing, and myriad other purposes. John Grace's firm in San Francisco was well situated, and well experienced from the Meiggs railroad-building era, to supply lumber from the great forests of the Northwest. In mid-1884 W. R. Grace & Co., on behalf of J. W. Grace & Co., entered into negotiations with the Panama Canal Co. to supply the necessary timbers.

The original supplier of lumber for housing for the Panama Canal Co. had been the Franco-American Co. When that company defaulted on its contract in early 1884, Furth & Campbell in Panama contacted W. R. Grace & Co. with a proposal that a joint bid for the business be made by Grace and Furth & Campbell.[35] Since most if not all of the wood for the building of railroads in Peru and Costa Rica had come through the hands of the Graces in the 1870s and 1880s, Furth & Campbell's approach to W. R. Grace & Co. was not an unlikely one.

William Grace and his people in New York studied the proposal by Furth & Campbell in detail. They went over the plans and specifications for the sanitarium and house contracts and studied previous bids made by the Franco-American Co. They kept in daily communication with the San Francisco house by wire and closely reviewed and compared all previous contracts and prices.[36]

Then, at the last moment, Grace withdrew from the bidding.

He decided that the contract and the plans and specifications differed too drastically and that even their experts could not produce estimates without great discrepancies. Under these uncertain circumstances, Grace decided at the very last moment that it would be entirely unsafe to bid on the house contracts with such information as he had at hand.[37]

This was a typical decision in a business built largely on speculation, but on speculation well-thought out and with a decent chance of success. The earlier bids for the housing made by the Franco-American Co. were described by the Graces as nothing more than "leaps in the dark," and that although they undoubtedly would have made some profit on the contract had it been carried out, it was absolutely impossible to calculate from the data in their possession and from the uncertainty of the plans and specifications whether the profit would be 2 or 20 percent.[38]

Also typical of Grace was having someone on site with a

thorough knowledge of the ongoing commodity being traded or project being contemplated. A man was to be sent to Panama to make a professional appraisal of the situation, but the vagaries of a still rudimentary cable system fouled the plan. New York cabled Furth & Campbell to extend the deadline on the bid. The cable, however, arrived at Panama in a mutilated state, and the delay in sorting out the message pushed them past the bid deadline.[39]

That they could not bid was a bit frustrating, since the overall business of building the canal was booming and Grace would have liked a part of it. But the proposed housing business struck Grace as too filled with uncertainties and too vague and lacking in details.[40] However, another aspect of the business appeared more promising.

The Franco-American Co. had not only defaulted in its delivery of wood to build houses, but failed to deliver over two million feet of lumber as well. When the firm could not meet this obligation, it approached W. R. Grace & Co. and offered to sell its contract outright, but asked for such a figure that Grace could not entertain the proposition at all.[41] Furth & Campbell, however, was advised by Grace in New York to try and obtain this contract, for it looked promising from two points of view: one, that firm knew the details; and two, it could fulfill it with ease.[42]

W. R. Grace kept J. W. Grace in San Francisco closely apprised of the negotiations, and asked the San Francisco house to be ready to get the best bids possible on short notice.[43] In case of doubt on requirements or specifications, the Panama Canal Co. should be given the benefit of the doubt, "inasmuch as we wish to assume no risks whatever for rejections of the work . . . in a word, we want to give them every benefit, and a first-class and satisfactory job, without any scrimping whatever."[44]

These efforts of Furth & Campbell and W. R. Grace & Co. to get the bids on the lumber failed, but the experience proved valuable as far as Grace was concerned. Most of the correspondence issuing from New York carried the signature of William Ivins, who, although not a partner, was developing as one of the most reliable and inventive individuals in the organization during the decade of the 1880s.

By June 1884 it was clear to Grace and Furth & Campbell that they would be unable to obtain the Franco-American Co.'s contract to supply large quantities of pine and redwood.[45] Occasional sales of coal to the isthmus were nonetheless made in 1884 by the Graces, even though their ventures in housing and lumber did not get off the ground.

Perhaps it was just as well from William Grace's point of view, for he, as others, seriously doubted the financial integrity of Lesseps' grand venture. The problems of digging in the tropics through jungles and mountains were proving much more demanding than simply spading up a ditch through the flat desert at Suez. Furthermore, pestilence and an unrelentingly wet climate took a terrifying toll on workers, many of whom were recruited from English-speaking Caribbean islands and fought with the native Panamanians.

In July 1884 William asked Michael, then in London, to query his London and Paris friends closely on the financial condition of the Panama Canal Co. William, a studious and conservative businessman, saw waste and extravagance in the canal project. It was also turning into one of the longest and costliest projects of the century and William Grace thought it prudent to inquire "from time to time into the condition of the company's exchequer."[46] Yet, if the lumber business with a shaky French company did not materialize, coal sales to Panama and other parts of Latin America were secure and profitable. That was the nature of this firm, one of the earliest diversifiers with multinational tendencies.

A major buyer of Grace coal over the years had been United States Navy steamers calling on West Coast ports. Then suddenly in early December 1884, shortly after Grace had been elected mayor of New York for a second term, Admiral Upshur, in command of the U.S. squadron on that station, issued a peremptory order prohibiting the purchase of any goods whatsoever, including coal, from the house of Grace.[47] Adding to this indignity was Upshur's followup order: in the future all goods should be bought from Thomas Shute & Co., an English firm. Incensed, William Grace shot a letter off to Secretary of the Navy William E. Chandler on December 9, advising the secretary that this act amounted to the "proscription of the only American house at that station and to the preference of an English concern."[48] The latter act really brewed up the Irish in mayor-elect Grace, who rather bluntly told the secretary that "these orders . . . are so unusual as to be practically unintelligible to us."[49]

William Grace wanted to know why the action had been taken and demanded that Upshur's order be countermanded. Grace had done business for many years with the navy on the West Coast and never heard a complaint. The firm had always furnished supplies "to the best advantage," and could not fathom the abrupt cancellation of its business with the navy. Competition always stimulated William and his response was no different in this instance. "We are not only satisfied to compete, but we may state that we will supply goods for the use of the navy as cheaply as it is possible for any other concern in Callao to do so . . . we feel our house has been unjustly treated, and without the ascription of any good or sufficient reasons."[50]

Ivins personally followed his boss's note to Washington on December 9 to present the Grace case more forcefully. While never residing permanently in Washington, Ivins nonetheless was the first major Grace lobbyist in the capital, for his presence there was crucial during the rest of the decade when the Grace Contract was being thrashed out.

Ivins contacted the secretary, who explained the admiral's point of view, decidedly at odds with one expressed by the mayor, as one might suspect. The fact that Upshur was a senior officer and station commander with wide latitude was impressed upon Ivins not only by Secretary Chandler, but also by the judge advocate general, William B. Ramey, with whom Ivins consulted at length as well. The judge advocate was involved in the case since Upshur's proscription of Grace Brothers, Callao, resulted from a judicial proceeding dating back to September 1882, when the admiral first arrived on station.

The admiral had discovered that the costs of fresh provisions obtained for his flagship, USS *Hartford*, were inordinately high and he concluded that the navy was being grossly overcharged.[51] Upshur decided to investigate the matter and to force some competitive bidding. Soon after, Grace Brothers and Thomas Lawler & Co., the two traditional suppliers of the U.S. Navy, lowered their prices. The admiral became suspicious and he convened a more formal inquiry. This hearing revealed—with the help of testimony gladly offered by competitors of Lawler and Grace—that the U.S. Navy had consistently paid prices higher than those paid by other nationalities.[52] Grace and Lawler were accused of monopolizing the market and excluding smaller suppliers who were willing to provide the goods for lower prices. Then the admiral set in motion an eighteen-month investigation.

The investigation showed that supplies of coal, wood, flour, and other staple articles purchased from Grace Brothers & Co. and from Lawler & Co. varied from 25 to 300 percent over lowest market rates.[53] The investigation was conducted by a formal board of inquiry, but in describing the proceedings to

Ivins, the secretary hedged somewhat with a few "appears," which provided Chandler with some room to maneuver if necessary: "The investigation appears to have been thorough and was openly conducted by a Court of Inquiry . . . it also appears that there was ample opportunity for the firms above named to tender such explanations or evidence respecting the transactions referred to . . . it further appears that one of the immediate effects of the investigation ordered by Rear Admiral Upshur was a saving, on six staple articles alone, of over $8,000.00, in a fortnight's supplies for a portion of the squadron."[54] Admiral Upshur reported all this to the Navy Department and issued orders to secure some competition and lower prices in the business of provisioning the ships of the fleet.[55] This pleased the secretary, who sent Upshur a long, flowing commendation for his efforts in behalf of the government.[56]

What the secretary did not anticipate was Upshur's prohibition of Grace Brothers from bidding, a rather bare contradiction of his announced aim of fostering competition. That was the act that rankled William Grace in early December when he heard about it. The secretary had to back off in the face of this strong remonstrance by the Graces. He promised to correct the error if any injustice appeared to have been committed.[57] Ivins was in Washington through the Christmas season and into January 1885 attempting to bring about precisely a correction of the "error."

One of the first steps was to secure the service of a good lawyer to represent the Grace interests before the government. Ivins found the ideal type: a prominent Washington attorney who was a personal friend of both President Chester Arthur and Secretary Chandler.[58] However, the need for such a well-placed lawyer never became necessary, for by February 20, 1885, the Upshur order discriminating against Grace Brothers was rescinded.[59] Secretary Chandler had obviously been persuaded by two factors: one, the pressure brought to bear by the mayor, and, two, the subsequent award of an exclusive three-year contract for servicing the fleet to the *English* firm of Thomas Shute & Co. This contract was modified to a one-year basis and free bidding was guaranteed in the future. Politics and patriotism were blended into a satisfactory, commonsense solution from the Grace point of view.

That Grace Brothers and Lawler in Callao charged the fleet a handsome price for goods and produce was probably true. But they were certainly willing to modify their prices when faced with losing the navy's business. William, as well as Michael, Ned Eyre, and the other partners and associates, was more than happy to knock heads with other merchants and entrepreneurs and lower or raise prices to achieve the best position. What fueled William's temper was being peremptorily eliminated from the competition. He was willing to bet and win or lose, but he felt it was wrong to be barred from betting. And he was right. Besides—here we see some of those intangibles at work that favored the Graces throughout the latter half of the nineteenth century—a new administration William Grace had helped elect (Grover Cleveland) was about to be inaugurated in March 1885. William Grace was not in the habit of soliciting unearned favors, but it did make sense to argue for competition. And it made especially good sense to argue for favoring Americans—even though naturalized and possessing a nice Irish brogue—at the expense of the English.

The whole business of servicing steamships operating between Europe, North America, and Latin America, whether queens of the Pacific Mail Steamship Co. plying between the Isthmus of Panama and the United States, or American warships on station in the Pacific, heightened William and Michael Grace's awareness of the inexorable replacement of sail by steam. Additionally, new and improved cable services provided near instantaneous communications, enhancing the capability of steamships to operate with timeliness and predictability.

By the late 1880s the Graces were seriously entertaining the idea of establishing a steamship service between New York and the West Coast of South America. It would roughly parallel the Merchants Line already supplying service to the area and, perhaps most important, would be the first steamship line along the route.[60] The Graces were aware that the pioneer on this stage would have the upper hand. They were also aware that steamship operations were expensive and almost invariably necessitated some form of government subsidy to survive and be profitable. They entered into negotiations with a British steamship line, Greenock Steamship Co. of Greenock, Scotland; the Chilean national steamship company, Compañía Sudamericana de Vapores; and the governments of Chile and the United States to explore the possibilities.

Greenock owned a fleet of eleven steamers and had two under construction in 1889, and was a likely partner in establishing a new line from England to New York and the West Coast of South America. William C. Tripler made the initial contact for Grace in September 1889, and convinced Greenock of the feasibility of the undertaking based upon the potential freight along such a route.[61] Greenock, like Grace, wanted to study the potential business carefully before making any commitments. It was especially interested in rates, cargoes, and the profit margin forecast. Its insistence upon detail was matched easily by the Grace penchant for thoroughness.

Of course, there could be no guarantee of how well a steamship line might do since the trade had so far been done entirely by sailing ships. Grace began cautiously. Actual experience with the steamers could alone definitely establish the local expenses of such a business.[62] But, W. R. Grace & Co. could produce some detailed estimates and persuasive reasons for establishing such a line.

The potential expenses of steamshipping from New York were covered with Grace's typical attention to the smallest detail. On wharfage, "we would say that, especially at the outstart, ten days should be calculated for steamer's loading, and it would be necessary to engage a covered wharf, with privilege of accumulating cargo thereon for, say, one week prior to steamer's arrival."[63] Stevedoring or loading general cargo "would be 40¢ to 45¢ per ton weight or measurement; as likewise for putting on coal."[64] Coal for the steamer would cost about $3.25 per ton of 2,240 pounds, laid alongside the ship. These were figures provided by people immersed in the shipping world of New York. William Grace had not only operated windjammers for many years before 1889, but also occasionally chartered steamers and ran them to all parts of Latin America. Nonetheless, there would be little room for error in the establishment of this new line, and nowhere was the guesswork—based on experience—more important than in estimating the types and quantities of cargo available for any such new service.

The leading commodities being shipped from New York were lard in kegs, nails in kegs, refined petroleum in cases, rosin, and refined sugar, all of which, being bulk items, of low value, could not stand high rates.[65] Other products such as agricultural implements would be charged slightly higher rates.[66] Grace emphasized that while the business in the beginning might be modest, direct steam communication with the West Coast would attract much merchandise that was presently shipped via Panama, and also via Liverpool and Hamburg.[67] In other words, create the means, and the means will stimulate new business. The Graces sounded a note of urgency in attempting to persuade Greenock to join them in setting up such a line. It was inevitable that steam communication would soon become established with the West Coast, and it was thus imperative to pioneer the route and ensure a commanding influence.[68] Besides, the Graces' Merchants Line was being hotly challenged by a new sailing line that might itself soon expand into steam. What made the matter even more prickly for the Graces was the name of their new competitor, Charles Flint.[69]

Flint and his partners in this new "West Coast Line," Hemenway and Grown, quickly grabbed the lion's share of a contract with the North & South American Construction Co. to ship 14 locomotives, 115 construction cars, and 200 freight cars to South America.* Michael Grace visited with Hemenway to feel out this new competitor, who said that he had no wish to harm the Graces, a demurral in which Grace "had no faith, for the opposition has been undertaken in obvious antagonism, and we must now prepare to meet the issue."[70] Flint might well next undertake the establishment of steamship service, and this would be intolerable to William and Michael Grace, already stung from being shoved out of the lucrative rubber business in Brazil by the brilliant and adroit Flint.

Greenock, however, did not share the same sense of urgency. It wanted to study the matter more, especially since it did not anticipate a rapid rise in the rates, which were far from remunerative at that time.[71] Tripler, Grace's advocate before Greenock, continued to present a sanguine picture of the potential new business, pointing especially to the very probable increase in the shipment of manganese ores from the West Coast to North America. Greenock was skeptical of Tripler's rosy picture, especially with regard to manganese. It was a bulk cargo that merited only low rates, and Greenock thought Tripler was exaggerating the potential.[72] So, no steamers were forthcoming from Greenock in the year 1889, although company officials did look forward to meeting Michael Grace when he next appeared in London.[73]

If a line of steamers were to be established, with or without Greenock's assistance, the first ports of call on the West Coast would be those of Chile, and the Graces were very interested in obtaining some form of subsidy from the Chilean government, or entering into a partnership with the Chilean national steamship company, the Compañía Sudamericana de Vapores.

The Compañía Sudamericana was one of the oldest steamship companies in operation in the Pacific, preceded only by

---

*This turned out to be a pretty poor deal, since the construction company never built a mile of railroad because of its fraudulent nature. See below in this chapter.

the British Pacific Steam Navigation Company.[74] The Suda-mericana had been formed in 1872 by consolidating several smaller companies, and it was controlled by the Lyon family. The general manager in 1889 was Heraclio Lyon.

In approaching Lyon, Grace once again stressed the importance of being first before they were preempted by some Tom, Dick, or Harry, or Charley Flint. Grace might have been thinking: "We apprehend that the West Coast service may be spasmodically opened by some transient steamer, and we do not know how soon."[75] Grace proposed to Lyon that the Suda-mericana and W. R. Grace & Co. enter into a joint venture.[76]

Grace furthermore sought an operating subsidy from the United States or Chilean government, or from both, the company's premise being that such a steamship service would benefit both countries. The issue of subsidies was related, once again, to the necessity of pioneering the service. "The question of increased commercial relations with South America facilitated by steam communication, is now a subject of much discussion in this country and this fact, together with the immense advantage of being first in the field, indicates the desirability of prompt and active efforts to secure a business which has such a promising future."[77]

How much of a subsidy was necessary? Grace suggested that four or five steamers be built especially for the service, and that a subsidy of £2,000 to £2,500 for each round trip be provided; another alternative would be for the Chilean government to guarantee 6 percent of the capital of the company.[78] Grace was also actively soliciting a subsidy from the United States government, hoping that the new Republican president, Benjamin Harrison, would promote a discussion of subsidies to new lines of American steamers.[79] The ideal situation for Grace would have been for Chile and the United States to subsidize jointly a mixed line of steamers under the Chilean and United States flags, owned by either the Compañía Sudamericana or W. R. Grace & Co. The important point was to get started and be the first in the field.

Grace also projected for Lyon the size of the potential new steamers, the traffic, the cargo, rates, and other germane matters. The steamers should be capable of carrying three thousand to four thousand tons mixed weight and measurement cargo, with a speed of about ten knots, and power to increase to about twelve knots. Such steamers could be built, thoroughly equipped for use, for not over £50,000; overall capital required would be about £200,000 to £250,000.[80]

There would probably be enough cargo obtainable in New York to load the steamers entirely for the West Coast and operate them on a monthly basis. They could steam direct from New York to Punta Arenas on the Straits of Magellan with sufficient coal on board to carry them to Aranco Bay, making the trip between New York and Valparaiso in thirty-five to forty days. If occasionally sufficient cargo was not offered for the West Coast, they could easily fill up with cargo for Montevideo and Buenos Aires, calling there en route. For the return voyage they would probably have to carry nitrate of soda, wool, and perhaps other Peruvian products; when pressed for freight, some manganese ore could be loaded. If still with incomplete cargoes, they could call in at Santos, serving São Paulo, or at Rio de Janeiro, during the season, to fill up with coffee, or at Bahía or Pernambuco for sugar.[81]

It was an optimistic picture, but one reinforced by trade statistics that Grace supplied Lyon. On sailing vessels alone, over 25,000 tons of goods were shipped annually from New York to Chile; from New York to Peru, 17,500 tons; the tonnage moving from the East Coast of North America to Chile and Peru was over 54,000 tons per year. Furthermore, shipments of general merchandise to the River Plate from New York alone were running at 60,000 to 75,000 tons of general cargo per annum.[82] On the overall scene, trade was increasing, and the thrust of Grace's message was to persuade Lyon and the Chileans to move with speed.

Lyon and the Compañía Sudamericana were already making their own plans, some of which proposed to parallel existing routes between Chile and Europe, and others to establish services between Chile and Central America. Although the Sudamericana usually competed fiercely with the imposing Pacific Steam Navigation Company, which pioneered and dominated steam operations in the Pacific, the Chileans sought an accommodation with the PSNC in the establishment of these new services. In 1889 the Sudamericana was already negotiating with the PSNC to establish a line of steamers from Valparaiso to Liverpool.[83]

The Chileans also had a service to Panama which had been inaugurated in 1874 with a generous subsidy of a hundred thousand pesos supplied by the Chilean government, renewable every ten years.[84] Only with such subsidies could the Chileans compete effectively against the PSNC, whose size and British government support endowed it with a competitive advantage.

One other central factor underlay Grace's interest in pioneering steam service from the East Coast of the United States to the West Coast of South America: the future isthmian canal. If the Panama Canal were ever completed, or, alternatively, a canal were to be cut through Nicaragua, the accessibility of the South American West Coast to the United States East Coast would be dramatically improved by halving the time needed to trade between the two areas. The English PSNC had proven conclusively that its pioneer services gave it a huge advantage over later competitors, and Grace meant to repeat that success.

Always thinking on several fronts at once, Grace urged the Sudamericana not only to join the Graces in establishing a service from New York to the Pacific through the Straits of Magellan, but to consider a Panama route as well. Grace suggested to the Sudamericana that it team up and challenge the monopoly held by the American-owned Pacific Mail Steamship Co. across the isthmian route by virtue of an agreement with the Panama Railroad Co.

Although the New York to the West Coast line via the Straits of Magellan would be the pioneer, Grace could eventually follow it up by running a couple of steamers to Colon, the Atlantic terminal of the Panama Railroad, to connect with the existing Sudamericana service from Chile to Panama. The overall suggestion came from Grace's knowledge that the Panama Railroad Co.'s contract, which gave the Pacific Mail Steamship Co. a great advantage, was due to expire, and a strong probability existed that the railroad company would not renew it.[85] The arrangement between the Panama Railroad Co. and the Pacific Mail Steamship Co. was not in fact broken until 1897, and then only because of the intense pressure put on them by the PSNC. But William Grace obviously had wind of the forthcoming changes.

In spite of attempts by the Graces to keep their ideas confidential, the Panama Railroad Co. and the Pacific Mail Steamship Co. were suspicious of overtures by Grace and the Sudamericana to pioneer new routes or parallel old ones that would compete with the Panama route.[86] The Chileans were as aggressive as the Graces, planning a new line with government subsidies to engage in the Valparaiso to Liverpool run. President Jorge Balmaceda was personally interested in this project, since it promised, among other things, cheap transportation for colonists and immigrants.[87]

Although the Chilean project was not realized until after World War I, the threat it posed to Panama's interests was considerable, since any new line would deflect trade away from the isthmus. So would the new line of steamers that W. R. Grace & Co. was proposing between the East Coast of the United States and the West Coast of South America via the Straits of Magellan.

The arrangements with the Chileans ultimately bore no more fruit than had earlier negotiations with Greenock in Scotland. W. R. Grace & Co. nonetheless moved ahead, effectively taking its own advice: if we do not initiate the business soon, it will fall to others. In 1890 and 1891 the firm chartered two British cargo steamers, the *Mount Tabor* and *Balcarres Brook*, loaded them at New York, and sent them through the straits to Chile and Peru.[88] The tryout proved a success, and in 1893 the British steamer *Bayley* was bought and renamed the *Coya*. It was the first steamship of the New York & Pacific Steamship Co., Ltd., organized by W. R. Grace & Co. and incorporated in England in late 1892.[89] In 1893 three more steamers were ordered built in England, the *Condor, Capac,* and *Cacique,* each with a carrying capacity of about four thousand tons. The New York & Pacific Steamship Co. was the direct predecessor of Grace Line

Why build in England? Why incorporate in England? William and Michael Grace were both naturalized American citizens. William was especially attached to the United States and W. R. Grace & Co. was well entrenched in New York. One can clearly discern here the emergence of a multinational characteristic which tends to reduce the effects of national boundaries and priorities as much as possible, and to accent a global perspective. Yet, another more immediate factor persuaded the Graces to look abroad as they diversified into steam. The sad fact was, the United States had failed to provide American shipbuilders and shippers with the incentives to make steamshipping competitive with the English and other major maritime powers.

Writing to Lyon in 1889, the Grace firm adumbrated its plans: "In putting the cost of the steamers at £50,000, it is of course contemplated to build them in England."[90] American law since 1789 had forbidden ships from operating under the United States flag if purchased or built abroad, so the New York & Pacific steamers entered the Grace service by sporting the Union Jack from their stern masts.

The American merchant marine had slipped precipitously since the Civil War, during which more than half of the imports and exports had been carried in American bottoms. By the end of the nineteenth century, less than 10 percent of American trade was being shipped in U.S. flag carriers.

The 1789 law had been enacted to promote the American shipping and shipbuilding industries, and for the next sixty years it fulfilled the goal nobly. But, since the Civil War, Americans were slowly driven away from their own flag by the increasing difference in costs to build and operate ships between the United States and, say, Great Britain, which actively subsidized its merchant marine. So, like today, when shipowners often operate their vessels under flags of "convenience," such as the Liberian or Panamanian ensigns, sentimentality played small part in organizing the New York & Pacific Steamship Co. William Grace may have preferred to operate his steamships, like his downeasters and windjammers of the Merchants Line, under the American flag, but with no subsidy from the United States government there was no reasonable alternative but to incorporate and register one's ships in England.

W. R. Grace & Co. continued to press its case for United States subsidies, and persistently lobbied for the cause of an American merchant marine languishing in the early twentieth century. Moreover, the British registry of Grace steamers sometimes complicated their positions when the American government did consider subsidies during that period. For example, in 1907 a bill was debated by Congress to encourage fast mail service in American bottoms between the United States, Hawaii, Cuba, and South America.[91] No vessel was to be entitled to a subsidy, contemplated at five dollars for every knot traveled in the service, unless it could run at sixteen knots, and the ships had to be fitted to carry mail and passengers. Naturally, only steamers built in the United States would qualify for the subsidies.

Grace ran slow steamers around the Straits of Magellan to the West Coast. Would they be threatened by the new bill? William Grace's son, Joseph Peter, by then a vice president of the firm and soon to become president (William R. Grace died in 1904), thought not, because the subsidy would not apply to steamers running through the Straits of Magellan.[92] How would the fast, new American vessels contemplated stack up against Grace's slow steamers running under the British flag? Again, Joseph Grace figured the contents of the proposed bill would not stimulate challengers to Grace's slow British steamers.[93] If, on the other hand, the San Francisco–South American West Coast trade were to grow, Joseph Grace thought that some time in the future Grace should consider taking advantage of the subsidy by running sixteen-knot boats from San Francisco to Panama and then along the West Coast of South America, in opposition to the Compañía Sudamericana de Vapores and the

Pacific Steam Navigation Company, which "give such a very indifferent service at present."[94] While the United States procrastinated in support of its merchant marine, Grace certainly did not dally in anticipation of American subsidies. The establishment of the line in 1894 attests to that. Nor did Grace give up on obtaining a Chilean subsidy.

Chile, in fact, had always represented a fertile field for investment by W. R. Grace & Co., if we exclude the fractious decade of the 1880s, when Michael Grace was so deeply involved in negotiating the Grace Contract that somewhat abused Chilean sensibilities. Although the alliance with the Compañía Sudamericana had not worked out in 1889, Grace again petitioned the Chilean government for a subsidy in 1902.[95]

The Grace request was for £25,000 to establish a service between Valparaiso, Punta Arenas, and Brazil. By then the New York & Pacific had increased its fleet to six steamers, having added the *Cumbal* and the *Cuzco*—4,259 and 4,302 tons, respectively—to the original four. According to Claudio Veliz, Chile's most distinguished maritime historian, Grace offered to put this fleet under the Chilean flag and to establish a regular service between Valparaiso and the United States, with stops at Punta Arenas on the Straits of Magellan, Brazil, and other intermediate points.[96] As concessions to Chile, the Grace steamers would carry two Chilean officers and two Chilean engineers, Chilean mail would be transported at no expense, and Chilean state employees would receive a 50 percent fare reduction. The proposal was signed by John Eyre and dated December 18, 1902.

Then a rival firm made a counter offer. Beeche, Duval & Co. promoted itself as a Chilean company, located in Chile, and with the majority of its shares held by Chileans. The ensuing dispute between Beeche and Grace reflected a rivalry that will be dealt with in a later chapter. The immediate upshot of the competing proposals was that the Chilean government rejected them both.[97]

Two important points emerge from this incident. One, Grace was determined to make the steamship business work and work well between the United States and the West Coast of South America, regardless of which flag had to be flown. Second, relations between the house of Grace and Chile had thawed considerably in the last decade of the century.

The cordiality that developed traced ironically to the souring of relations between the United States and Chile that almost brought them to war in 1891–92. Once again the Graces moved into a dangerous diplomatic wrangle which thrust them onto center stage of inter-American relations. What followed was a virtuoso performance of tact, pressure, and compromise.

9

The Balmaceda Revolution

Chile's relations with the United States turned cool during the course of the War of the Pacific and remained chilled for most of the decade. The United States had made intensive efforts to mediate the war and, until early 1882 at least, to help prevent Peru from losing substantial territories to Chile. After the war, Chilean nationalists moved to harvest the fruits of the victory over Peru and Bolivia and to raise Chile into the ranks of a major power in the hemisphere. If this alienated Argentina, Brazil, the United States, or any other contender for influence in the Americas, so be it. Chile had demonstrated its prowess and stood by its ability to defend and indeed project its interests with strength and success.

The circumstances and proceedings of the First International American Conference (the forerunner of the Pan-American Union, now renamed the Organization of American States), which convened in Washington in October 1889, demonstrated full well, from Chile's point of view, the ill will and jealousy borne by such major states as Argentina and Brazil toward Chile. That the conference was the inspiration of Secretary of State James G. Blaine—an old friend of Peru—and that it was held in the capital of the United States merely tended to reinforce Chile's distrust of Washington.

Briefly, Chile agreed to attend this conference only if the agenda was kept clear of discussing international arbitration as a means of settling international disputes—past, present, and future.[1] The Chileans were sure that Argentina, Brazil, Peru, Bolivia, or even the United States would take advantage of the conference to meddle in the Tacna-Arica dispute between Chile and Peru, and in other unsettled affairs originating from the

War of the Pacific. The United States persisted in including Chile in the conference and promised that the agenda would include only relatively innocuous questions of economic and commercial content. Chile agreed to attend under these circumstances.

From October 1889 to January 1890 the conference went well, discussions being limited to various aspects of rules and procedures and other non-controversial matters. Then Argentina and Brazil, the latter having just overthrown its monarchy and seeking a new era of conviviality with its fellow republic to the south, jointly sponsored a resolution calling for international arbitration in all matters of territorial transfers issuing from acts of war between nations in the hemisphere. Not only was this resolution to apply " 'to differences that may arise in the future, but also in those that . . . are now under actual discussion.' "[2] Chile was indignant, and the United States faced the potential embarrassment of hearing the Treaty of Guadalupe Hidalgo discussed publicly and officially once again.[3] The Mexican–American War had yielded immense territories to the United States (California, Arizona, New Mexico, to mention a few), and that subject—as far as the U.S. was concerned—was closed.

Blaine called the delegates of Mexico, Argentina, Brazil, and Chile together on February 19, 1890, to try and reach some form of compromise. The Chileans obtained the removal of the most obnoxious portion of the arbitration proposal—the retroactive clause—but then Chile abstained when the Arbitration Treaty was signed in May 1890. Argentina refrained from signing as well. The treaty was never ratified by any of the seven countries that signed it.[4]

Chileans were outraged that such a resolution had even been introduced by Argentina and Brazil. It was direct intervention in their internal affairs—the Tacna-Arica dispute being considered in that category—and totally unacceptable. That the United States might have suffered potential embarrassment as well was too bad. It was clear to Chileans that "American conferences had come to be associated with pro-Peruvian intervention in settling the Tacna-Arica controversy," and this was waving the red flag before the bull.[5]

Within a year of the conclusion of the First International American Conference, Chile's congress revolted against its president and touched off a domestic crisis of immense importance. The civil war that erupted between the president, José Manuel Balmaceda, and the Congressional party, was widespread and quickly involved Grace & Co. in Valparaiso as

well. How William and Michael Grace and their various Eyre
cousins and nephews threaded through this crisis is fascinating.
Not only did they support the winning side, the Congressionalists, but they also got in a good lick at their old nemesis
Charles Flint, *and* managed to increase their credibility and
stake in Chile at a time when that country was turning more
and more to Europe to counterbalance the growing influence
of the United States in South America.

The Grace house had been established in Valparaiso on October 19, 1881.[6] Like the other Grace houses, it was a partnership, in this instance shared by Noel West, the manager; John
W. Grace and Edward Eyre, both in Lima at that time; and
William Grace, Michael Grace, and Charles Flint, then in New
York. Although Grace-Chile initially faced a somewhat hostile
attitude from Chileans who remembered the Grace association
with Peru during the War of the Pacific, the cultivation of business and goodwill by West and his successor, John Grace, led
Grace & Co. to a position as leading exporter of nitrates and
wool to the United States by 1890.[7] John Grace left Chile in
1887. After a short interim under a rather unsuccessful manager
named George Duval, a nephew from the Eyre tribe, William,
was sent from Lima to take charge in 1890.[8]

Grace also had a claim against Chile stemming from the 1877
concession by Peru to Grace for the exclusive sale of nitrates
in the United States from the province of Tarapaca. Tarapaca
had, of course, been transferred to Chile after the War of the
Pacific. Subsequently, Chile was sued by Grace to honor that
contract. About a dozen such claims by American citizens
against the spoliation of their property by the Chileans were
eventually filed by the United States government in the mid-
1880s. The suits produced very little compensation when finally
settled in 1894, but their existence tended to remind Chileans
that Grace had been very much a Peruvian house before and
during the War of the Pacific. Grace's problems with the Chilean
government were nothing, however, when compared with the
intransigent congress that President Balmaceda faced in Santiago in 1891.

★ ★ ★

Balmaceda had been elected to the chief magistracy of Chile
in 1886 after a distinguished public service career. He was descended from colonial aristocracy and possessed autocratic in-
clinations that did not augur well in a country then pushing
for more parliamentary control of the nation's destinies. Never-

theless, Balmaceda was very much a liberal who had absorbed the ideals of Rousseau, Montesquieu, and other enlightened thinkers. Economically, he skirted away from the classic nineteenth-century liberal doctrine of laissez faire, further complicating his character. He was a proselytizer for active state intervention in the economy to stimulate and guide it toward definite goals. This philosophy clashed with a majority of Chile's influential capitalists, for the moneyed class promoted an open marketplace economy. Their power was centered in the congress and it became the focus of discontent. Much like the circumstances surrounding the English Civil War of the seventeenth century, which pitted an unyielding, authoritarian monarchy (James I and Charles I) against an equally inflexible legislative body (the Parliament that eventually gave rise to Oliver Cromwell), there existed other complex factors of major importance.

Balmaceda not only offended the congress, but his suppression of a massive general strike by nitrate workers in Iquique in 1890 with federal troops aligned him against the aspirations of the growing labor movement in the north. Copper miners, longshoremen, and other working-class sectors allied themselves sympathetically with the nitrate workers against Balmaceda.

In another realm, Balmaceda worked actively against a plan by the Conservative and Radical parties to increase municipal autonomy at the expense of the national government. Balmaceda opposed this plan to dilute the executive authority and criticism of his regime grew more and more strident. In response, Balmaceda vitriolically denounced his critics and purged those in government agencies under his control.[9] By late 1890 Balmaceda's opposition included most of the important members of all political parties and even the hero of the War of the Pacific, Gen. Manuel Baquedano.

In disgust with Balmaceda, congress unilaterally adjourned and simply left the scene early in January 1891, especially antagonized by a speech the president delivered on January 1. In this address—Balmaceda's "Manifesto to the Nation"—the president recycled last year's budget for the coming year since congress had refused to pass the appropriations bill presented to it earlier. Besides, Balmaceda observed, congressional elections would take place in two months and voters could then ratify or reject his acts. Provoked to its limits, congress marched off to Valparaiso and boarded naval vessels under the command of Capt. Jorge Montt, who transferred the angry legislators north to Iquique. There congress denounced Balmaceda and called for the restoration of constitutional government. Balmaceda secured the temporary allegiance of the army by sweetening their salaries 50 percent and the civil war was joined.[10]

The American minister in Santiago was a naturalized citizen from Ireland, appointed to his post in 1889 as a reward for political services to President Benjamin Harrison. Patrick Egan had been a lieutenant of the flamboyant Irish nationalist leader Parnell. Hotheaded and rebellious, Egan made a good Irish patriot, but he eventually had to flee in 1882, one step ahead of the English authorities. A successful businessman in Ireland, Egan repeated the act in the United States. He settled in the Midwest and staunchly supported the Republican party. In 1886 he became a citizen and in return for his loyalty and support in the presidential election of 1888, Harrison appointed him minister to Chile.

William Grace was satisfied with the appointment of Egan to the post. Egan's antipathy toward the British might, after all, help the cause of the United States in Chile and perhaps even facilitate a prompt and just settlement of the nitrate claim that Grace held against Chile.[11] Grace provided Egan with letters of introduction to friends in Chile to smooth the new minister's arrival. Then the revolution erupted in 1891 and Egan rather blatantly sided with Balmaceda.

Egan figured the Congressionalists were pro-British. After all, they espoused the cause of parliament over the executive authority and launched their revolution from the north of Chile where the British presence was prominent. Conversely, Balmaceda was considered pro-American by Egan and his dispatches back to the United States reflected this bias.[12] Egan had also been snubbed by the British commercial establishment in Santiago, further reinforcing his natural penchant—being a good Irish nationalist—to despise the English nation and distrust its alleged agents, the Congressionalists.

The U.S. State Department was inclined to accept the opinion of its minister in Santiago. On the other hand, Pedro Montt, the minister sent in June 1891 by the Congressionalist party to Washington to represent its cause, worked hard to deny what were considered Egan's false, misleading, and partisan reports from Chile.[13] The American press soon entered the act as well. The *Boston Herald* "attributed the inaccurate accounts on the Chilean civil war given out by the State Department to the partisanship of Egan, adding that it was disgraceful for any man who had worked so hard for the cause of Irish independence to have endeavored to saddle the Chileans with tyranny."[14]

Some discerned a more material motive behind Egan's support of Balmaceda. Egan's son had served as a lawyer for a railroad company, the North & South American Construction Co., which had received large railroad contracts from Balmaceda's administration. Although the company never laid a mile of track, Egan's son profited from the commissions and many attributed his gains to his father's close association and support of Balmaceda.[15]

Egan's anglophobia was well known by the Chileans even before the civil war erupted. When first named to the Santiago post in 1889, the Chilean minister to Washington, Emilio C. Varas, described Egan as one of the most notorious home rulers whose Irish nationalistic sentiment was common knowledge.[16] Newspapers questioned the wisdom of sending such a passionate critic of England to a country with a large British commercial population; the *Omaha Herald* commented cryptically that it hoped " 'Egan would remember when he is in Santiago that he is not the leader of an anti-British crusade, but the representative of this republic instead.' "[17]

Nothing else exacerbated the ill will between the Congressionalists and the United States government more in this initial stage of the civil war than the issue of arms. Arms and munitions are crucial in any great struggle with a military dimension and the Chilean civil war was no exception.

In anticipation of hostilities, Balmaceda's representative in Washington, Prudencio Lazcano, had promptly placed an order of arms with the firm of Flint & Co.[18] One could almost anticipate that William and Michael Grace would support the Congressionalists' cause, if for no other reason than that Flint was selling arms to the Balmacedistas.

Pedro Montt, the Congressionalists' representative in Washington, had been joined by Ricardo Trumbull, a Yale-educated Chilean and a member of the distinguished Trumbull family of Connecticut.[19] Trumbull was charged with securing arms for the Congressionalists, and upon his arrival in May 1891, he stopped in at W. R. Grace & Co.

William Grace was traveling around the country and John Grace was temporarily minding the store. His instructions were to deal with the Congressionalists cordially and supply them with anything, except arms and munitions. There were no reservations, however, on supplying Trumbull with good advice and recommendations; and W. R. Grace & Co. had some experience in the arms trade.

Not only had the Graces assisted Peru during the War of the Pacific, but they also helped Peru rearm in the middle and late 1880s. Rifles, carbines, muskets, cartridges, primers, Gatling guns, and other tools of the business had been ordered—sometimes to specification—and purchased for the Peruvian government by the Graces.[20] In the course of this business the Graces dealt frequently with such prestigious armorers as the Winchester and the Remington firms in the United States, as well as with several abroad.

Conversant with the trade, the Graces certainly could put at Ricardo Trumbull's disposal a great deal of practical experience. Grace & Co., Valparaiso, it will be recalled, was also the leading exporter of nitrate of soda in 1890 to the United States, and all of Chile's nitrates were mined in the northern provinces then under the control of the Congressionalists. Although William Grace described his sympathies publicly as "neutral," they could be construed as friendly toward the Congressionalists, especially in the light of Trumbull's subsequent efforts to ship arms directly from California to Iquique in northern Chile. William Grace's firm assisted them, but the episode turned into a bitter and frustrating experience for the Congressionalists.

The United States had been caught in a somewhat delicate situation by the civil war in Chile. Revolutions, by their very nature, are seditions against legally established or traditional governments. Only when they succeed do they pass into legitimacy that validates their principles and goals. Foreign governments professing neutrality have one of three choices: maintain relations only with the legitimate government; recognize the revolutionaries as belligerents and decide the merits of each request in the light of the ongoing situation; recognize both contenders as equals. In mid-1891 Secretary of State Blaine opted for the second course. Although the United States declared itself neutral, Blaine also ruled that anything, including arms and munitions, was a legal article of trade between the United States and the two contending factions in Chile.

While several steamers chartered by Grace were loading on both American coasts with goods for the Congressionalists, Trumbull traveled out to California in May. There he intended to organize a shipment of arms so desperately needed by the Congressionalists to launch an offensive strike from strongholds in the north of the country.

To this end the Congressionalists bought a steamer from the Compañía Sudamericana de Vapores and dispatched it north to San Diego to pick up munitions to be purchased by Trumbull.[21] The *Itata*, flying the Chilean flag, arrived at San Diego on May 3. Its captain declared he was en route to San Francisco from Iquique with a load of merchandise and passengers, and, furthermore, that the *Itata* was owned by W. R. Grace & Co. While reprovisioning, it was seized on the afternoon of May 5 by a federal marshal.[22]

William Grace disclaimed ownership of the *Itata*, admitting only that his firm served as agents in the United States for the Compañía Sudamericana de Vapores, the previous owner of the impounded steamer. Newspaper headlines stated that the *Itata* was seized for violating neutrality laws. Meanwhile, Trumbull was busy in San Francisco preparing a small coasting schooner, the *Robert & Minnie*, to sail with a most valuable cargo for the Congressionalist cause.

Schooners such as the *Robert & Minnie* were not required to register goods or file a manifest since they were involved in the domestic coastal trade. Trumbull felt fairly secure as he quietly supervised the loading of her unmarked cargo only recently shipped by rail from New York: fifty thousand rifles in two hundred fifty cases and two million rounds of ammunition in two thousand boxes.[23] Trumbull intended to rendezvous off the coast of Southern California with the *Itata* and transfer this precious cargo to the steamer.

He loaded the *Robert & Minnie* as secretly as possible, hoping to maintain the element of surprise for the Congressionalists. The ultimate strategy of the Congressionalists was to transport rapidly their army south and capture Santiago. Speed and secrecy were essential, especially since Congressionalist control of the sea was being threatened by two new cruisers the Balmacedistas had received from England. Equipped with new torpedoes supplied by Flint in Montevideo, they had steamed through the Straits of Magellan and sunk the Congressionalists ironclad *Blanco Encalada*, a noble veteran of the Chilean cause from the War of the Pacific.[24]

Trumbull, however, was tailed by a private detective, and Flint's agent in San Francisco, J. F. Chapman, soon spread the word of the planned rendezvous between the *Robert & Minnie* and the *Itata*. On Flint's advice, an international lawyer and former American minister to Mexico, Russia, and Spain, John

W. Foster, was hired by Prudencio Lazcano, the Balmacedista minister to Washington, to block this possible rendezvous. The *Robert & Minnie* managed to escape in time. But, as noted above, the *Itata* was boarded by a federal marshal in San Diego, acting on Foster's judicial motion maintaining that the *Itata* was intent on violating American neutrality laws.

Before the courts could hear the case, the *Itata* dramatically broke loose. On the second day of her seizure, the federal marshal left the ship in the hands of a deputy while he chugged out in a tug to pursue the *Robert & Minnie*. The *Itata*, its steam still up, slipped its lines and got under way with the deputy aboard, contentedly drinking and playing poker below decks. Three days later U.S. marshals boarded the *Robert & Minnie*, but it carried no arms or munitions.[25]

While the case for impounding the *Itata* in San Diego had been weak to nonexistent, a real infraction of the law was committed when it broke arrest. The American press was outraged by this insult of American laws and dignity. "Chilean pirates" were scourged in editorials and the Congressionalist cause certainly was tarred by the *Itata*'s escape.[26]

Immediately after *Itata* broke arrest and headed for the rendezvous with the *Robert & Minnie*, the U.S. attorney general and the secretary of the navy ordered the cruiser *Charleston* in pursuit.[27] It sortied from San Francisco and there was some speculation of an impending sea battle between the *Charleston* and any warship dispatched by the Congressionalists to escort the *Itata*.

The possibility of a shootout on the high seas and the complete rupture of relations between the United States and the Congressionalists prompted William to send Michael to Washington posthaste. When Michael confirmed that the *Charleston*'s orders were indeed to take the *Itata* under any circumstances, he prevailed upon Pedro Montt to persuade the Congressionalists to promise to give up the *Itata* as soon as it reached Chile.

The chase of the *Itata* became more of a race, the *Charleston* arriving in Iquique on June 4, one day ahead of the Chilean steamer. It was given up as promised, along with the arms and munitions, and escorted by the *Charleston* back to San Diego. The two ships had to leave Iquique under the cover of darkness to escape Chileans enraged by the incident.[28] The United States district court at San Diego "eventually acquitted the *Itata* of violation of American neutrality laws on the grounds that a foreign ship, even though it had violated international law within the territory of another nation, could not be pursued by that nation beyond its territory into any part of the high seas."[29]

That ruling only served to vindicate the Congressionalists' contentions.

Minister Egan intruded into the scene about this time and characteristically offended the Congressionalists even more. Before the *Itata* was removed from Iquique by the *Charleston*, Isidoro Errazuriz, then conducting foreign affairs for the Congressionalists, unsuccessfully appealed to Secretary of State Blaine to allow the *Itata's* cargo of guns and munitions to remain in Iquique in the care of Adm. M. B. McCann commander of the United States Pacific Squadron, pending disposition of the case in San Diego.[30] This failed, but the disappointment of the Congressionalists was nothing compared to the anger provoked by a letter sent by Egan to Errazuriz.

In an attempt to mediate the civil war, Egan dispatched a message to Errazuriz through Admiral McCann, then in Iquique. The note contained the opinion that Balmaceda could not be dislodged, with the qualifying phrase, "if the army remained loyal."[31] In relaying the message, McCann neglected to add that phrase. The truncated letter infuriated Errazuriz and caused him to wonder "what good could come from United States good offices if its envoy had already made up his mind as to the outcome of the struggle." The congressional forces never forgave Egan—even when they learned the original, complete text of his letter.[32]

The failure of the *Itata's* mission only temporarily set back Congressionalist plans. A shipment of arms from Germany reached the Congressionalists shortly after the *Itata* incident. With these arms and a growing momentum in the Congressionalist favor, an army was embarked and transported south in August. It came ashore at Quintero Bay just north of Valparaiso on August 20. Observing the scene out of curiosity and to keep abreast of the war was Adm. George Brown aboard the *San Francisco*.[33] He sent a dispatch to the Navy Department routinely reporting the landing. Somehow the contents of this cable were leaked in Valparaiso, and the ever suspicious Congressionalists accused Brown of spying for the Balmacedistas by reporting on Congressionalist troop movements, concentrations, etc.

The fall of Balmaceda followed shortly after the Congressionalist army invaded the rich Central Valley of Chile. Santiago and Valparaiso rose against the president and much of the army deserted to the cause of the Congressionalists. Balmaceda took refuge in the Argentine embassy and waited until his legal term of office was completed. Honor and propriety satisfied, the president then put a bullet through his head. The Congressionalists assumed power early in September. They were rid of Balmaceda, but kept on feuding with the irascible Egan.

The new Congressionalist minister of foreign relations, M. A. Matta, had been dumbfounded by the alleged espionage of Admiral Brown during the the Quintero Bay landings. Egan was equally and characteristically intemperate and complained to Matta "about the scandalous charges that had been voiced against Brown, saying that they constituted 'a studied insult to the navy and the flag of the United States.' "[34] So began the relations between the new Chilean government and the United States minister to Santiago.

Back in the United States, Flint and the Graces jockeyed for advantage as matters rapidly developed in Chile. After the capture of the *Itata*, Flint gained the momentum and was named Balmaceda's consul general in New York (a position that Flint had held at the outbreak of the War of the Pacific). Then the fortunes of the Congressionalists began to ascend, and so did the Graces' prestige, culminating with the Congressionalist victory in early September. William Grace sent messages of congratulations to leaders.[35] Flint, meanwhile, attempted to discredit the Grace sympathy toward the Congressionalist cause. He produced evidence that implied W. R. Grace & Co. had dealt in arms with both the Balmaceda government and the Congressionalists.

Flint, in an interview with the *New York Herald* on September 22, asserted that his interest in Balmaceda was purely of a mercantile nature. Flint & Co. had sold arms to the Balmaceda government and reaped a commission, and so had W. R. Grace & Co., and at the same time.[36] Grace denied the charge, whereupon Flint supplied the *Herald* with facsimiles of bills of sale from the Winchester Co. to the Balmaceda government, each with the notation "paid by check W. R. Grace & Co."[37]

The money had indeed come from the treasury of W. R. Grace & Co., but it had belonged to the account of the Balmaceda government's legation in Washington, which had maintained a balance with Grace. William's firm promptly made public the check in question, drawn on W. R. Grace & Co. and payable to the order of Manuel J. Vega. Vega had been a subordinate of Balmaceda's minister in Washington, Lazcano. Vega had endorsed the check, for $6,900, to the Winchester Repeating Arms Co. While Grace and Flint traded jabs in the United States, Egan continued almost deliberately to bait the Congressionalists governing Chile after the middle of September.

The immediate issue centered on defeated Balmacedistas who took refuge in the United States legation early in September.

Egan also helped a number escape to board the American warship *Baltimore*, then in Valparaiso. While other legations in Santiago also accepted political refugees, Chilean animus was
directed toward Egan and the Americans. Egan and Matta, the
new minister of foreign relations, pelted each other with more
than two dozen angry and provocative notes during September
and October. Egan complained bitterly of the gross misbehavior
of Chilean authorities harassing the American legation, while
Matta asserted that the United States was harboring criminals
and subversives who were hatching plots under Egan's protection.[38] Egan demanded safe-conduct passes for many of the
hostages, and these requests were promptly denied by Matta.
Demonstrations by the public outside the legation and the arrest
and detention of people seen entering or leaving the legation
outraged the American minister. For example, on September
25 Egan shot off one note to Matta stating that "activities of
Chilean officials stationed in the vicinity of the legation were
'so extraordinary and incredible that I do not know of any
similar instances having occurred in any part of the world toward the legation of a friendly power.' "[39]

In Washington, Blaine and Harrison tended to support their
minister in Santiago. Blaine sympathized with Egan's anti-British sentiments, and the secretary felt it was especially important
to keep Egan on the post now that the Congressionalists, who
were pro-English, were in power. Blaine did nothing to mend
the already frayed relations between the two countries when
he repeated allegations made by Egan that the Chilean government planned to execute all those who had taken refuge in
the United States legation and then confiscate their property.[40]

Nothing of the sort was ever committed, but the American
public believed Blaine. At one point late in September, when
Egan was adamantly resisting Chilean demands to hand over
some of the refugees, President Harrison rattled the saber by
dramatically summoning his secretaries of war and navy. The
newspapers, perhaps rehearsing for the great outpouring of
jingoism that would precede the Spanish–American War at the
end of the decade, defined the issue for their readers with
characteristic and simplistic boldness. The *New York Evening
World* asked, "Will Warships Go to Chile?" And the *New York
Journal* observed, "It Looks as Though We Were Ready to
Fight."[41] Then, on October 16, a bar brawl between some
American sailors and Chilean civilians in Valparaiso almost
touched off the powder keg.

One hundred sailors had been granted liberty by the captain
of the *Baltimore*, Winfield S. Schley, and like sailors all over the

world, they took their liberty in exaggerated fashion. Drinking and carousing in the rowdier sections of Valparaiso led to inebriated bravado and then to a fight that erupted in one bar and poured out into the street. Before the Chilean police finally quelled the riotous sailors, American and Chilean, two of the *Baltimore* sailors had been killed and seventeen wounded.[42] One Chilean was wounded and ten Chileans and thirty Americans were hauled off to jail.

Two versions of the fight rapidly emerged, and they agreed on little more than the date of the incident. Captain Schley conducted an investigation within four days of the fracas. He reported to Washington on October 22 that the *Baltimore*'s sailors, unarmed and orderly in their demeanor, had been brazenly attacked by armed Chileans in large numbers. Furthermore, the police deliberately beat up the Americans while breaking up the fighting mob. *El Mercurio* reported a slightly more credible version. The American sailors, some armed, had earlier in the day been taunting Chileans and declaring there would be a good fight that evening. A donnybrook ensued in a bar, drawing many Chileans out of the surrounding saloons to join the action. Outnumbered, the Americans naturally got the worst of the combat before Chilean police managed to quell the brawl.[43]

Accepting Captain Schley's report uncritically and without corroboration from the Chilean authorities, William F. Wharton, acting as the interim secretary of state during an illness of Blaine's, instructed Egan to remonstrate with the Chilean government over the incident, obviously inspired "by hostility to the sailors as representatives of the United States government."[44] Egan sent a note to Matta on October 26. He demanded full and prompt reparation and the punishment of those guilty of perpetrating the premeditated, brutal attack on the innocent sailors of the *Baltimore*.

Matta replied the next day. The authority to investigate the matter lay with the judicial system of Chile. Santiago would await the official inquest to be made by the criminal court of Valparaiso, presided over by Judge E. Foster Recabarren.[45] Besides, the United States had only a few months before sent a similar, blunt note to Italy to keep cool while the American court system heard a case concerning the killing of certain Italian citizens by an American mob in New Orleans. What was good for the goose was good for the gander.

An off-year election was approaching in the United States and some political wags viewed the ensuing publicity given to the increasingly strained relations between Chile and the

United States in late October and early November as good elec-
tioneering. President Harrison would probably seek renomination in 1892 and the *New York Times* cynically headlined that
the *Baltimore* incident was "A Very Opportune Broil," adding,
"A Little Display of Jingoism Just Before the Election Thought
to Be Beneficial to the Party."[46]

The proceedings of the court presided over by Judge Recabarren in Valparaiso were "as distinguished for [their] length
as the Schley proceedings had been for their brevity."[47] No
report was available until late December, and Matta blamed the
tardiness of the court to uncooperative Americans, including
Egan, the *Baltimore's* crew, and the American consul at Valparaiso. There was no lack of finger-pointing as the fabric of
Chilean-American relations rapidly unraveled.

In New York William Grace received frequent communications from the Valparaiso house that the situation was growing
more difficult day by day.[48] Persuaded by responsible citizens
on both sides, Grace traveled to Washington to speak with
Blaine and Montt. Long conversations with both produced the
following impressions, which William sent to Michael on November 16: "Montt is a cold, careful man of great caution, very
slow & I think stubborn, patriotic, honest & . . . he does not
understand the American character."[49] Montt told Grace he was
convinced the United States had acted in bad faith by blatantly
favoring Balmaceda during the civil war. Grace agreed, except
he attributed the United States behavior not to bad faith but to
"bad information" from Egan.[50]

Blaine, on the other hand, was sick, and his illness condi-
tioned his erratic behavior. "His mind works differently under
his physical troubles from day to day."[51] Yet Blaine was to keep
the jingoists and the war hawks in Harrison's cabinet from
gaining the upper hand, while sustaining United States honor
and prestige in the face of the *Baltimore* incident.

Grace persuaded Montt to impress Santiago with the necessity of offering reparations and an apology if the impasse was
to be broken. He conveyed Montt's promise to do so to Blaine,
adding that Montt's cousin Jorge had just been elected president of Chile and had publicly expressed himself in a friendly
fashion toward the United States.[52] Grace conferred on a daily
basis with members of Harrison's cabinet and other friends and
advisers of the president in the attempt "to influence them in
favor of Chile."[53] He also interceded with the press to put the
best possible light on developments between the two countries,
while acting as unofficial liaison between Montt and Blaine,
promoting a conciliatory mood that only an individual with

sympathies and understanding of both sides could hope to accomplish.

Grace's campaign demonstrated a virtuosity born of a dozen years' experience in American politics at the very highest level. For example, when the *Itata* decision was finally rendered in December by the district court in San Diego, Grace persuaded the press to note that the Chilean version of the incident had been upheld by the United States judiciary.[54]

Grace also counted on Andrew Carnegie as a good friend, especially since both shared a deep interest in inter-American affairs. Carnegie had been in England when the *Baltimore* affair exploded. He immediately wired Harrison to treat Chile liberally and with every consideration, and when the powerful Carnegie returned from London, Grace convinced him to present these views personally to Harrison and Blaine.[55]

Harrison, however, was not disposed to view the *Baltimore* incident from Blaine's, Carnegie's, or Grace's more conciliatory angle. The president delivered his opinion in the annual message to Congress on December 9. Irritated by the delay in the promised report from the Recabarren court in Valparaiso, Harrison impatiently demanded a "satisfactory" report promptly or he would prepare another message shortly for Congress. Grace thought this portion of Harrison's speech "moderate"; unfortunately, other references to the incident and its principals infuriated the Chileans.[56]

Foreign Minister Matta in Santiago wired Montt in Washington to protest the errors or deliberate inaccuracies in portions of the speech.[57] Matta was particularly irate over Harrison's implication that refugees in the United States legation had been in physical danger and that Egan had been the subject of calculated provocations. He also took strong exception to Harrison's view that Chilean sailors and police had assaulted the *Baltimore*'s crew in a cold, premeditated fashion.

Montt knew the volcanic effect such a note would have on the United States and he wisely kept it private. He also had that day received from William Grace an important message urging him once more to do his best to persuade his government to make some concessions.

Grace solicited advice and sounded the waters often among newspapermen and government officials in the wake of Harrison's message of December 9. Among those he spoke with was Stephen B. Elkins of West Virginia, who had just been offered the cabinet post of secretary of war by President Harrison. Grace knew Elkins from their business relations. Elkins produced coal and Grace had on many occasions shipped Elkins' coal to ports on the West Coast of South America. They were on familiar terms and when Elkins went to Washington to accept the post he arranged for a private appointment between Harrison and Grace to discuss the matter.

Even before Grace met with Harrison, it was clear to the ex-mayor that the American mood was growing truculent. Sensing an ugly outcome to this affair, Grace sent Montt a frank letter urging him not to underestimate Harrison's brinkmanship. As noted, Grace's plea for concessions arrived on Montt's desk on December 13, the very day Montt received Matta's incendiary cable.

Grace told Montt that most Americans believed the attack had been deliberate and unwarranted, and that Congress was predisposed warmly to support Harrison in seeking satisfaction from Chile.[58] It was imperative to persuade Santiago to urge the Recabarren inquest to a rapid conclusion, to offer an apology or express regrets, and, furthermore, to agree to arbitration by a mutually agreeable party or court. With Matta's message before him, and Grace's opinion that the United States would accept nothing less than an apology and reparations, Montt was called upon to exercise the highest statesmanship and diplomacy. Then Matta's message was revealed to the American public.

Matta had been asked by the Chilean Senate on December 11 to report on relations with the United States. He read his latest instructions to Montt—the cable—and on December 12 *El Ferrocarril* published the full text. The next day it was being reported in the American press.[59] Egan severed relations with the Ministry of Foreign Relations on the basis of the Matta note, and was notably absent from the December 25 inauguration of President Jorge Montt.[60]

While a real chill set in between Egan and the Chilean government in Santiago, William Grace and others in New York and Washington pushed even harder for a reasonable resolution. Montt was persuaded by a string of emissaries from the business and diplomatic world that the United States had no intention of backing down. In Europe, Chilean diplomats were advised by France and Germany that should hostilities break out between Chile and the United States, no aid would be forthcoming.[61] Montt was not about to be stampeded into a humiliating admission on behalf of Chile, but he was a realist. He used the presidential inauguration of his cousin in Santiago as an excuse to throw a party in Washington on December 26. Blaine came with his daughter, who substituted for his ill wife. Ricardo Trumbull was there, William Grace attended, and several prominent members of the Senate Committee on Foreign Relations and the House Committee on Foreign Affairs were present.[62]

After the party a reporter asked Grace if he thought "the Chilean government is ready to accede to our demands." Grace answered tactfully, "I believe they are willing to do what is right and I am sure the United States will only ask what is right."[63]

The Christmas spirit must have softened the negotiators at this moment late in the year, for within a few days of the party, New Year's Day 1892, Montt advised Blaine that Chile would accept arbitration.[64] Blaine was pleased with this turn of events, of which Grace had been apprised from private cables from Chile. Other news was equally optimistic. Among President Jorge Montt's new cabinet members were two of Egan's personal friends. The belligerent Matta was replaced by Luis Pereira as minister of foreign relations. Pereira possessed a much more conciliatory attitude toward the United States.

Harrison had, in the meanwhile, taken a step in the opposite direction. Recabarren's aggravatingly slow inquest finally ended in late December and the judge released his findings. Basically he substantiated earlier conclusions reached by other Chilean authorities: the fight had been caused by drunken sailors, Chilean and American, and the Chilean police had not deliberately provoked or beaten the Americans with premeditation.[65] Harrison found the report sorely wanting. On the same day, January 1, 1892, that Montt advised Blaine that Chile was willing to submit to arbitration, Harrison's private secretary wrote, "The President stated that all the members of the cabinet are for war."[66]

Paradoxically, Egan in Santiago was enjoying slightly improved relations with the Chileans these first few weeks of the new year. The last of the Balmacedista refugees had been allowed to leave his residence quietly and the police watch on the American legation was lifted.

Meanwhile, Blaine and Montt were working in Washington to produce the details to a solution. They had agreed by January 19 to accept arbitration by a third power, and to withdraw the offensive portions of the Matta note of December 11.[67] Egan still extremely irritated Chilean sensibilities and the Chileans wished him removed as part of the deal. Blaine agreed to this request on January 20. For its part, Chile agreed not to advertise Egan's partisan behavior during the civil war as the reason for the request.[68] But Harrison was on the "warpath . . . and fancied war would reelect him."[69]

Buoyed by the jingoistic mood of the country, Harrison instructed Blaine to dispatch an ultimatum, which the president himself had probably prepared.[70] The United States was in no way persuaded by the findings of the Chilean judicial investigation, which contradicted the American version of the *Baltimore* incident. Chile was still obligated to apologize and provide adequate reparations.[71] Harrison also demanded retraction of the objectionable portions of the Matta note, "which under ordinary circumstances would have justified United States severance of relations."[72] If prompt action was not taken by Chile, Harrison would go to Congress and ask for the termination of diplomatic relations and the immediate power to support United States demands.

This note was transmitted to Foreign Minister Pereira by Egan on January 23. Two days later Harrison sent Congress a fourteen-page message. He called on the lawmakers to take action to enforce American demands and complained that Chile was dragging its feet in responding to the January 21 ultimatum.[73] He should have been a trifle less impatient. Chile, in fact, had reiterated its willingness to disavow the offensive portions of the Matta note and to submit the dispute to arbitration. This response, which only reflected earlier agreements between Blaine and Montt in Washington, was communicated to the United States the same day, January 25, that Harrison was prodding Congress to more drastic steps.[74]

Chile was willing to let the United States Supreme Court, or any other body chosen by Harrison, arbitrate the matter and admitted that the Valparaiso court's pace might not have "been as rapid as the president of the United States could have desired."[75] But the Chileans denied that the attack on the *Baltimore* represented a premeditated offense against the government of the United States.[76] Nonetheless, Harrison was mollified. He informed Congress on January 28 that the Chilean response was satisfactory. The crisis passed. Within a year Chile provided an indemnity of $75,000 for the families of the dead American sailors.

The legacy of Patrick Egan and the *Baltimore* affair was frostiness and alienation between the United States and Chile for many years to come. Egan remained at his post until September 1893 and became involved once more in giving asylum to Balmacedistas implicated in a brief unsuccessful plot. The ensuing flareup, almost inevitable, between Egan and the government

prompted Eduardo Phillips, chief of the diplomatic section of
the Ministry of Foreign Relations, to summarize general feelings
about a man most Chileans detested: Egan was a person "utterly lacking in all elements of culture and courtesy, and ever
ready to descend to the level of invective and calumny."[77]

Why did the Harrison administration blow the *Baltimore* incident all out of proportion? What appears like a relatively
minor fracas that should have been dealt with easily by two
friendly, sovereign nations was in reality an *opportunity* sensed
by one on the make.

The grand era of United States imperialism culminating in
the Spanish–American War was about to hit its stride and the
United States would announce to the world in 1895, through
Secretary of State Richard Olney, that its will was practically
law in the Western Hemisphere. Chile, on the other hand, was
riding a crest of its own, but Chileans could not have withstood
the sustained enmity of the United States. Or could they? Pedro
Montt had amid the crisis asked a British attaché, perhaps rhetorically, "The Americans would never dare [attack us], would
they?"[78] The uncertainty of such an outcome, especially given
the stated neutrality of all the major European nations, and the
extreme vulnerability of Chile's northern provinces (rich in nitrates) to assault from the sea, led to Chile's decision to avoid
the confrontation.

William Grace would have preferred a less dramatic ending;
Harrison's saber-rattling ultimatum set everyone on edge.
Grace predicted the Chileans would not soon forget their humiliation of having to buckle under and apologize. Grace's role
in helping mediate the crisis, however, endowed him and his
firm with a more positive image among Chileans, an image that
worked to the advantage of both company and country in the
coming years.

The negotiations that led to the resolution of the crisis took
place at the ministerial level between Blaine and Montt, and a
constant presence between the two was William Grace. He
spoke with the voice of conciliation and compromise, viewing
a war between Chile and the United States as abhorrent. The
bellicose roaring of Harrison, prodded on by such jingoists as
his secretary of the navy, Benjamin Tracy, was considered nothing short of outrageous by Grace. The ex-mayor was no less a
patriot than his president, but a war with Chile over a prickly
sense of nationalism seemed utterly irrational. And Grace was

still a good businessman who viewed war as disruptive, and productive of nothing but lost opportunities and lost fortunes.

Grace's role in the Balmaceda affair also evinces his maturity as a formidable influence in the making of inter-American policies. His intimacy with Blaine and Montt, his cautionary voice with Harrison, his ability to persuade the likes of Andrew Carnegie to lend his weight in the affair, his constant search for the middle ground—all testify to his influence. His talents as a politician honed in the New York world of Tammany and Jay Gould sustained him well in 1891–92. It was a most exciting moment in American history as the United States entered its great age of imperialism.

10

Shaping the New American Empire

GRACE FROM THE GILDED AGE THROUGH WORLD WAR I

Du}}uring the decade and a half on either side of the turn of the century, the United States projected itself dramatically beyond its borders and joined the ranks of the great powers in influencing world developments. Nowhere else was this vigorous American brand of imperialism more evident than in the Western Hemisphere. The crisis between the United States and Chile in 1891 certainly represented a clear harbinger of the new American mood that culminated at the end of the century in the Spanish–American War.

The expansionist wave was made not only of a political and moral ethos—perhaps best characterized by Rudyard Kipling's remark about the "white man's burden"—but also by commercial links being forged by such people as William and Michael Grace. In other words, the forerunners were not simply naval planners and thinkers exemplified by the great Alfred Thayer Mahan, who championed a mighty presence on the sea, taking England as his example; they were not limited to expansionists who viewed islands and ports around the world as mere coaling stations on the road to an imperial America; they were not social Darwinians alone who sought to civilize the world in the American mold; nor were they fatuous jingoists who only sought overseas adventures for their own advancement, political or commercial. They were all of the above and more.

James A. Field, Jr. came closest to defining the real origins

224

of American imperialism, which he ascribed to individual initiatives and acts rather than to governmental prodding: "Generally, it may be said, these relations [between the United States and other nations] were far more individual than governmental . . . explorers, tourists, art collectors, philanthropists, missionaries, synarchists, railroad promoters, and mining engineers" led the field.[1] Technological advances, such as the extension and improvement of cable service, further assisted Americans in penetrating markets abroad with speed and efficiency. Direct investments increased as communications improved and American capital and American entrepreneurs sought opportunities and profits abroad. Indeed, the prosaic trader, the flamboyant railroad builder, and the venture capitalist formed the cutting edge of American expansionism. William and Michael Grace were in the vanguard of that group.

By the early 1890s the range of the Grace brothers' public and private interests and their ability to translate these interests into actions had been boldly demonstrated. William Grace had served two terms as mayor of the great international trading metropolis New York; Michael had almost single-handedly forged the Peruvian Grace Contract; and the brothers had fought a drawn-out battle with Charles Flint over the pioneering rubber business in Brazil. Furthermore, they were squarely in the center of the most important crisis of the era, that between the United States and Chile. And William continued to be involved in domestic politics, maneuvering with dexterity and influence at the highest levels.

In 1898 the Graces challenged the Panama Canal interests by organizing an immensely popular drive to build a canal across Nicaragua, even while their diversified business empire based on trade, but certainly not limited to simple trade, continued to expand, doing so through World War I. William Grace, fondly referred to as "our chief" in much of the correspondence, remained at the heart of things through the twilight of the nineteenth century.

William's personality, like Michael's, was a complicated compound of strong virtues and occasional vices, best exemplified by the periodic eruption of a flashing temper. His single-minded determination could produce extraordinary results for his firm and the public commonwealth—such as during his terms as mayor—but it could also lead him to tempestuous rivalries with Charles Flint and Joseph Pulitzer.

Perhaps no other observer caught the ambivalent nature of William Grace more than his own brother Morgan, who made his life as a surgeon and public servant on the remote island of New Zealand. Morgan occasionally traveled to the United States to visit his numerous kin in their new American homes. After one such visit he wrote William a typically garrulous, analytical description of his impressions, demonstrating not only a good grasp of William's character, but a pleasant literary style.

> The gothic structure of your eccentricities has reached my heart. A more thoroughly illogical man when angry or excited I don't know. A more humble-minded rational citizen when "compos mentis" I never met. . . . Who so liberal as you but my dear old Father who is dead; who so economical but Uncle William. You are a regular bundle of incongruities, and I never met a man I would rather be quizzing, bullying and coaxing, chiefly because there is always an element of danger in the pursuit.[2]

Morgan counseled William, then approaching forty-five, to back away from business, which was consuming him, often to the exclusion of his wife Lillius and the children:

> After all, what does business matter with Lillius bright and happy, Alice growing amiable, Agnes bright & loving, Joe well & strong, Lillie affectionate and the baby bawling [the year was 1876]. We are all too solicitous about business. . . . If it does not remit about forty, man is likely to become a slave to it. . . . By all this, I mean to advise you to ease off. Your children are growing up and they and your wife require a great deal of your attention and will repay it. I propose following this course myself.[3]

In early 1884, just after William was reelected for his second term as mayor, he and Lillius lost another child, this time their beloved sixteen-year-old Agnes. The stabbing pain of her death following a short illness finally gave way to the grief of parents who would always remember. Poignantly and sadly William wrote his brother John that "my wife can't get over . . . the loss of our girl. . . . Whenever I see Agnes' photo about the house I kiss my hand to it & say God bless my baby, just as if she were there in person for I can't feel that she is gone."[4]

Grace was, in truth, devoted to his family, notwithstanding Morgan's injunctions to pay them more heed. He wrote a letter to an Irish niece in 1891 describing some of his brood, and Grace's observations reflect the eye of a loving father who nonetheless could list the strengths and foibles of his children with pragmatic certainty:

> Lill [Lilias] is much taller than her Mother, is a fair French scholar and has a great taste for painting, and [is] a very manageable girl and not much of a kicker. Joe [Joseph] is short, not very manly looking, but is considerable of an athlete, moderate in his views, a good steady worker, likes his study and keeps at it; he is a moderate-tempered fellow, good natured, but with an opinion of his own and firm. Lu [Louise] is younger and less settled; she is tall, strong, well-built and rough, very nervous, much inclined to catch cold, very affectionate but sensitive and hates to be demonstrative; very proud but I think entirely conscientious and truthful. Russ [William Russell] is a long boy for his age, quick-witted, very good tempered, very affectionate, mischievous, very cautious, a poor student and a poor scholar, finds it very disagreeable work to have to study. All go regularly to their monthly communion. Russ being the only one who needs a reminder.[5]

The Gracefield estate at Great Neck was always bustling with children swimming, playing polo, tennis, golf, or riding from a large and well-kept stable. Poker was learned by all the children, although the stakes were low and Grace taught them the consequences, as well as the game. Losses came out of moderate allowances, which were sometimes advanced but never increased to meet gambling obligations. Grace had learned to play poker from Americans back in his early days in Peru, and part of training his children was to bring them up in the world of realities. Although Grace himself was nearly a teetotaler, Joseph's undergraduate days at Columbia, and at New York University while reading law, were often interrupted by long sessions of poker, beer drinking, and camaraderie. William Grace's philosophy was regarded by some as indulgent and perhaps even extravagant. His answer to one such accusation of spoiling his children at Gracefield was "not a bit . . . it keeps 'em home."[6] He could be almost parsimonious in other dealings, but never so with his family and children.

He never forgot that the source of his wealth was his business, which had grown from close attention to detail and a studied frugality. Yet, unlike so many famed misers of fact and fiction, Grace was loving and generous to his family and could often turn this generosity and sensitivity outwardly as well. In one instance he reprimanded his superintendent at Gracefield for a questionable expenditure of $12.50; later he assisted the man's son in obtaining an appointment to West Point and gave the superintendent a bonus.[7]

Grace perfectly embodied his generation's attitude toward women. His eldest daughter, Alice, married William C. Holloway, who later was unable to provide for Alice's medical treatment during a prolonged recovery following the birth of their first child, William Grace Holloway. William gave his son-in-law an allowance to cover the cost, observing that "it has occurred to me that a woman is always better subject to her husband in all things and dependent on him alone for all financial help. . . . I am a little old-fashioned in my ideas, and I want my daughter to feel toward her husband as I like to have my wife feel toward me, dependent on me and me alone."[8] That statement, the antithesis of today's liberationist movement, was mainstream America at the turn of the century; then the nation was dedicated to the family as the keeper and propagator of society's morality, education, and order.

In his public and private philanthropy Grace might well have been described as a soft touch, for his loyalties to old friends and Roman Catholic causes often contradicted his pure business instincts. The adage that charity begins at home certainly had no other practitioner better than William Grace. During the course of his long career he took care of his parents, brothers, nephews, nieces, and other relations, not only of his immediate family, but of his "extended" family as well. Charley Flint had at one time been treated almost as a son, while many ship captains, wives of absent business partners, and sundry widows always could count on friendship and assistance from William and Lillius. This couple's warm and generous nature radiates through the old, dry letterbooks in silent but unquestionable testimony to their goodness.

On one occasion Capt. L. H. Stevens promptly received a check from Grace for the amount mentioned in the following note: "My dear wife died suddenly yesterday, and I have not the means to give her a respectable burial. Will you . . . let me have $150.00 and greatly relieve and oblige."[9]

In many other instances the Grace houses served as post offices for husbands and wives, mothers and sweethearts separated by long sea voyages. Not only did their letters pass through the Grace offices in New York, but worried relatives sought advice and information from William. "Has . . . the ship *Genecole* of Liverpool from the Brazills . . . arrived at New York. . . . My son Christopher Hass is a seaman onboard of her . . . If you will be kind enough to write it will be a great consolation to a troubled widow."[10] Others wondered how well their husbands were faring in foreign ports under the temptations of loose women and strong drink. Mrs. M. E. Weymouth wanted to know if her husband, a captain, had really behaved as a "half crazed . . . beast" while ashore in Callao.[11] William answered tactfully. Certainly no such exaggerated report had been received from Callao, although Captain Weymouth "was a little sick from causes supposed to be liquor, but . . . [he has] entirely reformed."[12]

Grace's public philanthropy was expressed largely through the Roman Catholic church. Helping the church satisfied Grace in two ways: he was always interested in promoting the opportunities and goals of young people; and he liked to do it within the framework of organized religion, for he was a devout, if not dogmatic, Roman Catholic. He gave regularly to good causes, helped traveling members of the clergy with his special knowledge and friendships around the world, and capped it all in 1897 with the creation of the Grace Institute.

The origins of the Grace Institute arose from a long, frustrating strike against the Ingersoll-Sargeant Drill Company in Easton, Pennsylvania. Grace had invested in Ingersoll-Sargeant in 1890 and had effectively taken over its management. During the course of the strike he became aware that working-class girls and young women had little opportunity to learn the traditional skills of home and hearth, or the new skills demanded by this industrial age. If taught sewing, cooking, and stenography, for example, Grace thought they might be better prepared to seek employment now and be better homemakers in the future.

Grace consulted with Grace Dodge, the first woman member of the New York Board of Education. He had appointed her during his second term as mayor. Dodge and other specialists put William in touch with the Catholic Sisters of Charity, an order that was already conducting classes in cooking and dressmaking for girls in Jersey City. William and Michael appropriated $80,000 for the project and the Grace Institute was founded and incorporated by the legislature in 1897. The Sisters of Charity provided the instruction in the institute, which was open to girls of all creeds or no creed, since Grace wished to combine the best of a Roman Catholic environment within a nonsectarian framework. No religious instruction would be given in the institute, but one could hardly divorce the Sisters from their profession, of course.

An old mansion on West Sixtieth Street was purchased and remodeled in preparation for the first class of three hundred girls. The institute opened in January 1898. By its second year of operation, five hundred girls were enrolled not only in cooking and sewing classes, but in learning millinery, stenography, and bookkeeping.[13] It was a satisfying contribution to bettering his world by making opportunities for young people.

★ ★ ★

Nowhere else was Grace's dedication to the above principle more apparent than in his own business. Almost all of the rising associates, family and other, in the 1880s and 1890s had started out as office boys in the mailroom or apprentices of some sort in the business. Grace not only expected them to work hard, but also advised them on all matters, business and personal. Typically, he provided John F. Fowler, who later rose to vice president, with the following message in 1893, when Fowler was sent to Valparaiso as a junior partner: "Be prudent, modest and graceful, and you are sure of success. But if you should become inflated with a notion of your own abilities you can be pretty certain that disaster will follow any such idea. The men who are really successful are those who do not overestimate their own abilities. . . . I think if you confer with that good, sensible wife of yours from time to time . . . you will probably find that in her you have a pretty safe adviser."[14] A good leader is measured in part by his ability to select good subordinates, and to delegate responsibilities with confidence. That gift Grace possessed.

When Lawrence Shearman was elevated to the head of the Lima house at the turn of the century, Grace was promoting not only a young man who had started out with W. R. Grace & Co. in New York, but one who could be trusted wisely to counsel others beneath him. Shearman supplied Grace, for example, with a detailed analysis of the character and promise of a young Eyre in Lima in 1899 in response to an informal questionnaire prepared by Grace. On Eyre's judgment Shearman wrote: "I don't think he is possessed of either remarkably good or bad judgment. At times he has a tendency to let his prejudices get away with his judgment but this is usually in little things and I don't think he does so to such an extent as to amount to a serious matter." On his devotion to business and success: "his best point is the interest he takes in the business and his readiness to serve it day and night when occasion requires and to the best of his ability." Was he shrewd? "No. In my opinion he is a man of ordinary ability who has the interests of the house at heart, is willing to work hard and will with time get on. I don't think he will ever be possessed of anything like the ability of Don Eduardo [Ned Eyre] or the hard commonsense shrewdness and energy of Jack [Eyre]. His worst point, that is the most dangerous to himself, is a tendency to a 'big head.' "[15]

The probing for the character of a man was a legacy William Grace bequeathed to his successors, especially to his son Joseph Peter and Joseph's closest friend, David Stewart Iglehart, both of whom later became presidents of the company. Like William, they and others in high positions always scrutinized their subordinates with care in detail to uncover both strengths and weaknesses.

Joseph, although still a young man himself in 1900, cultivated his father's habit of seeking out good young people and testing them at the bottom rung. To Shearman in Lima, Joseph noted that "as you know it is very hard for anyone to get into this office except by way of the mail bag." He, Joseph, would keep "on the watch for one or two really bright fellows from the Under Dept. here"; Shearman had indicated a growing need for some good young associates in the Lima office.[16]

Once a bond of trust was established—based on ability, attitude, loyalty, and performance—relationships flourished as within a family, with all the idiosyncrasies that characterize family affairs. Until 1929, however, the head of the company was always a Grace or an Eyre, for, as in ancient kingdoms, blood still separated royalty from the peerage. But, unlike ancient hierarchs, William Grace was close to the people in the 1880s and 1890s following his service as mayor.

He never lost the ambition to serve publicly again, and sought various political offices between 1888 and 1894. The growth and influence of W. R. Grace & Co. was still wedded to the growth and influence of William R. Grace himself in this period, and it is important to note the closeness by which William Grace remained near the sources of political power in the United States. That closeness enabled him and his family, especially Michael, to make extremely important contributions in the realm of inter-American affairs and, indirectly, to develop and foster the growth of the company itself. Grace's political ambitions, as will be seen below, brought him into contact with various people he might not have met as a mere businessman, people who further broadened not only his horizon but that of his company as well.

In 1887 and 1888 a boomlet for William Grace's election as governor of New York surged and gained some momentum, but it failed ultimately from lack of support from President Cleveland. Without Cleveland's active intercession in New York State politics, Grace and the reform elements were unable to unseat the incumbent governor, David B. Hill.

Hill had created an efficient and corrupt political machine during his term as governor commencing in 1884, and it was against this machine and its leader that Grace began to direct his attention in 1887. Grace was particularly nettled by Cleveland's unwillingness to challenge the Hill machine in patronage and other matters deemed important to Grace and like thinkers such as his successor as mayor of New York, the crusty Abram Hewitt. Cleveland had hedged and vacillated on recommendations from Hewitt, prompting an irritated Grace to remark sarcastically to Cleveland's private secretary, Daniel S. Lamont: "I write you thusly, hoping that my recommendation in this case may not be too deeply buried in 'careful consideration' as to be lost sight of."[17]

Cleveland's reluctance to be forceful in New York Democratic politics nonetheless did not discourage Grace from contemplating a run for the governorship, figuring that Cleveland needed him more than vice versa in the forthcoming national election year of 1888.[18] Grace sounded out old allies, such as Oswald Ottendorfer, who offered their support. By early 1888 he committed himself to the race, although Cleveland still dallied.

A splendid presidential reception in honor of the Supreme Court justices on February 3, 1888, brought Grace and some of his major supporters together at the White House. Several nights of dining out and politicking in Washington, including an additional evening at the White House, produced no commitments from the implacable Cleveland. In early spring, Grace traveled to Europe on behalf of the negotiations for the Grace Contract and was away for six weeks. By the time he returned in early May, the Hill forces had advanced considerably. They demonstrated their power by gaining almost complete control of the New York delegation to the Democratic National Convention which met in St. Louis in June and renominated Cleveland.

An old scandal involving the aqueduct commission resurfaced in July and broke the Hill momentum temporarily, prompting Grace once more to appeal directly to Cleveland to part with Hill. "I am thoroughly & deeply interested in your election but not sufficiently so to induce me to sacrifice my own conscientious convictions. . . . I never belonged to a political gang & . . . I think it only fair to let you know how I feel."[19] Grace clearly felt that Cleveland should honor his own "conscientious convictions" with respect to Hill.

Cleveland did not see it that way and again refused to be a party to the factionalism produced by the Grace-Hill rivalry.[20]

Without Cleveland's support, Grace acknowledged defeat and Hill was easily renominated for the governorship by the New York Democrats.

Then the policy of nonentanglement backfired on Cleveland. Hill turned against Cleveland when the president refused to endorse him publicly, while independents like Grace and Hewitt were outraged by Cleveland's professed neutrality. On election day Hill was carried back into office by a nice margin. On the other hand, the Republican presidential candidate, Benjamin Harrison, rolled up thirteen thousand more votes in New York than the incumbent and led the Republicans back into the White House.

In 1890 Grace again toyed with the idea of running for mayor but instead backed a reform candidate nominated by a coalition of Democratic liberals, independents, and Republicans. The strategy was to get his candidate elected as a steppingstone to gaining the full support of the Republican state organization in Grace's bid for a seat in the U.S. Senate.[21] However, the incumbent mayor, Hugh Grant, was reelected rather easily with Tammany's support, and Grace looked down the road to the year 1892.

Cleveland had backed the reform mayoralty ticket quietly in the election of 1890, and was again the probable Democratic presidential candidate in 1892. Although Grace still smarted from Cleveland's lack of support in the preelectioneering maneuvers of 1888, a rupture had never occurred between the two men. They saw each other occasionally in New York; Grace did the former president some small favors, like sponsoring him for membership in the Manhattan Club, and they maintained a cordial but polite relationship.[22]

Hill challenged Cleveland for the Democratic national nomination in 1892, but his effort was quickly crushed in the first ballot, which gave the ex-president an overwhelming majority. Grace had joined with other independent Democrats in the preceding months to contest Hill over New York's delegation to the convention held in Chicago, but Hill's power and Cleveland's assurance of the nomination without New York's delegates combined to defeat the Grace interests.

However, the popular support that Grace and the State Democracy—as the anti-Hill forces were styled—had been able to muster in opposition to Hill helped Cleveland by breaking Hill's early momentum toward the nomination. Over two hundred

thousand signatures were obtained in the campaign to dispute
Hill's control and influence over New York Democrats, and this
popular manifestation smoothed the way for Cleveland by dis-
crediting Hill's power. Grace's many speeches and travels in
behalf of Cleveland throughout New York and other states were
well publicized.[23]

Cleveland was elected in November by a comfortable margin,
but Grace's aspirations for a Senate seat from New York were
not supported by the president-elect.

In truth, Cleveland orchestrated the feuding New York Democrats in a masterly fashion and William Grace involuntarily
played an important part in Grover Cleveland's symphony. As
long as Grace could be counted upon to support Cleveland
steadily, the presidential patronage could be distributed to
those groups—for example, among Tammany Hall and Hill's
supporters—which were more likely to bolt from Cleveland's
discipline. Thus, patronage in New York after the
election—postmastership of New York City, commissionership
of immigration, collector of the port of New York, civil service
commissioner, and many others—was divided among reformers, independents, and Tammany with little regard, in Grace's
opinion, for the loyal support reform Democrats had given to
Cleveland.[24] Although he remained on friendly terms with the
president, Grace turned his attention more directly back to state
politics and away from the national scene in 1893 and 1894. He
worked hard as the chairman of the State Democracy in its
efforts against Tammany and Hill. Rallies at Cooper Union, the
tedious but necessary spadework at the district level, the cultivation of friendships and political alliances, they all occupied
his attention.[25]

Grace enthusiastically endorsed the election of a State Democracy candidate, William L. Strong, for mayor in 1894. He
campaigned hard for Strong and the balloting in November
propelled Strong into the mayor's office with a generous margin
of forty thousand votes.[26]

In the most ironic twist of the period, in March 1895 Tammany offered Grace its leadership, perhaps bowing to one of
the most obvious Democratic powers then extant in the state.
Grace declined. He also resigned the chairmanship of the State
Democracy that year, once again suffering from an attack of
Bright's disease. At the age of sixty-three, his body no longer
recovered with the resiliency of youth and his political activities
slackened.[27]

One of the first four Grace steamers, Coya, Condor, Capac, *and* Cacique; *one bought and three built in 1893, England, as the core of the New York and Pacific Steamship Co. Incorporated in Great Britain, wholly owned by Graces. Three thousand tons.*

Four photographs of the destruction caused by a massive earthquake which struck Valparaiso in 1906. Gaston J. Lipscomb, head of W. R. Grace & Co.'s first engineering department, survived this earthquake while working for Grace in Chile. A major fund-raising effort in the United States

was led by Joseph P. Grace to provide relief for the victims. Tens of thousands of dollars were raised and were used to assist people such as those shown in the inside of a warehouse, left homeless by the disaster. The other three photographs are awesome testimony to the power of the quake.

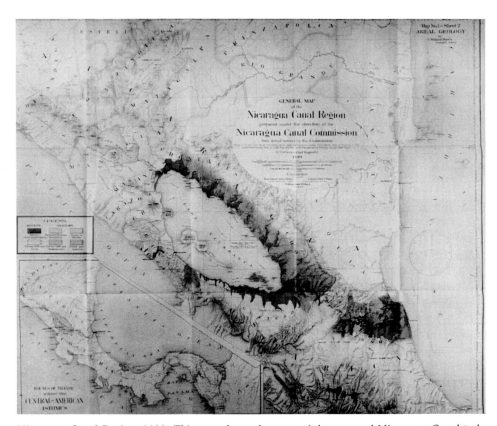

Nicaragua Canal Region, 1899. This map shows the route of the proposed Nicaragua Canal to be built for $100,000,000 by a syndicate of U. S. investors organized by William Russell Grace. The Nicaraguan route was most favored by Americans in the nineteenth century and the debate in Congress between the proponents of Nicaragua and those of Panama captured the attention of the nation at the turn of the century.

Joseph P. Grace, son of William Russell Grace and president of W. R. Grace & Co., 1907-1929. Joseph guided Grace through the First World War and the commodities crisis of 1920 which almost destroyed the company. A graduate of Columbia, class of 1894, he became one if its greatest supporters, serving as a member of the Board of Trustees. Under Joseph Grace, Grace Line was formed, Grace went heavily into the nitrate business in Chile, and the company's multifarious interests in Peru were expanded.

Analysis of Profit and Loss account of W. R. Grace & Co., for the year ended December 31, 1891.

STATEMENT OF CONDITION

SEPTEMBER 8, 1917

OF

W. R. GRACE & CO'S BANK

7 HANOVER SQUARE

NEW YORK, N. Y.

LETTERS OF CREDIT

CABLE TRANSFERS

BILLS OF EXCHANGE

—

EXCEPTIONAL FACILITIES FOR COLLECTING AND
TRANSFERRING FUNDS IN CENTRAL
AND SOUTH AMERICA

Statement of Condition of W. R. Grace & Co.'s Bank, September 8, 1917. The bank was established in 1914 to do the banking business W. R. Grace & Co. had traditionally handled for its customers but which it could no longer do because of the Federal Reserve Act of 1914. W. R. Grace & Co.'s Bank evolved into the Grace National Bank in the 1920s and constituted one of the steadiest and most profitable branches of the multifaceted company.

W. R. GRACE & CO'S BANK

STATEMENT OF CONDITION, SEPTEMBER 8TH, 1917

RESOURCES		LIABILITIES		
Bonds, Securities, etc. - - -	$1,496,226.60	Capital Stock - - - - -		$ 500,000.00
Loans, Discounts and Bills purchased	4,374,374.07	Surplus Fund - - - -		500,000.00
Customers' liability on acceptances -	3,650.00	Undivided Profits - - -		113,062.69
Accrued Interest - - - -	28,304.79	U. S. Government Deposits $ 410,000.00		
U. S. Government Certificates of		Deposits subject to checks 3,471,676.25		
Indebtedness - - - -	815,000.00	Certificates of deposit 2,035,000.00		
Cash on hand and in Banks - -	629,526.47	Cashier's and Certified		
		Checks outstanding 32,341.70		
		Due Banks and Bankers 78,762.40		
				6,027,780.35
		Acceptances of drafts payable at a		
		future date or authorized by		
		letters of credit - - -		184,966.68
		Accrued interest and unearned		
		discounts - - - -		21,272.21
	7,347,081.93			7,347,081.93

Callao harbor, 1908. A steamer, possibly owned or operated by Grace, is tied alongside the far pier, while in the right side fishing smacks lie at anchor. A small, one-masted schooner is almost awash in the left foreground, either on the verge of sinking or, more likely, loaded down to the scuppers with a heavy cargo.

The dock area of Callao, 1908, demonstrating a typical mixture of the old and the new. Railroads and coal cars curling out to docks accommodating sailing ships tied alongside.

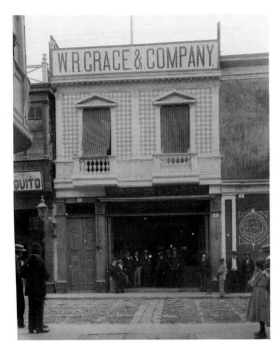

W. R. Grace & Co., Callao, 1908.

Street and plaza in Lima, circa 1908. The new streetcars bespoke of a modern city, while the horsedrawn cart and the unpaved streets indicated more properly a city and a nation in transition. The Graces were heavily involved in electrification at the turn of the century and were one of the principal investors in this new form of energy applied to such activities as mass, public transportation.

The port of Callao, 1908. Sailing ships still appear in some number, recalling the age of sail that had not quite yielded up totally to the age of steam. Modernization of the port had already advanced to the stage where piers and jetties were being serviced by rail lines, facilitating the loading and unloading of merchant ships.

Santa Clara, *freighter built by Cramps, Philadelphia, August, 1913, 6310 tons gross. Operated by Atlantic and Pacific Steamship Co., Sisters:* Catalina *and* Cecilia. Santa Clara *was one of the first commercial ships to pass through the formally opened Panama Canal going north on June 18, 1915.*

Santa Clara, *on the rocks at Mindful Shoals, English Narrows, in Smythes Channel, the Straits of Magellan, December 30, 1915. Part of the perils of the sea.*

Santa Ana. *First passenger ship built for Grace Line. Launched from Cramps Shipyards October 13, 1917. Carried 100 passengers and 5400 tons of cargo.*

Santa Rosa. *Named after patron saint of Lima, Peru. Shown in 1918 returning home with American troops from France.*

The Santa Cruz, *an American-flag ship, was the first in Grace Line to use the "Santa" prefix and was built in February 1913 in Cramps Shipyard in Philadelphia, for use by the newly formed Atlantic & Pacific S. S. Co., in the intercoastal trade with the* Santa Catalina, Santa Clara, *and* Santa Cecilia, *built later in the same year. The* Santa Cruz *had accommodations for fifty passengers but was not used as a passenger ship until later when she entered Grace's transpacific service. The ship was sold in 1930 to the Bull Line and renamed the* Barbara.

Laborers on Hacienda Cartavio, circa 1900, unloading sugar cane to be processed in the mill. A large percentage of the workers were still Chinese coolies. The steam locomotive on the left hauled cane from the fields on portable tracks. Cartavio was W. R. Grace's first direct investment in the sugar industry of Peru.

Port of Huanchaco, for more than three hundred years the port for both the Chicama and Moche Valleys. By 1930 it was abandoned in favor of Salaverry and Puerto Chicama. Note the heavy surf and the old church back of the town which had served for centuries as a landmark for ships. The very exposed roadsteads are characteristic of most Peruvian ports and made lighterage service very important. Grace Line provided not only lighterage service for its own vessels but served ships of many different lines.

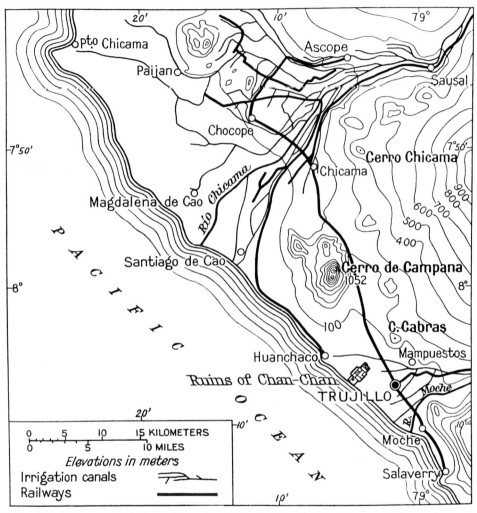

Map of the Chicama and Moche Valleys, circa 1930, showing the Rio Chicama which was the main water source for Hacienda Cartavio and the other sugar plantations of the area. The railroads serving the sugar industry are shown in bold black lines. Sugar from Cartavio was sent by rail to Salaverry for shipment.

Hacienda Paramonga, 1930. This is the earliest aerial photograph of the plantation after it was acquired by Grace in 1927. It may be the first aerial photograph as well. It shows the administrative center of the estate built on a plateau above the irrigable level of the valley with the sugar mills and the railway to the port of Supe in the foreground.

Grace Line steamer unloading freight into launches at Callao harbor, 1930. The open roadsteads of Peru almost invariably necessitated this type of cargo transfer requiring extensive lighterage service, much of which Grace provided not only for its own ships but as agents of other lines. Sugar, cotton, copper, and silver were the principal exports through Callao.

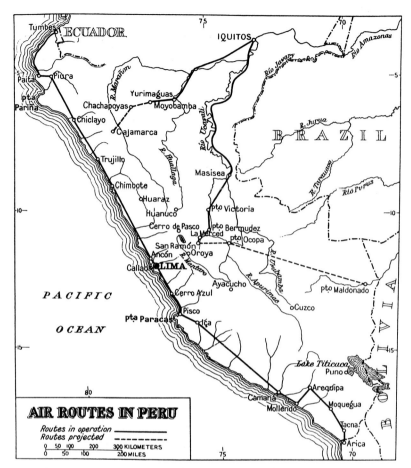

Map of air routes in Peru, 1930. The main north-south route along the coast was operated by Pan American-Grace Airways, incorporated in early 1929. Projected routes are marked in broken lines. Service from Lima north to Panama and south to Santiago was offered on a weekly basis.

Panagra Ford Tri-Motors in flight along the edge of irrigated fields of the River Rimac delta which contains the capital city of Lima, 1930. These airplanes of Panagra were among the first to inaugurate international air service between the West Coast of South America and Panama with through service to Central America, Cuba, and Miami. Panagra was a joint venture of W. R. Grace & Co. and Pan American World Airways.

PAN AMERICAN AIRWAYS, Inc. *PAA*

General Offices—122 East 42nd Street, New York City

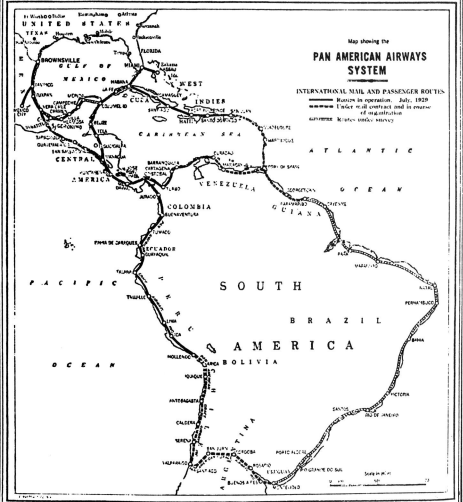

The Pan American Airways System map, August, 1929, shows the Panagra route already opened between Cristobal, Panama Canal Zone and Mollendo, Peru. Panagra would soon extend the route down through Chile to Argentina and Uruguay.

PAN AMERICAN AIRWAYS, Inc.

MIAMI
Southbound (Read Down)

CRISTOBAL, C. Z.

MIAMI
Northbound (Read Up)

TABLE 81

Tuesdays, Thursdays, Saturdays	STATION		Mondays, Saturdays, Thursdays
7 00	Lv	Miami	Ar	5 30
9 45	Ar	Havana	Lv	2 45
10 45	Lv	Havana	Ar	2 00 ET
12 15	Lv	La Fe		No Stop
12 45	Lv	La Fe		
1 45 CT	Ar	Cozumel	Lv	9 00
2 15 CT	Lv	Cozumel	Ar	8 15
4 30	Ar	Belize	Lv	6 00

Wednesdays, Fridays, Sundays	OVERNIGHT STOP		Sundays, Fridays, Wednesdays
7 00	Lv	Belize	Ar	1 00
8 30	Ar	Tela	Lv	11 30
9 30	Lv	Tela	Ar	10 30
1 00	Ar	Managua	Lv	7 00

Thursdays, Saturdays, Mondays	OVERNIGHT STOP		Saturdays, Thursdays, Tuesdays
7 00	Lv	Managua	Ar	3 00
11 30	Ar	David	Lv	10 30
12 30	Lv	David	Ar	9 30
3 00	Ar	Cristobal	Lv	7 00

PAN AMERICAN-GRACE AIRWAYS, Inc.

(Schedule Guayaquil-Mollendo—Connecting with Boats)

(Contractor F. A. M. Route No. 9—Cristobal, C. Z. to Santiago, Chile.)

PERUVIAN AIRWAYS CORPORATION
CHILEAN AIRWAYS CORPORATION

DIRECTORS

J. T. Trippe,   R. F. Hoyt   R. H. Patchin   W. F. Cogswell

F. A. M. ROUTE No. 9
CANAL ZONE TO MOLLENDO
North and Southbound Departures Fridays
(For Mail only)

TABLE 82

(FAM 9)

SOUTHBOUND 1st Day	Tuesday	1st Day	Sunday
Lv. Cristobal, C. Z.	8 00	Lv. Santiago, Chile	
Ar. Buenaventura, Col	1 00	Lv. Chanaral, Chile	
		Lv. Antofagasta, Chile	
2nd Day	Wednesday	Lv. Arica, Chile	
		Ar. Mollendo	
Lv. Buenaventura, Col	8 00		
Ar. Tumaco, Col	10 15	2nd Day	Monday
Lv. Tumaco, Col	10 45		
Ar. Esmeraldas, Col	11 45	Lv. Mollendo, Peru	9 00
Lv. Esmeraldas, Col	12 30	Ar. Lima, Peru	3 30
Ar. Guayaquil, Ecuador	3 00		
3rd Day	Thursday	3rd Day	Tuesday
		Lv. Lima, Peru	8 00
Lv. Guayaquil, Ecuador	7 00	Ar. Trujillo, Peru	11 30
Ar. Talara, Peru	9 30	Lv. Trujillo, Peru	12 30
Lv. Talara, Peru	10 30	Ar. Talara, Peru	3 45
Ar. Trujillo, Peru	1 45	Lv. Talara, Peru	4 30
Lv. Trujillo, Peru	2 30	Ar. Guayaquil, Ecuador	6 00
Ar. Lima, Peru	5 15		
4th Day	Friday	4th Day	Wednesday
		Lv. Guayaquil, Ecuador	8 00
Lv. Lima, Peru	8 00	Ar. Esmeraldas, Col	10 30
Ar. Mollendo, Peru	2 30	Lv. Esmeraldas, Col	11 15
		Ar. Tumaco, Col	12 15
5th Day	Saturday	Lv. Tumaco, Col	1 00
		Ar. Buenaventura, Col	3 15
Lv. Mollendo			
Ar. Arica, Chile		5th Day	Thursday
Lv. Antofagasta, Chile			
Lv. Chanaral, Chile		Lv. Buenaventura, Col	8 00
Ar. Santiago, Chile		Ar. Cristobal, Canal Zone	1 00

DELTA AIR SERVICE, Inc.

General Offices—Monroe, Louisiana. Tel. 1631

OFFICERS

D. Y. Smith, President
C. E. Woolman, Vice-President and General Manager
Captain Harold R. Harris, Vice-President
Travis Oliver, Secretary-Treasurer
J. S. Fox, General Traffic Manager

TABLE 83   DALLAS—JACKSON

Read Down	(Daily)		Read Up
8 30	Lv	Dallas	Ar	4 00
10 50	Lv	Shreveport	Lv	1 45
11 50	Ar	Monroe	Lv	12 15
12 15	Lv	Monroe	Ar	11 50
1 30	Ar	Jackson	Lv	10 30

FARES

		Dallas	Shreveport	Monroe
Shreveport	O. W.	$21.50	......	......
	R. T.	38.00	......	......
Monroe	O. W.	34.00	$12.50	......
	R. T.	63.00	20.00	......
Jackson	O. W.	47.25	25.75	$13.25
	R. T.	90.00	46.50	21.50

Baggage Allowance—25 pounds free. Excess at 25c per pound.

WEDELL-WILLIAMS AIR SERVICE, Inc.

605 Whitney Bldg., New Orleans, La.
City Office, Tel. RA. 1086.   Field Office, Tel. CR. 1150

TABLE 84   NEW ORLEANS—ST. LOUIS

Read Down Friday			Read Up Saturday
9 00	Lv	New Orleans	Ar	5 00
11 00	Lv	Jackson	Lv	3 00
1 00	Ar	Memphis	Lv	1 00
2 00	Lv	Memphis	Ar	12 00
5 00	Ar	St. Louis	Lv	9 00

FARES

	New Orleans	Jackson	Memphis
Jackson	$20		..
Memphis	40	$20	..
St. Louis	60	45	$30

TABLE 85   NEW ORLEANS—SHREVEPORT

Read Down Sat. & Mon.			Read Up Sat. & Mon.
8 30	Lv	New Orleans	Ar	5 30
9 30	Lv	Baton Rouge	Lv	4 30
10 45	Lv	Alexandria	Lv	3 15
12 00	Ar	Shreveport	Lv	2 00

FARES

	New Orleans	Baton Rouge	Alexandria
Baton Rouge	9	..	..
Alexandria	20	11	..
Shreveport	30	25	15

NEW ORLEANS—GRAND ISLE

Amphibian Service

Lv. New Orleans 1:30 P.M., 3:00 P.M., Saturday; 8:30 A.M., 10:30 A.M., 2:00 P.M.; 4:00 P.M. Sunday.

Lv. Grand Isle 2:15 P.M., 3:45 P.M. Saturday; 9:15 A.M., 11:15 A.M., 2:45 P.M.; 5:00 P.M. Sunday.

Passenger Rates—New Orleans-Grand Isle: $6.00 One Way, $10.00 Round Trip.

Baggage Allowance—25 pounds baggage free.

One of Panagra's first schedules, August, 1929. This page from The Official Aviation Guide of the Airways (Chicago, Illinois: John R. Fletcher, 1929), p. 26. shows the schedule for the Miami to Panama stage of the route operated by Pan American and, coincidentally, one of the first schedules of Delta Airlines, whose founder, C. E. Woolman, played a role in the early development of Panagra.

Grace's public service had never been limited to city, state, or even national politics. Some of his strongest contributions, as already noted, were in international politics and commerce, although they were considerably less celebrated in the American press than his more famous jousts with the likes of Honest John Kelly, David B. Hill, and the many minions of Tammany Hall. In fact, no other man in the United States was better versed in the business and politics of the Latin American world than William Grace, which makes it, on first glance, peculiar that he was not included among those American delegates named to the First International American Congress of 1889.

A congress of American nations had first been invited to convene in 1881 by Blaine, then serving as Garfield's secretary of state. A few months after Garfield's death, Blaine was replaced in office and the momentum for the congress dissipated. But when recalled to serve as secretary of state by Harrison in 1889, Blaine resurrected his idea of a pan-American congress.

Blaine was interested in fomenting trade between the United States and Latin America as a basis for closer bonds among the nations of the American continents. Blaine's vision may have been premature, for while over forty million potential Latin American customers and large potential markets existed south of the United States, American enterprise was generally satisfied to exploit the rapidly expanding domestic market.

Yet another forceful wind was blowing America's social and political sails, turning men's minds rather to the world than to the continent. Imperialism had taken hold of many Americans in the late 1880s and early 1890s. Although Blaine and Grace were moderates on this front, one must recognize that the complicated American character of the era embraced expanding United States power beyond its immediate borders. Although William Grace certainly was no saber-rattling jingoist of the decade, he firmly believed in the extension and development of ties between the Americas to facilitate the growth of a greater United States. He thus very much supported Blaine in his efforts to launch the First International American Congress, which finally convened in October 1889 in Washington. Delegates from eighteen countries attended.

Ten Americans represented the United States. Included among these were Andrew Carnegie and Charles Flint. The head of the American delegation was an ex-senator from Missouri, John B. Henderson, who had little or no experience with Latin American matters. William Grace was not included precisely because he was at the opposite end of the spectrum from somebody like Henderson. Grace was " 'too largely involved

in Chilean and Peruvian affairs to act as American Commr.,' "
and thus was compromised by his very closeness to Latin
America.[28] Besides, Grace had supported Cleveland in 1884
against Blaine's presidential attempt and Grace's mainstream
position in the Democratic party almost was guaranteed to produce a certain coolness in Republicans Harrison and Blaine,
who conferred closely on the selection of the American delegates.

Grace was peeved at his exclusion and later let off some steam
to a *New York Times* reporter in March 1890.[29] He criticized the
Latin American delegates, mostly lawyers and diplomats, who
possessed little commercial experience, while snorting that
most of the United States delegates were largely ignorant of
Latin American ways, language, customs, and culture. The congress had accomplished little in key commercial matters, in
reducing mutual tariffs, or in fomenting trade. After the article
appeared in the *Times*, Grace lamely excused himself to Blaine,
explaining that the interview had been confidential and not
meant for publication.[30] He subsequently gave several other
interviews, published in the *New York World* and *Export and
Finance*, for example, praising the work of the congress.

Ten years later Grace immersed himself in the most impressive American undertaking of the era with respect to Latin
America, and this time no excess of involvement in "Chilean
and Peruvian affairs" kept him out. Indeed, his experience in
Latin American affairs was his most prominent asset in the
maneuver to gain control over the building of a transisthmian
canal in Nicaragua in 1899. It was the most ambitious venture
ever attempted by William and Michael Grace and it placed
them squarely in the center of American dreams and aspirations
in an age when few things seemed impossible.

Until the middle of the nineteenth century, little energy,
other than on some thinking, scribbling, and scrambling about
jungles, had been expended in the construction of a canal across
Central America or Panama to connect the Atlantic and Pacific
Oceans. Nature's obstacles were impressive and man's capa-
bilities limited. Dreamers as far back as the sixteenth century
had turned over the possibilities, but the project never advanced beyond idle fancy. Even those who pondered it seriously in the early nineteenth century—the great German
explorer Baron Alexander von Humboldt for one—did not necessarily agree on the placement or route of such a pathway
between the seas.

Some, notably Humboldt, viewed Nicaragua as the most practical route. Others championed Panama, or the Tehuantepec region of southern Mexico. They even differed on the potential site for the canal *within* Panama, Nicaragua, or Tehuantepec. Various rivers, mountains, and lakes, most of them never seen by the armchair engineers, represented opportunities or barriers, depending on which route one espoused.

The Nicaragua route became known as Humboldt's, for the German scientist celebrated its virtues in an essay first published in 1811.[31] That Humboldt had never set foot in Nicaragua seemed to disturb no one.

Aside from some reports and books by a few itinerant archaeologists and diplomats who discoursed knowingly, but unprofessionally, on the virtues of the Nicaragua route in succeeding years, it remained a backwater—like most of Central America—in the American mind of the nineteenth century; that is, until 1848 when gold fever snapped the nation's head to the west.

The news of California's goldfields was confirmed in the East by late 1848 and the rush was on in 1849. Nicaragua was but one route to reach the West, but it proved to be an attractive one compared to sailing around the South American continent or sweating through Panama.[32] Nicaragua offered cheaper transportation, a healthier climate, and sometimes even abundant provisions. One embarked on a steamer from New York or New Orleans, landed at San Juan del Norte at the mouth of the San Juan River, rowed, kedged, poled, or (later) steamed up the river to Lake Nicaragua, transited that lake to the city of Granada, and then crossed by stagecoach or mule the 134 miles north to Realejo (modern Corinto) on the Pacific. At Realejo one reembarked and continued to San Francisco. By 1851 one could book passage from New Orleans to San Francisco via Nicaragua for about $180.00 in steerage and $300.00 in cabin. The entire trip, including the 376-mile passage across Nicaragua, could take several weeks or months. It depended upon the direction one was going and the availability of transportation at the time one happened upon the scene, be it at the humble port of San Juan del Norte on the hot Mosquito Coast or at remote waystations along the rapids of the San Juan River mobbed by gringos on their way to make it rich.

The rush to California drew the attention of both capitalists and diplomats to Nicaragua. Commodore Cornelius Vanderbilt established in 1851 a line to transport passengers speedily and comfortably from the East Coast to California. A year earlier the United States and England had negotiated a treaty binding both nations to neutrality and joint control over any canal built in Central America or Panama.

Most specifically, the Clayton-Bulwer Treaty read that neither England nor the United States " 'will ever obtain or maintain for itself any exclusive control over the said Shipcanal; agreeing that neither will ever erect or maintain any fortifications commanding the same, or in the vicinity thereof, or occupy, or fortify, or colonize, or assume or exercise any dominion over . . . Central America. . . . ' "[33] The treaty would cast a long shadow over the last half of the century, especially as Americans came more and more to resent the binding portions with respect to a canal. But it did have the effect, through other provisions, of limiting the extension of the powerful British presence in Central America by barring further British expansion of its dominions centered in British Honduras.

Vanderbilt was interested in more than merely transporting Americans from coast to coast via Nicaragua, although his line made a good profit and rivaled the Panama route. For example, he transported almost twenty thousand people to Panama's twenty-seven thousand in the year 1853.

In 1850 Vanderbilt created the American Atlantic & Pacific Ship Canal Company and hired Col. Orville W. Childs to survey the route for a canal. The concession from Nicaragua to build the canal had already been secured by a Vanderbilt-led syndicate in 1849. The second step was the engineering survey and the third was raising the capital. Childs would do the engineering and Vanderbilt was already priming such firms as Baring Brothers and Rothschild to start the capital flowing from London to Nicaragua via New York.

Childs took fourteen engineers and surveyors with him to Nicaragua in August 1850. He was well qualified, having only recently served as chief engineer for the enlargement of the Erie Canal in New York, considered to be one of the marvels of the century.[34] While some of the engineers busied themselves clearing the major obstacles—such as rapids—on the San Juan River, the surveyors ranged over the narrow twelve-mile hilly neck of land dividing the closest point on Lake Nicaragua, Virgin Bay, from the town of San Juan del Sur on the Pacific. Vanderbilt himself made a trip to Nicaragua in late 1850 and was convinced that the construction of a canal across Nicaragua was feasible.

When Childs' report was officially tendered in March 1852 Vanderbilt was buoyed with enthusiasm.[35] The canal not only was a practical vision but could be constructed for about thirty-one million dollars. The stock of Vanderbilt's Canal Company soared, and it seemed another, more immense, fortune, based on the noble act of linking the oceans for the good of all mankind, was in the making. But the English bankers did not buy the idea. They refused to invest in Vanderbilt's proposed canal, objecting particularly to the relatively shallow seventeen-foot depth projected. To have enlarged and deepened the canal to accommodate the transoceanic traffic that interested Europeans would have meant increasing the costs to over a hundred million dollars. The United States simply did not have the capital to go it alone on such a grand project and the canal stock plummeted as fast as it had risen.

American visions of a canal persisted, notwithstanding. The next major steps in the making of the Nicaragua canal paradoxically were taken by a young brevet captain in the United States Army crossing the isthmus of Panama the same year Childs presented his engineering report to Vanderbilt and the United States Congress.

When Ulysses S. Grant slogged across Panama in 1852 with his unit, the Fourth U.S. Infantry Regiment, the toll from the jungle, its fevers, its heat, and its misery appalled him. More than a hundred men perished, principally from cholera, and Grant never forgot that passage, maintaining for the rest of his life an interest in building an interoceanic canal.[36] When he became president in 1869 he did something about this interest. Seven surveying and engineering expeditions sponsored by the American government were sent to Central America and Panama in the early 1870s to identify the best route by rigorous scientific examination.

Two separate naval expeditions made the survey of Nicaragua in a laborious exploration that lasted over a year from 1872 to 1873. Nicaragua took its toll of Americans. Comdr. Alexander F. Crosman and five sailors were drowned early in the course of the first expedition, which was completed under the command of Chester Hatfield. The second expedition was led by Comdr. Edward P. Lull. Like his fellow officers, Lull was dedicated to the building of an isthmian canal to enable the navy to pass freely and rapidly from one ocean to the other and to link the American coasts as well.

At the head of the overall effort Grant placed an old friend and confidant, Rear Adm. Daniel Ammen. He presided over the three-member Interoceanic Canal Commission, established in 1872, which received all the reports and was charged with rendering a final opinion on the suitability of the various routes. In 1876 the Ammen commission unanimously recommended the Nicaragua route, but by then the Grant administration was on its way out and the momentum fizzled. Furthermore, by the end of the decade the irresistible Ferdinand de Lesseps was in Panama with his legions and the world watched the French attempt to cut the big ditch through that hot, pestilential isthmus.

Americans by and large remained skeptical of this heroic French effort to conquer the Panama route. They demonstrated their pessimism by investing little in the Compagnie Universelle du Canal Interoceanique and clucked their tongues collectively as Lesseps' grand project slowly mired inself in the muck and jungles and fevers of Panama. William Grace did some business with the French in Panama in the mid-1880s (see Chapter 8), but had also cautioned Michael to keep a sharp eye on the Paris bourse for any sign of financial weakness. When the French failed in the late 1880s, Americans once again refocused with energy on the "American" route.

First Childs' report in 1852 and then Ammen's commission in 1876 demonstrated beyond any doubt the superiority of the Nicaragua route. It would involve fewer engineering problems, the cost would be less, the climate was salubrious, the Nicaraguan government amenable, and it would be closer to the United States. The French failure at Panama underscored the horrors—medical, social, and technical—of that route. Everybody knew that Nicaragua would be where American engineers laid the capstone of American enterprise, ingenuity, pluck, and perseverance.

An attempt to begin the great project was made in the late 1880s. The Maritime Canal Company was formed in 1886 by a group of American investors presided over by Hiram Hitchcock, the company's first president. The company petitioned for and received a national charter from Congress in 1887, signed a contract with Nicaragua to build the canal, and began digging in 1890. It spent over six million dollars before 1893, when the financial panic that year coincided almost precisely with Maritime's attempts to refinance the enterprise, and the project collapsed.[37] A leading supporter of Maritime was Sen. John Tyler Morgan of Alabama. Senator Morgan continued to attempt a revival of Maritime with government support, hoping to transfer the initiative and control from private enterprise to the public domain. That philosophy inevitably clashed with William Grace's distrust of government sponsorship of any great project. But, while Grace and Morgan debated in 1898 and 1899 over the means, public or private, to build a canal across Nicaragua, both avidly preferred that route to the French one in Panama.

Morgan was one of the most powerful men in the Senate. He chaired the Senate Committee on Interoceanic Canals and was considered by many to be the premier expert on everything from grand designs to the nuts and bolts of a transisthmian canal. A thin and frail appearance only served to mask an indomitable character. As a Confederate officer during the Civil War, Morgan distinguished himself in a cavalry charge at the Battle of Chickamauga, finishing the war as a brigadier general.[38] Trained as a trial lawyer, he made a formidable opponent of any foe in the Senate, to which he was elected in 1876. As David McCullough described him, Morgan "was watchful, uncompromising, fiercely independent, nearly always irritable . . . he was also scrupulously honest . . . [and] the two greatest pleasures in Morgan's life, it was commonly said, were work and a good fight."[39]

On the Nicaragua canal, Morgan was nearly fanatical. "He knew the reports of every surveying expedition to Central America, the findings of the several successive canal commissions since the Grant administration . . . he had worked longest and hardest for congressional support for the ill-fated Maritime Canal Company, . . . had been the author of several canal bills . . . had done more to inform the public, heard more testimony, read more, asked more questions, and had more information on the entire subject of an interoceanic passage than any figure of either party. The canal was the dream of his life and he was certain as he could possibly be that it might be a Nicaragua canal."[40] Like many southerners who reach national stature, he remained loyal to his beloved South, even while occupying the limelight in Washington. Happily for Morgan, the Nicaragua canal also augured prosperity for the states of the old Confederacy. Mobile, New Orleans, Galveston would all become major entrepôts based on their proximity to the canal and to the natural resources of the South. Coal, cotton, lumber would flow in abundance from Gulf Coast ports to the Pacific and give muscle to the rise of the New South from the ashes of defeat.

Morgan's allies in promoting the Nicaragua canal at the end of the century were no less persuasive or powerful than the senator from Selma, Alabama. Adm. Alfred Thayer Mahan's

The Influence of Sea Power upon History was published in 1890 and, together with popular articles in *Atlantic Monthly* and other widely circulating magazines, roused the American imagination into thinking in worldwide terms. Great Britain had built an empire on the backs of its fleets and the United States was no less a power whose destiny was even greater. The Caribbean should become an American ocean with a canal piercing Nicaragua to provide for rapid transport and communications, commercial and naval, between the Atlantic and Pacific shores. The youngish assistant secretary of the navy in 1897, Theodore Roosevelt, ardently supported a greater America whose influence would be projected vigorously beyond our borders, and the Nicaragua canal was an integral part of Roosevelt's vision.[41]

The flush of victory from the Spanish-American War of 1898 brought the Nicaragua canal project to center stage. America needed a two-ocean navy; that much had been demonstrated by the naval battles off Cuba and the Philippines, battles which effectively dispatched the Spanish navy and secured victory in the war. No less paramount was the construction of a canal to reduce the long, wearying, and even dangerous voyage around the Horn. The battleship *Oregon* had steamed flat out all the way from San Francisco to the Caribbean upon the outbreak of war. The nation's hopes rode on the dash of the *Oregon* and a collective tension followed its progress as it plunged and drove down through the Pacific, around the Horn, and up the South Atlantic across the equator once again, finally arriving off the coast of southern Florida sixty-seven days out of California![42] The twelve-thousand-mile voyage would have been only four thousand miles with a canal through Nicaragua. It had to be built.

In late summer 1898, after the formal end of the war in July, Wiliam Grace decided to enter the lists. If a canal were built across Nicaragua, then he would do it. Edward F. Cragin, formerly associated with the Maritime Canal Co., became one of Grace's partners in the enterprise. Their intention was to substitute themselves for Maritime, obtain new and better concessions from Nicaragua, and proceed to build the canal, charged as they and the country were from the war and its repercussions.

The Nicaragua Canal Syndicate was formed in late August to further this goal and fifteen individuals subscribed one thousand dollars apiece immediately and promised an additional ten thousand for the project.[43] To put this act into contemporary perspective, one must consider two basic premises upon which William Grace was operating. One, the project had to be privately financed and built since the Clayton-Bulwer Treaty of 1850 prohibited the United States government from directly undertaking such an endeavor. Two, the Maritime Canal Co.'s concession from the Nicaragua government lapsed on October 9, 1899, opening the road to the Grace syndicate. Maritime had ceased operations in Nicaragua after the panic of 1893. The Nicaraguan government on the other hand was anxious to get started once again and was fully prepared to void the contract between it and Maritime when it expired in 1899. The Grace syndicate promised action, whereas the Maritime had gone moribund. The stage was set.

Satisfied that a good beginning had been made, Grace sent Cragin and Eyre to Nicaragua to negotiate a new concession in September, while he went off to Europe for a vacation. Grace suffered a slight stroke abroad which necessitated a period of convalescence in France. But Michael, as on other occasions, was able to take up where William left off, traveling to the United States in October to pursue the project with his characteristic energy.[44]

Cragin and Eyre were welcomed warmly in Nicaragua by President José Santos Zelaya, who was eager to negotiate with the Grace syndicate. However, Senator Morgan and Maritime's lobby in Washington were by no means to be discounted since they still wished to revive Maritime's work. Zelaya was caught in a squeeze between the Grace syndicate and Maritime. He did not wish to offend Maritime and its powerful friends, but he did wish to promote the most practical route for a Nicaragua canal.[45]

The negotiations Eyre and Cragin undertook in Nicaragua soon dampened their warm welcome. Not only was Maritime's lobby in Nicaragua, represented by the United States consul Chester Donaldson, strong, but Eyre and Cragin had to consider a proposed Central American union of Nicaragua, El Salvador, and Honduras, which was expected to come into being on November 10, 1898, as the Republic of the United States of Central America. On that date Zelaya would lose his power to negotiate such contracts to the new federal government with its capital at Chinandega. A union of all Central American republics, including Guatemala and Costa Rica, had been the dream of many political idealists since the era of independence in the 1820s, and this effort was but one chapter in that promising but frustrating dream.[46] Furthermore, Nicaragua and Costa Rica had been bickering for years over their common frontier running along the San Juan River. Any Nicaragua canal was posited on the use of that river so negotiations had to occur concurrently with Costa Rica as well as Nicaragua. To accomplish this end, a colorful colleague named Alexander S. Bacon traveled from Panama through Costa Rica to Nicaragua in September and October beating the drums for the Grace syndicate while Cragin and Eyre hammered out the details of the concession from Zelaya.

Bacon's task was to secure the rights of passage in Costa Rica, and he moved with cocky aplomb through the ports and presidential palaces of Central America. He left Panama from the city of Colón in early September, disgusted with the filth and unsanitary conditions "which breed yellow fever and had given the Isthmus its bad name."[47] After taking pictures from a small sailboat, which carried him up part of the unfinished canal, "we were rash enough to take 12 o'clock breakfast at the Swiss Hotel, which is called the best in Colón. The dining room looked inviting enough, but I had occasion to use the toiletroom, and its filthy condition was sufficient to breed fevers enough to exterminate a nation. The second course was fish. Mr. Diaz discovered that part of his fish was taking a cake walk on its own account, and he ate no more breakfast. As I am an old traveler, not averse to a mixed diet, I continued the program to the end."[48] Sang-froid in the tropics!

From Colón Bacon took the steamer *Alexander Bixie* to Puerto Limón on Costa Rica's Atlantic coast. The passengers slept on deck, showered night and day by cinders from the boilers, and broiled by the heat during the day. Puerto Limón was little improvement. A drenching, steamy, downpour bathed Bacon on the train trip up to the capital, San José. Once there Bacon and his traveling companion were rather politely shunned for a few days. Yellow fever had been raging in Puerto Limón and new arrivals from the coast were always slightly suspect of being carriers. However, Capt. William Merry, the American minister to Nicaragua then in Costa Rica, received them cordially.

Bacon recognized that Captain Merry was interested in the Maritime Canal Co. and owned his present position to its lobby in Washington. He hoped to persuade Merry to support the syndicate, but what Bacon did not know was that Merry was in close touch with both Senator Morgan and Hiram Hitchcock, the president of Maritime, and was still decidedly a Maritime man. Whether Merry deliberately misled Bacon or was simply acting out the role of helpful diplomat is not known.

Within a few days Bacon secured interviews with the minister of foreign affairs and the president of Costa Rica, Rafael Iglesias. Their first meeting lasted five hours, from eight in the evening until one the following morning, testifying to their community of interests. They talked over the Maritime Co.'s failure, the Grace syndicate's grand possibilities, the uneasy state of relations between Costa Rica and Nicaragua, and the president's two other pet projects—a new bank to get the country back on the gold standard and the completion of the railroad to the Pacific Coast. Bacon may have also reminded President Iglesias that the Graces had been Minor C. Keith's principal agents in the United States during the early epoch of railroad building in Costa Rica, and Minor Keith had achieved the stature of a near hero in his adopted homeland. The next mornng Bacon delivered a copy of the draft canal concession to Iglesias.

A major stumbling block still remained—the potential bid by the United States government to take over Maritime and build the canal itself. Bacon thus spent a large part of his time arguing that the United States could not build the canal in this generation, whereas the syndicate was prepared to start at once.[49] Bacon had succeeded in convincing himself of this argument, and now he had to weave the spell in Costa Rica. Iglesias was able, agreeable, polite, and ambitious. Bacon reported to Cragin that "we both spread it on pretty thick, and the passages at arms in that line were a draw . . . whether he or I am superior in the diplomacy of taffy has not been determined by our single interview."[50]

Well aware of the effect of a good show, Bacon "carried out the program of assumed magnificence." He frequented the opera, courted the president's family, and cultivated the image that "I am a wonderfully rich man."[51] He also kept his ear to the ground and his antennae sharp, meeting frequently with Minor Keith, whose wife also happened to be Iglesias's aunt. These impressions of the Costa Rican mood were then passed on to Cragin. The important negotiations, however, were proceeding in Nicaragua and Bacon was anxious to learn how negotiations were developing there "as I think Costa Rica will be guided largely by what Nicaragua does."[52] Bacon moved on to Nicaragua in early October to work more closely with Cragin and Eyre, having worn out his suit but not his welcome in San José. "As the principal people have laid themselves out to make it pleasant for me, the time [was] very agreeably spent . . . we [threw] on all the magnificence we knew how and my dress suit is about worn out. . . . "⁵³

In Managua it was Ned Eyre who was worn out, not his attire. The pressure from Donaldson to stall or somehow break off negotiations with Eyre and Cragin prompted Zelaya to a new tactic. He upped the ante from $100,000 to $200,000, payable in gold by the Grace syndicate to Nicaragua upon ratification of the contract. This, to Eyre, seemed a not unreasonable offer, but he was nearly spent by the protracted negotiations and was sick enough to be bedridden. He was now, in fact, carrying out negotiations with Zelaya's principal negotiator, Dr. Matus, from bed. Eyre urged that the concession as now written should be speedily approved. It was especially imperative, given the imminent ratification of the new Central American union; Eyre did not think similar concessions could be obtained from the proposed new union as had been negotiated with Zelaya.⁵⁴ Sick and pessimistic, Ned was even dubious of bringing the present discussions to a successful end. Indeed, Eyre had already decided to quit Nicaragua and go home as soon as possible, "no matter what the outcome may be."⁵⁵ At this juncture, Ned Eyre was fed up with Nicaraguan politics and canals, and was eager to throw the whole thing over for a steamer away from Nicaragua.

Michael Grace, however, blew up at Zelaya's new demands. He wrote a stinging note to President Zelaya. Even couched in polite language, the message must have smarted. The members of the syndicate would simply not accept this new alteration, especially since they had agreed to a great many other modifications already suggested by Nicaragua.⁵⁶ It was imperative for Zelaya to realize that the members of the syndicate would bow out of the negotiations in a moment's notice, since they had only entered into this agreement at the insistence of Mr. Cragin, "and if nothing is realized, the small loss incurred in expenses up to now won't bother them—they won't even think again of the Nicaragua canal." That was upping the stakes with a bluff, but Michael was a master at the game.

It would be a sad mistake to throw away the future of Nicaragua for the temporary advantages being sought by Zelaya. Furthermore, many in the United States were pushing for a government-sponsored canal, a proposition which Grace knew was perceived by Zelaya not to be in the best interests of Nicaragua. Finally, the president was importuned to change his mind "para que 'el pan no se queme en la boca del horno.' "[57] Michael's use of the Spanish *dicho*, or adage, was characteristic of the Graces' fluency in their adopted tongue. Loosely translated, it urged Zelaya not to burn the bread at the door of the oven. If the concession were not approved now with the $100,000 price tag, the opportunity might never again offer itself.

In Managua Eyre and Cragin wore down the president as well, returning always to the dismal record of the Maritime Canal Co. and the growing threat from Panama. Lose another ten years and Nicaragua will lose the whole game, not just a few innings. To keep stringing along with Maritime was a bad proposition for Nicaragua, whose future was at stake as the crossroads of the world. Zelaya finally relented and agreed to sign a "promise" of contract with Eyre and Cragin. Donaldson, however, interceded three times and the president's signature was withheld at the last moment. Zelaya then accepted the Eyre offer to pay for a necessary extra session of congress. Zelaya faced a dilemma. But as the November 1 deadline approached, Zelaya's defenses against the Grace syndicate's arguments crumbled in the face of the harsh realities: Maritime had failed to deliver while the Grace interests produced cash backed by a powerful syndicate of some of the wealthiest and most powerful men in the United States. Zelaya signed, on October 27, 1898, the promise to contract, which gave the syndicate the concession to build the canal when the Maritime concession officially lapsed on October 9, 1899.

Both parties were pleased with the agreement. Immensely relieved by his decision, Zelaya addressed an extraordinary session of the Nicaragua congress, characterizing the Grace syndicate as a "well organized and strong company which has many elements of power and abundant capital, as it has conclusively shown by the signatures of the sundry influential men who recommended it, and by the deposit of $100,000 in gold."[58] After garnishing his address by noting various other improvements of the new concession over the Maritime Co.'s old contract of 1887, Zelaya struck home by extolling the virtues of private over public initiative in the history of the United States. "The fertile initiative of the United States of America . . . is, beyond a doubt, destined to open the way between the two oceans, as that way has been marked out by the lavish hand of nature. All our people feel confidence in that initiative; yet some among us prefer the initiative of the government to that of private parties, thus forgetting the antecedents of that great people among whom governmental initiative is of little value when compared to private initiative, this latter being the powerful lever which has accomplished in that emporium of national life the most astonishing improvements in our time."[59] Those words must have rung sweetly in William Grace's ear. To Senator Morgan, Zelaya's speech, if he read it in translation, was only so much rhetoric. By the end of 1898 Morgan was preparing another bill for action by the U.S. Congress to rescue the Maritime Canal Co. And Morgan was a formidable opponent.

The Grace syndicate then attempted to gain control of Maritime by buying its depreciated stock. The idea was, almost predictably, Michael's; he possessed a well-known penchant for dramatic, even flamboyant, solutions. In this instance, the move, which would have brilliantly preempted the scene, failed. The Maritime Co. was still being championed by Senator Morgan and the shareholders felt Morgan's bill, once passed, would redeem them all.[60] William had returned from Europe in October to help Michael with this increasingly complex affair. He reorganized the syndicate, dropping some disaffected members such as Charles Flint, adding others with equal if not greater resources and prestige.[61] Once more animated by a good fight, William Grace, now sixty-eight and still weak from the stroke suffered in Europe, threw himself in with vigor.

It was important to maintain open channels to Nicaragua and Grace kept Zelaya advised of progress with letters considerably more tactful and less blustering than Michael's earlier communications with the president. The Maritime Co. still had a strong lobby in Central America and it was crucial to keep Zelaya and Nicaragua loyal to the syndicate.

Grace told Zelaya that Maritime was on its last legs and Morgan's bill stood little chance of passage. It only "lives in the region of illusions," and Senator Morgan's florid rhetoric and endless speeches are producing a negative effect on the American public.[62] Intemperate remarks by the senator should be dismissed by those like yourself who are above such crass polemics. Nicaragua is a sovereign state and Senator Morgan and Maritime simply cannot act in the absence of serious consultation with Nicaragua on such matters of transcendent importance. It is highly unlikely that the Morgan bill will be approved, for no amount of hysterical oratory will convince the American public to pay the expenses of a company that went bankrupt and completed few of its obligations. Besides, the American people are firm believers in private enterprise and are not likely to support such a large venture based on government sponsorship.

Those supporting the Panama route must still, of course, be reckoned with since they have enlisted some of the most important railroad owners in the United States and have other powerful interests behind them. But the syndicate, Grace assured Zelaya, has also attracted some major railroad entrepreneurs in the course of an October 1898 reorganization and the Panama interests will not challenge it seriously.

Costa Rica will have to be dealt with as well, since portions of the canal might impinge on its territory. However, no serious problems are presented in that area. The syndicate has already been dealing with Costa Rica and as soon as President Iglesias returns from Europe early in 1899 those matters can be brought under control.

Grace offered his regrets that the projected Central American union had not materialized. "Perhaps this noble work could be accomplished in the future."

Nicaragua was also interested in refinancing its internal and foreign debt, and William offered Michael's experienced services for this contemplated endeavor.

As Christmas 1898 neared, the Grace syndicate had a full head of steam up and William Grace assured Zelaya that the Morgan bill to support Maritime would not pass. He proved right on that point, but less prophetic on another: "Interest here as in England in a canal grows every day, and even though the friends of Panama work without rest, they will obtain nothing."[63]

Already by the end of the year the Graces were receiving job applications from engineers, surveyors, railroad men, and even inventors inquiring about the Nicaragua canal project. Writing for employment was obviously not a time to be bashful about one's merits. J. R. Whittle of Nashville, Tennessee, wrote:

> Dear Sir:
> I am a young man with a good business training familiar with bookkeeping and general business correspondence; with few bad habits and a large capacity for hard work. If you need the services of such a man when you begin work on the Nicaragua canal I should be glad to correspond with you.[64]

Others who inquired were veterans of the jungles and fevers of Panama and Central America, intoxicated once more by a grand design.

> Gentlemen: from the late papers I learn that your company has secured

the concession for the building of the Nicaragua canal and I write this to make application for a position in the machinery department when your works begin. I am a locomotive engineer but have had long experience with dredging machinery both with suction and bucket dredges. I have lived 20 months in Nicaragua [and] am familiar with the route. Had the yellow-fever on the Panama Canal; am therefore immune. At present am a civil service employee of the U.S. Engineer department on furlough and can enter your employ at any time. Can furnish testimonials to my standing as a sober industrious and skillful man. I also speak Spanish sufficiently to be of service.[65]

Henry Curtis Spalding suggested that an invention of his might be of direct assistance in the new venture:

I have long been a student of canal questions, especially as to construction and management, and am now concerned in one of the most important canal projects in this country. The needs of this enterprise have led me to renew the search for a better method than has yet been found for quickly and safely transferring ships from one level to another when the difference in levels exceeds the ordinary lift of a canal lock. I have, at last, found a method and am preparing to patent it. This method would be a great service to any who are interested in the American isthmus transit. Therefore I mention it to you for your consideration.[66]

Spalding's approach was coy and secretive. He offered the possibility of a technological breakthrough for a project everyone knew would require the highest degree of imagination and inventiveness.

From Jamaica, William H. Orrett offered his services to provide something more immediately necessary than the patent for a new lock:

I notice by our cablegrams that your esteemed Senior, Mr. W. R. Grace, is at present [November 15, 1898] in London arranging to carry thro' the Panama or Nicaragua canal, and, if he succeeds, you will no doubt require a General Agent in the West Indies to procure and ship Laborers to the works, as well as supplies, and generally to protect your interests, and I should therefore be glad if you would kindly use your influence on my behalf, which I feel sure that you will do.[67]

While offers of inventions, labor contractors, experienced and jungleproof engineers poured in, William and Michael Grace were still at odds with Senator Morgan and his support of their rival, the Maritime Canal Co. A trip to Washington in November 1898 by Michael produced few results, although he chatted with President McKinley and Secretary of State John Hay, and parlayed for over four hours with the main obstacle, Senator Morgan. The old Alabamian proved remarkably tractable in their conversation, agreeing that the Grace concession from Nicaragua was much better than Maritime's and that he personally favored private enterprise over a public effort. Yet Morgan urged the Grace syndicate to come to terms with Maritime and thus present a united front. Such an effort would have a much better chance in Congress. That body wished a government-sponsored canal built by a company with a national charter such as Maritime possessed. Michael left the interview somewhat frustrated, but feisty as usual.

Although Morgan refused to budge from his support of Maritime, he admitted the small probability of his bill passing Congress.[68] Morgan was right. His bill failed to pass Congress in 1899, but the decision by the government to support a Nicaragua or Panama canal was no nearer to being made. Pushed by the Panama lobby, Congress kept the competition open between the two routes by commissioning a million-dollar study to survey both routes intensively and to recommend the best. Rear Adm. John G. Walker was appointed head of this Isthmian Canal Commission, which began its work in summer 1899, building on the work of the earlier Nicaragua Canal Commission, also headed by Walker. Then Congress waited on the results to be tendered by the Isthmian Canal, or second Walker, Commission.[69] That report would not be submitted until late 1901.

In the meantime, William Grace once more reorganized the syndicate early in 1899 to bring in more subscribers and strengthen its public and financial position. Among the twenty-six members subscribing $10,500 apiece were John A. McCall, president of New York Life Insurance Co.; George Westinghouse; Levi P. Morton, ex-vice president of the United States and a major banker in New York and Europe; G. G. Williams, president of Chemical National Bank; James Stillman, president of National City Bank; John Jacob Astor; and Warner Miller, ex-senator.[70] Ever the tactician, Michael also reminded William about the existence of a contract between Nicaragua and an English company to navigate on Lake Nicaragua that could complicate matters for Maritime and Washington.[71] As the adversaries sparred in public and private forums in New York, Washington, and London, those following the flow of events from Managua were equally absorbed in the complex battle.

Pedro Gonzalez, the syndicate's lawyer in Nicaragua, continued to face a very unfriendly Merry, who spoke of the syndicate with some disdain. He dwelled on the fact that the syndicate had no contract with Costa Rica, which continued to be a major obstacle in their way.[72] While Merry was being watched closely by Gonzalez, rumors ricocheted in Nicaragua, a nation soon expecting to be chosen as the site for the crossroads to the world. Gonzalez begged for news from New York to provide besieging reporters, and to offset contrary propaganda issuing from Merry, Weissen, Gomez, and other opponents of the syndicate.[73]

On October 9, 1899, the Maritime Co.'s concession automatically terminated, seemingly clearing the air. According to the terms of the syndicate's contract with Nicaragua, an interoceanic canal company "shall be organized within six months" from the time the Maritime Co.'s concession lapsed, and "within four months from the organization of the [Interoceanic Canal] Company it shall deposit in the General Treasury on Nicaragua four hundred thousand ($400,000) dollars, American gold."[74] The syndicate fulfilled the first obligation, but failed in the second. After August 10, 1900, the Interoceanic Canal Company forfeited its concession to build a canal across Nicaragua by failing to pay the $400,000. What happened?

The mood of the country, titillated by the Spanish-American War and driven by the imagination and verve of Teddy Roosevelt and other expansionists, certainly desired a canal. It was a challenge fit for titans, and Americans were firmly convinced of their collective destinies. Toward this end, the obstacles standing in the way of an American canal were being rapidly cleared as the century drove to its conclusion.

One of the most obvious was the old Clayton-Bulwer Treaty, binding the United States to British agreement and participation in any canal endeavor. Shortly after the end of the Spanish-American War, McKinley instructed Hay to begin negotiating with Great Britain on a treaty to supplant the Clayton-Bulwer agreement. The English were approached at a good time, bogged down as they were in the Boer War. Central America no longer represented a major sphere of interest.[75] Accordingly, a treaty was signed between Hay and Sir Julian Pauncefote, the British ambassador to Washington, early in February 1900. Submitted to the Senate for its advice and consent, it was rejected in subsequent deliberations.

That august body objected strenuously to the clause providing for a neutral canal with no fortifications, open with free access to all vessels, merchant and naval alike, in times of war and peace. Although the United States would have the exclusive right to build and operate the canal, that British concession did not satisfy expansionist powers in the Senate like Henry Cabot Lodge and John Morgan. From his post as governor of New York, Teddy Roosevelt sounded the clarion call for the opposition, claiming that such a treaty would be next to useless and a positive menace in time of war. If we are able to build a canal, then let us guarantee its utility during war by fortifying it and denying it to the enemy.

Although temporarily demoralized by the defeat in the Senate, Hay returned to negotiations with Pauncefote. A second treaty was agreed to, omitting the clause on no fortifications, and signed on November 18, 1901. The deletion of the offending clause and the insertion of an article permitting the United States to protect the canal against "lawlessness and disorder" was a tacit admission of the United States' right to arm the canal. The treaty was ratified by the Senate on December 16.

Two months before, President McKinley had been assassinated by a mad anarchist named Leon Czolgosz. He was shot twice on September 6 in Buffalo, New York, while attending the Pan-American Exposition. Eight days later McKinley expired and Vice President Theodore Roosevelt bounded into the White House, at forty-two the youngest president in history.

Late in November Admiral Walker delivered his commission's report, and Senator Morgan prepared to bring it before his Interoceanic Canal Committee early in 1902. In December 1901 a bill introduced by Representative William Peters Hepburn of Iowa passed the House of Representatives. It called for the construction of a canal sponsored by the United States government in Nicaragua. When a formal agreement was signed between the United States and Nicaragua on December 10 with the same end in mind, the stage seemed set. Now it was simply the job of the Morgan committee to endorse the preliminary Walker Commission report tendered in November which favored the Nicaragua route.

By then the Grace syndicate and the Interoceanic Canal Company had been buried in the sentiment of the hour. Not only had their legal concessions expired by failing to deliver the $400,000 in American gold, but William Grace finally recognized that they had been swimming against the tide. "It was not expected when this matter was taken up by the Syndicate that the intention of having the canal built by our own Government would have manifested itself so strongly."[76] This strong manifestation, perfectly evident to the investors in the Interoceanic Canal Co., had prompted the failure to produce the $400,000 security and, by extension, the collapse of the Grace plan to build the canal across Nicaragua with private initiative and private capital.

Grace was convinced of the inappropriateness of a publicly sponsored project of this dimension. It would turn into a slow, political morass, lacking the continuity and steadfastness of a private venture. Nicaraguan sovereignty (for everyone, even in early 1902, still expected the canal to pierce through Nicaragua) would be seriously compromised. Costs would be extremely exaggerated. The construction of the magnificent capitol building at Albany struck Grace as a good example of a bad practice. It took thirty years to complete and cost twenty million dollars, and Grace figured it was worth three million at the most.[77]

Resigned by 1902 to having lost a grand opportunity, Grace must have looked on with some humor as his old rival, Senator Morgan, also succumbed to destiny. The one certainty virtually all had agreed upon changed dramatically. Instead of consistently supporting Nicaragua, the Walker Commission recommended Panama. Instead of voting for Nicaragua, the Senate voted for Panama. Instead of sending the dirt flying along Lake Nicaragua, American engineers plowed where few had envisioned, along the old French route festooned with disease, death, and failure.

The Walker Commission was persuaded to change its recommendation by two events. One, the French more than halved their original asking price of $109 million for all their excavations, their equipment, the Panama Railroad, their maps, surveys, drawings, and records.[78] Theodore Roosevelt and the powerful senator from Ohio, Mark Hanna, thought $40 million—the new asking price in January 1902—opened the door to Panama. With Roosevelt's gushing enthusiasm and energy, the momentum began to swing. Then nature added a tremendous clout when Momotombo, a volcano in Nicaragua, erupted on May 14. Only a few days before, Mt. Pelee had exploded on the island of Martinique in the Caribbean destroying the city of St. Pierre. Thirty thousand souls perished. When Momotombo rumbled in Nicaragua, the Panamian lobbyists, especially the enterprising Philippe Bunau-Varilla, drove home the lesson by distributing Nicaraguan stamps to senators on June 16, three days before the final ballot. The one-cent stamps showed a picturesque Momotombo erupting behind a wharf with a railroad in the foreground. On June 19, 1902, the Senate voted forty-two to thirty-four in favor of the Panama route.

Like the fight with Charles Flint in the late 1880s over the rubber business of Brazil, the failure of the Nicaragua canal venture was a debit on the Grace ledger in the nineteenth century. But the successes more than overcame the defeats and the growth of the company was steady. In 1891, for example, an analysis of the profits and losses of W. R. Grace & Co. reported a net profit of $69,998.39 based on a variety of enterprises now characteristic of the company's operations.[79] Among the items listed on the report were trade in nitrate of soda, wool, cotton, flax, "sundry shipments of merchandise," lithography for Peruvian bonds, venture for S.S. *Sirius* (one-third profit on shipment from San Francisco to Iquique), profit on exchange, chartering, Merchants Line, salaries, and apportionment of profits. In the last category, the three main partners, W. R. Grace, M. P. Grace, and J. W. Grace, each received 30 percent of $45,000, or $13,500 each. Edward Eyre received $4,500, which represented a 10 percent interest in the partnership, and J. F. Fowler, F. Dunloo, and A. Falcon (a Peruvian) each received a percentage of the profits amounting to $1,500–$2,000 each.

In 1894 W. R. Grace & Co. was incorporated in West Virginia with a capitalization of three million dollars. All original thirteen stockholders were members of the family. The executive body consisted of President William R. Grace, First Vice President Michael P. Grace, Second Vice President John W. Grace, Secretary Edward Eyre, and Treasurer J. Louis Schaefer.[80] The board of directors included Lillius Grace along with the above-mentioned officers.

In 1899 the company was reincorporated, this time in Connecticut, and the capitalization was doubled to six million dollars. Shareholders were increased to nineteen, but all were still members of the Grace clan. Yet, as noted in the analysis of the ledger of 1891, nonmembers of the family were already being included in sharing profits. This practice continued under the new incorporations, 34.75 percent of the dividends of the corporation under the Connecticut statutes being paid out as profit sharing to twenty managers and submanagers. Fourteen of these—among them David Stewart Iglehart, Louis Schaefer, Maurice Bouvier, Lawrence Shearman, John Fowler, Alberto Falcon, Federico Wightman (Chilean), and John Rossiter—were not members of the family.

Incorporation in the 1890s had been a natural transition for the company. The partnership form of association had served well up to then. Partnerships were contracts governed by common law and possessed the virtue of simplicity. Each partner had the power to speak or make contracts for the firm and to handle the company's business as though it were his own. On the other hand, the drawbacks in an age of increasing business complexity were numerous. No partner could dispose of holdings without the consent of all the others, and the death of any one of them dissolved the whole agreement.

By incorporating, continuity of the firm under one legal entity was accomplished. Furthermore, this very legal entity, W. R. Grace & Co., protected the Grace family members from personal liability for the company's debts, an important consideration and distinguishing feature of corporations.[81]

By the end of the decade Joseph P. Grace was assuming more and more responsibility as his abilities were clearly demonstrated. In 1897 he was made secretary and in 1899 promoted to second vice president. While William and Michael sparred with Senator Morgan and pushed for the hundred-million-dollar canal enterprise across Nicaragua, Joseph was taking charge of W. R. Grace & Co., working closely with his cousins and contemporaries such as D. Stewart Iglehart in the continued expansion of the business. He was a most appropriate executive for this developing multinational, for the range of his interests and activities was eclectic, always sharpening old businesses and constantly searching for new areas for investment. His management of company affairs at the turn of the century reflects his nature and the nature of the company—diverse, aggressive, a penchant for strong personal loyalties, and much in tune with the expanding American empire.

As one of the major officers of W. R. Grace & Co., Joseph had dealt directly with Theodore Roosevelt in the early stages of the Spanish-American War. The young assistant secretary of the navy was desperate to enlarge the American navy as rapidly as possible for the anticipated conflict with Spain and he asked Grace to inquire if the Argentines or Chileans would be willing to sell their newly commissioned cruisers, *San Martín* and *O'Higgins*, to the United States.[82] Urgent inquiries through the Grace offices in Valparaiso produced a negative reply and disappointed Joseph Grace's efforts to acquire the two cruisers for the United States.[83] While the outcome of the war was really never in doubt, Roosevelt's friendship with and confidence in the Graces was nonetheless confirmed by this incident. Old William and young Teddy had been allied in spirit as political reformers in New York since the 1880s, and Roosevelt maintained his good feelings toward William's successors.

New horizons always attracted the Graces. Joseph Grace was no exception. The business was already well established on the

West Coast of South America, and it was only natural to extend it into Argentina, then one of the most dynamic countries in Latin America, enjoying a surge of European immigrants, largely from Italy, and a rapid expansion in its basic agricultural and cattle industries. The Graces intended to open a house in Buenos Aires, and they characteristically studied the project in some detail.

John (Jack) Eyre, Joseph's cousin, was then running the Valparaiso house and he was consulted closely by Joseph Grace in early 1900.[84] Could Eyre spare John Fowler (in Chile since 1893), who had been very successful in working up new business both in merchandise and in produce? Would Fowler be enthusiastic about taking up new duties in Buenos Aires? There was no use in sending a man who was not enthusiastic about going.[85] Who would work with Fowler? Joseph Grace suggested Frank Grace, experienced in accounts and in handling the Antwerp Line business in San Francisco, for general produce, and D. Stewart Iglehart for merchandise. Grace admitted his general unfamiliarity with Argentina and so probed for good answers from cousin Jack in Chile. "I am the one who is accused of pushing for a house in Buenos Aires but of course know nothing about the conditions there or even in a similar market like Valparaiso, so if anything is to be done we must depend on you to go into the thing very carefully and advise us whether we had better go into market . . . what men . . . [etc.]"[86]

Grace wanted reports and a thorough study, but apparently he got more than he bargained for. Six months after the initial probe was made in February, Grace was still receiving reports, but nothing had been done to put the plans into action.[87] Grace asked that Fowler be sent to Buenos Aires armed with letters of introduction and charged with giving a final report. Iglehart was to accompany him to Buenos Aires since he was always a source of good ideas. But Fowler never made it past the high Cordilleras to Argentina. Grace was doing such good business in Chile that the Argentine project was allowed to lapse. Or as Joseph Grace phrased it nicely in April 1901, "We are so bully with other things the idea of opening a house there [Buenos Aires] has taken a back seat for the time being."[88]

A good business environment, of course, attracts strong competitors and the skills of the Grace managers in Chile were constantly honed by their rivals. The major competitor in 1900 was a Chilean shipping and trading firm named Beeche, Duval

& Co. The successor to Beeche & Co., Browne, Beeche & Co., and Hemenway & Co., Beeche, Duval & Co. was as much English as Chilean.[89] It chartered or rented steamers from the West Coast to Europe and North America and provided the most formidable nose-to-nose battle for business with the Grace steamers and windjammers at the turn of the century.

Like other major competitors, Beeche was watched like a hawk and attacked whenever possible. In May 1900 Joseph Grace reported to Lawrence Shearman, managing the Grace house in Lima, that "we are holding down Beeche and Co.'s business in Guayaquil. Juan Parodi, we understand, has rejected the lard they shipped him by the 'Queen Margaret,' and we are now gunning for their last regular customer, C. Ninci and Co. You, no doubt, will do your part to keep down their business in the northern Peruvian ports, which have been their stronghold from a freighting point of view."[90] Grace cautioned Shearman to make sure that every article handled showed at least some small profit. There was no margin for any guesswork and your salesmen "must be careful and accurate, as one bad 'bull' would eat up all the percentages on all the rest of the business."[91] Characteristically, Grace also provided other bits and pieces of news and ended with a few questions. He was pleased with sugar profits, solicitously asked how Mrs. Shearman and the children were doing, and finally, but with a nice hint of prodding, asked, "Where is Lima's balance sheet? Valparaiso accounts are about a month ahead of you."[92]

To John Fowler in Valparaiso, Joseph Grace also demonstrated the warm, caring side of this growing enterprise, which still very much bore a family imprint. "I was very sorry indeed to see by the last mail that your wife had an attack of fever. I hope it will prove to be a very light attack." He continued the prologue with some news on his father's health, of concern to young partners and managers like Fowler and Shearman, who knew and respected William Grace not only as the head of the house, but as a strong father figure. "We received your cable inquiry for my father's health and he appreciated it very much. He is now able to be back in town again but the doctor does not wish to have him attend business more than one or two days a week."[93] Joseph Grace had himself been relieved of his appendix, "but am all healed up in good shape."

Major decisions in 1900 were shared by all the top managers, which included Joseph Grace, Edward Eyre, Michael Grace, John Fowler, Lawrence Shearman, Jack Eyre, John Grace, and Louis Schaefer. When a new addition to the fleet of six steamers was being considered, Joseph Grace, for example, naturally consulted Fowler. He thought the decline in steel and iron prices, coupled with an anticipated drop in freight rates because of the end of the Boer War in South Africa, should bring the price of steamers down considerably.

The balance sheet Fowler sent from Valparaiso pleased Grace. "The showing is a fine one. Glad to hear that there is a good outlook for business the present year."

On the Beeche company, Grace's favorite nemesis, Joseph Grace was cautious. Rumor was that Beeche had linked itself with the powerful Guggenheims, an arrangement that bore close watching. "Guggenheims have been kicking against the David coke we shipped them. Apparently they are pretty close to Beeche and Co. and we will only be able to get their business when Beeche is unable to supply their wants satisfactorily."

If the news that passed between the various houses was unspectacular, it was absolutely necessary for a business strung out across three continents. Grace kept Fowler and Shearman informed of current events and future trends in as much detail as possible.

In July 1900 the drop in iron and steel was creating a lively competition that was undermining business confidence, but the election of McKinley and Roosevelt was expected to restore it.[94]

The Boxer Rebellion in China, like the Boer War in South Africa, could affect prices and products. The Chinese "trouble" jacked up freights so that it was difficult to offer anything at favorable rates.

The steamer *Cuzco* was going out loaded to its marks with two thousand tons of rails for Quito and Guayaquil. The railroad builders in Ecuador had contracted to ship all their freight by the Grace Line, but the instability of that enterprise in Ecuador was to be watched closely.

Along with news of China, U.S. presidential elections, and the Guggenheims were judgments on the character and behavior of business rivals. "I do not think Hughes and Isherwood's opinions are worth the paper they are written on. They always seem to be looking for business rather than caring for the interests of their clients."

The Graces were never spongy in their advice on how to drum up business. "The way to beat our competitors is to get at rock bottom."[95] Joseph Grace was liberal with criticism as well as praise. On sugar prices and steamer arrangements in late 1900, he frankly advised Shearman in Lima, "I do not agree with you that this sugar arrangement is satisfactory. I think Valpo had their legs pulled in making an indefinite arrangement for the steamers . . . On a declining freight market it is most important to have sugar to fall back upon so that we can avail of cheap nitrate."

Hauling nitrates formed one of the principal activities of the Grace steamers in competition with Beeche. The rivals were watched closely as the new century dawned. If Beeche was selling nitrates for lower prices than Grace and shipping at higher rates, then Grace concluded with some satisfaction that it must have lost money.[96]

Then in late 1902 the Graces attempted a real coup. They petitioned for a subvention from the Chilean government for the operation of the Grace steamers, offering to place them under the Chilean flag and operate them as Chilean carriers.[97] The petition, signed by John Eyre, almost immediately drew a rejoinder from Beeche.

Crying foul, Beeche requested the subvention for itself rather than allow it to go to Grace. Beeche described itself as a Chilean house, located in Chile, and subscribed largely by Chileans. For these reasons alone, it should be favored over the Grace bid.

Eyre responded keenly in January 1903, calling attention to the fact that the Beeche "West Coast Line" was not even *owned* by Beeche. Beeche simply acted as the agent and consignee for goods shipped on the line's vessels, which were in fact largely British-owned. Jack Eyre conveniently supplied a list of the West Coast Line ships that had made stops in Chile over the past year, identifying their owners and nationality. With the exception of one Danish-owned ship, all the others (seven) were registered as British, three of them the property of Taylor & Sanderson Steam Shipping Co.[98] How could Beeche pretend to place its ships under the Chilean flag when it was simply the agent for foreign-owned vessels? The Chilean government rejected both petitions for subventions in 1903, a decision that Claudio Veliz, an eminent Chilean maritime historian, termed "Solomonic." Indecisive or Solomonic, it formed an interesting chapter in the development of enterprises on the West Coast.

★ ★ ★

No other business of the Graces was more important than their developing steamship services, and a large portion of that business was based on hauling Chilean nitrates. No wonder the Graces invested considerably in the nitrate industry between 1900 and World War I. It was but one example of horizontal integration by a company that stressed diversification into complementary activities.

Competition for the nitrate-producing areas located on the arid coast shared by Peru, Bolivia, and Chile had triggered the War of the Pacific. After 1883 the Chileans came into possession of the richest nitrate-producing provinces, Antofagasta and Tarapaca, by virtue of the Treaty of Ancón.

Grace, which before the war had acquired the exclusive right to distribute in the United States Peruvian nitrates from Tarapaca, hastened to get a firm edge into the buying and selling of nitrates in the 1880s and 1890s. The only difference was that one had to deal almost exclusively with Chile, rather than with Peru, Bolivia, and Chile. By 1890 Grace was exporting more nitrates from Chile to the United States than any other firm. The balance sheet easily demonstrated the importance of nitrates in the various Grace enterprises. In 1891 the profits of W. R. Grace & Co. from nitrate imports amounted to $23,267.42, or approximately 33 percent of the whole, and 47 percent of the profits were generated from shipping.

Overall production from the Chilean nitrate fields jumped from 20,682,000 quintals (22.2 quintals per ton) in 1889 to 60,266,395 on the eve of the outbreak of World War I.[99] It was obvious to the Graces at the turn of the century that while good profits were to be made from handling and shipping nitrates, to enter into production might be equally lucrative. They were already well-known promoters of the use of nitrate of soda in the United States, having helped sponsor an experiment in South Carolina in 1906, for example, dramatically demonstrating the efficacy of nitrates. Often the production of cotton and wheat could be doubled by the addition of nitrates and Grace occasionally distributed parcels of nitrate of soda for experimental purposes in agricultural work.[100]

In 1900 or 1901 the decision was reached to enter production by purchasing a nitrate property called Jazpampa Bajo in Tarapaca. Michael Grace bought the *oficina*, as a nitrate establishment was called, and when Joseph Grace went on an extended trip to South America in 1902, his itinerary naturally included a visit to the nitrate region and Jazpampa Bajo. Joseph sent "Uncle Michael" a long, detailed report of his visit, penned from the steamship *Alliance* at sea between Colon and New York.

With his usual thoroughness, Joseph Grace described, evaluated, and recommended on everything he ran across, from personnel to *maquinas* (the equipment of the *oficina*). He was very pleased at the appearance of the *maquina* and everything looked "very first class."

Water was always a problem in the nitrate pampas of Tarapaca and Antofagasta. About forty-six liters (approximately
twelve gallons) were needed in the process of refining each
quintal (100 lb.) of finished nitrate from *caliche*, or nitrate ores
extracted from the ground. Enough water also had to be found
for the men and animals and other facilities of the *oficina*. Grace
visited the Quiuna water supply near Jazpampa Bajo and scrutinized the springs, the flow of water, and the plans for opening
up new wells, making his own recommendations based on
these observations.

Important also to acquiring and working a nitrate property
was its access to the railways connecting the fields in the interior
with the small ports serving the industry. The Jazpampa Bajo
property lay close to the Nitrate Railway, owned and operated
by the British, who "seemed to be anxious to do everything
they could to accommodate us." In Iquique Grace saw a Mr.
Nicholls and asked him to give the firm a quotation of rails and
sleepers; at the port of Pisagua a Mr. Clarke told Joseph Grace
that the British would carry up free any material for the new
Grace siding landed at Pisagua. Clarke told Joseph Grace that
they would assign Grace a warehouse exclusively for Grace's
use and that Grace could ship off their pier, the charge being
one cent a bag for warehouse and one cent for pier. Grace
described in detail for his uncle the problems of building a
proper siding to connect the Jazpampa Bajo site with the main
line of the Nitrate Railway. He also estimated the costs of shipping nitrate to Pisagua, and added other details relating to the
oficina, including the richness and workability of its nitrate holdings.

On his trip back home Joseph traveled with three American
tourists who boarded the ship at Lima. Tourists were a "rare
species in South America" and Joseph noted that two were
"Brewsters interested in Standard Oil and the American Trading Co. and one is a Hare, whose father is I believe a director
of New York Central." Arriving late at Panama, Joseph nonetheless crossed the isthmus rapidly on the Panama Railroad
and made his connection with the steamer *Allianza*, which had
been held up for a few hours by the New York office.

Perhaps it was on this trip that Joseph Grace first saw the
possibility of entering the tourist trade, which became in the
1920s and 1930s the best known activity of the Grace steamers
in the minds of the American public. Regardless of when the

germinal idea took hold, his intensive exposure to Latin America and the Grace businesses located there was crucial. Although Joseph Grace would run the growing company largely from New York, he knew what to look for, what questions to ask, and understood the reports and letters and cables streaming between New York and South America. Already the pattern of twentieth-century operations had been set. Executives stationed in New York or San Francisco would routinely make extended tours of Latin America to keep abreast of affairs. Edward Eyre, by 1900 a senior member of the establishment, had promoted this concept with enthusiasm and it became a fixture of the business.[101]

The first decade of the twentieth century witnessed the continued increase of nitrate exports to the United States, more than doubling from 190,000 tons in 1900 to 535,000 tons in 1910.[102] Between 1910 and World War I exports leveled off, increasing only from 535,000 to 600,000 tons to the United States. Already artificial fertilizers were beginning to make their appearance. As early as 1900 the Haber-Bosch method of producing artificial nitrogen by extracting it from the air and then combining it with hydrogen to manufacture ammonia presented a potential threat to Chilean nitrates. Nitrates were, of course, also key ingredients in the munitions industry and their value to it made them a premium commodity during World War I.[103] The war ultimately produced an offsetting effect: it stimulated the natural industry of Chile but also hastened the German perfection and production of artificial nitrates.

Grace investments in the industry grew apace with the expansion during these years. In 1909 Grace consolidated its small offices in Iquique and Antofagasta into the Nitrate Agencies, Ltd., which grew rapidly with the purchase of the business of Clarke, Bennett & Co. Branches of Nitrate Agencies were not only located in Iquique and Antofagasta, but also extended to the important nitrate ports of Pisagua, Tocopilla, and Taltal.[104]

Nitrate Agencies did more than simply purchase and ship nitrates. It was the financial agent and general administrator for numerous other *oficinas* belonging to the English firms of Santiago Nitrate Co., Santa Rita Nitrate Co., San Patricio Nitrate Co., Ghyzela Nitrate Co., Laguanas Nitrate Co., and Tarapaca & Tocopilla Nitrate Co. By World War I Nitrate Agencies had developed into the most powerful of the agencies in the area, handling not only nitrates, but inward freight, cars, railway lines, steam cranes, lighters, and managing lighters, bodegas, and other business.

The management of Nitrate Agencies during these years was typically international. A Scotsman, J. McKinlay, ran the office of Antofagasta, a Swiss, Adolf Garni, acted in a similar capacity in Iquique, and an American, Gaston J. Lipscomb, and a Chilean, J. Rimassa, were officers in the Agencies office in Iquique with Garni.

World War I seriously disrupted the nitrate trade, the situation being especially aggravated as the war progressed and ships became scarcer. English firms were particularly hard hit, and when Tarapaca & Tocopilla Nitrate Co. faced bankrupcy, Grace bought it out in 1916 for $2,344,789 cash.[105]

Grace had been closely associated for many years with Tarapaca & Tocopilla. Both companies shared common principal stockholders; Grace was a major creditor of the English firm, and also acted as that firm's financial agent in London. In Chile, Nitrate Agencies managed the properties of Tarapace & Tocopilla. It was a natural acquisition for Grace, which then formed the Grace Nitrate Co. to handle the new business.

The major property was a brand new $1.5 million plant named Paposo, which soon became the largest American-owned nitrate plant in Chile, producing about four thousand tons of nitrate a month by 1917. The only other major American producer was the Du Pont Nitrate Co., which owned an *oficina* named Delaware in the Taltal district. Paposo employed over a thousand men in its plant and the *oficina* complex held a population of more than five thousand. It possessed about ten miles of its own railway, two schools, a theater, and a hotel, and shipped all of its product to the United States, mostly aboard Grace steamers.

The turn of the century was not only a dynamic period for the Grace businesses, but also a period that saw the old guard passing away. William Russell Grace died in 1904, having already effectively delegated control to his major partners, the more senior Michael Grace and Edward Eyre, and to the rising juniors like Joseph Grace and D. Stewart Iglehart.

The stroke William Grace suffered in late 1898 was compounded by a fall in 1900 which injured his shoulder and laid him up for quite a while. Joseph's letters from 1900 onward often referred to his father's vacillating state of health. Joseph reported—as was his wont—the most optimistic news possible:

"My father keeps pretty well and he, my mother, and John go to Maine Aug. 15 [1900] . . . he is really feeling pretty well but is very easily tired and has to take good care of himself. . . . "[106]

Yet William Grace's remarkable powers of recuperation restored him to a fairly active role in business affairs in 1903, especially in the management of Ingersoll-Sargeant, which grew and prospered under his tutelage.[107] He also spent a good deal of time dedicated to philanthropic endeavors, notably with the Grace Institute. Over a half million dollars was invested in the school, and a recently enlarged building testified to its success. But a cold caught late in 1903 developed into pneumonia early the next year. Although Grace survived that crisis, his kidneys began to fail and the combined ailments—new and old—proved too much for his weakened constitution. He died the morning of March 20, 1904, leaving a personal estate of ten million dollars. At his bedside were brother Michael, sons Joseph and William R. Grace Jr., three daughters, and Lillius.

The newspapers of the country and world ran long obituaries, invariably praising his life as an outstanding businessman and public servant. The *New York Evening Telegram* headlined, "Twice Mayor of New York, Mr. Grace Won City's Praise." The *Brooklyn Eagle* said, "End of a Lifetime Filled with Business Enterprise and Public Usefulness . . . A Man of Strong Ideas, Whose Business, Politics and Charity Were All on a Big Scale." The *New York Times* wrote:

> Even in this country of self-made men, of great business houses, and of great fortunes, the career of ex-Mayor William R. Grace was a conspicuous one . . . he developed markets, he established transportation lines, he embarked in mercantile ventures, and directed them with such skill that while he was building up a personal fortune he was also contributing to the expansion of the commerce of this country and of other countries . . . and whenever he took an active part in politics it was as a man of sound principles working in behalf of honesty and efficiency in public administration . . . ex-Mayor Grace's name is always mentioned as that of one of the three "best Mayors" the city has had within the memory of living generations.

And the *New York Daily News*, always with a penchant for the colorful, produced this epitaph: "Romantic life story of an Irish lad who ran away from home to be a Robinson Crusoe, who twice became Mayor of New York and died a multimillionaire."[108] That was the embodiment of the American dream at the turn of the century.

Upon William Grace's death Edward Eyre became president. He was succeeded in this position by Joseph Grace in 1907. Michael Grace continued to crisscross the Atlantic, but basically resided in England, where he ran Grace Brothers, the London branch of W. R. Grace & Co. With Ned Eyre, he maintained the role of senior partner of the multifarious enterprises until his death in October 1920. Eyre lived well into the 1930s, providing a living continuity with the past for Joseph Grace, Iglehart, Garni, E. T. Ford, John Kirby, and others then rising in the organization. This Grace organization inexorably became increasingly associated in the public mind with the operation of steamships at a crucial juncture in the history of the American merchant marine.

The short, victorious Spanish-American War in 1898 had created not only a heady atmosphere in an America dramatically emerging as a world power, but also anxious moments upon the discovery that our merchant marine was woefully inadequate to meet the navy's needs for auxiliary ships such as coal colliers, scouts, and supply vessels.[109] Admiral Dewey's victory at Manila Bay was credited, perhaps apocryphally, to having been refueled by a British collier at a crucial moment of the campaign. When President Roosevelt dispatched the Great White Fleet on a tour of the world, it steamed only by the grace of colliers and supply ships owned by foreigners. There were not enough fast American merchant ships to accompany the U.S. Navy at sea on this singular mission to "Show the Flag." An adage pointed to a nation's merchant marine as the cradle of a strong navy, but, patently, the American merchant marine was now sorely lacking.

One of the greatest drawbacks was the 1789 law forbidding the operation of foreign-built ships under the American flag. This regulation had forced the Graces in 1893 to organize and incorporate the New York & Pacific Steamship Co. in Great Britain where the first Grace steamers had been built. Shipbuilding costs in the United States often were 40 to 75 percent higher than in England or Europe. Consequently, not only the Graces but many other American shippers built and registered their vessels abroad. In 1901 over six hundred seventy-two thousand tons of shipping owned by Americans were registered abroad, an amount which equaled U.S. tonnage registered in foreign trade, and which was exceeded only by the tonnage of four other nations, Great Britain, France, Germany, and Norway.[110]

Solutions offered were often tinged by partisan politics. The Democrats and Republicans could not agree on whether to provide building subsidies or operating subsidies to overcome some of the disparities in shipbuilding and shipping costs between American-built and -operated vessels and those from abroad. Nonetheless, the expected completion of the Panama Canal in 1914 prompted numerous bills between 1912 and 1915 which provided the first solid inducements to restoring the U.S. merchant marine. Foreign-built ships could now be registered American, duties on all imported shipbuilding materials were removed, and preferential tariffs were given to goods imported on American vessels. (The last was overturned by a Supreme Court decision in 1915, but by then other government acts were aiding the merchant marine.) The trend toward assisting the merchant marine was accelerated by the effects of World War I.

As the major belligerents drew their ships nearer into the European theater of combat or assigned them only to routes deemed crucial to supporting the war effort, the United States, dependent as it was on foreign carriers for so much of its trade, was left desperately short of shipping. Rates soared, as did insurance, and the government took some emergency measures. It liberalized the rules for transferring American-owned vessels from foreign registry to American registry and allowed war-risk insurance to be written on all American-owned ships. In 1916 a more comprehensive shipping act was passed to meet the continuing war emergency. "It established a five-member Shipping Board as a permanent independent agency with broad promotional, investigatory, regulatory, and administrative powers. It authorized the board to organize and take a majority interest in a government corporation to implement its programs. It included an open-end authorization to purchase and construct vessels" and other features.[111] When the United States entered the war in April 1917, the Shipping Board embarked on the most massive shipbuilding program ever attempted. From the period of relative neglect at the turn of the century to the era of almost fanatical attention between 1917 and 1922 (when the Shipping Board's program was terminated), Grace shipping interests were deeply entwined with the fortunes of the American merchant marine.

Contrary to generally accepted notions, the Spanish-American War demonstrated not so much a crisis in the American merchant marine as a difference in emphasis between naval strategists and commercial shippers like W. R. Grace & Co. To make a profit, merchants preferred slow and efficient carriers capable of carrying everything from bulk cargoes such as nitrate of soda to typewriters for the secretaries of Santiago and Lima.

The Grace fleet at the turn of the century contained such versatile craft.

When the navy went to war in the spring of 1898, it needed fast, well-ventilated transports to ferry troops, refrigerated products, coal, and other necessities of a fleet on the make. Grace's steamers, like many other American ships under foreign flags, were not built for Theodore Roosevelt's navy, and thus the firm had to forgo potentially high profits from the sale of steamships to the government in the spring and summer of 1898.[112]

While free-trading Democrats and tariff-minded Republicans debated in Congress on how best to subsidize the American merchant marine in the first decade of the twentieth century, Grace steamers continued to build up the trade between the United States and Latin America. The most common voyage was from New York to the West Coast of South America through the Straits of Magellan. It took approximately thirty-eight days from Sandy Hook to the first port of call in southern Chile, Coronel. The steamer then proceeded to Valparaiso and could go as far north as Guayaquil in Ecuador, depending on the nature of its cargo.

On the outward voyage it might carry coal for the nitrate *oficinas* of Tarapaca as well as many other products from the United States for the markets of Chile, Peru, Bolivia, and Ecuador: kerosene, naval stores, typewriters, electrical machinery, sewing machines, lubricating oil, rails, and anything else that could be bought in the United States, loaded on a steamer and sold in South America. In return, not only nitrates but guano, manganese, copper, quinine, and other products from South America filled the holds, a typical round-trip voyage covering about twenty thousand miles. In 1900, Grace steamers were carrying about a hundred fifty thousand tons on twenty-two sailings a year, offering a service equal to that of its combined competitors.[113]

The constant premise upon which Grace expanded its fleet during these years was that "trade follows transportation facilities." Of equal importance after 1900 was the expected completion of the Panama Canal sometime after 1912. The voyage from New York to Valparaiso would be reduced from 8,350 miles by way of the Straits of Magellan to only 4,600 miles via the Canal. By comparison, it would reduce the distance from Valparaiso to Southampton and Cherbourg only from 8,500 miles via the strait to 7,100 via the canal. Not only would the United States be closer, but Europe would be relatively more distant. Simultaneously, the new canal would cut the distance between the East and West coasts of the United States by more than half.

Looking toward these improved communications between the coasts of the United States, Grace commissioned the construction of four new steamers in American shipyards in 1912, taking advantage of shipbuilding codes that favored the construction of vessels destined exclusively for the American intercoastal trade.

The first of these, the *Santa Cruz*, was launched from Cramps Shipyard in Philadelphia in February 1913. Along with sister ships *Santa Cecilia, Santa Clara,* and *Santa Catalina,* the *Santa Cruz* was intended for the trade between the East and West coasts of the United States via the Panama Canal. They were owned by the newly formed Atlantic & Pacific Steamship Co. and each had accommodations for fifty passengers, the first such Grace ships built specifically for passenger service. Passengers were not, however, carried aboard these ships until several years later when they entered the Panama (formerly Pacific) Mail Steamship Co.'s transpacific service. The Panama Mail was acquired by Grace in 1915.

The war years brought on a series of major changes and advances for the Grace steamships. The most superficial of these changes finally and formally introduced the name "Grace" into the various companies under which it owned and operated steamers. The Grace Steamship Co. was incorporated in 1916, bringing together the old entities of the New York & Pacific Steamship Co. and the Merchants Line. From this year onward one can properly refer to the Grace Line, and its services between the Americas began to be more widely recognized among the population of both continents.

The year before this incorporation five new steamers, equipped to carry a hundred passengers and fifty-four hundred tons of cargo apiece, were ordered. The first of these, the *Santa Ana*, was launched from the Cramps yards on October 13, 1917, six months after the United States declared war on Germany. The *Santa Ana*, along with sister ships *Santa Elisa, Santa Teresa, Santa Rosa,* and *Santa Paula,* was drafted into war service and served largely as a troop carrier until 1918 and 1919.

Additionally, in 1915 Grace and the American International Corporation, the international branch of the National City Bank, purchased the old Pacific Mail Steamship Co. This venerable company had pioneered American flag steamship operations in the Pacific in 1848 by launching service from Panama and Central America to California. It had also run steamers to the Orient since 1869, and one of its ships, the *General Grant*, carried the famed Phineas Fogg on the Yokohama to San Francisco leg of his legendary odyssey around the world in eighty days. The Southern Pacific Railroad had been forced to divest itself of the Pacific Mail since no ship owned by a transcontinental railroad was allowed to use the Panama Canal, according to the Panama Canal bill of 1915, enacted to prevent monopolies of trade and traffic between the coasts.

The Graces also owned another line known as the North Pacific Division of Grace Line. Established in 1903, it initially hauled goods between the Pacific Northwest and Chile, largely lumber going south and nitrates in return. Grace had long been in the business of chartering and operating ships from the West Coast of the United States to South America and the continuation and expansion of this service with steamships was a natural extension of early routes. Some of the steamers on this line were the freighters *Cuzco, Coya, Capac, Condor, Charcas,* and *Cacique.* The North Pacific Division ships maintained a varied schedule, often making as many as fifteen stops between major terminals, the coffee trade from Central America being but one example of the diversified business on the West Coast.

★ ★ ★

Of the individual histories of the Grace steamships in the prewar and war period, perhaps none other is more representative than that of the *Santa Clara,* since it served in so many ways and in such differing circumstances, much like the company it represented.

The *Santa Clara* was launched in August 1913 and measured 6,310 tons gross. Originally destined for the Atlantic & Pacific Steamship Co. for service between the East and West coasts through the Panama Canal, it nonetheless began its career by making the long voyage from coast to coast through the far Straits of Magellan, since the canal was not opened until 1914. The *Santa Clara* hauled lumber from the Pacific Northwest to New York City, where many of the western timbers were used in constructing subways.

The Panama Canal was officially opened in August 15, 1914, when the steamer *Ancon* crossed from the Atlantic to the Pacific. Actually, the first oceangoing ship to make the full transit of the canal was the cement boat *Cristóbal* on August 3.[114] The *Santa Clara* passed through the new works in June 1915, making it one of the first commercial vessels to utilize the canal.[115] Later that year the *Santa Clara* ran onto a more ordinary, but nonetheless exciting, problem. While going through the Straits of Magellan it grounded on the rocks at Mindful Shoals, English

Narrows in Smythes Channel. No life was lost and it was soon floated off to resume service, but cables burned the wires between the strait and headquarters in New York. To help pioneer a new route through the great ditch of Panama was marvelous; to run aground and incur costly delays and repairs was definitely bad for business, especially one that maintained strict timetables to keep the edge on competitors.

On November 7, 1917, the *Santa Clara* went to war. On that day it was requisitioned by the government and outfitted for transport service, suitably armed with a five-inch gun mounted aft and a three-inch gun on the forecastle to shoot it out with the kaiser's submarines.[116] Two dozen regular U.S. Navy sailors were added to the crew, and on November 28 it sailed from Hoboken, New Jersey, for France loaded with army supplies, including sixty automobiles lashed on deck.

It was a rough crossing, as the North Atlantic put up monstrous winds and seas. The *Santa Clara* sailed in a convoy of twenty-eight other transports, all of them shepherded by the cruiser USS *Des Moines*. On the second day out all hell broke loose; gale-force winds were blowing by afternoon, accompanied by driving rain and sleet. At nightfall the *Des Moines* ordered its rolling, pitching charges to heave to. Running without lights to escape submarine detection and tossed about like so much flotsam, the ships faced the danger of collision, which was compounded by another nightmarish situation, best described by Capt. F. S. Blackadar commanding the *Santa Clara*: "The deck load on board the *Santa Clara* was breaking adrift and about midnight No. 1 hatch was broken in by a sea, making it necessary to keep the ship away before the wind. In bringing the *Santa Clara* around she shipped a heavy sea amidships, carrying away two of the lifeboats on the upper deck and causing other minor damage."[117]

The storm abated at dawn and the *Santa Clara* was able to resume its station in the convoy. Two ships had been damaged badly enough to return to Halifax. One other was not so lucky, foundering in the violent storm. Indeed, of the original convoy of twenty-eight, only eight proceeded in the company of the *Des Moines*. The rest were scattered across the winter sea and had to steam on alone and vulnerable across the Atlantic. Three other storms struck the fleet before they finally arrived at the entrance of the English Channel. Only four ships of the original convoy remained together, although two other vessels were picked up on the voyage, stragglers from another storm-battered convoy.

Its job done, the *Des Moines* hoisted the letter *P* (disregard motions of escort), turned around, and steamed back through the convoy signaling "Goodbye, pleasant voyage." As Captain Blackadar remarked, "This was a great surprise to us who were making our first trip through the war zone, but we cheered ourselves by believing that our [English] destroyer escort was near at hand."[118] Two long days later, late in the afternoon, smoke smudged the horizon and signaled the arrival of the new shepherds, three British torpedo-boat destroyers. With three additional destroyers soon added to the convoy, they all proceeded up the Channel.

The next day "we were picking up SOS calls from ships being torpedoed or gunned by submarines, many of them in our vicinity." While listening to the voices of fellow sailors under attack, the *Santa Clara*'s skipper was ordered to take his ship that evening to its destination, St. Nazaire, with all due dispatch. American or French destroyers supposedly en route to escort it and another American ship to the French coast never showed up. The *Santa Clara* struck off as ordered.

That evening the harrowing reports of torpedoings and submarine warnings crackling through the wireless convinced Captain Blackadar to seek shelter in Brest after rounding Ushant. One can well imagine the rising anxiety as night fell and the wireless ceaselessly broadcast the frightening reports. Brest, however, had extinguished all its aids to navigation leading into the harbor, and as "the night was very dark and no one on board was acquainted with the port, and as we did not dare to anchor we cruised around at full speed, zigzagging all night. At daylight we saw a French destroyer coming toward us and signaling us to show our distinguishing flags. Upon answering her signal she ordered us to follow her. About an hour later we picked up a pilot who informed us that we had been cruising about all night over a mine field. December fourteenth at 8 A.M. we came to anchor in the harbor at Brest." The laconic Captain Blackadar noted that they completed their voyage to St. Nazaire the next day, and while "we were at no time during the [entire] voyage in any immediate danger, nevertheless a feeling of uncertainty was continually hovering around." That type of sangfroid was typical of the officers and men who manned the convoys of the war.

The *Santa Clara* made three other voyages to France as an army transport during the war, each one attracting a submariner's bead on the feisty Grace steamer. On a voyage to Le Havre, a submarine popped up its periscope directly between the *Santa Clara* and another vessel in the middle of a convoy. After a minute, the periscope disappeared and the submarine took a shot at one of the ships in the rear of the convoy, and missed. Not so lucky was an English tank steamer, which took a hit just ahead of the *Santa Clara* later during the voyage.

Returning from Marseille, the *Santa Clara*'s crew was treated to the unusual sight of a German submarine appearing about fifteen hundred yards off its port quarter while steaming along the Spanish coast. It did not attack. After that voyage, the *Santa Clara* was formally taken over by the government and commissioned a regular member of the United States Navy on October 10, 1918. Many of its officers entered the navy and were awarded commissions, remaining to serve on the *Santa Clara*.

It sailed alone on October 30, 1918, bound once again for Marseille. As the ship neared Gibraltar on the afternoon of November 11, the radio from Lisbon crackled with the news of the armistice signed that day, "the eleventh hour, of the eleventh day, of the eleventh month." Two or three days before, a submarine had taken a shot at the *Santa Clara*, sending a torpedo across its bow on a clear night. Those on watch observed the lovely, deadly phosphorescent trail of the underwater missile as it harmlessly drove past the bow and into the black waters beyond.

Once the war was over, the *Santa Clara* was rapidly refitted to carry eighteen hundred troops, and a sixty-bed hospital section for the wounded was also added. It made four round-trip voyages to France to bring the doughboys back. On August 19, 1919, the ship was honorably mustered out of naval service and returned to its owners, the Atlantic & Pacific Steamship Co.[119]

Immediately following the war Grace Line inaugurated the service for which it became most famed during the next half century: direct passenger service between New York, Callao, Valparaiso, and intermediate ports via the Panama Canal. Yet, while the traditional Latin Americn ties were thus reinforced, Grace had actually expanded far beyond its familiar boundaries during the course of the war.

The war had caused a severe contraction in the activities of the great international English trading firms and much of the slack had been taken up by American companies such as W. R. Grace.[120] In fact, by the end of the war Grace had emerged as one of the largest import-export firms operating in the United States, with offices in Australia, South Africa, the Far East, Europe, and the East Coast of South America.

The boom in commodities trading after the war propelled the

company even further in this direction. A partial listing of cities where Grace maintained offices reads like a travelogue of the world before it was riven by communism and the end of the great colonial empires: Havana, Managua, Port-au-Prince, Kingston, Tampico, Antwerp, Copenhagen, London, Marseille, Hamburg, Genoa, Petrograd, Barcelona, Stockholm, Cardiff, Colombo, Hangchow, Shanghai, Bombay, Calcutta, Karachi, Kobe, Osaka, Yokohama, Taipei, Vladivostok, and more.[121] Grace became a worldwide factor in rubber, sugar, hides, hemp, pig bristles (China), rice (Southeast Asia), and myriad other products.

Additionally, because of the creation of the Federal Reserve System in 1913, it was no longer possible for a commercial firm like Grace to do banking business. It had long taken care of family and client business as part of its general trading activity, and so in 1916 it established W. R. Grace & Co.'s Bank to continue tending to these needs. At this stage it was largely a private bank and did not particularly seek other business, but the seed of a new business had nonetheless been sown.

The remarkable growth of the company since the 1890s had taken it far afield, from the jungles of Brazil to the teeming marketplaces of India. This widespread net would prove too fragile to withstand a commodities crash in 1920, when the company nearly failed because of its overextension.

Yet, even though this first attempt at a truly global business failed in 1920, the company's commitment to trade and industry on the "coast," and more particularly to Peru, remained constant. W. R. Grace & Co. had become one of the main engines in the modernization of Peru, its destiny bound closely to that country by a persuasive mixture of sentimentality and hard business sense which motivated William and Michael Grace and their successors.

11

Sugar, Cotton Mills, and Modern Peru

H e was tall, and very serious, possessed a penetrating look, was a very hard worker, and had a tremendous discipline. He possessed great social and industrial connections with Trujillo, and a vision that was wide and varied.

He was in the office by six in the morning, ringing the bell for us, even though formal work did not begin until seven. He was in the fields by one in the afternoon, and, if there was a water shortage, he ranged on horseback up and down the river looking after Cartavio's water rights. He was the real organizer of Cartavio.

Enrique Gómez-Sánchez's memory of Coll MacDougall was clear and strong, even when interviewed at the age of eighty-three in the home of one of his daughters in a Lima suburb in summer 1980.[1] Diminutive and wiry, the Peruvian perhaps remembered the Scotsman as taller than he actually was. But the other descriptions fit MacDougall's deeds, for it was during MacDougall's tenure as manager of the W. R. Grace & Co.'s sugar plantation Cartavio that it was developed into a multi-million-dollar enterprise. It was also an era, from the 1890s through World War I, when Peru sprang back from the economic and political trough of the War of the Pacific and advanced rapidly into the world of electricity, tramways, and industrial prosperity. Peru's sugar estates expanded rapidly as well, as they became more thoroughly tied to a vibrant world economy.

The sugar industry and its role in the modernization of Peru are a valuable example of the process at work. An ancient industry, it was revitalized and improved by the rapid advances of technology made in the nineteenth century. Labor for the mills and fields of the plantations became more of a proletariat, dependent upon regular wages, tied to the rhythms of an industrial enterprise, and ever more conscious of its developing existence as a class apart from the capitalists in Peru, both domestic and foreign. New demands—for labor, capital, and technology—created new resources for labor, carved out new channels for capital, and stimulated the inventiveness of Peruvians and foreigners alike in transforming the country from a quiet, almost residual, member of Latin America into a nation echoing with the demands, problems, and strengths of the modern age. The Guano Era had provided some inkling of this radical new departure. In the sugar industry, where Grace played a demonstrably major role as well, we see once again the old stability and order, principally economic and social, crumbling under exciting and stimulating new trends.

The sugar industry in Peru, nonetheless, had been in existence since the sixteenth century.

No one will ever know with certainty when the first cane was brought from Panama or Mexico and planted in the rich soils of the valley of Chicama or Nasca or perhaps Lambayeque.[2] Don Diego de Mora had black slaves in his sugar-cane fields in the Chicama Valley by the middle of the century, and sugar became a staple of the maritime trade in the viceroyalty of Peru for most of the colonial period. The sugar mills on the coastal estates of Peru regularly sent their sweet products to Chileans, Argentineans, Bolivians, and Ecuadorians populating the vast viceroyalty. The disruptions caused by the Wars of Independence temporarily stalled the Peruvian sugar industry. Nonetheless, it was ideally equipped for the remarkable rise of sugar consumption by the Western world in the nineteenth century.

The rise in consumption had been especially rapid in England as the industrial revolution pumped up the standard of living with velocity. Between the 1760s and 1815 the average Englishman increased his annual consumption from eight pounds to seventeen pounds.[3] Prices rose commensurately, especially caused by shortages during the disruptive Napoleonic Wars. English men-of-war throttled Napoleon's major ports and forced Europeans to improvise by large-scale planting of sugar beets on the Continent. But this source was never more than an expensive substitute for sugar from cane.

The price of sugar peaked in the 1840s and thereafter slowly declined for the remainder of the century, as improvements and new technologies were applied to the ancient industry.

Steam, for example, was introduced in sugar *ingenios* late in the eighteenth century and by 1808 at least twenty-five steam engines were driving machinery in Cuba.[4] The first steam engine for grinding sugar was imported into Brazil in 1813, into the United States in 1822, and arrived on the subcontinent of India in 1836.

The Wars of Independence in Peru were followed by further political and economic disruptions in the 1820s and 1830s which tempered any rapid recovery of the industry. In 1834 the English firm of Gibbs & Co. shipped a load of some two hundred eighty tons of Peruvian sugar to Liverpool on the brigantine *Pacifico*. Although this example was not followed immediately, Peruvian plantations did begin other experiments in the era, most notably with the manufacture of rum, which found a more receptive market.

After 1839 the sugar industry entered into a phase of steady recuperation, based partially on the reopening of the old Chilean market, which had been closed by a prohibitive tariff. Other factors at midcentury, especially the massive importation of Chinese coolies after 1849, imparted momentum to the business as the sugar growers themselves became more export-oriented, more conscious of the potential in the world market. A slow growth in the 1860s was followed by an explosive growth in production in the 1870s. Production doubled from a base of 16,000 tons in 1873 to 34,000 the following year; it doubled again by 1876, reaching in 1878 a peak (85,000 tons) that was not surpassed until 1897.

By the 1870s certain dynamic foreigners were identifiable as prime movers in the success of the industry, especially among those plantations located in the Chicama Valley north of Trujillo. Over 60 percent of the Peruvian sugar industry came to be located in the Chicama Valley and the opportunities naturally attracted the bold, ambitious, and talented.[5] Two Italian brothers, Andres and Rafael Larco, made their way north from Lima to the Chicama Valley in the early 1870s after immigrating to Peru in the 1850s and accumulating a small fortune from trade in Lima and Trujillo. In 1872 they bought one of the largest haciendas in the valley, the 1,250-fanegada (one fanegada equals 1.59 acres) Chiquitoy, and immediately began to enlarge the space devoted to planting sugar cane.[6] Profits from Chiquitoy enabled them to purchase two other haciendas, Tulape and Cepeda, which were consolidated and renamed Roma in 1878.

While the Larcos came from the Mediterranean end of Europe, Johan Gildemeister issued from Bremen, Germany. He migrated to Brazil in the 1830s as a young teenager and there began a fascinating career.[7] From Brazil he sailed round the Horn to Chile aboard a small schooner laden with timber. He parlayed that profitable venture into a move to Peru, struck off to California during the gold rush, and finally returned to Callao, where he established an importing business. He made investments in the growing nitrate business in southern Peru before turning his attention northward to the Chicama Valley in 1888, attracted by the sugar industry. The hacienda Casa Grande was purchased and from that base the Gildemeister family began to extend its holdings in the same fashion as the Larcos, by purchasing smaller haciendas and *chacras* and planting more and more sugar on land previously devoted to other crops.

Financing the sugar boom in Peru required occasional large infusions of capital for major additions to the mills, for extending the railroads to carry canes from the new fields to the mills and sacked sugar from the mills to the ports, for improving harbors; in short, for all the infrastructure necessary to develop the industry. The Larcos, for example, were closely tied to Graham, Rowe, & Co. of Callao. One of the many talented Larco descendants, Rafael Larco Herrera, the son of Rafael, commented in 1923 that "during more than fifty years, the respectable commercial firm of Graham, Rowe, & Co. in Lima maintained close and cordial relations with the members of the Larco family, contributing . . . capital in moments of crises and providing avenues of distribution for our sugar crops by way of their commercial establishments in Liverpool, Valparaiso, and New York."[8]

★ ★ ★

Michael Grace had also been investing in the sugar industry in the early 1870s, turning profits made on the Meiggs railroad projects into large loans to the sugar planters. One planter in particular came to depend rather heavily on the Graces by the middle of the decade. In 1875 Guillermo Alzamora owed Bryce-Grace $285,000, a substantial mortgage that would soon lead to direct Grace participation in the thriving sugar business of the Chicama Valley.[9]

Alzamora, like many before him, had been attracted from Lima to the north and its opportunities. His first major inroad into the sugar industry was to rent the hacienda of Chiclin in the Chicama Valley.[10] Successful in this, he then bought the neighboring hacienda of Cartavio, which was devoted solely to the production of *pan llevar*, or truck produce. As at Chiclin, Alzamora began to plant sugar cane at Cartavio in small quantities. Alzamora also acquired Hacienda Arriba at this time, going rather steeply into debt to purchase Cartavio and Arriba. Cane from Cartavio was ground at Chiclin, for no mill yet existed at Cartavio.[11]

As early as 1875 a Bryce-Grace representative, Pablo de la Barrera, was stationed at Chiclin looking after the firm's interests.[12] The debts eventually proved too much for Alzamora and at the end of the decade Alzamora's mortgage on Cartavio was foreclosed and the property was effectively transferred to the hands of Grace (the transfer was officially completed in 1882). At that time Cartavio contained just over twelve hundred fanegadas and was valued at about £30,000. It still grew only a small amount of cane, was almost bereft of houses, and for the next decade represented something of a white elephant for the Graces.[13]

Insufficient labor remained a problem for all sugar planters through the 1870s, especially after the 1873 treaty between Peru and China effectively closed off the old coolie trade. While immigration of Chinese to Peru was still permitted, the greater controls to protect the Chinese precluded any significant additions after 1873. Nonetheless, in May 1879 Alzamora entered into a contract with Gabriel Larrieu of the "Empresa de Introducción de Asiaticos para el Fomento de la Agricultura en el Peru" ("Company for Introducing Asiatics to Peru to Develop Agriculture"). Larrieu promised to deliver a hundred Asiatics, healthy and capable of agricultural labor, between the ages of twenty and forty, to Alzamora in Callao.[14] These Chinese were to labor not only in the cultivation and cutting of cane, but also in all other aspects of the production of sugar. The contract was to run for five years, and each man was committed to a ten-hour day, six days a week. Article three specified their salaries as twelve silver soles per month, payable in equivalent currency if silver was not available. Alzamora was to supply two sets of clothes annually and provide his Chinese workers with good food, sufficient to maintain them. If sick, Alzamora's Chinese were to receive free medicine and medical treatment. In an afterthought, introduced as an "Additional Article," the two contractors, Larrieu and Alzamora, agreed that each coolie was obliged to work four hours on Sunday, from six to ten in the morning, in daily tasks without any increase in the wages agreed upon.[15]

It was a very rude life for the Chinamen, Enrique Gómez-Sánchez recalled years later. Gómez-Sánchez was born on Ha-

cienda Cartavio before the end of the nineteenth century. He
worked on the plantation for most of his life and he remembered well, or remembered the stories told him by his father,
of the existence of the Chinese in the flat, warm coastal valley
of Chicama.

The Chinaman was the Negro's substitute, and even though
the Chinamen came under a contract, in reality he was a slave.
He lived on the sugar plantations on a *galpón* (barracks-style
compound), worked from daybreak to sunset, was given one
hour in the fields to prepare and eat his lunch, and at night
was returned to the *galpón* to wash up, prepare his supper, and
be locked up until four or five the next morning.

The War of the Pacific rather abruptly severed the trade in
Chinese immigrants and gradually most of the Chinese became
free men. Yet shortages of labor in the plantations in the 1880s
and 1890s continued and prompted some of the more intelligent
and ambitious Chinese to invent a system for contract labor.

The more intelligent Chinamen went to the patrón (the
owner) of the plantation, and said, "You need more labor. I
have thirty fellow countrymen, now free, and I will represent
them. I'll present this group to you for labor on your plantation." The patrón accepted this arrangement, and would give
the contractor a commission. The contractor would see that the
laborers met their obligations.

As the system developed, the plantation managers would
pay the laborers through these *contratistas* ("contractors"). They
became the middlemen between owners and workers, both of
whom depended upon them. The owners and managers would
provide the *contratistas* not only with a commission but also
with an opportunity to have a *fondo*—a small restaurant—for
the workers, and next to it was located a *bodega*, or small store.

The sugar industry in Peru was able to sustain itself for many
years—up to 1912 at least—by this system of contracting free
Chinese laborers. But this source of Chinese labor was constantly diminishing, from old age, migration to the cities, and
so forth. The sugar growers then looked to the mountains of
Peru, populated by millions of Indians who represented a potentially rich source of labor. However, as in times past, the
problem was how to induce Indians from the neighboring Sierra
to come down and work on the coastal plantations. Gómez-
Sánchez recalls that "Peruvians then actually imitated the
Chinese *contratistas*. This is the way the *enganche* ['hooking']
system was was born. The Peruvian, who saw that the Chinese
contratista received a commission, possessed a *fondo*, and had
plenty of meat and rice, decided to do the same and bring

Peruvians from the Sierra. He would go to the Sierra, contract with twenty or thirty Indians, would advance them some money or chits on his *bodega*, and bring them back to the coast."

Since there was no housing, the Indians would be put up in the giant *galpones*. That's where the Indians arrived and started to work. Since the Chinaman had received—as part of his contract—meat, rice, and salt, which had been provided for him as a slave, the Peruvian Indian demanded the same. And that custom of giving the workers a portion of meat, rice, and salt exists in plantations today and is called *salario en especie* ("salary in kind"). In some cases other goods are now substituted for food.

The Indians were housed in *campamentos* or *girones* ("sections" or "streets"), which were assigned to each *contratista*. Today many of the streets still retain the names of the original *contratistas*—Calle de Ramos, Calle de Vazquez, etc.—who brought the Indians down from the Sierra to their *campamentos*.

The *enganche* system had disappeared by the 1930s, according to Gómez-Sánchez.

The *enganche* system's abuses and benefits have been the subject of political and academic scrutiny since the system evolved.[16] That Indians—later followed by their families—were brought to the coast from the 1890s onward to work on the plantations is indisputable. But everything else about the system is subject to interpretation. Its critics have focused principally on the debt-peonage dimension and on the gradual depersonalization of labor as the sugar plantations of the Chicama evolved into large agricultural industries in the early twentieth century.

Peter Klaren's thesis, well expounded, is that "this migratory flow . . . provided the basis for the emergence of a new rural proletariat in the north."[17] Klaren's bias is that "for the newcomer, plantation living and working conditions were harsh and oppressive, as might be expected,"[18] and that laborers were slowly acculturated and became "proletarianized" by their experience as wage laborers. Inevitably, strikes broke out and labor organizations and political institutions evolved to mirror the aspirations of this new proletariat. In this milieu there eventually developed the most radical and far-reaching Peruvian political party of the twentieth century, the Alianza Popular Revolucionaria Americana (APRA), founded by Victor Raul Haya de la Torre in the early 1920s.

But how low were wages, how bad were working conditions, how did debt peonage operate? Arnold Bauer questions all of the basic assumptions and does so equally convincingly. He begins by taking exception to the standard accounts. "The older reports on working conditions tended toward the muckraking variety of exposé in which writers, outraged by the direction Peruvian society was developing in the early twentieth century, chose the worst and most abusive examples to make a general case. Peter Klaren's work . . . reflects the conventional view of those sources that the new sugar plantations on the north coast imposed a harsh and cruel system of debt bondage through the *enganche* system of labor recruitment."[19]

Bauer says that "clear understanding of the system itself has been distorted by more than the ordinary volume of ideological fervor and charged language," and contends that "it now seems likely that they [the Indians] freely and knowingly chose to work on the coast, took advantage of competition for labor, and knew how to drive up the amount of wages that plantation agents had to advance. . . . The point here is that the closer the new sources enable us to get to social reality, the more there emerges a world of mutual adjustment and accommodation. . . . Instead of being passive victims, it seems more likely that workers saw their chance and took it."[20]

Bauer also seriously questions the direct relationship between debt and bondage. That the workers were often in debt—actually from the moment they accepted the *contratista*'s advance in the Sierra—is true. That they were in bondage is not true. Laborers were constantly in short supply, thus driving up their value and their bargaining power. "The fact that workers could insist on so large an advance [often up to six months' pay] suggests that there was competition for their labor and that they had certain cards to play in bargaining with plantations. In place of force and coercion, wage advances more likely testify to the landowners' lack of extraeconomic power and their need to play by the rules of a new and as yet imperfectly functioning labor market."[21]

A most incisive portion of Bauer's analysis lies in his comparisons between Peru (and Latin America in general) and England a century before.

> The years 1870–1930 represented a transition which in many ways is analagous to the period a century earlier in Great Britain and western Europe. During these sixty years, landowners and rural entrepreneurs managed gradually and incompletely, to tighten their control over production . . . labor contractors, *enganchadores*, paternalistic measures, wage increases, wage advances, and in rare cases debt bondage were

used to obtain the kind of labor needed by new types of plantations and haciendas . . . rural peoples are not merely passive victims; rather, they make choices, work out of self-interest. They and the landowners alike make compromises and strike accommodations which are often mutually beneficial.[22]

In yet another instance of the modern industrial process at work, time took on a different meaning for workers on the sugar plantations of the early twentieth century. Whereas the traditional passage of time was marked by agricultural tasks associated with the season—sowing, weeding, reaping, etc.—the industrialized sugar process demanded a new notion of time, based ultimately not on natural rhythms but on external demands like shipping schedules, price changes in the London sugar market, and machine breakdowns.

The accommodations made in the sugar plantations of Peru, and specifically at Cartavio, bear out much of Bauer's hypothesis about the changing world of Peru in the early 1900s. Certain changes had been catalyzed by the War of the Pacific.

General Lynch's Sherman-like tour through the coastal provinces of Peru during the war had had its desired effect. From a high of 85,000 tons of sugar produced in Peru in 1878, the war eroded the industry: in 1879, 81,280 tons were produced; 1882, 30,000 tons; 1883, 24,000 tons; 1884, 6,600 tons. As Peru languished in the wake of this disaster, so did the Graces' interest in Cartavio, which had never been desired in the first place.

All of Cartavio's cane was still being ground at the estate of Chiclin, now operated by the Larcos, and the inconvenience of this arrangement finally prompted Edward Eyre, then running the Lima house, to sound off to his uncles William and Michael in March 1887: "We require to come to some decision regarding the future of this estate, as to either a renewed arrangement with Larco H'nos [*hermanos*—"brothers"] to grind our cane, or erection of machinery—a course we trust we will not have to adopt."[23]

Michael Grace had already tried to sell Cartavio to the Larcos, threatening to put up a competing *ingenio*, or mill, if the Larcos rejected the offer. The Larcos called the Grace bluff. "Our Mr. M. P. Grace . . . informed Señor Jose A. Larco that if he would not purchase Cartavio, we would erect machinery, an offer Larco declined—and as time begins to press, we must come to some decision."[24] Ned Eyre was tired of playing the game. The tactic had failed and now it was time to make a decision on the machinery.

Eyre did not wish to start a sugar mill. Indeed, the very thought of becoming a factory operator caused Eyre to "shudder." Having to pay even a portion of the cost was an unpleasant notion to Eyre; having to shoulder the responsibility of actually running machinery was even more unpalatable.[25] Clearly, Eyre was not interested in branching out so far afield from the business he knew well, trade and commerce. However, that did not stop him from looking around, especially now that the Grace bluff had been called by Larco.

He inquired in Peru and came to the decision that the firm of Heaton, Cree, & Kerr of Callao offered the best arrangement.[26] What was most revealing came in the following observation by Eyre: "They could make as good machinery as we could import." Peruvian foundries had in fact been producing heavy equipment for the sugar industry and the railroads for several years before 1887.

One tends to think of the approach of the industrial age to Peru as strictly a twentieth-century phenomenon, and a late blooming one at that. Yet the evidence is that Peruvians, with European and American specialists, had already begun to develop a capital-goods industry in the second half of the nineteenth century. The sugar industry's spectacular growth (albeit interrupted by the War of the Pacific) was one of the key catalysts in this development.[27] Although Grace would be among the pioneers in industrializing the Peruvian economy during the course of the next two decades, Ned Eyre was still reluctant to make the plunge into the world of machinery, factories, and workers in 1887.

However, if a sugar mill had to be bought, Heaton, Cree, & Kerr in Callao could make it. That firm had put up a complete plant for Christian Schreitmuller on his estate, Melgarejo, near Callao, and in Eyre's judgment it was "the most simple and effective plant that we have seen."[28] Both Heaton and Kerr were experienced in manufacturing sugar machinery and Kerr was furthermore the best authority in Peru in the field.

Heaton, Cree & Kerr's firm, the Eagle Iron Works of Callao, submitted a proposal for the plan that Grace intended to use to bring the Larco brothers to terms. Meanwhile, Eyre asked the New York office to see what the cost would be in the United States of such a plant as Heaton, Cree, & Kerr proposed to erect.[29]

The Eagle Iron Works proposal was detailed and in two parts: the first was entitled "Specification of Machinery for Grace

Brothers Co.'s Sugar Estate, 'Cartavio,' " and dated March 4, 1887; and the second, "Pro Forma Statement of Arrangements Between Messrs. Grace Bros' & Co. and Heaton, Cree, & Kerr, for the Erection of Machinery on Estate 'Cartavio,' for the Grinding of Cane to Manufacture Sugar and Rum," outlined the arrangement for operating the machinery on the estate. It was similar to the one negotiated nine years later, in 1896, when the first machinery for grinding cane was actually installed at Cartavio.

The machinery proposed by Eagle included three boilers with a thirteen-hundred-square-foot heating surface to work with forced hot draft, one air-heating apparatus, one flywheel feed-pump cylinder, which was guaranteed "to work . . . without pounding," one chimney—adobe or iron—one fire pump and hose "for use in case of fire and for washing our apparatus and building," one mill, one steam engine, one juice heater, and dozens of other items for a sugar mill, including pumps, tanks, pipes, and one still for alcohol.[30] Also on the list of necessities—one "building framed in wood and covered with corrugated iron, columns stepped in cast-iron bases on stone or brick foundations." Four miles of portable track, three-foot gauge, one seven-ton engine, and wheels for twenty cane cars would also be required. The owners of Eagle Iron Works added optimistically that it "is presumed there is at present accommodation at 'Cartavio' for employees, and that it will not be necessary to erect buildings especially for this object."

How much would it cost to build and operate the mill? The following budget was suggested:

2,000 soles per month for 18 months	36,000
Importations, exclusive of timber	20,000
100,000 supl. ft. Oregon pine	4,000
To purchase cane mill	3,450
Corrugated iron for building	4,500
Foundations for building machinery	12,000
20 peones, 120 days at 60¢	1,440
2 sailors, 120 at $1	240
	81,630
Pitch, white pine, & red wood	1,500
	83,130

Added to this were the "expenses of transportation from Callao to estate 'Cartavio,' and food for men on estate. The making of the building and erection of the building (skilled labor) is included in the 2,000 per month."[31] So were, presumably, all the other costs.

To finance and operate the mill Grace Brothers would advance Heaton, Cree, & Kerr up to 82,000 soles, in silver, in cash, imports, labor and/or materials. This would be in the form of a 7 percent loan to be amortized by half the net proceeds from the annual operation of the sugar mill retained as Heaton's property. The machinery was to be capable of grinding the cane grown on two hundred fanegadas of land.

The procedure was simple enough: "Heaton, Cree, & Kerr will receive the cane at the conductor and deliver the sugar sacked, each party contributing their proportion of sacks, or other package." Cartavio would provide the water for the plant. If not enough cane were available from Cartavio, Heaton and associates were "empowered to grind any cane that may be offered other than that of 'Cartavio,' . . . and, if necessary, to work by day and by night to accomplish this object."[32] Although Grace never contracted with Heaton, the foundation for the improvements and additions to Cartavio date from this era as Ned Eyre's determination to get a decision pushed his uncles to a resolution of Cartavio's fate.

In 1891 Grace formed the Cartavio Sugar Company to manage the estate, and in 1896 a separate entity, the Ingenio Central de Cartavio, imported and erected the first mill. Included among the investors and directors of Ingenio Central were Antero Aspillaga, V. G. Delgado, and Luis Pardo, all Peruvians involved directly in the sugar business. The arrangements between the Ingenio Central and the Cartavio Sugar Co. were similar to those suggested back in 1887 by Heaton, Cree, & Kerr. From 1896 onward each company was operated separately, although the name Hacienda Cartavio has been taken historically to encompass both companies.

Cartavio was developed gradually by the Graces from the 1890s onward. The first major expenditure, $300,000, was made in 1893, signaling the intention to make sugar an integral part of W. R. Grace & Co.[33]

As with all nooks and crannies of the company, none was ignored by the management with respect to Cartavio. In August 1900 Joseph Grace observed that the current manager of Cartavio, a man named Leggath, "must be extravagant. Perhaps there is the same difference as exists between the gentleman farmer and the man who seeks out an existence of some little place. One buys the right kind of everything but spends more money than the farm could produce in years. The other gets the best he can with what he can afford."[34]

Although Joseph was usually a perceptive observer, his remarks on the man who helped build up Cartavio in this period, Coll MacDougall, missed their mark: "MacDougall seemed to be a rather ordinary type of man without much keenness or aggressiveness. . . . "[35] MacDougall, in fact, had a profound effect on the improvement of Hacienda Cartavio in all respects. A thorough review of Cartavio's operations made in 1909 by Lawrence Shearman so testifies.

The hacienda had been gradually enlarged from just over twelve hundred fanegadas when first acquired from Alzamora to about thirteen hundred fifty fanegadas by the purchase of Hacienda Saplan and several smaller surrounding *chacras* between 1897 and 1909.[36] Cartavio had been originally valued at less than $150,000 (£30,000) in the 1880s, whereas a detailed appraisal in 1909 including the value of the equipment, livestock, supplies, growing crops, and land exceeded $840,000.[37] Production of sugar had increased from 5,138 tons in 1896 to 13,800 in 1908, or almost 150 percent, while the *yield* per acre had doubled from 2.42 tons to 4.60 tons, a remarkable advance in efficiency and modernization. Similar improvements on other sugar estates in Peru corroborated the trend apparent at Cartavio.[38] In the same period, 1896–1908, sugar exports, for example, from Peru jumped from 71,735 tons to 124,892 tons.[39] Prices, on the other hand, actually decreased, from £10.56 per ton in 1896 to £9.58 per ton. Certain key external factors such as the Cuban revolution of 1895, which eventually led to the Spanish-American War, worked to Peru's advantage. Peruvian sugar made inroads into the American market as Cuban production fell off because of revolution in the last five years of the century.

The basis for improvements in crop production at Cartavio in the first decade of the twentieth century was the reinvestment of profits into the estate. In fact, no profits were paid out to the owners between the years 1896 and 1909. Yet, while the owners of Cartavio had not received dividends on their investment, no new moneys had been necessary to build up and improve the estate.[40] Between these years the Cartavio Sugar Co. produced about £44,000 in gross profits (the difference between expenditures and receipts), and the Ingenio Central generated about £110,000, all of which were plowed back into either amortizing debts or making improvements. About £4,000 was spent in the purchase of *chacras* and £10,000 was spent on building houses for peons, dwellings, stables, and on the general betterment of the estate; £10,000 was set aside for a special fund for the building of a new factory.[41]

Not everyone, especially the senior member of the firm in 1909, Michael Grace, thought the sugar business was a particularly wise or good investment. Shearman, on the other hand, was one of its defenders and he argued in its favor persuasively. "From your [M. P. Grace's] letters, and from those of Mr. Edward Eyre, it is clear that the exact present position of this business is not understood, and that in view of the fact that there has been no dividend and also that through the fact that the books in London are kept upon a most absurd basis, one which nowise represents the true condition of affairs, *you both feel that the business had been and is a bad one* [italics added]; of course if we had the money in our pantaloon pocket, I certainly would not recommend its investment in a sugar estate; but this is not the case, and after studying the figures herewith I think that you will agree with me that the business has not been so bad after all."[42]

Shearman supported his claim at some length with detailed facts and figures, already a penchant of Grace executives, and concluded, "I trust that the above figures [profits, losses, reinvestments, improvements, etc.] will be sufficient to convince you that this business is really not so bad as it is considered, and that if you have not received dividends in the past, you have, on the other hand, been capitalizing and building up a big property, which, if the same policy is pursued for the future, will ultimately prove a handsome business."[43] Shearman proved more prophetic than Michael Grace, for worldwide shortages in sugar caused by World War I rewarded the Grace investment many thousands of percent when Cartavio made profits in the millions in the late teens.

Shearman was clearly pleased with MacDougall, but sought one or two assistants to ease the burden on him, and, more important, to give Cartavio a "permanent organization." Shearman argued, "Now that we have the place on its legs, the question of a little administrative expense is nothing as compared to the losses which would be occasioned by a change of management. In a word, we must be in a position where managers and employees may come and go and the work continue without prejudice."[44]

Equally important for improving Cartavio was the application of advances in sugar technology. About 1900 Cartavio hired a sugar expert from Hawaii, Thomas F. Sedgwick, to study and recommend improvements for the estate. Hawaii was leading the world in yield per acre and the introduction of Hawaiian canes to Cartavio was one project suggested by his studies. Sedgwick spent almost three years at Cartavio and a small booklet published in 1905 described the hacienda in detail. Every aspect of sugar production was examined—soil analysis, crop records, yields, etc.[45] After finishing his consulting work at

Cartavio, Sedgwick went on to found Peru's first Agricultural Station, in 1906. This early example of Grace's successful use of technology ultimately had a wider bearing on Peru.[46]

While pioneering under an expert like Sedgwick, Cartavio nonetheless was plagued by problems common to all the growers in the valley; problems that in 1909 were as new as some of the solutions were experimental. The transformation of the Chicama Valley from small agriculturalists growing a variety of crops to large plantations dedicated to sugar cane strained the water resources far beyond expectations. Water for the crops on this rainless coast was drawn from rivers or wells, and a system for allocating river water to different parcels of land had existed as far back as the colonial period. Sugar production, however, demanded more water, and disputes over water rights led to a restructuring of the old codes in 1902.[47] That, of course, did not increase the supply of water. During droughts, the effects could be pronounced.

MacDougall, always determined to improve Cartavio's position, was especially frustrated by this problem, for Cartavio lay far downriver near the coast and was thus last man to receive its *toma*, or ration of water. In 1908 and 1909 the opportunity to buy the seven-hundred-fanegada Orbegoso family estate of Chicamita came up. MacDougall was enthusiastic and pushed for the acquisition, not on account of the increased acreage, but because Chicamita was located further up the valley with better water rights than Cartavio.[48] That the Gildemeisters of Casa Grande were also contemplating the acquisition of Chicamita tended to strengthen MacDougall's argument. Any increase in the size of Casa Grande made Cartavio's share of the major business correspondingly smaller and more vulnerable, especially with its relatively poor water rights.

Joseph Grace was predisposed to accept MacDougall's argument, even if oldtimers like Michael Grace and Ned Eyre were skeptical of the entire sugar industry. Joseph Grace visited Cartavio in summer 1909 and was led to believe that the Orbegosos were eager to sell. But he learned they were playing coy. "During my visit to Cartavio, Orbegoso [Carlos Manuel] never approached me on the subject of our buying Chicamita, although I saw him several times . . . on my last day on my way down from Trujillo to Salaverry [Trujillo's port] to take the steamer, a man named Loyer jumped on the train and told me he had been commissioned to approach me on the matter, to see if we cared to buy . . . [I listened] to what he had to say."[49]

The Orbegosos wanted £40,000 for Chicamita and "would undoubtedly give the preference to this house in the sale of

Chicamita, knowing that they would be paid in cash."[50] Earlier, MacDougall had escorted Grace through Chicamita and impressed his boss with the need to obtain Chicamita's water rights.

Chicamita was not destined to be part of Cartavio, however. It was purchased by Casa Grande, as the dynamic Gildemeister family continued actively to expand that estate, especially after 1910, when the family tied in more closely with its German partners, improving its capitalization and embarking on the construction of a large, new mill.[51]

A severe drought in 1907, together with falling prices and the rising cost of labor, prompted one of several proposals made at the time to consolidate all of the estates of the valley.[52] This was, after all, the modern age of trusts and monopoly makers and the spirit was caught by Victor Larco Herrera, the owner of Roma and then the most powerful landholder in the valley.

On May 3, 1907, he handwrote an eleven-page document on his Roma and Chiquitoy "Negociaciones Azucareras" stationery entitled "Ventajas que se Tendría al formar una sola negociación de todas las haciendas del valle de Chicama" ("The Advantages of Forming One Business from all the Haciendas in the Valley of the Chicama").[53] The advantages that occurred to Don Rafael were better governance of water resources, reduced cost of production, lessened transportation costs by utilizing Roma's port of Huanchaco instead of the more distant Salaverry, improvements in cane agriculture leading to increased yields, and various other ideas that clearly linked consolidation with efficiency.

The idea of uniting the planters of the valley surfaced again two years later.[54] R. Angus Clay, another hacienda manager, suggested to Lawrence Shearman, then passing through Peru on his way to New York after one of his periodic visits to Latin America, that most of the owners were willing "in principle to fall in with the idea of forming one big concern, together with 'Cartavio.' "[55] Although Clay had not yet consulted his superiors in Lima, he felt sure they would go along, and he was certain the planters would fall in place since most of those estates were mortgaged to his firm.[56] He even included the possibility of Casa Grande's adhesion to the plan, thus forming "one grand company comprising the whole valley, the advantages of which in the distribution of water, reduction of wages, and general cost of production, I need not mention to you who know them well."[57] Neither Grace nor the Chicama Valley was ready for the formation of "one grand company," although the very projection of these ideas symbolized the gradual change of the valley's economic structure from small agriculturalists to the larger combinations pieced together by the Gildemeisters, Larcos, and Graces.

MacDougall seems to have been much more preoccupied with administering Cartavio than with any grand designs coming from the pens of Larco and Clay; or perhaps he sensed that Casa Grande would have nothing of consolidation unless it was master. MacDougall really reflected a business philosophy Grace practiced with consistency in Peru: participate in as many endeavors as compatible with the company's projected growth, but without attempting to dominate any one. The exception was transportation, as noted in the previous chapter, for Grace Line developed into the indisputable sovereign of trade, commercial and tourist, between the United States and the West Coast of South America.

MacDougall's life on the hacienda, when not pressing superiors for permission to acquire more land such as Chicamita, was taken up with attention to crop analyses, harvests, labor shortages, water supplies, and the constants of modern industrial life, budgets. His four-page, single-space, typewritten narrative report for the year 1908 is detailed and candid. Severe cold and water shortages stunted portions of the crop, "so that returns for 1909 cannot be expected to be equal to those of 1908."[58] Water supplies, however, compared with the "years of 1905/6 & 7, were much better," signifying an end to the drought of 1907. An artesian well sunk at Nepen proved insufficient, but Casa Grande also drilled a clinker that same year. That at least cushioned the news that £4,500 had been spent by MacDougall on the "artesian well experiment."[59]

Some excesses in expenditures over the projected budget were accounted for largely by the necessity of combating an outbreak of bubonic plague:

> On 1st February, 1908, bubonic plague again broke out on the Estate, and, owing to our having so many old mud wall houses with straw roofs, epidemic spread very quickly, we having had 20 cases in February, 27 in March, 3 in April, 2 in May, and 4 in June, and were only able to stamp it out by taking all the people out of these houses, and burning roofs. These houses have all been rebuilt with adobes, and wild-cane matting put on the roofs, so that rats are now easily seen and destroyed, and do not think that we shall again have such a severe outbreak. From July 1908 to date of writing (April 1909) we have had only one case. Of the total 56 cases, one died on Estate, and 55 were sent to the Lazareto in Trujillo, 37 recovering and 18 dying.

One tends to equate modernization of an industry with equal progress made in all avenues of human endeavor, for example in medicine, habitability, and social services. But the transition from a basically rural, diversified, almost colonial life and spirit in the Chicama Valley to the single-crop, export-oriented, industrial-style economy of the twentieth century was gradual and often erratic. That the medieval specter of bubonic plague coexisted with Sedgwick's scientific reports on soils and productivity was one indication of a people and a nation in transition.

When not faced with water shortages, McDougall had to witness floods. "Owing to large quantity of water in Chicama river this year, some damage has been done to the Nepen property . . . .in one place water is butting right against the cane, eating away land toward an old barranca, and from information gathered from old inhabitants, river broke in to this same place some 38 years ago, washing away some ten *fanegadas* on land. To save this place, considerable expense will have to be gone to this year . . . money spent on river defense work is just like throwing it away, but it is an expense that cannot be avoided. . . . "[60] Other expenses listed for 1909 typified sugar plantation agriculture in the early twentieth century: Chinese contract, agricultural chemist, manure, packages, sugar, fuel, hospital and botical (pharmacy), locomotives and cars, maintenance railway, shipping sugar and rum, and rum packages.

From 1910 to 1913 the overall production and export of sugar from Peru continued to increase, giving further strength to Cartavio's position.[61] The hacienda had, of course, been producing profits, but these had been consistently plowed back into the estate. For several years before 1913 a special fund had been accumulating to erect a new mill and the final commitment was made in 1913. In 1914 a new English *trapiche*, or mill, was erected at Cartavio and put into operation in 1915, its completion hampered somewhat by growing wartime shortages.[62]

It was about this time as well that the Ingenio Central de Cartavio, the entity that erected the first mill in 1896, disappeared. Its shares were all purchased by Grace and the Chicama Central Sugar Factory took its place alongside the Cartavio Sugar Co.[63] Still, the books of the factory continued to be carried separately from those of the fields, a tradition born of the original separation of the two entities.

The installation of the new mill, substantially more efficient than the one it replaced, could not have been more opportune. While exports of Peruvian sugar continued to climb slowly during the war years, prices more than doubled between 1914 and 1919, transforming the formerly quiescent Cartavio into a leading money winner for Grace. War circumstances actually almost forced the union of Cartavio and Casa Grande, an event that would have created the most powerful sugar enterprise in the country.

The German-affiliated Gildemeisters, who owned Casa Grande, had become ensnared in American wartime regulations, violating the Trading-with-the-Enemy Act in one instance, and the United States began to pressure Peru to force the sale of Casa Grande to American interests.[64] At the instigation of the Department of State, Grace entered into informal negotiations with Casa Grande, but they never amounted to much. The Germans would not permit the Americans to inspect their estate. Not only were the Gildemeisters reluctant to part with their lucrative property but the Peruvian government was against the near monopolistic control that a basically foreign-owned combination like Cartavio–Casa Grande would have wielded.

More in keeping with the Grace business philosophy of maintaining a presence, but not an overwhelming presence, in any industry was the purchase of the smaller sugar estate of Infantas in the Carabayllo Valley near Lima in 1917. Grace then combined its sugar estates into one company, the Compañia Agricola Carabayllo, Sección Chicama (Cartavio) and Sección Infantas-Caudivilla.[65] Infantas was sold three years later to a Peruvian syndicate for about a 33 percent profit. But that was only a temporary move away from sugar. In 1926 the company bought Hacienda Paramonga, spread out along the banks of the Pativilca River in a rich valley about a hundred miles north of Lima.

The purchase of Paramonga culminated a long association between its owners, the Canaval family, and the Graces, an association dating back to the 1870s when Michael Grace's eclectic investment philosophy had led the company into sugar. Ned Eyre, still only in his twenties then, clearly remembered the period and Paramonga. In 1874 "I was away in the north at the time having been sent to hurry the shipment of sugar from the estate of Paramonga and then on to Chicama to expedite shipments from Chiclin."[66] The Canavals had also become solid debtors of Bryce, Grace & Co. in the 1870s.

The move into sugar by Grace in the 1870s was but one example of the diversified interests of the family. In the 1880s and 1890s Michael Grace's range and investments widened even more as his resources grew more ample and his vision more encompassing. The complicated negotiations that led to the Grace Contract involved him directly in two of Peru's most spectacular industries, railroads and mining. One was new and the other ancient, but together they constituted the most powerful engines of modern development for the nation as the twentieth century dawned.

In the final arrangements made with the Peruvian Corporation in 1890, Michael signed over to the corporation his rights to the Central Railway, his concessions to build the Rumillana Tunnel, and his rights to work abandoned or unclaimed mines in the Cerro region, all of which he had purchased from Meiggs's heirs in 1885. Between 1891 and 1895, however, the Peruvian Corporation and the government quarreled over their basic agreements, over how to interpret them, and each side accused the other of bad faith and contractual failures. The upshot was the Peruvian government's revocation of the corporation's rights to the Rumillana Tunnel, to portions of the Cerro de Pasco region's mines, and even to a small railroad already completed in the mining district. The corporation and Michael Grace sued the government for damages, and the proceedings dragged on through the turn of the century and well into the second decade of the twentieth.

Michael's determined pursuit of his rights in this protracted dispute well demonstrated the international breadth of his operations. Before it was over, appeals and arguments had been lodged with the governments of the United States and Great Britain. The case was eventually recommended to the Tribunal of Arbitrators of the World Court in the Hague for adjudication.[67] Ned Eyre, never one to mince words, summed up his opinion of these fractious proceedings nicely in a letter to Charles G. Bennett, then a member of the House of Representatives, while appealing for more forthright United States intervention in the matter: "If things were as they used to be in the good times of old, H. B. M. [His Britannic Majesty's] Government would put his big foot down and the matter would be adjusted, but John Bull's spinal cord on this continent has been interfered with by the accentuation of the Monroe Doctrine in later times and the old gentleman does not now amount to so much as he used to."[68] It never had been that simple, of course, but Ned Eyre knew the value of a little jingoistic appeal at a time the United States was exuding empire. Grace asserted that he had been despoiled of over $5 million owed to him and his old American associates allied in the 1885 syndicate to purchase and develop Meiggs's concessions.

Meanwhile, between 1899 and 1901, Peruvian contractors

were awarded the rights to complete the railroad from Oroya to Cerro de Pasco, and to finish the Rumillana Tunnel. Furthermore, a syndicate of Americans led by Alfred W. MacCune, James B. Haggin, Henry C. Frick, Mrs. Phoebe Hearst, and J. P. Morgan bought up most of the claims in the Cerro region and formed a multi-million-dollar syndicate in 1901, the Cerro de Pasco Mining Co., to exploit these silver and copper mines.[69] The Cerro Co. eventually finished the Oroya to Cerro railroad and emerged as the largest American corporation in Peru, a ranking based principally on its millions of dollars invested directly in the mining and smelting of copper ores.[70]

Eyre was involved in the last direct business Grace had with these railroads. He supervised the construction of the fifty-mile segment of the Central Railway from Chilca to Oroya under the contract arranged by Michael with the Peruvian Corporation in 1890.[71] Engineers such as H. D. B. Norris and John Thorndike of the old Meiggs group supervised the actual construction of the road, which included rebuilding the Verrugas bridge that had fallen in 1889, and nudging the railroad over the Continental Divide at an altitude of over fifteen thousand feet, the highest regular gauge railroad of the world.

Many essential building blocks make up a successful business, but two can be readily isolated in the growth of W. R. Grace & Co. in Peru in the period under consideration: the ability to be flexible and adapt to changing market conditions; and the willingness to invest in new ventures, often pioneering and taking risks (like establishing the first steamship service between New York and the West Coast of South America). The first ingredient derived from experience as international traders who could survive only by rapid adjustments, and the second from the nature of the men who ran the business. An important corollary was the nature of the times. Peru was being rapidly transformed by new technologies applied to old industries (mining and sugar, for example) and entirely new industries and services (electricity, tramways, cables, steamships) based on the transformation of the industrial revolution itself.[72] Guided by experience and imbued by an age that encouraged experimentation and technological improvement, Grace grew with Peru during the era, in many instances setting the pace rather than keeping it.

One of the oldest industries in Peru, one that dates back to antiquity, was that of textiles. During the colonial period, *obrajes*, or textile workshops, were organized by the Spanish to produce goods for both home consumption and export to other parts of the empire. Mechanization then transformed the industry in Peru in the late nineteenth century, just as it had in England (see Chapter 1).

A small mechanized mill had been first constructed in 1854 at Vitarte, a district about ten miles up the Rimac Valley from Lima, by a pioneering entrepreneur named Lopez Aldana. In this early period, Vitarte featured some fifty looms powered by a small hydraulic turbine.[73]

A village grew up around Vitarte, again remarkably resembling the beginnings of the textile industry in parts of Europe and North America. In 1890 or 1891 Aldana sold out to English capitalists who began to expand the mill. An English manager and two foremen were sent out by the Peruvian Cotton Manufacturing Co., organized by the British to administer Vitarte. During the next quarter century the small mill grew to seven hundred fifty looms, and by 1917 was producing a wide variety of products: ducks, tickings, fancy checks, cotton trouserings, osnaburgs, towels, wicking, and the like. Power was supplied partially by electricity and partially by a four-hundred-horse-power diesel engine set up in 1906, the largest in the area. A contemporary description in 1919 included the following:

> The little village had naturally grown in proportion [to the mill,] and now boasts electric lights, a first-class, if somewhat primitive, water and sewerage system, and a "movie." The millworkers' houses have all been built by the mill, and rents (figures to cover interest and depreciation) are perhaps worth mentioning; a family house, one story, two good-sized rooms, with a courtyard in back, followed by a kitchen and washroom commands about $4.50 a month. Other welfare activities of the mill comprise a church, school, drugstore, and a general holiday, with a bullfight thrown in, on that yearly date marked by the mill manager's birthday. The Vitarte Mill has about 15,000 spindles and the machinery used is all British.[74]

The normal work week was fifty-eight hours—a ten-hour day, except on Saturdays, when the mill ran only eight. In 1919 the mill employed about four hundred fifty operatives. But it was not the largest. That honor went to the Inca mill, built in the late 1890s by Peruvian capital. In 1902 Grace bought a one-third share in Inca and moved into textile manufacturing, a field leading in the industrialization of the country.

Between the 1890s and 1910 the production of textiles in Peru increased dramatically, doubling at a rate of about once every ten years.[75] Native production naturally began to displace imported textiles, the percentage of local textile production in the overall Peruvian domestic market rising from less than 5 percent in 1890 to 42 percent by 1906.[76] Almost all of the locally produced textiles were marketed in Peru, and, with few exceptions, much of the capital for these early mills was generated by Peruvians.

The Inca mill was owned jointly by Grace, the British owners of the Vitarte mill, and the Peruvians who owned La Victoria mill.[77] Within a few years Grace purchased the Vitarte mill. By 1910, then, Grace had a fair share of the sugar and textile businesses in Peru, both of which were being expanded and modernized.[78] Actually, by 1918 the Grace mills were producing 45 percent of the textiles in Peru, compared with 33 percent produced by the Peruvian-controlled mills, and 22 percent by Duncan Fox & Co.[79]

The move into the manufacturing and service industries by Grace in the twentieth century grew out of the firm's conclusion that the import-export business, the mainstay in the nineteenth century, was only a limited field.[80] Furthermore, Grace's ability to compete effectively against smaller houses was reduced by an increasing overhead. But, as the concern grew, so did its resources, and it was felt that advanced expertise and technical knowledge could be more effectively brought to bear in manufacturing and industrial production where Peruvian nationals might be limited.

We have here two themes clearly identified: one, the increasing influence of Grace in the modernization of Peru as the company diversified and expanded into new areas, often employing new technologies and advancements associated with the industrial revolution; and second, a business philosophy that directly contributed to the gradual transition of a trading company to a multinational corporation. The two men most responsible for producing this gradual transition were Joseph P. Grace, and his old Columbia roommate, David Stewart Iglehart. Grace anchored the New York office while Iglehart ran the West Coast business from Santiago and Lima in the early twentieth century. Introducing advanced agricultural techniques in Cartavio was one application of this philosophy. Investing in the electrification of Peru, a novel industry born of the industrial revolution, was another.

The first electrical plant erected in Peru was done in 1895 amid a traditional setting, reminiscent of another age. Lima, near the turn of the century, "was always conservative, [and] still bore many marks of the previous century. Bits of the [colonial] City Wall were still intact; the narrow streets were ill paved or unpaved; the Plaza de Armas or Central Square was an area of cobblestones. The only feminine headgear to be seen was the manto or mantilla; on the streets the poncho was nearly as common as the coat."[81] Yet more modern ways were creeping in. Horse races were becoming as familiar as bullfights. Flashy new coaches cruised the streets in imitation of Paris and New York. Horse-drawn streetcars on rails moved people about. Gaslighting adorned some houses and streets. Even Peruvian women were stirring as the first inklings of the feminist movement became apparent in the old viceregal capital.[82] Clorinda Matto de Turner not only championed the emancipation of women in a dignified fashion, but also was an early—perhaps the first—defender of Indian rights.[83]

Industrialization in Peru would also lead, as in other parts of the Western world, to disorientation, the creation of a new proletariat, and, inevitably, the rise of mass-based political parties. Turn-of-the-century polemicists like the vitriolic Manuel González Prada criticized the inequalities in Peruvian society and laid the intellectual foundations for such entities as the APRA. But, as the working classes slowly increased, so did those middle and upper classes actively contributing to the modernization of the nation.

While González Prada dissected society, investors such as Mariano Ignacio Prado y Ugarteche pushed the electrification of Lima into more advanced stages. The first plant erected in 1895 was called La Compañía Transmisora de Fuerza Eléctrica. It installed a Leffel hydraulic turbine at an old abandoned mill site on the edge of the city. The turbine was connected to a 75-kw General Electric generator and the power went largely to the Santa Catalina Woolen Mills about four kilometers away. Limeños were dubious about electricity's safety, looking on its wires as some form of unnatural menace.[84] Yet they adapted to the idea, albeit slowly.

The second stage in the development of the industry was the formation of the Empresa Eléctrica de Santa Rosa, a syndicate arranged by Prado y Ugarteche. The new Empresa Eléctrica absorbed the old Compañía Transmisora and began to expand its capacity at the end of the century, all the time selling the Lima public on the advantages of electricity, especially as a source of light for the city. When the city decided to install electric street lights, the water-driven turbines at the power plants were supplemented by a new McIntosh and Seymour cross compound steam engine directly connected to an equally new 400-kw General Electric generator. Steam provided for continuous power in the event water lines broke or the flow of water was interrupted as the motive for the older turbines.

The next step was electrification of public transportation.[85] Steam railroads already served the principal routes between Lima and Callao, and between Lima and Chorillos. The latter railroad ran through the suburbs of Miraflores and Barranco before reaching the small resort town of Chorillos on the Pacific. Since fares were high and service inadequate on these lines, the pioneering electrical entrepreneurs targeted these routes as particularly susceptible to competition.

In 1903 two companies were organized: the Transvía Eléctrica de Lima a Chorillos and the Ferro-Carril Eléctrico de Lima a Callao. Service on the Lima-Chorillos route began in 1904 on a double-track standard-gauge railroad over which ran five first-class open cars and five Stephenson closed-combination first- and second-class cars, all equipped with General Electric motors. For twenty centavos (about ten cents) one could clank along out to Chorillos in fifteen minutes, enjoying the best of the modern world. A comparable trip on the old railroad cost twice as much and forty minutes. Service on the Callao-Lima line operated by the Ferro-Carril Eléctrico de Lima a Callao also commenced in 1904, meeting with equal success and approval. The age of electric-powered mass transportation had arrived in the capital of Peru. Electric trolleys for Lima soon followed in 1905, and in 1906 all the electric enterprises in Peru were consolidated under one concern, Empresas Eléctricas Asociadas. The Graces were among the major initiators of and subscribers to this company.

The use of electricity expanded quite naturally in the succeeding years. Cotton mills, woolen mills, cotton-seed-oil mills, machine shops, breweries, and the Peruvian Central Railway shops became major users in addition to the trams and streetcars. Traffic on the existing streetcar service increased dramatically, prompting one rider to assure New Yorkers that even they would feel at home during the rush hour.[86] Nonetheless, the greatest expansion took place in domestic uses, electricity replacing gas and kerosene in many *limeño* homes by the war years.

The gradual displacement of English capital and equipment by American money and goods during this period in Peru was graphically exemplified by these pioneering innovations in electricity. All power units of the Empresas Eléctricas were American-made, as were all but six of the cars. One witness noted that "almost every piece of equipment and almost all of the accessories and supplies . . . in use came from the United States. The greater part of the company's equipment was supplied through the business cooperation of W. R. Grace & Co., who continually have on their staff of engineer salesmen in Lima a General Electric Company Engineer. . . . "[87]

Talk in the clubs and the news of the day in Lima around 1910 reflected the growing presence of North Americans not only in Peru but throughout Latin America. The progress of the Panama Canal always made good copy, occasional landslides and other reverses never puncturing for long the building swell of optimism for this great endeavor. A new journal appeared that year, *Peru Today*, dedicated to giving Peru greater publicity in the commercial world and to promoting the country's anticipated leap in prosperity when the canal was completed. A new drydock was brought to Callao to improve the port facilities; one of the backers was D. Stewart Iglehart.

Aviation, that fledgling, fragile harbinger of an industry that would transform world communications and world wars, was big news in 1910. Jorge Chávez, a young Peruvian aviator, thrilled the imagination of his countrymen before being killed while piloting a tiny craft through the mighty Alps. In 1928 Grace and Pan American would introduce the first international commercial aviation to Peru and continue the spirit of Jorge Chávez.[88]

World War I churned up the fields and spirits of old Europe, laid waste a generation of French and Englishmen, and midwifed Marxism in Russia. The United States and Latin America adjusted to the changes caused by the war by growing more closely together as old bonds between Latin America and Europe were frayed and even split by the catastrophe over there. In fashion with the times, Grace increased its investments in and commitments to Latin America, especially to Peru and Chile. The further enlargement and modernization of Cartavio and the purchase of the nitrate *oficina* of Paposo were but two examples.

By the end of the war, Peru had emerged from the long, century-old shadow of British dominance in foreign investments and foreign trade and, for better or worse, had become a client more of the United States than of Great Britain.[89] The presidency of Augusto B. Leguía between 1908 and 1912 had hastened this transition. Leguía's pro-American sentiments helped smooth the way for increases not only in United States investments in Peru, but in the esteem for Americans held by Peruvians. W. R. Grace & Co. was certainly most intimately associated with the United States, even though Michael Grace, living in England and presiding over extensive investments of his own and those of Grace Brothers, London, still imparted an old British hue to the firm in some circles.

Perhaps no other example better spotlights Peruvian esteem for Casa Grace—as the company was known on the West Coast—than the following anecdote from the war period. Jolted by the uncertainties of war, many began hoarding silver and gold in Peru. A severe shortage of currency ensued. Confident that American dollars were acceptable, U. S. bills were temporarily circulated by the government as legal currency. Still leery, many miners and mill workers accepted the currency only when someone suggested stamping the bills "Garantizada por la Casa Grace."[90]

Casa Grace, however, almost went under in 1920, buffeted by cyclonic winds of change. The decade of the twenties signaled an end to the old world of absolutes, peace, and harmony between man and much of his universe. It also opened up unparalleled opportunities for men. Casa Grace was caught in the whiplash of the age, an age marked by remarkably contrasting drives, some noble, some base, some divinely optimistic, some darkly pessimistic. But one thing the age was not—boring.

12

Joseph P. Grace and the Roaring Twenties

CRISIS MANAGEMENT AND THE
DEVELOPING MULTINATIONAL

Nineteen-nineteen. The "noble experiment," Prohibition, commenced, leading to another uniquely American invention, the speakeasy, to quench wet America's thirst in a land legally gone dry. Henry Cabot Lodge broke the spirit and back of the League of Nations in the United States Senate by leading the opposition to President Woodrow Wilson's dream of peace and democracy forever in the world. The Ku Klux Klan showed signs of reviving in a malevolent form and Red hysteria swept parts of the country as Americans faced the implications of bolshevism in Russia. But the main thrust was a triumphant nation's determination to return to normalcy.

In mid-decade another president, Calvin Coolidge, would pronounce solemnly, "The business of the United States is business." It indeed would be a splendid decade for businessmen, and the first year after the Great War seemed to augur the continued enlargement of hopes, profits, real incomes, and, perhaps most important for our story, American enterprise abroad. The United States, for all the isolationism of a Henry

Cabot Lodge, had replaced Europe as the world's creditor and vast sums of loan money and direct investments flowed from the United States.[1] It was in fact a grand year to be involved in international business, and W. R. Grace & Co. was then one of the leading commodities traders in the world. Together with healthy profits made from war shipping, Grace was booming along with America in general. In 1919 new Grace agencies were established at Milan, Hamburg, and Paris, to add to the almost one hundred fifty then extant worldwide. Trade in sugar, rice, jute, hides, tea, shellac, and coffee kept the Grace network busy and profitable in this postwar period, when the world's suppliers and buyers were still struggling to adjust to the shortages caused by the war.

United States investments abroad increased rapidly as well, especially in the mining sectors. Latin America and Canada were the principal areas of expansion, but investments on a smaller scale were also made in Europe, the Far East, and Africa. From these mines the raw materials of an industrial empire were being extracted: asbestos, bauxite, chrome, coal, copper, diamonds, iron ore, lead, manganese, nickel, nitrates, platinum, potash, tin, tungsten, vanadium, and zinc, and the more precious ones of gold and silver.[2] In her excellent general survey of the formation of American multinationals, Mira Wilkins wrote:

> United States investors . . . abroad shared the general business buoyancy. They extended their wartime investments as commodity prices in 1919 remained high. U. S. Rubber acquired the first plantation in Malaya in 1919. Soft drink producer Charles E. Hires purchased the Cardenas–American Sugar Company in Cuba in early in 1920. The Guggenheims put additional funds into their copper mining operations at Chuquicamata in Chile; Anaconda acquired a copper mining property in Peru in 1920. . . .[3]

Then, between May 1920 and June 1921, the postwar boom was punctured by a drastic price decline which halved prices and caused widespread unemployment and a mild depression in the United States. By now the integration of the world economy was so complete as to cause a similar effect on prices around the world, especially in commodities like rice and sugar. Grace, like many other international traders, took a nose dive.

Basically, Grace was overextended, caught with large stocks of commodities on hand that it could either not sell or sell at only catastrophically low prices. The crisis of 1920–21 was a real body blow for the company and especially so for the man at the center, Joseph P. Grace. On him were forced the decisions to close agencies, to release people (relatives were not spared in the draconian moves to survive the crisis), and to bargain with bankers for immense loans and credits. The son certainly proved to be a model leader. Throughout the crisis his letters counsel caution, boost morale, chastise those who have continued to overextend in spite of instructions, and call attention to the company's basically healthy body only temporarily afflicted by these postwar setbacks.

The crisis that Joseph Grace faced was in every respect as severe as the one weathered by William and Michael back in 1873 and 1874. Then, the negative Bryce connection and the collapsing Meiggs projects coincided unfortuitously with a worldwide depression that sent William traveling across three continents to shore up the dikes. By 1921, however, the stakes had increased immensely. Where the elder Graces had measured their losses in hundreds of thousands of dollars, Joseph had to accept the harsh reality that the company lost almost $26 million between 1920 and 1922.[4]

The major problem Joseph Grace faced in 1920–21 was part material and part mental. He had, on the one hand, to borrow enough cash to survive the shortfall and, on the other, to generate enough strength to overcome the crisis of confidence afflicting Grace managers around the world. November and December 1920 not only previewed the cold gloom of the coming season but ushered in a spate of rumors that threatened the company as much as the cash shortage. While Joseph Grace negotiated with a consortium of lenders, of which the National City Bank was by far the most important, panic spread among those closest to Grace from Santiago to Paris.

D. Stewart Iglehart, Grace's old classmate and certainly his closest and most trusted adviser in the company, reported from Valparaiso early in 1921 that the reaction to the rumor of imminent collapse in late 1920 did not appreciably shake the Chileans' confidence in the ultimate staying power of Casa Grace. One prominent banker told Iglehart "in a very friendly way that he did not consider all the talk that had been heard in this market had affected our standing in the least."[5]

Grace, of course, was not the only one afflicted by this worldwide phenomenon. More than thirty smaller firms had gone bankrupt in Chile in two months, having been caught with heavy stocks and insufficient capital to carry them through. Iglehart tightened Grace's credit policy since "business morale here seems to have entirely disappeared."[6]

In Paris morale dropped as precipitously as in Valparaiso. A. Barrelet de Ricou, the Grace manager in Paris, was beset by rumors among bankers and in the Bourse that Grace's financial position was perilous. Monsieur Barrelet de Ricou had been receiving newspaper clippings from New York since November reporting on a series of meetings between Grace and bankers (National City, J. P. Morgan & Co., and others), all with an eye toward averting a disastrous end for Grace.[7] While Barrelet tried to sound breezily confident, he was shaken by the news of the forthcoming demise of Grace and sought anxiously some reassurance from New York.[8]

Joseph Grace in New York fired off a telegram asking Ricou to name the New York correspondent who was supplying Paris with the premature notices of the fall of Grace. Ricou was placated but not particularly convinced by Joseph Grace's response. "I was very pleased indeed to hear direct from you that the reports on your house are untrue . . . it is most satisfactory to hear that your house has not one minute been shaken on its solid base."[9] Having whistled loudly in the dark, Ricou nonetheless could not hide his anxiety. Grace was closing trading offices all over the world and bankers in Paris, London, and New York viewed the retrenchment as symptoms of serious problems, "especially as the losses incurred by you in Spain, in Senegal, Japan, and Shanghai were of course known by the public."

Then Grace decided to close its Paris office as well. Ricou plaintively commented, "As for me, I still cannot explain to myself why you decided to withdraw from here. The rumors spread about your house have led me to think you needed your money elsewhere, but as it is not the case, it leaves the question still unanswered in my mind."[10] Ricou simply did not want to acknowledge the obvious, which he had so clearly stated but refused to believe. Grace had been shaken to its foundations and part of the solution was a radical pruning across the world. Paris was simply one of the offices that was lopped off to save the firm, whose principal efforts had historically been relegated to the Americas.

An equally troubled Sir William Maxwell, in charge of Grace Bros., Limited, Calcutta, received encouraging counsel from Joseph Grace. To kill rumors about the financial condition of the home office, Grace had Price Waterhouse, & Co. make up the balance as of October 21 and file a copy with the Federal Reserve Bank.[11] This he forwarded to Maxwell. Having assured Sir William of the solvency of W. R. Grace & Co., Joseph Grace also offered some advice on how to run a business in bad market conditions. A dull world market should force all managers to avoid long-term commitments. The Calcutta office made some blunders in contracting for freight under these circumstances and it cost it dearly.[12] Of course, the general market conditions beyond anyone's control had to be allowed for. Yet, Grace reminded Maxwell, "You promised me to reduce your debit balance to London to £200,000 promptly. I realize the difficulties you are up against but I rely upon you to get business down to this basis."[13]

The West Coast of South America, site of Grace's long and stable presence, helped steady the company. Iglehart, in his swing through Chile, Bolivia, and Peru, found that Grace's standing in Peru was solid in spite of the rumors.[14] Iglehart was, nonetheless, not one to gloss over difficulties. He was a tough businessman with perception and foresight. Since the depression had not struck Lima with force yet, he pressed William (Billy) Grace Holloway, then Grace manager in Peru, to squeeze on collections as much as possible. The bottom had dropped out of the cotton market, a sensitive business barometer since the Graces were building a commanding presence in the area of textiles.

Nevertheless, the sheer variety of Grace investments in Peru almost guaranteed that as least one or two major sectors would be clipping along well enough to buoy those others with problems. For example, sugar profits for 1920 were a little larger than anticipated, and, while the new mill at Cartavio had to be paid for, Iglehart remained high on sugar.[15]

Iglehart found Bolivia even less affected by the depression than Peru and Chile. Nothing looked bad, but his report was uncharacteristically but understandably short.[16] While in La Paz he suffered a bad case of *soroche*, or altitude sickness, that left him limp and weary.[17] Iglehart skipped Lima on his way to Cartavio, not wishing to get caught in the celebration of Carnival, a generally wild and ribald time. To Iglehart's mind, shoring up the business did not include wasting time on fruitless diversions.

★ ★ ★

By 1922 the crisis was weathered, although W. R. Grace & Co. had shrunk considerably. In May 1922 Joseph Grace could comment with some relief that "as far as business is concerned, it had been a year and a half of the hardest possible plugging, with very little show for the work put in. We have now got things on a good working basis and are well prepared to squeeze a little profit out of any of the sunshine which comes around the clouds which you say are now breaking."[18]

What had caused the worldwide depression? Correspondence between Joseph Grace and various relatives and colleagues dwelled on this question. From London, Gaspard Farrer wrote: "I am afraid one cannot get over the broad fact that 190 million people in Russia and almost as many more in Central Europe are temporarily knocked out as either consumers or producers, and the whole delicate structure of the world's commerce in prewar times was based and balanced on their inclusion."[19] Farrer had lucidly described a main cause. The only failure of his diagnosis lay in his misapprehension of the permanence of the Bolshevik Revolution that brought communism to Russia. The Soviet way would more than "temporarily" knock out those people from the world economy. But to have guessed otherwise in 1921 would have been unusual, given the newness of communism's rise to power in Russia and its failure to grip Germany as well.

Closer to home, the Red scare struck America in 1919 and 1920, and many radical, labor-based movements were implicated as destroyers of the world order and indirectly (sometimes directly) as agents of the 1920–21 depression. That the capitalist system itself was the cause of periodic recessions and depressions was ignored as Americans "seriously thought—or at least millions of them did, millions of otherwise reasonable citizens—that a Red revolution might begin in the United States the next month or next week, and they were less concerned with making the world safe for democracy than with making America safe for themselves."[20]

Across the sea, Ireland was producing a real nightmare for England. The Irish moved violently from 1916 through 1924 toward freedom from centuries-old English oppression. The Graces had always maintained close ties with their European kin and the correspondence in the early 1920s is especially rich with commentary on the progress, or deterioration, of politics and society. From England, Viscount Donoughmore, Michael Grace's grandson (from the marriage of Michael P. Grace's daughter Elena to the Lord Donoughmore of the Grace Contract), traded letters with Joseph Grace on a hodgepodge of business and personal matters. The woes of Ireland in rebellion, the fate of family properties in a future, independent Ireland, the onslaught of communism not only in America but among the workers in industrial England, and the doings of other family members in Great Britain and Europe caught in the postwar tumult were mixed with the current prices of nitrates and sugar on the Continent.

Until Michael P. Grace died in London in October 1920, he

was the leader of the clan in Great Britain. His mantle fell on the venerable Edward Eyre, who lived well into the 1930s and provided a living continuity with the Peruvian origins of the company. Eyre became the chairman of the board of W. R. Grace & Co. upon Michael Grace's death, but the title was more honorific in this period. The real leader of the house through the 1920s was Joseph P. Grace, whose nature combined the sound business sense of his father with the warmth and charity of his mother.

That he weathered the 1920–21 crisis certainly proved his tenacity and intelligence as a businessman. Yet he was more than merely the leader of a tough company with staying power. He was a warm, understanding father who could realistically size up the strengths and foibles of his beloved family. Perhaps his counsel to a growing Joseph Peter Grace, Jr. in the twenties best demonstrated the nature of the father.[21] Young Peter was not to let homesickness get him down while away at school. Time would heal the loneliness. To a tutor of Peter's he wrote that Joseph Peter Grace, Jr. is given to "argue." Peter was to work hard, and to keep in touch with mother and father, who cherish his letters.

Joseph and his wife Janet lost a child in 1922 and their sadness must have been crushing. A note from a close relative to the grieving parents surely reflected the parents' sorrow: "I just ache for you and dear Janekie just when everything seemed so lovely and you were so happy. I know how she feels as I lost my own wee one, but tell her to keep thinking of the three treasures she has and that helps a lot. He was a sweet, precious baby and so perfect . . . with dearest love to you both."[22]

Although the business was no longer the family affair it had been half a century earlier, talented relations—near and distant—were encouraged as always to develop themselves while contributing to the firm. One of the most successful relatives was William Grace Holloway, Joseph Grace's nephew. Young Holloway and Uncle Joseph enjoyed a confidence in each other that grows from long association built on mutual esteem and trust. A similar relationship existed between Grace and his old college roommate D. S. Iglehart. These personal and professional friendships mixed family, business, and politics in delightful fashion.

The engagement of a young American friend of the family in Lima to a Peruvian girl early in 1922 triggered an anxious inquiry from the father, a cashier of the City Bank in New York. Who was his boy marrying? Who indeed was Leolita del Campo, and, more important, what information could Holloway from Lima please supply Joseph Grace about her family and whether the marriage was likely to be a suitable one?[23] Billy Holloway did some investigating in Lima and wrote back to Uncle Joe that the cashier could put his mind at ease. Leolita's father, Arturo del Campo y Pesta, came from a good family in Peru and Ecuador. He lived on his income from real estate, and although not rich, he could be considered well to do. In short, he had a good reputation.[24] Don Arturo also had a dashing air about him. He once fought a duel and killed a member of the distinguished Porras family.[25] All in all, however, Holloway reported that an alliance with the daughter should be considered a desirable one. If Leolita was as passionate as her father seemingly was, the young American probably had found himself a good match.

Holloway added at the end of the short note reporting on the daring Arturo del Campo y Pesta that while business was still dull, the bottom had been reached and they were slowly climbing out.[26] Joseph Grace had carefully been following developments in Peru and he concurred. They still had some tough sledding ahead, but the worst was over.[27]

Matters of personnel were always of crucial importance. A. W. Parker, an Englishman who held a key accounting position in Holloway's Peruvian operations, had gone to England on vacation and sick leave in 1921 and his return was in doubt. The problem was his wife. She was born of English parents in Valparaiso and did not particularly like Peru. Parker loved Peru and his work with Holloway and Grace. The Englishman showed up unexpectedly in New York in late January 1922 and said he would be perfectly willing to sign a three-year contract and wished to return to Peru.[28] As for his Chilean-English wife, she was staying in England and would not join him until later.[29] That seemed to solve, at least temporarily, the domestic difficulty and Parker returned to Peru, much to the delight of Holloway, who reported in May that "Parker is a joy and we were very fortunate to get him back."[30]

In a long report on the general business of the company in 1928 Iglehart included the following:

> McOscar. Has decided to go to Colombia [where Grace had an extensive coffee-buying and export business] and feels that his wife will go and be happy there. I wish you would make it a point to have a talk with McOscar as I in my conversations with him have been impressed with the fact that he has a great deal of ability and that the trip has developed

him remarkably. I think he is a man we must keep our eye on for future development.[31]

Parker, McOscar, and others were indeed important to Grace's future development, and the identification and cultivation of such men were integral to the Grace management philosophy. Part of that philosophy was to pay them well, an issue of some controversy during the 1920–21 crisis.

The crisis produced, as could certainly be expected, a good deal of second-guessing and grousing by the stockholders. David T. Layman, Jr. accused Grace of forcing the stockholders to shoulder the brunt of the losses from the crisis while the managers were kept fat and happy.[32] Joseph Grace answered this charge at length, defending with conviction the basic philosophy that the "best results cannot be obtained from underpaid men."[33]

Profit sharing was one method, for "my father and Uncle Michael decided from the inception of the corporation that there would have to be a profit-sharing plan to provide the necessary incentive to develop men capable of running the business."[34] While Joseph Grace defended his men, he offered no excuses for lapses which obviously contributed to the crisis. "Most of the managers have given every day of their lives to the business. We are all to blame for allowing the business to extend beyond the point where we could give it close management, and we are not shirking any responsibility for it. It can hardly be contended, however, that the heavy losses made as a result of being unprepared for the world shrinkage of 1920–21 nullifies all the work that was done in building the concern in the previous years."[35] As it was, managers' pay had already been cut in conformity with the terms of the major bank loans taken out to weather the crisis. Profit sharing, however, paid out as percentages on dividends and stock ownership, was retained. Joseph Grace was emphatic in keeping this feature. "This may seem only a sentimental difference [as opposed to paying straight salaries] but the *spirit and ability with which men work makes the difference between the successful merchant* and those who are unsound or dry-rotted" (italics added).[36]

Nothing else symbolized this commitment more than the promotion of Luis Valverde of Valparaiso to junior partnership in the firm in November 1924. With the promotion went the right to receive seven eights of one percent of the dividends as his share of the profits.[37] Joseph Grace summarized much of his working philosophy toward colleagues and rising subordinates forcefully: "You are now recognized as one of those upon whom, to a great extent, the future of the House depends.

From the beginning of the House men have arisen as so-called junior partners whose function it has been to organize men, build up business and to be conservative at all times."[38]

And what did "be conservative at all times" mean? In fashion? Politics? Culture? Probably a bit of all, but it was principally aimed at one's business practices. And why not? After the near disaster of 1920–21, it was only natural to counsel a more conservative approach to business. Hence, the company withdrew from most of the world and concentrated on the Americas after 1922.

Unlike Southeast Asia or India, both areas from where Grace pulled out after the short experience that propelled profits and imaginations like a slingshot before the inevitable dropback to earth, the West Coast of South America was not alien to Grace. New York, San Francisco, Valparaiso, Callao, Colón—these represented the earth to Grace, with known factors and familiar cultures. After all, the company had been founded in South America, there it had sunk its roots, there it had promoted nationals based on talent and merit, there it was known and respected. Even during local political turmoil, Grace found this taproot strong and resistant.

The return to the coast was the homing instinct of the house of Grace. When Joseph Grace wrote Valverde in July 1921, he concluded thus: "If we can only increase the general business between our West Coast houses and New York, it is the most important thing that can be done today for the general organization. . . . We are anxious to increase our merchandise movement in Peru and Chile, where we get some benefit in carrying the freight and *where we have known market conditions and customs for years* . . . we are depending on you, when you come to New York, to increase the volume of business between this country and Peru and Chile" (italics added).[39]

Nitrates in Chile, sugar from Peru, textiles in both countries, ores from Bolivia, coffee from Colombia and Costa Rica—all these were commodities and businesses it had long experience with.

In the 1920s the nitrate business of Chile was especially challenging. Like all other commodities, nitrates went into a postwar slump, except the depression hit the nitrate industry precisely when the armistice was signed in November 1918. No longer needed for the production of ammunition to feed the arsenals of the combatants, production dropped radically since

existing surpluses in Chile and abroad more than met the agricultural needs of the world. From a high of 5,212,752 quintals,
production fell to 2,376,564 quintals in August 1919.[40] Only fifty
oficinas were left in operation in August, whereas 117 had been
operating in the preceding September.

Then the cycle of recovery began. As production rose to meet
increasing demands from abroad, the Association of Chilean
Nitrate Producers, formed in 1919 to promote the nitrate trade
by gathering information and fixing prices, contributed to the
rapid restoration of prosperity in the nitrate fields. During the
next decade nitrates generated large profits for its producers
and generous revenues for the Chilean government. The majority of the nitrate plants continued to be owned by English
and Chilean interests during the twenties. Only three plants
of 118 were American-owned in 1922, and they produced only
3 percent of the total. Yet 25 percent of overall Chilean nitrate
of soda production was exported to the United States. Of all
the *oficinas* Grace's Paposo was one of the largest single producers, and Grace Nitrate Agencies was the leading importer
of nitrates into the United States.

The prosperous operation at Paposo naturally drew rivals,
and none other challenged the Graces more hotly than the
Guggenheim family as it sought to add nitrates to its mining
empire. Led by Daniel Guggenheim, the immensely talented
and wealthy family divested its copper interests in Chile by
selling the largest copper mine in the world, Chuquicamata, to
Anaconda in 1923. The capital was plowed into the nitrate industry by buying control of the Anglo-Chilean Nitrate Company and the Lautaro Nitrate Company.[41]

The Graces kept close tabs on the Guggenheim incursion into
nitrates, especially in the early 1920s when the first moves were
being made. Joseph Grace advised Federico Wightman, Grace
manager in Chile, of the Guggenheim threat in January 1922.
Rumor was that the Guggenheims had developed a new process for making nitrates, and had interested some powerful
backers: J. P. Morgan & Co. and perhaps even Agustin Edwards, one of the leading industrialists in Chile. The Guggenheims believed it was an important process and expected to get
a foothold in the nitrate industry by this means.[42]

The Guggenheims had accumulated a vast fortune by bringing a potent combination of talent, energy, and innovation to
bear on mining industries in the Americas, especially in Mexico,
and Daniel Guggenheim figured improved methods of nitrate
production would eventually help natural nitrates overcome
the growing competition from synthetics. The new technology,

however, was perfected only in the 1930s, although Guggenheim experiments in the 1920s kept everyone, including the Graces, guessing. "The Guggenheim Bros. nitrate process is being made the mystery of the ages on this coast."[43] But the major Guggenheim thrust in the industry was made after 1930, after Grace had withdrawn from the field, and, more important, after synthetic nitrates had gained the upper hand on natural nitrates. While keeping an eye on the Guggenheims, Grace went ahead with its own experiments in developing Oficina Paposo and extending its marketing network over most of the southern and southwestern United States.

Meanwhile, although still largely known as merchants and shippers in the 1920s, Grace had also been selling and servicing machinery for more than three decades along the West Coast.[44] Beginning with the importation of agricultural machinery into Chile in the late 1880s, Grace handled such orders on a commission basis until the turn of the century.

Then in 1902 Grace arranged to be the exclusive agent for the General Electric Company in Peru, Bolivia, Chile. G.E. sent a sales engineer to help advise prospective customers and to supply technical information and service on the equipment. As the business expanded to include other classes of machinery—water wheels, steam engines, boilers, pumps, hoists, and general mining equipment—additional experts were taken on. In 1907 the Grace machinery business was extended to cover the nitrate district with technical organizations located at Iquique, Antofagasta, and in the mining districts of Bolivia.[45] A new technical department was established in New York to coordinate these services. In 1912 the business was organized as the International Machinery Company (IMACO). One of General Electric's engineers sent down before 1906 was a young, adventurous fellow from Demopolis, Alabama, named Gaston J. Lipscomb.[46]

Lipscomb graduated from Auburn University with a degree in electrical engineering. From there he went to work with G.E. in Schenectady, New York, continuing his education at nearby Union College.[47] Lippy, as he was known by associates and close friends, was then transferred to the tropical Canal Zone to supervise the nitrogen plant making ice to keep things cool for the builders of the canal under construction. While there he came down with a case of yellow fever, which almost killed him.

Luckily for Lippy, Dr. William Crawford Gorgas, the man

most responsible for eradicating yellow fever from the isthmus, was a close friend of the Lipscomb family, for Gorgas's home in Tuscaloosa was not far from Demopolis. As recounted by William H. Clayton, one of Lipscomb's brightest young subordinates to work with him later in Chile and Peru, "Lippy told me that if it had not been for this close family relationship he would never have pulled through yellow fever. Gorgas took special care and stayed with him practically night and day for several weeks until he pulled him through."[48]

From Panama Lipscomb was ordered south to Chile as the General Electric engineer. There he began his association with W. R. Grace & Co. as a sales engineer. Once again, as in Panama, Lippy almost perished, this time in Valparaiso in 1906 when a disastrous earthquake shook that lovely port city to rubble. He was a good survivor, however.

Lipscomb became a key figure in the Grace nitrate business and by the early 1920s was back in New York heading the small engineering department, consisting largely of himself and a secretary. Although industrial enterprises—best represented by the Grace investments in textiles, nitrates, and sugar—were but one part of a complex whole, they already were demanding a separate and distinct niche within the company, exemplified by Lipscomb's small office in New York. Grace's experience in developing Paposo provided the company with a wealth of experience for engineer-managers like Clayton, who represented, along with Lipscomb, this new industrial dimension.

The chief problem for Oficina Paposo and other nitrate establishments in the postwar decade was to remain competitive in the face of synthetic nitrates. It was recognized by some that the German development of fixing nitrogen from the atmosphere had been far enough advanced by wartime imperatives eventually to drive natural Chilean nitrates from the marketplace. But it was not a radical change; rather, it was one that proceeded slowly and was self-evident. Clayton, a chemist by training who worked in Paposo from 1923 to 1930, commented, "We always considered, or at least I always considered, when I went to Chile in 1923, that eight years would be as long as I could stay there because I thought that by that time the synthetic nitrogen would run us off. It so happened that that was the case." However, properly applied, new technology could prolong the viable life of the Chilean nitrate fields. It was an industry well worth preserving and improving, even in the face of predictable obsolescence. Between 1916 and 1930 the nitrate business yielded annual profits for Grace of over one million pounds sterling.

Improving the ability to deal with lower-grade ores and raw materials is a classic way of upgrading the efficiency of a mining industry. Between 1917 and 1919, a new plant was built at Paposo to handle the slimes, or slimy ores and nitrate muds. These slimes possessed only 13–14 percent nitrates as opposed to the 17–19 percent concentrations of most other ores in the area. To handle these muds and slimes, this plant was composed of filters designed by Edward Burt, an engineer-inventor, who had spent a long life in Mexico and South America in gold and silver mining.[49] He had gained some fame from inventing these filters to work the precious metals. Grace was the first company to try the filters in the nitrate fields. The only problem was, the plant had been a complete flop. And it had cost several million dollars.[50] Burt was sent by Grace to Paposo in 1923 to get the plant operating. When he finally did, Paposo became the most efficient of the nitrate *oficinas* on the pampas of northern Chile, helping prolong the natural nitrate industry in the face of growing German competition through the twenties.

Other innovations by Grace kept Paposo's balance sheets flowing nicely in the black throughout the decade. The ideas predictably flowed out of Mr. Lipscomb's small but inventive office tucked away at Seven Hanover Square, Grace headquarters in New York.

Potassium is an important ingredient in fertilizers and Grace discovered that it could produce at Paposo a fertilizer combining both potassium and nitrates. Luckily for Grace, Paposo's grounds contained a sizable amount of both iodine and potassium. Not many nitrate plants in northern Chile contained workable amounts of potassium. One of the first projects that Lipscomb's engineering department promoted was the production of a double-duty nitrate for the farmers of the United States. Being double duty, the product would have the same amount of potassium oxide normally contained in a potassium fertilizer and simultaneously would contain the same or practically the same amount of nitrogen that sodium nitrate carried. This, therefore, meant that if a farmer bought this nitrate, which Grace trademarked Nitrapo—or nitrate of potash—he would get for the same price two full quantities of two different plant foods: potassium and nitrogen.[51] Nitrapo was advertised widely throughout the United States as beneficial for tobacco (improves the burning quality), sugar beets (maximum sugar content), potatoes (size and quality), and, of course, cotton.[52]

Improvements were also instituted in human affairs at Paposo. The Grace management was the first to implement an eight-hour working day in northern Chile's nitrate *oficinas*, and it may just have saved a few lives as well as improved efficiency. By 1925 young Clayton had been promoted to manager of Paposo's plant, now employing more than one thousand six hundred laborers. Clayton, a South Carolinian of twenty-five, had been hired by Lipscomb in 1923 and sent to accompany Burt and a Swedish engineer, Ludwig Lumaire, as their assistant on their trip to get the fouled filters operating properly.

Clayton liked Paposo, but admitted "it was a tough place to live."[53] One could travel for hundreds of miles and never see a blade of grass, except maybe in the manager's back yard, where a few potted plants might exist on soil brought in from hundreds or thousands of miles away. People didn't stay there long; they didn't like the place, they didn't like the people, they didn't learn the language. Clayton, on the other hand, got along well and found the work extremely interesting.

Singling out good people was always uppermost in Grace management, and Billwiller, then running the Iquique office of Grace Nitrate Agencies, kept Clayton on and encouraged him in his work.[54] Part of that work included labor relations, one of the major challenges to managers of any industrial enterprise.

The Paposo plant had been operating on two twelve-hour shifts, a circumstance hard to handle for Clayton, who was running the factory by himself after he had been there two years. He also figured they were losing a lot of efficiency by trying to work people too hard. So he brought his crews together and told them he was going to put them on eight-hour shifts. However, with less men on each shift, they would have to put in some extra effort. But they would be earning the same daily wage for eight rather than twelve hours of work. The result? "I wasn't spending any more money and getting much higher efficiency. And I had people that were better satisfied."[55]

It was well that they were. Soon after the eight-hour day innovation was put into effect at Paposo, a labor strike erupted into violence on the nitrate pampas. A force of about two or three thousand miners came across the desert shutting down nitrate plants and calling for, among other demands, an eight-hour workday. Between one hundred fifty and two hundred *carabineros*, Chilean national policemen, were strung out across the mountain ridge to cut them off. They killed a dozen or two, but the workmen kept on coming; right up to the Paposo plant, where they climbed atop the "iodine house," in which finished iodine was stored. It had a big flat roof, and from there they made speeches and asked Paposo's workmen to go on strike with them.

But the appeal fell on deaf ears. Paposo already had an eight-hour workday and its workers "said it would be crazy for us to go on strike with you or go on a sympathy strike. So, my boys ran them right out. And they were armed. They had pistols, knives, and bayonets, and machetes."[56] Notwithstanding its eight-hour shift, Paposo was to enjoy a relatively short lifespan.

Always with an eye on the future, Joseph Grace wrote Gale Carter of the San Francisco branch in 1926 that the depression in the nitrate business did not augur well.[57] Joseph's concern with the fall in Chilean nitrate business in 1926 presaged the end of the Grace presence in the industry four years later.

In that year the Chilean government formed the Compañía de Salitre de Chile, COSACH, and bought out most of the nitrate companies then in existence, effectively nationalizing the industry with generous compensation to the former owners. Oficina Paposo was closed down, although all the equipment and the plant were left in a good state of preservation for possible future use. However, COSACH never reopened Paposo and within two or three years the entire plant was dismantled and hauled away. Today, Paposo is only a name.

"There's nothing, not one stick of timber or piece of iron or anything left at all. It's just flat, open ground. No vegetation, just desert . . . the only way you could recognize it would be by the hills."[58]

Far to the north of the barren hills of Paposo, the first American ace of World War I wrote to Joseph Grace in July 1922, from Hacienda Cartavio, surrounded by hundreds of acres of tall green sugar cane: "As for the living conditions, I guess I must be rather primitive in my tastes, for in spite of inconveniences I must say that life in the open air in quiet Cartavio is far more enjoyable than the frantic, steam-heated sardine existence which one leads in New York. Perhaps the most delightful part of it is that one can spend a couple of hours a day reading or writing, instead of using up all one's spare time on the subway."[59]

Douglas Campbell was the first American aviator in the war to have achieved ace status in an American uniform. An extraordinarily capable and resourceful person, he was recruited by Joseph Grace in April 1919 and first went to work in the mailroom.[60] From there he was promoted to the accounting department and in 1920–21 served as a nonstenographic secretary to Joseph Grace. In September 1921 he packed up and boarded a steamer for Peru and Hacienda Cartavio.

The original intention was to have Campbell serve as bookkeeper for a while and then have him take over the accountant's position on the hacienda. That man's contract was to expire in six months. It was well that Campbell was both resourceful and a hard worker. Three weeks after he arrived the accountant came down with typhoid and was shipped off to Lima and from there to the U.S., and he never returned. Campbell was now the accountant, knowing very little Spanish and much less about accounting. He had to work nights that first month, taking the previous months' accounts apart backward to find out how they were put together.[61]

Cartavio's ambiance could not have been more remote from the airdromes and skies of France in 1918, inhabited by flying machines and gallants whose very names—Baron von Richthofen, Eddie Rickenbacker, Billy Bishop—still elicit romantic visions of aviation's first heroes and villains. Campbell had served with the first American squadron, the ninety-fourth, to fly into combat. On the first day the ninety-fourth went into action, "two German airplanes came over to take a look at us and another guy and myself shot them both down, in a flight over the airfield that lasted four and a half minutes."[62] Five more air victories were added to this one before Campbell was wounded in June. Needing experienced pilots to train the new ones flocking to the standard back home, Campbell was sent back to the United States. The armistice was signed as he steamed back across the Atlantic to reenter the war.

Campbell lived in Peru for eleven years, eventually being promoted to administrator, the top post, of Cartavio at the end of the decade. Like Clayton in Paposo, Campbell prospered in the remote, faintly exotic setting of Hacienda Cartavio. Campbell was Harvard-educated and his father, a celebrated astronomer, was president of the University of California, Berkeley. Cartavio must have seemed doubly remote to a young man of such a cosmopolitan background. He also identified one of the main attractions when describing life far out of the mainstream of America and Europe: "But there were some compensations in this isolated life, other than *sheer interest in one's work* . . . there was little opportunity to spend any money and one could bank almost all of one's salary unless one wanted to spend it all on alcohol, and there wasn't much time for that anyway in a 6½-

day work week (on Sunday mornings the irrigations of the cane fields could not go without supervision, nor could the cleaning and repairing of the factory)" (italics added).[63]

Campbell, like most of the single young men (mostly Scots) who made up the small technical force of engineers and chemists on the plantation, lived in fairly primitive bachelor's quarters within sight, smell, and sound of the plant.[64] The quarters were built of adobe, with roofs consisting of planks with four inches of adobe on top of that. They had a shower and washstand in the back part of the house. Farther back in the patio was a two-holer. Each house had a houseboy provided by the hacienda; he made the beds and kept the place more or less clean.[65]

If one wished to get away from it all, the city of Trujillo was twenty-five miles away. However, since there were no roads, there were no automobiles, and in fact no means of going anywhere except on the daily narrow-gauge train, which transported the sugar to the port of Salaverry on the other side of Trujillo for shipment. Or one could travel on horseback. Campbell's first trip away from the property came fifteen months after his arrival. He made the fifty-mile round trip to Trujillo, on horseback and mostly at night, to go to a dance.

There was also an *autocarril*, a sort of automobile which ran on the railroad track, but in those days it was reserved almost exclusively for the use of the manager. Lima could be reached only by a steamer voyage of a day or two, but the schedules were such that the round trip could rarely be made in less than about ten days, and the management took a dim view of anyone being away from his job that long, except to go to the hospital.[66] The manager was still Coll MacDougall, thrifty as befits his origins in the hills of Scotland. While Cartavio was making profits of over a million dollars a year in the war and postwar period, MacDougall's habits and sense of order remained simple and disciplined.

So Campbell and the dozen or so other gringos worked most of the time. For entertainment, they read books, played bridge, or participated in an occasional very amateur soccer match.[67] Exercise came from two sets of tennis before sundown every evening, and on Sundays and on occasional mornings or afternoons during the week Campbell managed to get a good long ride to become better acquainted with the work in the field.[68] With his typical penchant for accuracy and self-effacement, Campbell did not claim to be much of a horseman yet, "as the only trotting horses we have here are a bit dopy, and while they can take a fairly wide ditch in good style, they wouldn't consider going over a fence."[69]

No piece of correspondence between Grace men seems appropriate without at least a small mention of business, and Campbell, as young to the company as he then was, naturally caught the spirit in writing to Joseph Grace of his existence at Cartavio in 1922:

> Things seem to be getting along here nicely at present . . . this will be the third week of over 12,000 tons grind, but of course the Fiesta of the 28th [Peruvian Independence Day, July 28] will bring the monthly figure down, as the loading gangs will start quitting a day or two ahead and will not show up in force until probably the 1st of August. . . .
>
> Labor troubles have been slight for many months. There was a slight flare-up in the first week of June, but I think we can expect that every so often. After they get the wind off their chest they seem to settle down for another fairly long period of steady work. . . .[70]
>
> If you can keep the demand for sugar at its present level, I think we can do the rest.[71]

MacDougall was pleased with the hard-working young man sent to him by Joseph Grace, who had taken a strong liking to Campbell. Grace wrote Campbell: "You have the qualities to really master the business from the ground up, if you have the temperament and the patience to stick to the game."[72] Campbell had been treated like a member of the family while working for Joseph Grace in New York, and so news of the children, tennis, and riding flowed easily from Grace's pen to Campbell in Cartavio: "Our tennis court has been rebuilt and is a great success. We had a family match the other day—Janet [Mrs. Joseph P. Grace] and Nora [eldest daughter] against Peter and me—and whichever side got the ball over the net once made the score."[73]

In the same letter, Joseph wrote: "Judging by your performance when you rode with me, I have no question about your horsemanship either on the flat or over ditches. Nora and Peter are both getting more at home in the art, but they still hold on the saddle with one hand when they go over a jump."[74] Peter Grace in fact later became an accomplished rider and polo player, and Douglas Campbell did indeed "stick to the game" and remained with Grace for the rest of his life.

In 1922 sugar production in Peru surpassed the three-hundred-thousand-ton mark for only the second time in history, having first hit that level in 1919. Production continued to rise slowly through the twenties and Cartavio shared in the general prosperity. Cartavio was the third largest plantation in the Chicama Valley after Casa Grande and Roma, and after 1927 would move into second place when the Gildemeisters absorbed Victor Larco's Roma.

Cartavio consisted of about thirty thousand acres, of which eighty-five hundred were devoted to growing sugar cane, the rest planted in other crops or used for pasture.[75] The pasture land was necessary to support the almost two thousand horses, mules, and oxen kept on the estate. It was really a sizable town, for its property included nine hundred seventy-five buildings, consisting of laborers' and employees' houses, warehouses, shops, two schools, a movie theater, church, and hospital. To haul the cane, four locomotives, one hundred twenty-five cane cars, and seventeen miles of portable track were employed. A population of about twenty-five hundred people completed the picture of a town oddly near self-sufficiency, but linked critically to the world market for its ultimate prosperity.

The mill was modernized once again in 1921 with the addition of a nineteen-roll mill built especially for Cartavio by the Fulton Iron Works of St. Louis. As in other areas of the Peruvian economy, the displacement of English and European machinery by American machinery took place in the sugar industry and contributed to the continued ascendancy of United States economic and political interests in Peru in the 1920s. With the addition of the mill, Cartavio's capacity was increased to twenty-five hundred tons of cane per day.

Competition with the two other main growers in the valley, the Gildemeisters and the Larcos, continued through the decade with both MacDougall and Iglehart taking aggressive stances. The rationale in 1924 was not too different from that twenty or thirty years earlier when MacDougall was commencing the slow expansion of the estate: water rights and ambitious neighbors. This time Iglehart and MacDougall wanted to buy the estates of Sintuco and Sonolipe for sixty thousand pounds sterling. They contained about forty-two hundred acres of land and a dozen *riegos*, or parceled water rights, which MacDougall especially wanted to acquire outright for Cartavio. Victor Larco was also attempting to acquire those smaller estates from their owner, Luis Jose Orbegoso. As Iglehart succinctly put it: "Larco *as an owner* would be a dangerous element for us" (italics added). MacDougall had a verbal agreement with Orbegoso to renew the lease on those estates for twenty years at 4,200 pounds annually. But, even if MacDougall got the twenty-year lease, he was pressing for authority to buy those estates whenever the opportunity arose. Without those properties or their water rights, MacDougall asserted that Cartavio would be obliged to abandon practically 50 percent of its present cultivation. The going price was a hundred pounds sterling per fanegada of land, which was considered a fair price in the valley. MacDougall also argued that Grace would simply be putting back part of that year's profits into the business.[76]

The sale of Roma in 1927 for thirteen million soles to the Gildemeisters ended Victor Larco's threatening posture toward Cartavio and the valley itself settled down to domination by Casa Grande.[77] Cartavio's competitive stance, however, remained strong, based on the large resources that Grace could bring to bear not only in modernizing production but also in competing against the Gildemeisters for the grinding business of the few remaining independent growers, such as Rafael Larco's Chiclin estate, which sent its cane to be ground at either Cartavio or Casa Grande.

Consolidation was not limited to the large planters in the 1920s. The incipient labor union movement in the Chicama Valley also matured in the decade, blossoming into prolonged and violent strikes in 1920 and 1921 aimed in particular at Victor Larco and his unenlightened policies at Roma.[78] Although several of the strikes proved contagious and spread to other estates, Cartavio, though not immune, was rarely singled out for attack.

What Grace at Cartavio and the Gildemeisters at Casa Grande did share, however, was the public association with foreign ownership, even though the Gildemeisters were second-generation Peruvians and Casa Grace had been founded in Peru. The radical political rhetoric of the period, inspired in part by Victor Raul Haya de la Torre's APRA party, founded in 1923, was intensely nationalistic and anti-Yankee (Yankee being equated with imperialism in all its virulent forms). There was simply no way the management of Cartavio could avoid the brickbats hurled by Haya de la Torre's partisans proselytizing for their point of view.

But a genuine effort was made to keep the managers of Cartavio *acriollado* ("creolized") as much as possible to "gain the workers' respect and even affection."[79] The son of Victor Larco was almost hired by Cartavio in 1927, so that "we may have somebody who can get opinions on the real feeling and sentiment of the people," although H. H. G. Redshaw, then managing Lima, added, "Of course, I know the whole valley is very much upset against Gildemeisters, and certain individuals lose no opportunity of working up public feeling against the gringos, the son of Victor Larco amongst them."[80]

Grace policy, in fact, had always been to identify strongly with the nations in which it operated, and this policy had led to the promotion of various nationals to head Grace operations in their respective countries. As early as 1896 Alberto Falcon served as general manager of W. R. Grace & Co. in Peru and was eventually promoted to vice president in New York in charge of the import business.[81] Federico Wightman rose to head the house in Chile and Jorge Zalles was doing the same in Bolivia in the 1920s. This general policy would be accelerated in the 1930s and 1940s, and one must certainly conclude the wisdom of such a course. Few major strikes and little violence centered on Cartavio in the 1920s.

The Grace sugar interests were rounded out in 1926 by the purchase of the Canaval family estate of Paramonga. The Graces were no strangers to the Canavals and Paramonga, loans having been made as early as the 1870s to help them expand their production.[82] As noted, in 1875 the Canavals owed Bryce, Grace $258,000, but had managed to whittle this down and enjoy the prosperity that came during and after World War I when production and profits soared. So did the Canavals' enjoyment of the world, however. By 1926, because of mismanagement and the family's profligate existence in Europe, the estate was again deeply in debt and badly run down. Grace bought it for $4.6 million.

Paramonga lies in the Pativilca Valley, about a hundred thirty miles north of Lima. In 1926 it contained 6,910 acres, of which only 3,900 were planted in cane. The mill, like the estate in general, was run down and the town unimproved and in sad need of renovation. The fields suffered from absentee ownership and neglect while many irrigation ditches were clogged, broken, and useless. Paramonga, in fact, lost money for the next fourteen years.

Why buy such a white elephant? One, the price was right, and two, sugar production continued to climb in Peru through the middle twenties. In 1928 production went over the four-hundred-thousand-ton mark for the first time and the promise was for increasing profits. How many years had Cartavio yielded nothing but "improvements to the plant and fields," with little to show the owners in dividends and profits. Yet the rewards had been rich indeed, and there was no reason to suspect that Paramonga could not be scientifically restored like Cartavio. Furthermore, no one in 1926 was clairvoyant enough to predict the crash of 1929 and the drastic drop in prices during the 1930s. Besides, Peru in the 1920s under the presidency of Augusto B. Leguía was probusiness, pro-American, and stable.

Paramonga would ultimately be the site of one of the most remarkable industrial experiments in the third world, and it would produce a cornucopia of benefits and profits for Peru and Grace. But that transformation did not occur until the late 1930s and 1940s. For the rest of the flapper decade, Paramonga attracted Grace technicians and engineers sent to study the problems and propose solutions. Among them, for example, was Douglas Campbell, who went there for a year and a half in 1927 and 1928 as an assistant administrator.

Not all investment opportunities in Peru attracted the Graces. One which promised to be lucrative and fell within an area of growing interest to the company, tourism, was rejected for reasons peculiar to W. R. Grace & Co.

Since the end of the war Grace had been expanding its passenger service aboard the *Santas* serving the West Coast from New York. Even though the majority of these passengers were technicians, engineers, accountants, and other managers of American and European enterprises in Latin America in transit, a trickle of real tourists was beginning to flow. To accommodate them in the City of Kings, Lima capitalists had already erected one splendid first-class hotel, the Bolivar, in 1922. In late 1924 another was proposed, this time more in the line of a club to put up "the young bachelor set who have [already] applied for accommodations."[83] Not only foreigners but Peruvians were keenly interested in the proposal being championed by W. C. Hebard, the vice president and manager of the Foundation Company in Peru.

The Foundation Company was a United States construction firm very much in favor in Leguía's Peru. Public works on a grand scale were an important part of Leguía's vision of a modern nation. Lavish expenditures on roads, irrigation projects, bridges, railroads, port facilities, and the like were made, and key American companies such as the Foundation benefited from generous contracts let by the pro-American Leguía. For example, they constructed a cement factory, helped reorganize a glass bottle factory, and contributed to a freezing works and slaughterhouse in Callao.[84]

But Mr. Hebard did not particularly like Peruvians. While many members of the prestigious Club Nacional had offered "their help in supplying the money" to build the new club, Hebard looked down his nose at "the Peruvian element."[85] As he put it:

Everything that has been started by or is in the hands of the Peruvian

element has been a failure, including the National Club itself so far as
its financing goes . . . therefore it is eminently desirable to keep the
control of this club and its urbanization in the hands of what we might
call the foreign element. . . . for this reason, I am particularly anxious
to have individual subscriptions from our Company, Grace, and Cerro
de Pasco. We can easily find all the money we need for this scheme
right here among the Peruvian element, but we do not wish to give
them control.[86]

Leguía's government was willing to help facilitate the matter
and has "offered us land at a price under which we contemplate
purchasing it."[87]

Hebard communicated all of this to his chief, Franklin Remington, in New York, who then solicited Joseph Grace's participation in the venture. The Foundation Company took out
an £8,000 subscription and Remington suggested that "it is
quite likely that it will be a very profitable venture."[88]

Grace waited until January 8, 1925, to respond, preferring to
consult with Iglehart before informing Remington of his decision. "With reference to our taking a subscription in the enterprise, we, after discussing it with our Directors, have decided
that it would be out of the established line of our activities to
do so."[89] Grace added a polite phrase or two justifying the
decision on the basis that "there is a tendency to go into [too
many] new lines, and we consequently have to hold to very
strict policy and keep all of our investments closely within the
limits of this policy."[90]

But the unvarnished fact was, Grace did not share Hebard's
contemptuous attitude toward "the Peruvian element." Hebard's letter to Remington, of which a copy had been sent to
Joseph Grace, must indeed have embarrassed the son of William Russell Grace, who bequeathed a legacy of respect for
people of different cultures. One could be, had to be, tough,
demanding, and keen in driving business bargains, motivating
people to superior performances, and managing a complicated,
multifaceted enterprise in a highly competitive world, but business decisions were not made in Casa Grace by invoking dis-
paraging stereotypes.

The company was no longer a family affair in the 1920s, but
strong and ambitious family members were still encouraged to
grow and develop within the company. One such was young
William Grace Holloway, who tackled all jobs with enthusiasm.
However, when Billy took on Japanese shipping interests in

the early 1920s he met an equally determined competitor with business acumen as sharp as those Holloway had inherited from his grandfather, William Russell Grace.

Holloway's oriental counterpart was Mr. Ota, the special representative of the Japanese Oriental Steamship Co., or Toyokisen, which had been operating between Japan and South America since 1905. Ota, based in Valparaiso, traveled to Callao in early 1921 to find out why his ships were paying double charges to unload at Callao where Grace was his agent.

He protested to Holloway vigorously and Billy balked, promising only to return to Toyokisen a part of the money, and this under protest. Ota refused to accept Holloway's excuses or money, demanding the full amount without argument.[91] After this spat, Ota and Holloway stopped talking and Ota fired off a telegram to Joseph Grace in New York. "Under the circumstances Ota [writing in the third person] feels Mr. Holloway does not treat Toyokisen fairly and there being no further talk possible between Mr. Holloway and Ota on this question, Ota wished you to immediately straighten the matter fundamentally."[92] Mr. Ota was invoking a tried and true formula—go to the top.

Joseph Grace perceived that his nephew had pushed Ota too far. He instructed Holloway to back off and remit the offending surcharge, an *aumento al flete*, to Toyokisen. Joseph Grace noted, however, that Ota should appreciate that in retaining the surcharge Holloway was simply following the established custom of steamship agents in the port of Callao.[93] Ota accepted the arbitration but proved flinty on Joseph Grace's invocation of "established customs" to defend Holloway.

"If it is an old established custom it must be abandoned, as many other customs which make of Callao a port a hundred years behind the times."[94] Furthermore, the feisty Ota lectured Grace, "I feel it is the moral obligation of the principal steamship concerns on this Coast, just like as your Company, to take the lead in abolishing such wrong practices and be persistent in so doing to eliminate them all if this is possible, but never to adhere to them."[95]

Ota warmed up, probably remembering a shouting match or two with Holloway, as he came to the end of a long letter to Grace summarizing the entire matter:

> I do not know what kind of service is given to the vessels of Grace Line, Johnson Line, etc. by your Lima and Callao Houses in operating the agency business of Callao, but so far as the TKK [Toyo Kisen Kaisha, full name of Oriental Steamship Co.] is concerned, I want good service and proper treatment. To tell you the truth our Principals in Japan

always instruct me to maintain friendly relations with your representatives in this Coast, but whenever I find that our Company is not treated by them fairly and properly, I must lodge a complaint, as I do now and expect to have both attention and redress.[96]

Having got it off his chest, Ota concluded by thanking Joseph Grace for his "courteous and prompt attention to this first matter I have taken the liberty of referring you to, and hoping that the relations of our two companies may continue to be pleasant and profitable, barring minor accidents."[97]

The drive to excel in international competition comes through Ota's correspondence like an airhorn in the night. Whether Holloway and his small adversary ever were reconciled is not known, but W. R. Grace & Co. and Toyo Kisen Kaisha continued to do business amicably all along the West Coast of South America and Central America as shippers and agents for the next four years, until 1925. Then TKK opened up its own agency in Callao and canceled its contract with Grace.

That move did not sever the long-standing business arrangements between Grace and TKK. President S. Asano advised President Grace that TKK wished to maintain all other agency contracts along the Central and South American coast. The opening of the Callao agency had actually been long promoted by the Japanese government and TKK had resisted the move over the years. But the pressure finally became too great and so Asano advised Grace of the act late in 1925. He added, "We beg to frankly state that we are most appreciative for all that you and your different Houses on the coast have done in developing our business during the past 20 years and are very much reluctant to make the foregoing change at this time."[98]

Grace accepted the Japanese explanation at face value, although the opportunity to point out the merits of doing business with Casa Grace in Peru were not missed. "We beg to call your attention to our very considerable floating plant in Callao which we shall continue to hold at your disposal so as to expedite the loading and discharging of your steamers, and we shall appreciate it very much if you will be good enough to instruct your agent to preferentially make use of our facilities provided our terms are as good as those made by our competitors. We know that the service we can render in Callao is superior to that of any competitor."[99]

The Japanese had been active on another front that competed with the Graces as well. Taking advantage of war shortages, they became active in the textile industry of Peru. By 1918 the Japanese had captured 8 percent of the textile import market and that percentage grew throughout the next two decades.[100]

In the same year Grace acquired the old Vitarte mill and increased its domestic textile production to 45 percent.

Ten years later the Victoria mill was added to the Grace textile holdings, and at the end of the twenties Grace mills accounted for 50 percent of Peruvian production.[101] Grace was in the rather peculiar situation of being not only the largest domestic producer, but also one of the major exporters of raw cotton, *and* an importer of finer foreign textiles. Casa Grace's basic point of view, with regard to textiles, nonetheless was Peruvian, calling for protection and supporting a tariff in 1927. The subject of cheap Japanese competition would continue to occupy space in the correspondence of Grace executives through the 1930s as the Greater East Asia Prosperity Society spread its interests, and with considerable success, beyond the mere confines of the western Pacific basin.

Always carrying the Grace flag in the public's mind were the stately *Santa* steamers plying between the continents of the Western Hemisphere. The public association of Grace with steamships coincided quite well with the reality of the company's existence. Nothing else captures this spirit better than an editorial in the company magazine, *Grace Log*, by its editor, Clayton Sedgwick Cooper, in 1921:

> Before the war no American passenger lines went further south than Panama or Venezuela. Today, both the West and East coasts of South America have direct, rapid and regular connections with New York by new, comfortable and attractive vessels under the American flag. The traveler can leave New York by the Grace Line and, passing through the Panama Canal six days later, can reach Callao, Peru, the port of Lima in thirteen days; and Valparaiso, Chile, in twenty. In three days more, he can travel by rail over the Andes and across the Argentine pampa, arriving at Buenos Aires the twenty-fourth day from New York. From there back to New York, via Montevideo and Rio de Janeiro on the Shipping Board vessels of the Munson Line, is seventeen days. It is, therefore, literally possible to travel entirely around South America in forty-one days. . . . The possibility of traveling from New York to Valparaiso without a change, whereas three were necessary before the war, is probably the most noteworthy advance over prewar communications. . . . Travel between the United States and South America is rapidly increasing and the mail service is greatly improved. . . . Freight service is, of course, notably more frequent; as a matter of fact, there are now more American ships than cargoes in the trade. Once seldom seen, the Stars and Stripes are now familiar in every port beneath the Southern Cross.[102]

The Stars and Stripes were not the only colors flying in ever increasing numbers beneath the Southern Cross. From his stateroom on the *Santa Elisa* going through the Panama Canal, R. H. Patchin reported in May 1924 to his chief, Joseph Grace, that since leaving New York he had witnessed overwhelming evidence of the increasing competition in passenger traffic. He saw or read about new German steamers, new Norwegian steamers, one new and one old Spanish ship, Japanese, Chinese, and Italian steamers all competing actively for coastal, Peruvian, and Panama Canal passengers, "to say nothing of the Chilean and British competition for through business."

Nothing else was guaranteed to stimulate Grace people more than tough competition and Patchin was clearly roused, especially since even the lion's share of existing business which Grace possessed would be too little to keep up passenger revenue with all those new competing steamers. One of his suggestions for improving passenger revenues is ironic, in the light of the Foundation Company's overture to W. R. Grace & Co. the same year about the new hotel-club for Lima. Patchin suggested that to increase tourist traffic, one must have first-class hotels. "Therefore I hope if we have a chance to participate in a hotel enterprise in Peru you will, provided it is sound, be not unwilling to [contribute] to a limited extent so we can influence its development."[103] The circumstances, of course, proved wrong in late 1924.

During the war and in the immediate postwar years the American merchant marine prospered from the monumental outpouring of resources made available by the United States after its entry into the war in April 1917. Even before then, however, tonnage shortages helped United States flag carriers like Grace Line increase their rates considerably during the war, especially after 1915, when the effects of the European conflict constricted the normal operations of European lines. After 1918 the postwar commodities boom carried the tide of profits to 1920. Between 1916 and 1920 "almost $27,000,000 gross profits were realized by the Grace shipping business in reflection of this general prosperity shared by all American shippers."[104] Then a combination of factors ended the euphoria in the American merchant marine.

The glut of ships produced by the U.S. Shipping Board brought down rates, and major foreign competitors began to recover from the war and to compete. For the past half century America's competitors had been able to build and operate ships with government subsidies more cheaply than their U.S. counterparts, and that trend was broken only temporarily by the conflict. Whereas the years 1916–20 had produced $27 million in profits, from 1920 to 1933 only $9 million was generated by the company, the gross profits per year dropping off to $400,000 annually after 1928.[105] But the Grace commitment to steamship operations between the Americas was solid and a mainstay of this emerging multinational.

From the end of the war through the twenties Grace lobbied actively for various bills to increase the competitive stance of American flag carriers.

In 1920 the Merchant Marine Act was passed by Congress. It was designed to help American shipping by providing certain aids like preferential railroad rates on goods exported or imported in American vessels; preferential customs duties on goods imported in American vessels; construction loans at low rates of interest for building new ships; revival of ocean mail contracts; and others. But the act was flawed in some respects and undone by vested interests in others. The mail contracts were to be renewed annually, hindering the ability of shipbuilders and shippers to make long-range plans. Preferential customs duties were not applied since the executive branch felt these would violate certain international treaties. The railroads logjammed preferential rail rates, explaining that they would upset existing rate structures. The situation of the merchant marine limped along until passage of the Jones-White Act in 1928, officially known at the Merchant Marine Act of 1928.

The 1928 act reaffirmed all the principles contained in the 1920 legislation, emphasizing the absolute necessity of supporting a first-class merchant marine, privately owned and operated, capable of carrying the greater part of the national commerce and of aiding the national defense. The English had summarized this guiding principle in the poetic language of the seventeenth century:

> As concerning ships it is that which everyone knoweth and can say: "They are our pleasures, they are our defense, they are our profit; the fortunate by them is made rich, the kingdom through them strong, the prince in them is mighty; in a word, by them, in a manner, we live, the Kingdom is, the King liveth."[106]

The Jones-White Act created a substantial $250 million construction fund to build ships in American yards. An important correction to the earlier mail-contracts deficiency authorized the postmaster general to make long-term contracts, not to exceed ten years, for the purpose of establishing fast, frequent, and regular shipping lines to all the world markets. Liberal rates were to be paid to encourage the building of larger, faster, and finer ships.

When the new *Santa Clara* slipped down the ways and splashed into the Delaware River on November 14, 1929, christened by young Nora Grace, Joseph and Janet's eldest child, it was the first passenger ship built exclusively for foreign trade under the provisions of the Jones-White Act.[107] It was no coincidence that Grace took the lead among American shippers in taking advantage of new laws and legislation. Part of the success of Grace shipping interests was to apply the old rule of getting there first with the best.

Grace maintained four distinct lines in the 1920s. The heart of the shipping organization was the Grace Line serving the West Coast from New York via the Panama Canal. From the end of the war to 1927 Grace Line operated four combination passenger-freight liners on this route, the *Santa Teresa*, *Santa Ana*, *Santa Luisa* and *Santa Elisa*, all measuring 5,232 tons deadweight and built before or during the war.

Service varied from fortnightly to every three weeks, with sailings originating in New York and calling at Callao, Mollendo, Arica, Iquique, Antofagasta, Valparaiso, and Talcahuano, stopping en route at Cristóbal and Balboa in Panama for passengers and mail as well.[108] If one sailed from New York on the *Santa Ana* on December 7, 1921, he could be in Iquique on Christmas Eve to celebrate Holy Night in a stark, desert setting, and disembark farther south at the lovely port of Valparaiso, with its steep hills climbing away from the sea, on December 27.[109]

Grace also put into service two new 6,800-ton (15,000-ton displacement) liners in 1928 named the *Santa Maria* and *Santa Barbara*, employing the latest in deisel-engine design and fostering the ambiance of the floating hotel so popular with ocean travelers of the era.[110] Averaging sixteen and a half knots, they represented the fastest service between the Americas, while combining it with every luxury of shipboard life: all cabins with windows, beds instead of berths, social hall, smoking room, children's dining and play rooms, swimming pool, and orchestras and motion pictures. On the *Santa Maria*'s maiden voyage in May and June 1928 perhaps the ultimate encomium was paid to its dining room, often the scene of worst suffering for landlubbers. It was declared "absolutely free from odors of any description, was light and airy and this combined with the steadiness of the ship and the lack of vibration made passengers' meals so pleasant that many said that they seemed to be dining at a hotel instead of on shipboard."

★ ★ ★

Let's board the *Santa Maria* on its maiden voyage, begun on a brilliant day in May in New York. After a short cruise down the Atlantic coast we put in at Havana to the first of many festive welcomes. The captain, officers, and men turned out in their dress uniforms to entertain the city and government dignitaries trooping aboard.

From Cuba we steam through the diamond bright Caribbean Sea toward the Isthmus of Panama, first crossed by Balboa in 1513 on his way to discovering the Pacific. Passing through the Panama Canal always produces pride and wonder among Americans traversing this most famous engineering feat of the modern world. Special lectures by the ship's company enhance the passage.

Moving south on the tropical Pacific we cross the equator and are initiated with outlandish costumes and unceremonious gags into that select portion of mankind King Neptune welcomes into his realm. Even during the hottest portions of the voyage as we slice through the equatorial seas off Colombia and Ecuador, we are kept cool by the new Thermotank Punkah Louvre ventilation system, which forces fresh air into all parts of the ship. This is a great improvement over the old-fashioned system of simply stirring stagnant air of the cabins and public rooms by an electric fan.

We put in at Talara in northern Peru. There the International Petroleum Company, Limited (Standard Oil) has large works pumping out and refining black oil, the energy source of the modern world. Most everybody from the oil camps turned out to see the *Santa*. One happy driller wrote, "An excellent buffet luncheon was served to all on board which was thoroughly enjoyed, and, as it was served in the manner for which the Grace Line is renowned, further comments are needless."

Then down along the barren, brown Peruvian coast toward Callao, in a voyage that often lasted months for the sixteenth-century sailors trying to buck the winds and currents perpetually flowing northward. We arrive in Callao on May 23, barely two weeks after cruising out through the Narrows of New York and only about thirty-six hours after weighing anchor at Talara.

The newspapers of Callao and Lima feature the *Santa Maria* in columns and pictures, and enthusiastic guests swarm over the ship shortly after eleven in the morning, "putting the launches and motorboats of the Grace Agency to feats of speed to carry all these people onboard. . . ." Everyone is curious about the elegant, luxurious touches to this grand modern leviathan built especially to connect better the ports of South

America with New York. Yankee ingenuity and entrepreneurship are celebrated in the press and many Peruvians are no
doubt attracted to make the voyage the next time the *Santa
Maria*—or the sister ship *Santa Barbara,* due to join the Grace
fleet in September—makes the run between the continents.

The mayor of Callao, the prefect, and other government dignitaries are feted at a luncheon presided over by the general
manager of Grace in Peru, Redshaw. A toast and impromptu
speech by the minister of the navy, Dr. Núñez-Chávez, sets
the tone of the Peruvian welcome to the *Santa Maria.*

The scene is repeated down the coast, at Mollendo, Arica,
Iquique, Antofagasta, Coquimbo, and finally Valparaiso, where
we arrive on the exact hour of the day scheduled, punctuality
being a byword of *Santa* steamers. Only now everyone aboard
is bundled in sweaters and coats, braced against the winter
winds whipping up from the Antarctic Ocean. Storm-tossed
Valparaiso postpones the welcoming celebration until June 1.
This time it is transferred to the more stable dining room of the
Astor Hotel, where the minister of foreign relations, the American ambassador, and other officials are feted by the Grace
organization in Chile.[111] From here we can return to New York,
completing the round trip on June 25, or disembark and train
across the Andes to Argentina, to steam up the East Coast from
Buenos Aires on the ships of the Munson Line; or, we could
have gone touring inland from any of the ports visited en route
down the West Coast. Grace Line was ready to arrange for
"cruises of rare delight to Panama, Peru, Chile and Bolivia, an
ideal vacation trip for yourself and family amid the finest accommodations afloat and ashore and with a complete sight-
seeing program. Visits in foreign lands. Many optional sidetrips
arranged."[112]

But the bread and butter produced by Grace Line came not
from its passenger service, notwithstanding its growing fame.
Only 27 percent of total revenues was generated from carrying
passengers. What determined the profitability, and hence vi-
ability, of Grace Line were its mail contracts negotiated in 1928
according to the provisions of the Jones-White Act, and, most
important, its freight services connecting ports strung out along
the coasts of North America, Central America, and South
America.

In addition to the major north-south run by the luxurious
Santas from New York to Valparaiso, Grace Line operated six

other ships in 1927 between New York and ports in Panama, Colombia, Ecuador, Peru, Chile, and Argentina, all carrying freight with limited passenger accommodations as well. The scheduling varied through the 1920s, but one could depend upon a Grace ship servicing the following ports on the average of at least once a month: Cartagena, Buenaventura, Guayaquil, Paita, Eten, Pimentel, Pacasmayo, Salaverry, Coquimbo, Valparaiso, Talcahuano, Bahía Blanca, Port Madryn, Punta Arenas, Corral, and Coronel.

From the northwest coast of the United States to the West Coast of South America Grace maintained its North Pacific Division with an average of six steamers in the 1920s. These vessels carried the oldest steamship names associated with Grace: *Cuzco, Coya, Capac, Condor, Charcas,* and *Cacique.* Although the ships were largely dedicated to freight, limited passenger accommodations were sometimes available on these runs from Seattle and San Francisco to the ports of Ecuador, Peru, and Chile.

The North Pacific Division was officially organized in 1903 to carry lumber from the ports of the Northwest in return for nitrates from Chile. The business rapidly diversified and by the 1920s was competing for traffic with three other lines, two Norwegian and one Japanese.[113]

The North Pacific Division was the best example of a steamship line dedicated to the movement rather of cargo than of people. Its ships were constantly being rotated and its routes adjusted to meet the demands of the trade.

For example, during the war its three main steamers, *Colusa, Cuzco,* and *Cacique,* averaging 7,500–9,000 tons deadweight, were taken off the North Pacific run and put on the Orient and India trade to take advantage of that lucrative market. Three smaller steamers, *Santa Alicia, Santa Rita,* and *Santa Inez,* whose total deadweight was but 8,800 tons, were purchased to cover the routes of the larger vessels. The capacity of these small vessels was insufficient, but, because of wartime exigencies, no others were available. So the bark *Belfast* and the schooner *W. J. Pirrie* were bought and put into service as tows for the small steamers, augmenting the carrying capacity of the North Pacific Division by more than half.[114] The five-masted *W. J. Pirrie* was furthermore fitted with a 1,500-ton oil tank to supply the Grace bunker fuel stations at Callao and Arica.

At the end of the war the United States Shipping Board steamer *Delrosa* was purchased and put into service, the *Colusa* returned to its normal run, and so forth. This was the essence of a cargo line: adjustments, improvisations, imagination.

More romantic than the North Pacific Division was Grace's control and operation of the venerable Pacific Mail Steamship Co. from 1915 to 1925. The line ran ships around the world, inaugurating the service in 1920 when the S.S. *West Kasson* returned to Boston on July 29 after circumnavigating the globe on a through schedule via a fixed route.[115] Seven other Pacific Mail steamers joined the *West Kasson* in this service, which dispatched a ship around the world every three weeks from the Golden Gate of San Francisco. They followed in the *West Kasson's* tracks, calling at Honolulu, Yokohama, Kobe, Taku Bar (Tientsin), Darien, Shanghai, Hong Kong, Manila, Singapore, Calcutta, Colombo, Bombay, Suez, Port Said, Alexandria, Genoa, Marseille, Barcelona, Valencia, Balboa, Boston, New York, Baltimore, and, via the Panama Canal, back to San Francisco.

The Pacific Mail was most famed for its pioneering transpacific service, also maintained by Grace. Advertised as the Sunshine Belt to the Orient, the Pacific Mail maintained a regular passenger and freight service from San Francisco to Honolulu, Yokohama, Kobe, Shanghai, Manila, and Hong Kong, with luxury vessels such as the *Golden State* and *Empire State*, each measuring 12,600 tons deadweight. Grace lost the mail contract for this transpacific route in 1925 to the Dollar Line. However, Grace retained the route of the Pacific Mail between the East and West coasts of the United States. With services to Central America, this route was naturally more consistent with Grace's historic interests.

This line was renamed the Panama Mail S. S. Co. and was eventually fully integrated into the Grace steamship operations in 1931 as the Panama Mail Service of the Grace Line. The Panama Mail not only ran a complete service between both coasts of the United States and Central America, but in 1928 connected the East Coast of Colombia with San Francisco. By the end of the decade, Grace was operating eight vessels—six steamships and two motorships—over this line, which brought some of the best Central American and Colombian coffees into the United States.

Certainly it was not unusual for Grace itself to be a buyer and packager of coffees. As one advertisement in 1928 noted, Grace Milds moved directly from producer to roaster to distributor and provided the American drinker with superior quality. From Colombia Grace packaged four different brands, Gracebest, Gracefine, Gracefancy, and Grace Claro. Coffees were also exported from all the Central American producing countries: Guatemala, Nicaragua, El Salvador, and Costa Rica.[116]

For those wishing to tour, the Panama Mail offered a package to California from New York, advertised as "the most economical and most interesting trip of the season." One embarked at New York and steamed south to the "tropic seas" with "ports of call at Panama, Colombia, Nicaragua, El Salvador, and Guatemala, including [visits to] the capitals of the two latter countries."[117] Upon disembarking on the West Coast about three weeks later, one returned home via the railroad. For $350.00 and up one could sail on the popular Panama Service steamers *Venezuela, Colombia,* and *Ecuador*. The ticket included all meals and "a Simmons bed on steamer—first class—and first-class railroad transportation. Swimming tank. Deck sports. Orchestra for concerts and dancing. All outside rooms with two beds—no upper and lower berths. Electric fan in every room."[118] The sailings were every three weeks.

Only the Gulf Coast was not serviced by Grace steamers before World War I, but in 1918 that lacuna was filled by the establishment of the New Orleans & South American Steamship Co. (NOSA Line). It was the first line to offer a direct service between Gulf ports and the West Coast of South America. The opening of the Panama Canal had been the stimulant to this service, which offered sailings every three weeks aboard NOSA's six ships. Ports of call were in Colombia, Ecuador, Peru, and Chile. The line was reorganized in 1931–32 and it became the Gulf & South American Steamship Co. in which Grace held a 50 percent interest.

A list of routes and ports of call is, of course, but a poor portrayal of a steamship company, especially of one operated by such a competitive team presided over by Joseph Grace and D. Stewart Iglehart. Perhaps they were not all as combative as Billy Holloway, but the success of the company certainly testifies to the acumen and energy of the Holloways, the Lipscombs, the MacDougalls; and of men like Adolf Garni, John Kirby, and Andrew Shea, who came into positions of leadership, along with Holloway, in the decades after the 1920s.

Iglehart perhaps best exemplified a manager who brilliantly joined ideas with action. As Grace Line moved more deeply into the passenger-carrying business, publicity naturally became critical. As early as 1928 we can discern the germination of a massive publicity campaign that Grace Line launched in the coming years, helping not only to popularize the *Santas,* but also to draw the American public's attention to South America.

Grace had sunk four million dollars in building the *Santa Barbara* and *Santa Maria* and had included the most modern comforts and attractions. Iglehart was sure there were "people to fill these boats provided we can appeal to them and get them to travel on them." Grace best knew the ins and outs of travel and tourism on the West Coast and Iglehart was inclined to make an important investment on advertising for at least a year to promote the ships and tourism in South America. Halfway measures would earn them little increase on their present business; what Grace needed to do was "pull up our socks and lay out an advertising and publicity campaign that would make a real dent."[119]

While beating the bushes for passengers in the United States, one continued to keep a sharp eye on the competition from abroad, especially since the American merchant marine was vulnerable to foreign competition. When two Chilean steamers, the *Teno* and *Aconcagua* of the Compañía Sudamericana de Vapores (CSAV), came up for sale in 1926, Grace seriously considered purchasing and incorporating them into the North Pacific Division, specifically to forestall the British Pacific Steam Navigation Co. (PSNC) from putting on two "new steamers to fill the gap formerly occupied by the CSAV."[120]

Meeting competition in the rather complicated world of shipping was no simple matter, as this zigzag reasoning testifies:

> The immediate danger in our buying the Chile boats is that it may force the PSNC to put on two additional passenger steamers they have been thinking about in which case the trade would be spoilt for everybody and our only consolation would be that we would lose less money than they did so we should in the end get out on top in the fight. On the other hand, if the PSNC really intend to put on two big steamers now before our new steamers are ready, we could give them a much harder fight if we owned the Chilean steamers and could run six steamers to their four. The real danger in the purchase of the Chile boats is that we are committing ourselves to run six steamers in the West Coast passenger and freight trade. . . .[121]

The PSNC was an old competitor and one Grace could spar with knowledgeably. However, the business got very sticky when an American company not celebrated for steamship operations, but certainly celebrated for success and size, pushed into Grace territory in late 1929. After General Motors was advised by Grace that it could not handle G.M.'s cargo, G.M. went to Du Pont, which in turn went to the Guggenheims. The upshot was that Du Pont started a regular line based on the support of G.M. and Guggenheim. The latter then contracted with Du Pont for 180,000 tons of nitrate homeward and agreed to give it a minimum of 80,000 tons of cargo outward in the first six months of 1929. The Du Ponts appeared to have joined the steamship business, and with the backlog that they had obtained under favorable charter rates, they would not be easy to dislodge.[122] That the Du Ponts had gained control of General Motors by 1922 and were probably the richest, and certainly one of the most powerful, business clans in the United States sent shivers through the smaller, more vulnerable Grace organization.

Since it was not thought the Du Ponts could be dissuaded from their commitment to shipping, the next best thing was to contain them as best as possible. Joseph Grace suggested that the Du Ponts could probably be persuaded to enter the appropriate shipping conference and to limit their sailings to Baltimore and Philadelphia; and, most important, to agree to keep out of New York.[123]

The very diversity of the Grace organization continued to be its strength. If the Du Ponts threatened to upset the rate structure and spoil the business for everyone in Chile, then Colombia was enjoying an upturn in its economy. Grace started to equip itself with lighters on Colombia's principal Pacific coast port of Buenaventura and looked to an increase in freight and passengers from Colombia to make up for the problems with the Chilean nitrate trade.[124]

If Grace lost the Pacific Mail Steamship Co.'s transpacific and around-the-world routes in 1925, then other opportunities would surely emerge, no matter how risky they might be. Aviation seemed to combine all those perils in the 1920s, and the attraction proved irresistible to the successors of William and Michael Grace.

On September 13, 1928, pilot Dan Tobin started the two-hundred-horsepower Whirlwind engine on a small, four-passenger monoplane built especially for the occasion by the Fairchild Aircraft Company. After a brief salutation to the crowd gathered at the Santa Beatriz racetrack in Lima, Tobin taxied out to one end of the straightway, normally reserved for thoroughbreds in full gallop. He warmed up his engine for a few moments, checking the instrument panel as the small plane trembled from the roar of the engine. Satisfied, he rolled down the makeshift runway and into the air, turning north as he gained altitude. A few hours later he landed in Talara, six hundred miles north on the desert coast of Peru, inaugurating the first scheduled air service on the West Coast of South America. A new era in transportation and communications for that part of the world had begun.

Like railroads half a century earlier, airplanes implied progress, prestige, and a more modern nation. They could knit together isolated parts of the national territory, provide for better defense, extend the benefits of modern civilization to vast areas only remotely touched by modern science, and put travelers in rapid contact with the world. Little wonder then that Chile, Peru, Ecuador, and Colombia eagerly anticipated the flying machines.

In 1928 and 1929 W. R. Grace & Co. and Pan American Airlines jointly sponsored an airline, Pan American–Grace Airways, to link Argentina and the West Coast of South America with the United States. Behind that bare fact lies a history of entrepreneurship the like of which had not occurred on the American stage since the end of the nineteenth century. Foremost among the actors was Harold R. Harris. He flew bombers in the Italian theater during World War I, bombed captured German capital ships anchored in the Atlantic during Billy Mitchell's celebrated demonstration of air power in 1921, and made the first successful free-fall emergency parachute jump in 1922.

Harold Harris was a born pioneer. In 1910 he witnessed an airshow at Long Beach and was hooked.[125] The next year at the same show he watched Arch Hoxie in a Wright Flyer descend from an altitude attempt, go into a vertical dive, and plow into the ground. "I was horrified when the crowd rushed out to the crashed plane and tore the clothing off his body for souvenirs!"[126] However, that tocsin served only to encourage Harris's determination to man a marvelous flying machine.

After graduating from Manual Arts High School one year ahead of Jimmy Doolittle's class, Harris enrolled in the Throop College of Technology to study mechanical engineering. Throop later evolved into the prestigious California Institute of Technology. In 1916, Harris entered military aviation, as it then existed. He went to Monterey and the Citizen's Military Training Camp (various ones were organized around the country by the government), which had an aviation unit. There he became the engineering officer of the First Provisional Aero Squadron, which operated two biplanes and one monoplane on loan to the army by their private owners.

It was the responsibility of the engineering officer to keep the craft flying, so Harris tested them frequently. "Whether one of these planes could fly was determined by tying a spring balance to a fence post and the other side of the balance to the tail skid. At full throttle, if the balance showed 50-lb. pull, the plane could take off."[127] A nice short checklist.

When war was declared in April 1917, Harris jumped into the Army Signal Reserve Corps, then housing the air arm of the army, and was assigned to the first class in ground school at the University of California at Berkeley. Coincidentally, another California native son, Douglas Campbell, was fleeing Harvard to get "over there" in an American airplane as well.

For his flight training, Harris was shipped out to Europe, where he was assigned to the Eighth Aviation Instruction Center of the American Expeditionary Force organized at Foggia, Italy. Harris advanced from apprentice pilot to chief instructor in the year he spent in Italy flying the Italian bombers to which he was assigned. Capt. Fiorello LaGuardia, commanding the second detachment, reached Foggia shortly after Harris.

One day Harris watched as the future mayor of New York practiced landings. "LaGuardia was getting instruction in a Farman [single-engined plane] from an Italian pilot. We watched the plane come in for a landing, very slow and flat, and about to spin. It hit the ground flat, bounced several times, and finally stopped. The two men jumped out screaming at each other in Italian. It turned out that each thought the other was making the landing."[128]

In the summer of 1918 Harris, along with some other flying officers, was posted back to the United States as a test pilot and instructor for big Italian bombers slated to be manufactured by the Fisher Body Company in Detroit. From Detroit Harris was detached to the Wilbur Wright Field in Dayton, Ohio, as a test pilot. There, within sight of the original barn utilized by the Wright brothers, and later at McCook Field, also in Dayton, Harris was stationed for the next seven years, becoming chief test pilot for the air service in 1920. There he pioneered the free-fall parachute jump; made one of the first, if not the first, pressurized cabin flights in the world; set ten world and fifteen American records by 1925; and managed to survive more crashes than he will admit to. When the opportunity came to participate in another new area of aviation, commercial, Harris struck off again, this time moving closer to the orbit of Grace and South America.

The development of commercial aviation between the United States and Latin America was largely the work of one ambitious and talented man. Juan Terry Trippe, in spite of his Hispanic forename, was descended from a long line of distinguished and wealthy Americans; his father was a banker and member of the New York Stock Exchange.[129] Juan attended Yale after prepping at Hill School and, like Campbell and Harris, jumped into the war when American entered; only Trippe chose naval aviation, even more daring—if possible in this early age of flying—than land-based aviation.

After returning to Yale, and graduating in 1922, he combined a social knowledge of wealthy people with his love of flying and started his own company, Long Island Airways. It failed and Trippe joined another outfit in the Northwest for a short while. Then in 1927 he set his focus on the Caribbean and gained control of a small airline, Pan American. Pan Am had been awarded the mail contract from Key West to Havana, launching the first regularly scheduled air service in the Caribbean.

The same year, 1927, Charles Lindbergh soloed across the Atlantic and captured the imagination of the world; he also undertook a spectacular flying tour of Mexico, Central America, Panama, Colombia, Venezuela, and the Caribbean, covering over nine thousand miles. Feted, mobbed, and adored, Lindbergh further popularized the promise of commercial aviation in Latin America.

When Lindbergh landed the *Spirit of St. Louis* in Paris in May 1927, Harold Harris was already in Peru pioneering some early commercial uses of aviation.

Harris had gone to Peru to kill army worms in 1927. Controlling insects from the air had only lately been combined into the art, or science (it was a bit of both in this early stage), of crop dusting, and Harris, in the employ of the Huff Daland Company, had been dispatched in December 1926 from New Orleans with four crop dusters to introduce this new technology to the cotton growers of Peru.[130]

The founders of the firm, Thomas H. Huff and Elliot Daland, had been building trainers for the U.S. Navy when business got sluggish. In searching for alternative ways to use their planes, Tom Huff discovered that the U.S. Army, in cooperation with entomologists at Tallulah, Louisiana, had become involved in experiments to dust cotton by airplane to combat the boll weevil. In 1925 Huff persuaded Harris into joining them to administer Huff Daland's new crop-dusting business and Harris took a year's leave of absence. As Harris recalled, "I went into it and liked it and found that I'd better resign my commission, which I did in 1926, and went into the dusting business."[131]

The next question Harris and his associates faced was what to do with the crop dusters during the fallow winter season in the United States. One had idle airplanes and equally idle pilots. Why not try the Southern Hemisphere where the seasons were reversed? Peruvian cotton was suffering from the army worm during the American winter, so C. E. Woolman, an enterprising Louisiana entomologist and later the founder of Delta Airlines, joined the effort to spread the benefits of crop dusting and sailed to Peru in 1926. There he arranged for the first crop-dusting contract in South America.

The first dusting, which took place largely in the Cañete Valley south of Lima in 1927, was a great success even though Harris learned the hard way how long it took to get parts, mail, and supplies from the United States by sea.[132] After the season was over, he took a trip beyond Peru to scout out other dusting jobs and to reconnoiter potential commercial air routes. After touring through Bolivia, Argentina, Uruguay, and Brazil, Harris returned to New York and began to beat the drums for the establishment of a good air route from the United States to South America. He proved prophetic in his timing.

Not only was Lindbergh charging the public's imagination, but entrepreneurs like Trippe were launching airlines as fast as new technology produced the equipment to span greater and greater distances with increased payloads and comfort. Furthermore, French and German aviation companies, notably in Colombia, Argentina, Bolivia, Brazil, were sponsoring fledgling airlines, perceived as threatening to United States commercial and political interests in Latin America.[133]

Harris found a receptive audience in New York, especially among persons like Trippe, who was actively seeking new postal routes to extend his airline. Harris was introduced to Trippe by Richard F. Hoyt, a member of the investment firm of Hayden Stone, which was financing both Pan Am and the Keystone Company. The Huff Daland crop-dusting service had been only recently purchased by Hoyt's firm.

Dick Hoyt was an enthusiastic supporter of aviation, and when Harris produced a small map of Latin America with the potential air routes inked in based on present and future aircraft performance, Hoyt was captivated. "He turned to his secretary and he said get Trippe on the phone. I'd never heard Trippe's name until that moment, but he got Trippe on the phone and he said, 'Trippe, come over here; I got a fellow here who's two years ahead of us.' "[134] It is hard to believe that anybody was two years ahead of Juan Trippe, but the goad by Hoyt produced the necessary effect.

When C. E. Woolman returned to Peru in 1928 to renegotiate the crop-dusting contracts, he was also seeking a concession from the Peruvian government to operate an international airline service. Woolman had to contend with several other competitors for this potentially lucrative concession, although he did have the support of Harold B. Grow, an American naval aviator who had risen in President Leguía's regime to become coordinator of all Peruvian aviation by 1928.[135] Grow managed to throttle the German attempt to gain the concession, but Woolman still had to overcome a bid by Elmer C. Faucett, another pioneering American aviator in Peru.

Slim Faucett had landed in Peru before Harris and Grow; in fact, before most other gringos. He had become somewhat legendary, leaving not only a legacy of rich stories, but an airline still operating today that bears his name, Faucett International Airlines. Faucett began his career as a mechanic at Roosevelt Field on Long Island and from there naturally advanced from tinkering to flying.[136] Although he got fired for taking off on one of the Curtis Wright planes one day—Faucett's first unauthorized solo—the daring young man managed to attach himself to another branch of the Curtis Wright group then preparing to take a team of pilots, mechanics, and planes to South America to drum up some business.[137] The tour went bankrupt and among its uncompensated personnel was young Slim Faucett. In lieu of cash, Faucett was given one of the demonstrating airplanes in Lima in 1924.

Faucett made a living with this plane by offering various services. It was only natural for him to seek the international concession in 1928 when the issue arose. Although he lost to C. E. Woolman and Huff Daland, Faucett went on to found his own airline and to pioneer many routes over Peru's large and challenging national territory, which ranged from the bleak, arid coast to the high, snowbound sierra and dense jungles of the east.

Woolman, a magnificent salesman, however, *was* successful and the concession was granted by the Leguía regime in May 1928. It permitted Huff Daland to carry mail, passengers, and cargo. The concession was soon absorbed by Pan Am in league with the largest United States concern interested in transportation on the "coast," W. R. Grace & Co.

The transfer of the Huff Daland concession to Pan American and Grace was facilitated largely through the offices of Hayden Stone. Richard Hoyt and Juan Trippe were the principal agents for Pan Am's interests, and Harris acted as the go-between for Pan Am and Grace.[138]

What was Grace doing in the aviation business? The answer is uncomplicated. Any improvements or innovations in transportation or communication in South America were of vital interest to the leading shipper from the United States to the West Coast. Furthermore, certain of the Grace organization—like R. H. Patchin, a vice president of Grace Line, and Burt Pageant, then in charge of public relations—were aviation enthusiasts.

Trippe would have preferred to go it alone, but was ultimately dependent upon Grace's vast network of ships, people, friendships, and information to provide the support needed for a route that by 1930 would be the longest in the world, forty-five hundred miles from Buenos Aires to Panama.[139] To appreciate Trippe's acceptance of the Grace offer to become a partner by funding half of the new enterprise, one only has to take into account some of the following: the average range for the best planes then available was about six hundred miles; there was no radar, indeed virtually no radio communication; only the most makeshift landing fields existed; and only a pioneer's knowledge of flying weather in the Southern Hemisphere was available. Grace, in turn, was blocked by Trippe and Pan Am from extending any potentially independent South American operation sponsored by Grace past Panama to the north to Miami and New York. It was an accommodation made by both Grace and Pan Am to existing realities.

Each partner of the new entity inheriting the Huff Daland concession, Peruvian Airways, Inc., subscribed $25,000. Harris, then in the United States, became vice president and general manager of the new company, and in summer 1928 got together with a Dutch engineer handling Pan Am's operations to order a special plane from the Fairchild Aircraft Company to launch the new service.

The new plane, modeled on one Sherman Fairchild had built for his own photographic work, carried the pilot and four passengers. It was powered by a 200-hp Whirlwind engine, certainly proved reliable by Lindbergh's *Spirit of St. Louis* on its historic trip across the Atlantic. While it was under construction, the former test pilot insisted on including a toilet in the rear of the plane. Already passenger comfort was rating a high priority with the founders of Peruvian Airways. Indeed, it may have been the first toilet installed in a U. S. commercial airplane, although the English and French were ahead of the Americans in commercial aviation and may have already provided such accommodations. The windows on this small plane could be lowered for passengers wishing some fresh air, as if to reinforce the rather primitive image of this diminutive but sturdy pioneer. It also possessed the added advantage of collapsible wings for easy transportation. "You didn't have to have any crates or anything of that sort. So it was a question of ten or fifteen minutes after you got the airplane off the ship and on to a place where it could take off, unpull the wings, put some fuel in the tank, and take off."[140] Harris sent the completed Fairchild on ahead to Peru on a Grace steamer in late August 1928.

On September 13 this little monoplane, with pilot Dan Tobin (ex–crop duster for Huff Daland) at the controls, took off from the Santa Beatriz racetrack in Lima. His six-hundred-mile flight to Talara inaugurated the first scheduled air service on the West Coast of South America. The flight was made weekly to Talara, the headquarters of IPC in Peru and a regular port of call for the *Santas.* The airplane schedule was set up to coincide with steamship arrivals and departures for better mail and passenger connections.[141]

In the meantime, Woolman had traveled north to Ecuador from Peru in July to seek a similar concession from the Ecuadorian government. Scadta, the Colombian airline with a heavy German influence, had just secured a concession to extend its route from Buenaventura in Colombia to the Ecuadorian coast, and the Americans were anxious to get a foot in the door as well.[142] However, Woolman failed and returned to the United States, permanently leaving the Latin American scene.

Harris took up where Woolman left off in Ecuador. A goodwill trip to South America by President-elect Herbert Hoover touched in at Ecuador and Peru in December and helped smooth Harris's approach. Harris the aviator met Hoover the engineer and Hoover assured the vice president and general manager of Peruvian Airways that the United States government fully supported efforts by commercial aviation to grow and expand internationally. With this assurance, relayed by Harris to New York, the decision to order several larger Fairchilds—equipped with 400-hp engines and capable of carrying six passengers—was made. Yet Harris still had to get the Ecuadorian concession if Peruvian Airways was to expand according to the routes he had drawn on that small Latin American map shown to Richard Hoyt in 1927.

Harris first contacted the Grace representative in Guayaquil, who promptly tore up Harris's business card identifying him as the vice president and general manager of Peruvian Airways Corporation. Harris, the experienced aviator, was told brusquely that "no Peruvian can get anything in Ecuador" because of the poor political relations between the two countries. After this brief lesson in the politics of doing business in Latin America, Harris and the Grace man traveled up to Quito to begin negotiations for the concession.[143]

They succeeded in Quito and the concession was signed on February 22, 1929, paving the way for extending air service to Ecuador. The day before, Pan American and Grace had announced the formation of Pan American–Grace Airways, Inc. to succeed Peruvian Airways. Panagra's official existence commences from that date, although Peruvian Airways and Huff Daland's crop dusters were all direct predecessors, each one contributing the experienced men and legal concessions eventually absorbed by Panagra.[144]

The formation of Panagra facilitated the rapid extension of its routes beyond the confines of Peru. It would be much easier to negotiate concessions and permissions from South American governments with the entity Pan American–Grace Airways, which was not associated directly with a Latin American nation—such as Peru—by name or implication.

These negotiations for concessions were largely accomplished in the year 1929, perhaps the most important one of the decade as a multitude of national and international companies jockeyed for position at the start of what everyone knew was the beginning of a major new industry.

In the United States, the crucial award Panagra needed, and obtained on March 2, 1929, was for postal contract number FAM9 to carry U.S. mails from Panama south along the West Coast and thence across the Andes to Argentina and Uruguay.[145]

Juan Trippe was gradually convincing the United States Department of State and other departments, such as the postal service, which made major decisions of an international nature, that if the United States was to compete effectively against such entities as Scadta (German-influenced) and Aeropostale (new French service to Brazil and Argentina, established in 1929), it needed to favor one "chosen instrument." That chosen instrument should be Pan American. Panagra naturally benefited from this successful lobbying by Trippe, although in the critical negotiations with the postal service in 1928 and 1929, Robert Patchin of Grace was equally persuasive in championing Panagra over other potential American competitors.

While this intensive effort proceeded in Washington, concessions also were being negotiated from the Latin American nations. Colombia gave PAA and Panagra landing rights and a few other privileges in exchange for allowing Scadta similar concessions in the Canal Zone. That cleared the path for flying from Peru through Ecuador and Colombia to Panama. PAA already was sewing up the routes from Panama north to the United States.

To the south, Chile proved the toughest nut to crack. An intensely nationalistic country, Chile was in no rush to grant to foreigners any concessions that might adversely affect its own fledgling aviation services, largely operated by the armed forces at this stage. Furthermore, relations between Chile and the United States had always been more formal than warm, and the ticklish American arbitration of the long-standing Tacna-Arica dispute between Chile and Peru was only now moving to its concluding stage (finally ratified in July 1929).[146] However, a concession was finally received on June 24 allowing Panagra to carry passengers, mail, and freight into and out of Chile.[147] Although more limited than rights received in other countries, the concession opened another leg on the route envisioned by Harris.

By the end of the year the Argentine and Uruguayan concessions had been settled as well, and Panagra was carrying mail all the way from the southern cone to Panama. Each new leg added to the route, each new plane added to the fleet was a cause for promotion and celebration as the crucial year 1929 unwound. These pioneers, unlike many others through the ages, were acutely conscious of being at the cutting edge of a new industry and, indeed, at the edge of a revolutionary new era. Not given to inordinate amounts of modesty, these early aviators and their backers enjoyed their work and its fabulous reception by the Latin American public immensely.

Panagra rapidly progressed from the single-engined Fairchilds to Ford trimotors in 1929, then representing the newest and finest commercial aircraft in the air. For the long pull between Panama and Guayaquil, Ecuador, two twin-engined amphibian Sikorsky S38s were also utilized for a time in this early period.

The first Ford trimotor was shipped to Guayaquil and assembled there in August. It seated twelve passengers and was the pride of the fleet. In Lima it was welcomed as such, and in an elaborate christening ceremony presided over by the archbishop of Lima, Monsignor Emilio Lisson, it was baptized the *Santa Rosa* by the daughter of the president, Carmen Rosa Leguía de Ayulo.[148]

Each new trimotor added to the fleet that year was christened and named after the patron saint of a country serviced by Panagra. Thus the second was christened the *San Cristóbal* in September in a similar ceremony in Santiago. The third trimotor was to be similarly affixed with the name of an Ecuadorian saint, only Ecuador did not have any saints. As Harris remembered, "They had a woman who had been beatified and was about to be sanctified, so we went to the archbishop there in Ecuador and asked him if it would be all right if we would name one of our airplanes Santa Mariana, even though she was still on the way up. He said yes. It didn't fool the Ecuadorians; that airplane was always called Santa Mañana."[149] *Santa Mariana* or *Santa Mañana*, it mattered not. It was the heyday of American aviation and the mood was buoyant.

For the inaugural flight of weekly mail service early in October 1929 between Buenos Aires and New York via the Panagra route, John D. MacGregor, the general manager of Panagra, hopped the plane as the first passenger. This first mail run was notable enough to prompt an exchange of congratulatory telegrams between President Hoover and President Hipolito Irigoyen of Argentina.[150] A week later Junius B. Wood, correspondent of the *Chicago Daily News*, took off from Buenos Aires on the second run; he was carrying a letter mailed to himself in the United States. Wood also left us a newspaperman's vivid observations of the aerial odyssey.

The *San Cristóbal*, piloted by Raymond Williams and carrying his mechanic, Peter Prokup, and their one intrepid passenger, Junius Wood, took off promptly at eight o'clock on the morning of October 19 from the bucolic Pacheco airfield ten miles outside Buenos Aires.[151] It was pouring, "but what has bad weather to do with keeping a schedule?"[152] They bumped into the air and settled in for the long haul across the pampas to the first stop, Mendoza, at the foot of the Argentine side of the high Andes. Wood soon discovered that the weather could indeed overrule the schedule. "A raging blizzard that had forced its way over the Andes prevented further flight that day, but next morning at 8:12 the plane again took off to cross the Andes via Uspallata Pass to Chile."

This pass was about eleven thousand feet above sea level. Mount Aconcagua formed one of its sides, soaring to over twenty thousand feet. Wood recorded only an ordinary passage, the *San Cristóbal* rising to 20,700 feet and crossing the pass comfortably with heaters to keep crew and passenger warm, "although the sliding glass windows were frozen shut." An early pilot, John Shannon, remembered the pass differently. One really never knew if the pass would be clear, so the only way to be certain was to fly up there and take a look. "If it was clear you flew through; if it wasn't you went back down."[153] Very simple. Not until 1932 was a small weather station established in the heart of the pass at an old travelers' rest, the first of many navigational and safety aids put in by Panagra along its routes.

Wood landed in Santiago about two hours after leaving Mendoza, remarking that the same trip by train—when the passes were not blocked by snow—took ten hours. The hardy traveler then continued on to a Chilean army field farther north, changed planes and pilots, and flew north to Copiapo, the last stop of the day. They had covered 736 miles since leaving Santiago. On October 22 Wood reached Lima, three minutes ahead of scheduled time, having continued north from Copiapo with the sacks of mail to Antofagasta and Arica in Chile, with stops at Tacna, Ilo, Mollendo, Arequipa, and Camana in Peru before touching down at the capital.

The next morning, with a new pilot, Lloyd (Dinty) R. Moore, and another plane, the trip continued, this time with two other passengers to pass the time of day. After an overnight stop at Guayaquil, then entering its hot and steamy season, they flew on to Buenaventura in Colombia.

During the morning the plane crossed the equator. Here is how Mr. Wood describes it:

> "Where is the Equator?" I shouted into the ear of pilot Clark [another new one]. He referred to the charts and made a computation with a stubby pencil. "We cross it at 9:33 A.M.," he announced, and a half-hour later we were probably at that point, but the waves looked like the other waves and the shores looked the same as many other shores with steep wooded hills in the background, not even a signpost marking the place where the seasons change.[154]

Cristóbal in the Canal Zone was reached after a day of the worst kind of weather, and then Wood continued up the Pan Am route through Central America to Mexico, Cuba, and Miami. Nine days, seven hours, and fifty-five minutes had elapsed since leaving Buenos Aires. He flew aboard another airliner from Miami to Atlanta, but then had to train from there to Chicago since the weather had grounded the mail planes. The last extension of the basic Panagra mail route was made in late 1929. On November 30, the *San Cristóbal* lifted off from the grassy field of the Melilla Aviation School near Montevideo, bound for Buenos Aires, Santiago, Lima, Cristóbal, and all the short but vital stops in between.[155]

By 1930 the marriage of necessity between Grace and Pan Am was already producing friction between the partners. Trippe was near to acquiring the route down the East Coast of South America in a tough battle with another American competitor, and Joseph Grace wrote Iglehart that now "Trippe seems very anxious to buy us out."[156]

Grace already had the measure of Trippe. "As you know, he is not very liberal handed and the best he has indicated so far is $750,000. [Harold] Roig's ideas are, the company should be worth $5,000,000 and that we should not consider any overtures from Trippe unless he were willing to give us a ten-year or longer agency contract, pay us back the money we have put up, and give us something like $2,000,000 in Pan American stock at a figure under the present market."[157] Trippe would get no bargain from Grace.

Panagra's operations, however, were little affected by its sometimes quarreling founders and owners. Under the direction of John MacGregor, general manager, and Harold Harris, anchoring the South American operation from his headquarters in Lima, the firsts continued to be recorded as the Roaring Twenties relinquished their sway to a more dismal decade. In July 1930 a new schedule reduced the trip from New York to Buenos Aires to six and a half days. New planes, improved models, new services were continually being inaugurated.

The rest of the world was not doing so well. The stock-market crash in October 1929 precipitated a depression that eventually rippled through and engulfed most modern nations. From London, the venerable Ned Eyre predicted the worst and outlined the course to follow for survival: "I must be like the lunatic who believes everyone mad but himself. I am convinced that the worldwide business depression is with us for a long time, that its effects will be far reaching, and that all along the line the cry should be, run to cover. Keep on doing business by all means but no long commitments."[158]

It was good advice, balanced, like the company itself at the end of the decade. By now, of course, it was more than simply a firm doing business between the Americas. Steamship operator, sugar planter, coffee importer, equipment exporter, nitrate producer, banker, aviator, and trader par excellence, Grace was one of the major institutions linking the Americas. The substance indisputably matched the image.

Epilogue

Today Grace in Peru consists of one small room in a large, modern office building in Miraflores, a suburb of Lima. It is staffed occasionally by one or two older, loyal managers of the company, Peruvians and semi-retired, who are basically caretakers of a legacy. No more Panagra DC-8 jets, the last of a long line of distinguished predecessors, swoop down daily out of the west to approach the airports of Lima and Callao with their cargoes of passengers from New York or Buenos Aires or Miami. No more stately steamers of the Grace Line, smokestacks coated in the familiar Grace colors of white and green, ply the coasts of Colombia, Ecuador, Peru, and Chile, hauling in the trucks and derricks and refrigerators of North America and returning with the ores and sugar and bananas of South America. The headquarters of Casa Grace in Lima, dedicated in 1922 and built in almost the same style as the main headquarters at Seven Hanover Square, New York, now rate only a reminder by tour guides: "Casa Grace was once located there." Any Peruvian and most South Americans from Chile, Bolivia, Peru, Ecuador, and Colombia would nod their heads and take note. Very few were untouched by the enterprises created by Casa Grace along the West Coast of Latin America in the decades following 1930.

In any final reckoning of the impact of Grace on Peru and Latin America one must ask what difference the presence of this multinational made on the national life. It contributed to the modernization of several industries, it introduced new ones—steamships, airplanes, and tourism—and more than anything else, it was an agent for change and conveyed the industrialized world's vision and priorities to Latin America. It did all this within a Peruvian or Latin American context, which was sometimes hostile and critical of the "benefits" of foreign capital, foreign priorities, and foreigners in general. These were often perceived as the precursors or outriders of an aggressive capitalistic world, which only stripped the developing nations of their resources and pride.

But Casa Grace was not so perceived by Latin Americans. It

plowed its profits back into Peru—witness Hacienda Cartavio—selected its managers and employees from among nationals, and enhanced a legacy from William Russell Grace that was
perfectly embodied by his son Joseph Peter: work with and
respect your people—be they Peruvians, Americans, Chileans,
or others—as equals.

The company was not made of saints. Profits and prosperity
were high on its list of priorities. There was nothing sinful in
making good profits. Indeed, success in business was perceived
not only as a sign of personal determination, hard work, and
"sticktoitiveness," as Lillius Grace once instructed a young Ned
Eyre, but also as a path to a better and richer society. If Grace
ships ran on time and made good profits, they also contributed
to the growth and prosperity of Peru. Young managers like
Billy Holloway were fierce competitors, but so was William
Grace. To strike a good bargain, to underbid another firm, to
get ahead—these were part of the business credo of the times.
They still are today, and one must conclude that Grace managers were no better or worse than their peers.

Did Grace bring wealth to South America or was it simply
another multinational corporation, like Cerro de Pasco or the
International Petroleum Company, dedicated largely to exploiting the natural resources of the region? Grace did haul
away guano, nitrates, and tin in its *Santa* steamers; in some
instances, the tin was from its own mines and *oficinas*. But it
also created a vast wealth-producing infrastructure devoted to
producing, manufacturing, and marketing in its host countries.
Sugar and textiles come readily to mind. By itself, or in con-
junction with institutions like National City Bank, Grace participated in financing, promoting, building, and improving
railroads, harbors, light and power facilities, and other structures of a modernizing nation.

These were goals desired by a majority of South Americans
who sought to bring "progress" to their lands. (*Progress*, of
course, represents a two-edged phenomenon. Automobiles, for
example, both improve transportation for the masses and pol-
lute.) Furthermore, while new wealth was being generated in
South America, it was not being equitably distributed in societies ruled by small elites and only witnessing the emergence
of a middle class at the turn of the century. Nonetheless, if we
judge the *overall* improvement of the norms of living in the
nineteenth and twentieth centuries as positive—better public
services, improved medical care, increased material benefits,
and a general improvement of well-being by new capital and
technologies otherwise unavailable to the underdeveloped na-

tions of South America—then Grace's contribution was unusually positive.

Michael Grace had long been governed by the principle that what was good for him was good for Peru. Even after Michael died in 1920, one could recognize this guideline in the philosophy of the company. Wealth produced and reinvested in Latin America was wealth for Grace, as well as wealth for Peruvians, Chileans, Colombians, Ecuadorians, and Bolivians. The West Coast of South America was not an area one abandoned with an easy conscience, for Grace was profoundly rooted in Latin America, a claim few if any of the early multinationals could make.

What made Grace more successful than its competitors? It was an amalgam of those good business practices that bring success to any company: good management, hard work, successful risk-taking, and superior men and women. But there is another element: the Grace family structure.

Like earlier commercial and trading families, the Graces maintained their business through agents and partners in distant ports. Frequently those posts were for younger relatives training grounds for everything from basic accounting to warehousing. Given the distances involved, young business partners learned to take risks on their own and to reach decisions in a decentralized fashion. This type of arrangement continued through the turn of the century even as the company diversified and outgrew its simple mercantile nature, and it added a quality to the company that enhanced its competitive stance in the twentieth century. Managers in Valparaiso or Callao or Paposo or Buenaventura, although no longer family in the strictest sense, were encouraged to take initiatives and were supported in their decisions. Furthermore, few major decisions were made without a good thrashing-out of the problems and possibilities, preserving a strong sense of participation within the company.

Joseph Grace's concern with the wives and families of his employees was more than an expression of his warm personality. It was the Grace "family" structure in operation, perhaps a holdover from another age and outdated in the twentieth century, but nonetheless a source of great strength to the company. Along with other more concrete features such as profit-sharing, this structure encouraged and rewarded initiative and loyalty. Initiative and imagination played especially important roles in moving the company in new directions in the 1930s and 1940s.

Looking for alternative uses of sugar and its byproducts, Grace engineers and technicians, spurred by Gaston Lipscomb from his cockpit in New York, developed the first commercial process employing bagasse, the fibrous residue left after the juices had been ground out of sugar cane, to make paper. After several years of experimenting at the small chemical laboratory at Cartavio and then at a pilot plant in Whippany, New Jersey, Grace ordered a paper machine to specifications from Germany. It was shipped from Europe in 1938 and installed at Paramonga in 1939. Paramonga, unprofitable since bought by Grace in 1927, turned the corner in 1940 and never looked back. The immediate success of the first paper machine prompted the expansion and development of the papermaking facilities at Paramonga until by 1968 five machines were on line producing tons of paper for Peru.

Paramonga represented more than profits and paper for Grace. It marked a definite juncture in the company's evolution from merchant and trader to manufacturer and industrial producer. The nitrate fields of Paposo, and the sugar fields of Cartavio were the predecessors of this new direction, but the success of Paramonga really signified the turn. Not only was everything from toilet paper to cardboard lining being produced at Paramonga in the 1960s; in keeping with a tradition, other byproducts of the sugarmaking process had been utilized by Grace's innovative chemists and engineers to produce polyvinyl chloride, or PVC, one of the basic plastics of the modern world. For a long time Grace was the only producer of paper in Peru and was certainly the only pioneer producing PVC in the country. The Paramonga paper mills indeed became showcases for Peru, visited by technicians and engineers from all over the world.

Even as Paramonga became synonymous with Grace industry in Peru in the post–World War II decades, investments in other manufacturing and industrial enterprises kept pace, not only in Peru, but in Colombia, Ecuador, Bolivia, and Chile as well. Paint, candy, edible oils, all grades and qualities of paper, and myriad other items were being produced. To be sure, Grace Line and Panagra continued as viable components in the Grace Latin American empire, but the emphasis was on manufacturing.

Yet, while one revolution in direction was being wrought in Latin America, Grace was performing another remarkable turn under the leadership of Joseph Peter Grace, Jr., grandson of William Russell Grace and the new president as of 1945. He took the formidable assets bequeathed to him and turned his focus toward the United States. Peter Grace was especially impressed by the counsel offered by Raúl Simón, a brilliant Chilean economist who had been with Grace in Chile since the 1930s. Simón said profits were to be had not in the "developing" Latin American world, but in the United States, then leading the free world in almost every economic category imaginable.

Peter Grace explored the investment possibilities in petroleum but found it too tightly controlled by the seven sisters. The electronics industry seemed too esoteric. The chemical industry was selected as the optimum field and beginning with the purchase of the Davison Chemical Company and Dewey and Almy in the early 1950s, W. R. Grace & Co. broke into the circle of chemical producers. It was a startling switch for the old Latin American hands; a switch that caused not a little disruption and some hard feelings, but one that was pursued vigorously and profitably by Grace from the 1950s to the present.

Today, in fact, W. R. Grace & Co. is the nation's fifth largest chemical producer and represents a major presence in the agricultural and specialty chemical fields. It has branched out also into retailing and restauranting, and has become such a diversified concern as almost to defy Wall Street analysts attempting to identify the "real" Grace.

But, of course, the real Grace, even going back to the late nineteenth century, was always a diversified company that only appeared conservative and traditional. The actions of a Michael P. Grace, a D. Stewart Iglehart, a Joseph P. Grace were almost always dynamic, in some cases visionary, in others disastrous, but never dull. Even before World War I, Grace had been producing textiles, sugar, and nitrates in Latin America, all the while expanding Grace Line and looking for new avenues of investment and profit.

Yet, we return to the small office in Miraflores. What happened to Casa Grace? It became a casualty of another revolution, every bit as dramatic as the one wrought by Peter Grace in the 1950s and 1960s, but in this instance W. R. Grace & Co. was diminished, not enhanced. On October 3, 1968, the constitutional government of President Fernando Belaunde Terry was toppled by a military coup led by Gen. Juan Velasco Alvarado. The revolution was committed to state control of major enterprises in the nation and to widespread agrarian reform. It was an extreme expression of nationalist sentiment mandated by a group of military officers imbued with socialistic ideals.

They first, almost immediately, nationalized the property of the International Petroleum Company (IPC), a subsidiary of Esso, and certainly the most visible of foreign enterprises in Peru. Then, on June 24, 1969, Velasco nationalized the large productive estates along the coast in a sweeping agrarian reform announced on a day in Peru known as Indian Day. It was a day of promised redemption for the Peruvian peasant; a day of hubris for the Velasco government; a day of consternation among the people of Casa Grace, for it meant that the agricultural portions of Paramonga and Cartavio would be stripped away and distributed to people's collectives. Without definite control over the raw material, sugar, Grace decided to sell the industrial sectors of its estates in Peru and eventually to dispose of all its other productive enterprises in the country.

By the late 1960s, however, divestiture had been proceeding in other Latin American countries where Grace possessed a long record. When the socialistic government of Salvador Allende Goosens was inaugurated in Chile in 1970, Grace had already sold virtually all of its properties, certainly with some foresight in this instance, since the Allende government nationalized on an even grander scale than Peru between 1970 and 1973. Grace had been gradually pulling out of Latin America since the late 1960s, selling its properties and enterprises, valued at more than $70 million, piecemeal to its old employees.

Peru had been the exception. In Peru Grace was still expanding. Peru was thus an anomaly in the restructured W. R. Grace & Co. of the 1960s. A company that had sold Grace Line in 1969, sold its portion of Panagra in 1966, divested throughout Latin America, and become an enterprise drawing its resources and profits largely from the developed rather than the developing world, that company was still thoroughly a part of the Peruvian national life in 1968. Why?

Good profits and sentimentality combined to produce a sense of well-being and perhaps even artificial euphoria among those managing Grace in the 1960s. Why leave a country where one's name was almost synonymous with good products and good service, and was so intimately tied with the economic and technological development of the country? Casa Grace was more than that. It was so much a part of the culture as to be taken for granted, an ancient presence that would surely persevere into the future.

We return to William Russell Grace's letter to his brother John written almost a century earlier, enjoining John to think well of the people of any nation and the sentiment will be reciprocated. That had been the case of Grace in Peru.

The Velasco government nonetheless acted from a different set of imperatives, no less persuasive to its proponents than the commitment of Grace people to enterprise unfettered by government intervention. Perhaps it was inevitable that the chapter be closed stridently, dramatically, with hard feelings on both sides.

Curiously, in 1980, Peru ended its twelve-year experiment with the forms of socialism and statism espoused by Velasco. Fernando Belaunde Terry was again elected the constitutional president and the military retired to the barracks. Once again, steps were taken to dissociate the state gradually from intrusion into the economic life of the nation. The Velasquistas were thoroughly discredited; the extreme left in Peru was splintered and small; and the moderate majority was pressing for progress, emphasizing the old economic dictums commensurate with the principles of free enterprise and a pluralistic government. One of President Belaunde's closest advisers, Manuel Ulloa, was a former member of Casa Grace. Ironically or prophetically, many of the principles that had guided Grace for over a hundred years in Peru were again in vogue, perhaps testifying to the axiom that history repeats itself. Although it does not truly repeat itself, history does move in cycles that bear remarkable similarity to one another.

The experience of Grace in Peru through 1930 marked one distinct cycle in the modernization of the world. It was a period of invention, capital formation, technological breakthroughs, and rapid transformations in the economic nature of man and his society. Grace helped pioneer Peru's transition into this age. Although not the sole handmaiden as Peru passed through this critical period, Grace was a leading institution to that end.

Grace's multinational dimension was itself an efficacious instrument of modernization. It was an international firm almost from the very beginning, but its immensely varied investments, its many commercial and industrial activities, and its vision of a world market evinced a multinational nature. Even though principally directed to trade and industry in the Western Hemisphere, the company possessed a multinational's point of view that transcended national boundaries and prejudices.

Finally, Grace's founders were men of strong feelings and distinct convictions. They shied not from the pulls and tugs of the political world—whether of New York City politics or of the politics of Peru's debt renegotiation—and thus were active in late nineteenth-century politics across the Americas. It was a period of rapidly changing inter-American relations which saw the United States emerge as the colossus of the Western Hemisphere, and the Graces, especially William and Michael, acted therein with vision and tenacity not only in pursuit of their legitimate economic interests, but often in the public interest. They helped promote a just peace in the wake of the

War of the Pacific, facilitated the renegotiation of the Peruvian debt, mediated between Chile and the United States during the Balmaceda Revolution, and counseled and acted on many other fronts.

Although of strong principles, the company's founders and successors nonetheless demonstrated remarkable adaptability and inventiveness. In many ways, they were extraordinarily modern in their ability to move rapidly with the flow of history, often initiating pioneering changes themselves. Yet they were also imbued with the principles of loyalty, hard work, personal integrity, and Christian morality. They were, in fact, among the most important makers of our modern American world.

Notes

Chapter 1

1. Edward Eyre, a young nephew of William's, first went to Peru in 1867 and left his recollections of this era in the form of a 34-page, typescript, unpublished memoir titled 'Early Reminiscences of the Grace Organization.'' I have used the Eyre account throughout this first chapter for some of the detail and ambiance of Grace in Peru in this era. Marquis James, "Merchant Adventurer: The Story of W. R. Grace" (book-length manuscript, 1948), pp. 5–5½ (the book is in galleyproof stage and pagination progresses by half numbers); *History of W. R. Grace & Co. in Peru, 1854–1972,* inhouse history in typescript, p. 7; "Casa Grace," *Fortune,* December 1935, pp. 95–164; William S. Bollinger, "The Rise of United States Influence in the Peruvian Economy, 1869–1921" (M.A. thesis, University of California at Los Angeles, 1971), pp. 99 ff.

2. Eyre, "Reminiscences," p. 14.

3. Joseph Wilhelm, *The Family of Grace: Pedigrees and Memoirs Collected and Edited* (London: Kegan Paul, Trench, Trubner & Co., 1911).

4. E. J. Hobsbawn, *Industry and Empire: The Making of Modern English Society, Vol. 2, 1750 to the Present Day* (New York: Random House, 1968), p. 1.

5. Ibid., p. 47.

6. Ibid., p. 97.

7. George Macaulay Trevelyan, *British History in the Nineteenth Century and After (1782–1919)* (New York: David McKay, 1962).

8. E. L. Woodward, *The Age of Reform, 1815–1870* (Oxford: Clarendon Press, 1938), p. 323, a part of the *Oxford History of England* under the general editorship of G. N. Clark.

9. R. B. McDowell's "Ireland on the Eve of the Famine" in R. Dudley Edwards and T. Desmond Williams, eds., *The Great Famine: Studies in Irish History, 1845–1852* (New York: Russell & Russell, 1956), pp. 7–9.

10. Alfred W. Crosby, *The Columbian Exchange: Biological and Cultural Consequences of 1492* (Westport, Conn.: Greenwood Press, 1972).

11. Oliver MacDonagh, "Irish Emigration to the United States of America and the British Colonies During the Famine," in Edwards and Williams, *The Great Famine.*

12. Woodward, *Age of Reform,* p. 338.

13. Ibid., p. 341.

14. From Appendix I, a table titled "The Volume of Overseas Migration," in Oliver MacDonagh, "Irish Emigration to the United States of America and the British Colonies During the Famine," in Edwards and Williams, *The Great Famine,* p. 338.

15. Edward Eyre to Joseph P. Grace, Sr., July 28, 1930, Grace Papers, Rare Book and Manuscript Library, Columbia University, New York (hereafter cited as GP/C).

16. Ibid.
17. Eyre to Grace, July 28, 1930 (GP/C).

Chapter 2

1. Carlos Daniel Valcarcel, *Tupuc Amaru* (Lima, n.d.) and other works by Valcarcel on Tupuc Amaru II. See John Leddy Phelan, *The People and the King: The Comunero Revolution in Colombia, 1781* (Madison: University of Wisconsin Press, 1978), for the revolt in Colombia that occurred contemporaneously with the Peruvian revolt. Lillian Fisher, *The Last Inca Revolt, 1780–1783* (Norman: University of Oklahoma Press, 1966), deals with the Tupuc Amaru II revolt in English.
2. Most of the account that follows was drawn from one of the three following: J. J. von Tschudi, *Travels in Peru, on the Coast, in the Sierra, Across the Cordilleras and the Andes, into the Primeval Forests*, trans. Thomasina Ross from the German (New York: A. S. Barnes, 1847); G. W. Peck, *Melbourne and the Chincha Islands, with Sketches of Lima and a Voyage Around the World* (New York: Charles Scribner, 1854); A. J. Duffield, *The Prospects of Peru: The End of the Guano Age and a Description Thereof* (London: Newman & Co., 1881).
3. D. C. M. Platt, *Latin America and British Trade, 1806–1914* (London: Adam & Charles Black, 1972; New York: Harper & Row, 1973), p. 4.
4. Von Tschudi, *Travels*, pp. 63–64.
5. Ibid., p. 63.
6. Peck, *Melbourne*, p. 143.
7. Ibid., p. 149.
8. Only with the constitution of 1856 did the church lose, for example, the privileges–or *fueros*—of maintaining its own courts and the right of ecclesiastics to be elected to congress; on the other hand, the Roman Catholic faith continued to be the official state religion; see David Werlich, *Peru: A Short History* (Carbondale: University of Southern Illinois Press, 1978), pp. 85–86.
9. Peck, *Melbourne*, pp. 236–37.
10. Frederick P. Bowser's major study of blacks in the early Peruvian colony, *The African Slave in Colonial Peru, 1524–1650* (Stanford, Stanford University Press, 1974).
11. Von Tschudi, *Travels*, p. 74.
12. Pablo Macera, *Trabajos de historia*, 4 vols (Lima: Instituto Nacional de Cultura, 1977), includes a lengthy sociologically and economically slanted disquisition on slavery in mid-nineteenth-century Peru in vol. 4.
13. Fredrick B. Pike, *The United States and the Andean Republics: Peru, Bolivia, and Ecuador* (Cambridge: Harvard University Press, 1977).
14. Von Tschudi, *Travels*, pp. 80–81.
15. Ramón Menéndez Vidal, *The Spaniards in Their History* (New York: W. W. Norton, 1950), for a short, brilliant, inductive essay on this counterpoint in the Spanish character.
16. J. David Suárez-Torres, "Clorinda Matto de Turner," *Americas* 31, no. 8 (August 1979).
17. Peck, *Melbourne*, pp. 248–49.
18. Von Tschudi, *Travels*, pp. 68–70.
19. Ibid., p. 39.
20. David A. Robinson, *Peru in Four Dimensions* (Lima: American Studies Press, 1964), p. 131.
21. Most of the following discussion comes from Robinson's *Peru in Four Dimensions*, pp. 153 ff., an extraordinarily perceptive and detailed fountain of information on Peru.
22. Ibid., p. 183.
23. Ibid., p. 185.
24. Jonathan V. Levin, *The Export Economics: Their Pattern of Development in Historical Perspective* (Cambridge: Harvard University Press, 1960), especially chap. 2, "Peru in the Guano Age," pp. 27–123; W. M. Mathew, "Peru and the British Guano Market, 1840–1870," *Economic History Review* 2d ser. 23, no. 1 (April 1970): 112–128; "Foreign Contractors and the Peruvian Government at the Outset of the Guano Trade," *Hispanic*

American Historical Review (hereafter cited as *HAHR*) 52, no. 4 (November 1972): 598–620; "A Primitive Export Sector: Guano Production in Mid-Nineteenth Century Peru," *Journal of Latin American Studies* (hereafter cited as *JLAS*) 9, no. 1 (May 1977): 35–57; and Ernesto Yepes del Castillo, *Peru, 1820–1920: un siglo de desarrollo capitalista* (Lima: Instituto de Estudios Peruanos, 1971). With the exception of the most current literature which largely focuses on changing interpretations of the impact of the Guano Era on Peru, such as Heraclio Bonilla's *Guano y burguesía en el Perú* (Lima: Instituto de Estudios Peruanos, 1974), most of the relevant historical documents and books on guano are cited or utilized by the above-mentioned sources.

25. Louis Clinton Nolan, "The Diplomatic and Commercial Relations of the United States and Peru, 1826–1875" (Ph.D. dissertation, Duke University, 1935), offers a description of the trade and its importance to the U. S. market, especially pp. 187–215.

26. W. M. Mathew, "Foreign Contractors and the Peruvian Government," *HAHR*, 600.

27. Yepes del Castillo, *Peru*, pp. 67 ff.

28. Susan Ramirez Horton, *The Sugar Estates of the Lambayeque Valley, 1670–1800: A Contribution to Peruvian Agrarian History* (Madison, Wis.: Land Tenure Center, 1974).

29. Pablo Macera, "Las Plantaciones Azucareras Andinas (1821–1875)," in *Trabajos de historia*, 4 vols. (Lima: Instituto Nacional de Cultura, 1977), vol. 4.

30. Yepes del Castillo, *Peru*, p. 75.

31. For the importation and life of the Chinese coolies, see some of the following: Arnold J. Meagher, "The Introduction of Chinese Laborers to Latin America: The Coolie Trade, 1847–1874" (Ph.D. dissertation, University of California, Davis, 1975); Watt Stewart, *Chinese Bondage in Peru: A History of the Chinese Coolie in Peru, 1849–1874* (Durham: Duke University Press, 1951); Lawrence A. Clayton, "Chinese Indentured Labour in Peru," *History Today* 30 (June 1980): 19–23.

Chapter 3

1. William S. Bollinger, "Rise of United States Influence in the Peruvian Economy, 1869–1921" (M.A. thesis, University of California at Los Angeles, 1971), p. 101, fn. 9.

2. Louis Clinton Nolan, "The Diplomatic and Commercial Relations of the United States and Peru, 1826–1875" (Ph.D. dissertation, Duke University, 1935), pp. 187 ff.

3. Marquis James, "Merchant Adventurer: The Story of W.R. Grace" (ms., 1948). James had access to certain sources no longer available, among the most important a manuscript titled "Reminiscences of Mrs. W. R. Grace, May 24, 1921," taken from Mrs. Grace's dictation, and a manuscript by Lilias Grace Kent, "Recollections." Lilias was a daughter of William Russell and Lillius. James also depended upon the unpublished manuscript biography of William Russell Grace by Katherine Burton, "Anchor in Two Continents: The Story of William Russell Grace." For details of life aboard ship, see Basil Greenhill and Ann Giffard, comps., *Women Under Sail: Letters and Journals Concerning Eight Women Travelling or Working in Sailing Vessels Between 1829 and 1949* (South Brunswick: Great Albion Books, 1972).

4. Original pledge in GP/C, dated October 8, 1828.

5. *The Grace Log* 5, no. 6 (November–December 1922): 160.

6. Lillius Grace, "Reminiscences."

7. Lilias Grace Kent, "Recollections."

8. James, "Merchant Adventurer," p. 11½.

9. The packet of letters—more than a dozen—dating from February 23, 1861, to July 28, 1865, from James Lawler to members of his family belong to a descendant of Lawler's, Mrs. Edward Dwyer Sullivan of Ann Arbor, Michigan. Mrs. Sullivan transcribed the letters into typescript and made their contents available to J. Peter Grace, Jr., president of W. R. Grace & Co., in spring 1980. Copies of these transcriptions were used to write the following passages. These copies were donated to the Rare Book and Manuscript Library of Columbia University along with the Grace papers. My thanks to Mrs. Sullivan for making the letters of her predecessor available to us, and especially for the loving labor of having transcribed them.

10. "Casa Grace," *Fortune*, December 1935, p. 158.

11. Morgan S. Grace, *A Sketch of the New Zealand War* (London: Horache Marshall & Son, 1899), p. 9.

12. See Charles G. Summersell's edited version of the diary of George Fullam, *The Journal of George Townley Fullam: Boarding Officer of the Confederate Sea Raider Alabama* (University, Ala.: By the Friends of the Mobile Public Library through the University of Alabama Press, 1973).

13. A. B. C. Whipple, *The Whalers* (Alexandria, Va.: Time-Life Books, 1979), p. 156.

14. William C. Davis, *The Last Conquistadors: The Spanish Intervention in Peru and Chile, 1863–1866* (Athens: University of Georgia Press, 1950); James W. Cortada, "Diplomatic Rivalry Between Spain and the United States over Chile and Peru, 1864–1871," *Inter-American Economic Affairs* 27 (Spring 1974)· 47–57; Alberto Wagner de Reyna, *Las relaciones diplomáticas entre el Perú y Chile durante el conflicto con España, 1864–1867* (Lima: Ediciones del Sol, 1963); Mark Van Aken, *Pan-Hispanism: Its Origin and Development to 1866* (Berkeley: University of California Press, 1959); and David Werlich, *Peru: A Short History* (Carbondale, Ill.: University of Southern Illinois Press, 1978), pp. 90–91.

15. James, "Merchant Adventurer," pp. 13–13½.

16. This and following from Fredrick B. Pike, *The United States and the Andean Republics: Peru, Bolivia, and Ecuador* (Cambridge: Harvard University Press, 1977), p. 126.

Chapter 4

1. Jonathan V. Levin, *The Export Economies: Their Pattern of Development in Historical Perspective* (Cambridge: Harvard University Press, 1960), pp. 69 ff.; and Heraclio Bonilla, *Guano y burguesia en el Peru* (Lima: Instituto de Estudios Peruanos, 1974), pp. 69 ff.

2. Bonilla, *Guano y burguesia*, p. 79, and Pablo Macera, *Trabajos de historia*, 4 vols. (Lima: Instituto Nacional de Historia, 1977), vol. 1, *Los archivos de la Casa Dreyfus y la historia del Peru republicano.*

3. Bonilla, *Guano y burguesia*, "novedades de todo genero, tintes y mantenimientos," p. 79.

4. Levin, *Export Economies*, pp. 98–99.

5. Most of the following on Pardo from Bonilla, *Guano y burguesia* pp. 98 ff; who in turn drew heavily upon the biography of Pardo by Jacinto Lopez, *Manuel Pardo* (Lima: Imprenta Gil, 1947).

6. Bonilla, *Guano y burguesia*, p. 99, quoting from Lopez.

7. Ibid., p. 58, quoting from Lopez.

8. Watt Stewart, *Henry Meiggs: Yankee Pizarro* (Durham: Duke University Press, 1946).

9. Levin, *Export Economies*, p. 101.

10. Werlich, *Peru*, p. 94.

11. Levin, *Export Economies*, pp. 103–4.

12. Marquis James, "Merchant Adventurer: The Story of W. R. Grace" (ms., 1948), pp. 17–17½.

13. Ibid., p. 41½. Also see William S. Bollinger, "Rise of U. S. Influence in the Peruvian Economy, 1869–1921" (M.A. thesis, University of California at Los Angeles, 1971), pp. 105–6.

14. M. P. Grace to W. R. Grace, September 22, 1871, and Bryce, Grace & Co. (Michael's handwriting) to W. R. Grace, October 21, 1871, GP/C.

15. Bryce, Grace & Co. (Michael's handwriting) to W. R. Grace, November 21, 1871, GP/C.

16. Levin, *Export Economies*, p. 103.

17. From S.S. D. Hazen to W. R. Grace, June 14, 1872, GP/C.

18. James, "Merchant Adventurer," p. 24½, from Michael P. Grace to W. R. Grace, June 23, 1872, GP/C.

19. These scenes reconstructed from various sources, among them Werlich, *Peru*, p. 96; James, "Merchant Adventurer," pp. 27½–28; Ernesto Yepes del Castillo, *Peru: 1820–1920, un siglo de desarrollo capitalista* (Lima: Instituto de Estudios Peruanos 1972), pp. 105–10.

20. S. D. Hazen to W. R. Grace, July 27, 1872, GP/C.

21. Levin, *Export Economies*, pp. 107–8.

22. W. R. Grace to M. P. Grace, February 12, 20, 1873, GP/C.

23. Ibid.

24. W. R. Grace to M. P. Grace, April 12, 1873, GP/C.

25. Bollinger, "Rise of U. S. Influence," p. 110.

26. Lawrence A. Clayton, "Private Matters: The Establishment and Nature of United States–Peruvian Relations, 1820–1850," to appear in *Americas* in 1985.

27. Most of the following and preceding analysis of the United States vis-à-vis Latin America in 1870 from David M. Pletcher's "Inter-American Trade in the Early 1870s: A State Department Survey," *Americas* 33, no. 4 (April 1977): 593–612.

28. Nolan, "Diplomatic and Commercial Relations," p. 224; also Bollinger, "Rise of U. S. Influence," p. 111.

29. James, "Merchant Adventurer," pp. 16½–17½; Bollinger, "Rise of U.S. Influence," p. 105.

30. M. P. Grace to W. R. Grace, Callao, September 4, August 21, 1872, GP/C.

31. Ibid., December 21, 1872, GP/C.

32. Ibid.

33. James, "Merchant Adventurer," p. 22½.

34. Edward Eyre, "Early Reminiscences of the Grace Organization" (unpub. memoir), p. 30, GP/C.

35. M. P. Grace to W. R. Grace, Callao, September 13, 1872, GP/C.

36. Ibid.

37. Ibid.

38. Ibid.

39. The preceding and following on Eyre taken from his "Reminiscences."

40. Ibid.

41. Ibid.

42. Ibid.

43. Ibid.

44. Ibid.

45. Ibid.

46. Ibid.

47. From autobiography of Charles R. Flint, *Memories of an Active Life: Men, and Ships, and Sealing Wax* (New York: G. P. Putnam's Sons, 1923), p. 4.

48. Ibid., p. 5.

49. Ibid.

50. Ibid., p. 10.

51. Ibid., p. 49.

52. James, "Merchant Adventurer," p. 44, original sources in GP/C.

53. Ibid., p. 43½, original sources in GP/C.

54. M. P. Grace to W. R. Grace, Callao, December 21, 1872, GP/C.

55. Ibid., and James, "Merchant Adventurer," p. 47½, original sources in GP/C.

56. Ralph Lee Woodward Jr., *Central America: A Nation Divided* 2nd Ed. (New York: Oxford University Press, 1985), for the best general survey of Central American history.

57. James, "Merchant Adventurer," pp. 25–25½, original sources in GP/C.

58. See Watt Stewart's excellent biography of Keith, *Keith and Costa Rica: A Biographical Study of Minor Cooper Keith* (Albuquerque: University of New Mexico Press, 1964).

59. Thomas Karnes, *Tropical Enterprise: Standard Fruit and Steamship Company in Latin America* (Baton Rouge: Louisiana State University Press, 1979), is an excellent introduction to the rise of the banana trade, although by one of Minor Keith's competitors.

60. Flint, *Memories*, for his role in this phase of Costa Rican history.

61. Ezekiel Gutierrez (secretary to H. M. Keith) to W. R. Grace, October 12, 1872, and W. R. Grace to Guillermo Nanne, October 24, 1872, GP/C.

62. James, "Merchant Adventurer," pp. 39–39½, original sources in GP/C.

63. Ibid., pp. 40–41½, original sources in GP/C.

64. Some of the following from an unpublished, typewritten "Statement of Cerro de Pasco Claim, London, 28 January 1909," which is a full record of the Oroya Railroad, Rumillana Tunnel, and Cerro de Pasco mines projects, drawn up with the intent of

substantiating claims to the Cerro de Pasco mines on behalf of Michael P. Grace. It has 395 pages and is located in GP/C.

65. James, "Merchant Adventurer," p. 39½.

66. Werlich, *Peru*, pp. 100–101; Yepes del Castillo, *Peru, 1820–1920,* pp. 75–76.

67. James, "Merchant Adventurer," pp. 44½–45, from "various cables and letters exchanged among W. R. Grace & Co., Grace Brothers & Co., and Baring Brothers & Co., November 1878 to February 1879; see especially W. R. Grace & Co. to Grace Brothers & Co., December 26, January 8 and 9; to Baring Brothers & Co., January 8; see also W. R. Grace to C. R. Flint, December 24, 1878, GP/C.

68. Ibid.

69. James, "Merchant Adventurer," pp. 39, 42, 65. See chap. 11 for Grace and the sugar industry in Peru.

70. James, "Merchant Adventurer," pp. 10, 34, original sources in GP/C.

71. Bollinger, "Rise of United States Influence," p. 112.

72. W. R. Grace to John W. Grace, December 20, 1879, GP/C.

73. Ibid.

Chapter 5

1. Marquis James, "Merchant Adventurer: The Story of W. R. Grace" (ms., 1948), p. 48½, from W. R. Grace to Morgan S. Grace, November 15, 1879, GP/C.

2. Robert D. Parmet, "Cleveland, Blaine, and New York's Irish in the Elections of 1884" (M.A. thesis, Columbia University, 1961), p. 4.

3. For more on Tweed, see Leo Hershkowitz, *Tweed's New York: Another Look* (Garden City, N.Y.: Doubleday, Anchor Press, 1977), and Seymour J. Mandelbaum, *Boss Tweed's New York* (New York: John Wiley & Sons, 1965).

4. Parmet, "Cleveland, Blaine," p. 16.

5. This section on Kelly's Tammany procedures drawn largely from an excellent work by Robert H. Muccigrosso, "Tammany Hall and the New York Irish in the 1884 Presidential Election" (M.A. thesis, Columbia University, 1961).

6. James, "Merchant Adventurer," pp. 49–50.

7. Parmet, "Cleveland, Blaine," p. 6.

8. James, "Merchant Adventurer," pp. 49–49½.

9. Ibid., pp. 50–53, for material on Pratt candidacy.

10. W. R. Grace to H. H. Rossiter, July 8, 1880, GP/C; independent corroboration of William Grace's role in the 1880 nominating convention is offered by another political observer who was there. In Matthew P. Breen's autobiography, *Thirty Years of New York Politics, Up-to-Date* (New York: published by author, 1899), he wrote: "The first time I had the pleasure of meeting that gentleman [William Grace] was at the Presidential Convention, at Cincinnati, in 1880, when I found him actively engaged in a canvass to secure the nomination for President of his friend Judge Calvin E. Pratt, of Brooklyn . . . Judge Pratt was a worthy and capable judge, but he certainly lost his head when he became an aspirant for the President" (p. 683).

11. W. R. Grace to M. P. Grace, July 12, 1880, GP/C.

12. The account of the *Sewanhaka* incident from James, "Merchant Adventurer," pp. 53–53½, from W. R. Grace to M. P. Grace, June 28, 1880, GP/C. Various editions dated June 29, 1880, of the *Brooklyn Eagle, New York Evening Mail, New York Herald,* and *New York Times* were consulted by James.

13. Various sources describe this tactic, among them: Florence E. Gibson, *The Attitudes of the New York Irish Toward State and National Affairs, 1848–1892* (New York: Columbia University Press, 1951), pp. 317–18; Breen, *Thirty Years,* pp. 620–21; and Gustavus Myers, *The History of Tammany Hall* (New York: Boni & Liveright, 1917), pp. 260–61.

14. *New York Times,* October 19–20, 1880.

15. *New York Times,* October 19, 1880.

16. Gibson, *Attitudes of the New York Irish,* p. 317.

17. *New York Herald,* October 30, 1880.

18. Gibson, *Attitudes of the New York Irish,* p. 318, from *Irish World.*

19. *New York World,* October 24, 1880.

20. "Casa Grace," *Fortune,* December 1935, pp. 94–164; also from Katherine Burton manuscript (in galleyproof stage), "Anchor on Two Continents."

21. Account of this allegation and its outcome from James, "Merchant Adventurer," pp. 55–55½, from *New York Tribune,* October 27, 1880; *New York Times,* October 28, 1880; *New York Tribune,* November 1, 1880; and W. R. Grace to M. P. Grace, September 25, 1880; W. R. Grace to W. D. English and J. H. Rossiter, November 6, 1880, GP/C.

22. *New York Tribune,* January 6, 1881.

23. Gibson, *Attitudes of the New York Irish,* p. 318. David M. Pletcher, *The Awkward Years: American Foreign Relations Under Garfield and Arthur* (Columbia: University of Missouri Press, 1962).

24. W. R. Grace to J. H. Rossiter, November 6, 1880, GP/C.

25. *New York World,* October 24, 1880.

26. Ibid., p. 57, from Burton manuscript and Joseph P. Grace to Marquis James.

27. Much of account from following sources: *New York Tribune,* March 2, 1881; *New York Times,* May 25, June 5, August 24, 1881; *New York Herald,* March 19, April 7, 9, 13, 15, May 25, June 5, August 24, September 15, 1881; *New York World,* April 7, May 4, 25, June 5, 1881; W. R. Grace to F. A. Prince, March 19, 1881, GP/C.

28. James, "Merchant Adventurer," p. 58.

29. From "Letters to Mayor Grace," January–June 1881, Early Mayors' Papers, Municipal Archives and Records Center, New York City, Location 6130. My thanks to Mr. Idilio Gracia Peña of the Municipal Archives, who led me to these papers in June 1978.

30. Ibid.

31. Ibid.

32. Ibid.

33. James, "Merchant Adventurer," p. 57½.

34. The account of the elevated railways is drawn from Breen, *Thirty Years,* pp. 683–85, and James, "Merchant Adventurer," pp. 58½–59, which draws exclusively on newspapers as its sources.

35. *New York Herald,* June 1, 1882.

36. Breen, *Thirty Years,* p. 684; *New York Herald,* October 15, 24, 1882.

37. Breen, *Thirty Years,* p. 685.

38. Justus D. Doenecke, *The Presidencies of James A. Garfield and Chester A. Arthur* (Lawrence: Regents Press of Kansas, 1981), p. 76.

39. *New York Evening Post,* December 30, 1882.

40. *New York Staats-Zeitung,* December 3, 1882.

41. For the most comprehensive biography of Cleveland, see Allan Nevins, *Grover Cleveland: A Study in Courage* (New York: Dodd, Mead, 1933).

42. Much of the following comes from Parmet, "Cleveland, Blaine," pp. 20 ff., and from Muccigrosso, "Tammany Hall and the New York Irish," also pp. 20 ff.; the two works parallel each other closely on subject matter although differing in interpretation occasionally, and are essential sources for the 1884 election.

43. Parmet, "Cleveland, Blaine," p. 25.

44. Ibid., p. 26.

45. Muccigrosso, "Tammany Hall and the New York Irish," p. 74.

46. James, "Merchant Adventurer," p. 67½.

47. Muccigrosso, "Tammany Hall and the New York Irish," pp. 79 ff.

48. Parmet, "Cleveland, Blaine," pp. 71, ff.

49. Quoted in Muccigrosso, "Tammany Hall and the New York Irish," from William C. Hudson, *Random Recollections* (New York: Cupples & Leon, 1911), pp. 209–10.

50. H. Wayne Morgan, *From Hayes to McKinley: National Party Politics, 1877–1896* (Syracuse, N.Y.: Syracuse University Press, 1969), pp. 212–13, 538.

51. James, "Merchant Adventurer," p. 68½; it is rather strange that James omitted much if not all of the Cleveland-Blaine campaign history, which ultimately swung on the vote of New York. No mention was made in the James manuscript of "rum, romanism, and rebellion," the Blaine appeal to the Irish, and so forth.

52. *The Union,* December 1884; Letters to Mayor Grace, January–March 1885, Municipal Archives, Location 6132.

53. James, "Merchant Adventurer," p. 58½.

54. *New York Sun,* August 10, 1886, and *New York Telegram,* July 20, 1886.

55. See William Ivins, *Machine Politics and Money in New York City* (New York: Harper Brothers, 1887), for Ivins' account of his years with William Grace. Strangely, this work was not consulted by James or mentioned in his bibliography. It is even an odder omission when one recognizes that Professor Jonathan Grossman, then of Queens College, did some impressive spadework for James's chapters on William Grace's public career.

56. *New York World*, November 30, 1885.

57. *New York Tribune*, December 5, 1885, and *New York World*, December 9, 1885.

Chapter 6

1. Much of discussion on boundary disputes leading to the War of the Pacific are from following two sources: William Jefferson Dennis, *Tacna and Arica: An Account of the Chile-Peru Boundary Dispute and of the Arbitration by the United States* (New Haven: Yale University Press, 1931), and Herbert Millington, *American Diplomacy During the War of the Pacific* (New York: Columbia University Press, 1948).

2. Dennis, *Tacna and Arica*, p. 38.

3. Ibid., p. 55; Thomas F. O'Brien, "The Antofagasta Company: A Case Study of Peripheral Capitalism," *Hispanic American Historical Review* 60, no. 1 (February 1980): 1–31.

4. Robert N. Burr, *By Reason or Force: Chile and the Balancing of Power in South America, 1839–1905* (Berkeley and Los Angeles: University of California Press, 1965), pp. 57 ff.

5. For Chilean and Peruvian navies during this period, see Donald E. Worcester, "Naval Strategy in the War of the Pacific," *Journal of Inter-American Studies* 5 (January 1963): 31–38. The description of the *Huascar* drawn from Pedro Espina Ritchie, *Monitor Huascar* (Santiago: Editorial Andres Bello, 1974), pp. 25–26.

6. Marquis James, "Merchant Adventurer: The Story of W. R. Grace" (ms., 1948), p. 18½, from J. A. Garcia to W. R. Grace, May 26, 1869, GP/C.

7. Ibid., pp. 18½–19; see p. 114½, fns. 14, 15, of James ms. for original sources now in GP/C.

8. Worcester, "Naval Strategy," p. 34.

9. Millington, *American Diplomacy*, p. 24.

10. Dennis, *Tacna and Arica*, p. 55.

11. Ernesto Yepes del Castillo, *Peru, 1820–1920: un siglo de desarrollo capitalista* (Lima: Instituto de Estudios Peruanos, 1971), p. 118.

12. Jonathan V. Levin, *The Export Economies: Their Pattern of Development in Historical Perspective* (Cambridge: Harvard University Press, 1960), p. 109.

13. James, "Merchant Adventurer," pp. 44½–45; for details, also William S. Bollinger, "Rise of U. S. Influence in the Peruvian Economy, 1869–1921" (M.A. thesis, University of California at Los Angeles, 1971), pp. 114–15.

14. Much detail of these events from David Werlich, *Peru: A Short History* (Carbondale: University of Southern Illinois Press, 1978), pp. 109 ff.

15. Charles R. Flint, *Memories of an Active Life: Men, Ships, and Sealing Wax* (New York: G. P. Putnam's Sons, 1923), p. 85.

16. Ibid.

17. Ibid., pp. 85–86.

18. W. R. Grace to M. P. Grace, April 14, 1879, GP/C.

19. Flint, *Memories*, p. 86.

20. Ibid.

21. Ibid.

22. Account of this engagement from Worcester, "Naval Strategy," pp. 35–37.

23. The battle account from two sources principally: Espina, *Monitor Huascar*, pp. 57 ff., and Gonzalo Bulnes, *Resumen de la Guerra del Pacifico*, 3 vols. (Santiago: Editorial del Pacífico, 1976), pp. 51 ff.

24. James, "Merchant Adventurer," p. 45½.

25. Flint, *Memories*, p. 87.

26. James, "Merchant Adventurer," p. 46; Flint, *Memories*, illustrations facing p. 86.

See also L. Francis Herreshoff, *Captain Nat Herreshoff, the Wizard of Bristol: The Life and Achievements of Nathaniel Green Herreshoff* (New York: Sheridan House, 1953).

27. James, "Merchant Adventurer," p. 46; see p. 116½, fn. 13 for original sources in GP/C.

28. The episode of the Herreshoff boat drawn largely from James, "Merchant Adventurer," pp. 46–46½; see p. 116½, fn. 15 for original sources in GP/C.

29. Flint, *Memories*, p. 87.

30. James, "Merchant Adventurer," p. 46½; p. 116½, fn. 18 for original sources in GP/C.

31. Flint, *Memories*, p. 87.

32. James, "Merchant Adventurer," p. 47; p. 116½, fn. 21 for original sources in GP/C.

33. Ibid.

34. The account of the Battle of Angamos from several sources: Worcester, "Naval Strategy," p. 36; Dennis, *Tacna and Arica*, pp. 104 ff.; Pedro Espina's delightful and well illustrated *Monitor Huascar*, pp. 93–98; and Gonzalo Bulnes, *Resumen de la Guerra del Pacífico*, pp. 71–78. The *Huascar*, incidentally, is now preserved at Talcahuano by the Chilean navy as a national historic monument, and the men, both Peruvian and Chilean, who served and died aboard it during the War of the Pacific are remembered with equal pride.

35. Worcester, "Naval Strategy," p. 36.

36. Some important works on the War of the Pacific: Bulnes, *Guerra del Pacífico*; M. R. Paz Soldan, *Narración histórica de la guerra de Chile contra el Peru y Bolivia* (Buenos Aires, 1924); Clements R. Markham, *The War Between Peru and Chile, 1879–1882* (London, 1882); Tommaso Caivano, *Historia de la guerra de America entre Chile, Peru y Bolivia*, 2 vols. (Iquique, 1904); and Edmundo Civati Bernasconi, *Guerra del Pacífico* (Buenos Aires, 1946).

37. James, "Merchant Adventurer," p. 48; p. 116, fn. 27 for original sources in GP/C.

38. Ibid.

39. Millington, *American Diplomacy*, pp. 38–39. See also David M. Pletcher, *The Awkward Years: American Foreign Relations Under Garfield and Arthur* (Columbia: University of Missouri Press, 1962).

40. See an excellent article by Heraclio Bonilla, "The War of the Pacific and the National and Colonial Problem in Peru," *Past and Present*, no. 81 (November 1978): 92–118.

41. Ibid., p. 99.

42. Ibid., p. 101.

43. Werlich, *Peru*, p. 116.

44. Allan Peskin, "Blaine, Garfield and Latin America: A New Look," *Americas* 36, no. 1 (July 1979): 79–89.

45. Ibid.

46. Quoted in Bonilla, "War of the Pacific," p. 95, as presented by V. G. Kiernan, "Foreign Interest in the War of the Pacific," *Hispanic American Historical Review* 35 (February 1955): 14–36.

47. Bonilla, "War of the Pacific," p. 92.

48. Ibid., p. 105.

49. James, "Merchant Adventurer," p. 63, from p. 117½, fn. 2, for original sources in GP/C.

50. Millington, *American Diplomacy*, p. 42.

51. Dennis, *Tacna and Arica*, p. 136.

52. I. P. Christiancy to J. G. Blaine, May 4, 1881, United States Department of State, *Papers Relating to Foreign Relations, 1881.*

53. Peskin, "Blaine, Garfield," pp. 79–89.

54. James, "Merchant Adventurer," p. 63½; p. 117½, fn. 4 for original sources in GP/C.

55. M. P. Grace to Petrie, July 12, 1881, GP/C.

56. Millington, *American Diplomacy*, pp. 96–97.

57. Morton Keller, *Affairs of State: Public Life in Late Nineteenth Century America* (Cambridge: Harvard University Press, Belknap Press, 1977), p. 267.

58. Ibid.

59. James, "Merchant Adventurer," p. 64; p. 117½, fn. 6 for original sources in GP/C.

60. Ibid., p. 64; conversation reported in John Grace to Michael Grace, April 8, 1882; original sources in GP/C.

61. Bonilla, "War of the Pacific," p. 113.

62. Ibid., p. 109.

63. Millington, *American Diplomacy*, p. 142.

64. Bonilla, "War of the Pacific," p. 116, citing figures from chart in Jose Clavero, *El tesoro del Peru* (Lima, 1896), p. 51.

65. Dennis, *Tacna and Arica*, p. xii.

66. Ibid., pp. 220–24; James, "Merchant Adventurer," p. 64½.

Chapter 7

1. Jorge Basadre, *Historia de la Republica del Peru*, 6 vols., 5th ed. (Lima: Ediciones "Historia," 1962), 6: 2749.

2. Ibid., p. 2750; the original text in Spanish reads: "¿Estaba obligado el Peru a pagar la deuda externa, despues de que, con el tratado de paz, habia passado a poder de Chile el territorio en el que se encontraban los mas importantes depositos de guano?"

3. Most of the information above was derived from two valuable typewritten documents in the GP/C: "Cerro de Pasco Claim. Memorial of Michael P. Grace, April 5, 1911" (44 pages), and "Statement of Cerro de Pasco Claim, London, 28th January, 1909" (395 pages).

4. Marquis James, "Merchant Adventurer: The Story of W. R. Grace" (ms., 1948), pp. 65–65½; p. 119, fn. 12, for original sources in GP/C.

5. Ibid.

6. Ibid.

7. "Cerro de Pasco Claim . . . 1911," p. 9.

8. Ibid., p. 12.

9. Dale William Peterson, "The Diplomatic and Commercial Relations Between the United States and Peru from 1883 to 1918" (Ph.D. dissertation, University of Minnesota, 1959), quote extracted from *Dissertation Abstracts International*; see also pp. 64 ff. of Peterson's work for detail on Buck's fractious relations not only with Peruvians but with superiors in Washington.

10. "Cerro de Pasco Claim . . . 1909," p. 120.

11. James, "Merchant Adventurer," p. 80; p. 119, fn. 8 for original sources in GP/C.

12. "Cerro de Pasco Claim . . . 1909," p. 121.

13. Much of following discussion of bondholders is from an excellent article by Rory Miller, "The Making of the Grace Contract: British Bondholders and the Peruvian Government, 1885–1890," *Journal of Latin American Studies* 8, no. 1 (May 1976): 73–100.

14. Ibid.

15. "Cerro de Pasco Claim . . . 1909," p. 76.

16. Ibid., pp. 76–77. Marquis James missed the significance—indeed, he does not mention the government decree at all—in his account of what attracted Michael Grace to the railroads.

17. Basadre, *Historia*, 6:2750.

18. Ibid., p. 2751.

19. Miller, "Making of Grace Contract," p. 80.

20. Ibid.

21. "Cerro de Pasco Claim . . . 1909," p. 129.

22. James, "Merchant Adventurer," p. 79½; p. 119, fn. 7 for original sources in GP/C.

23. Ibid.

24. M. P. Grace to Denegri, February 20, 1888, GP/C.

25. James, "Merchant Adventurer," p. 78½; p. 119, fn. 2 for original sources in GP/C.

26. M. P. Grace to chairman of Bondholders Committee, May 18, 1885, GP/C.

27. "Cerro de Pasco Claim . . . 1911," p. 17, quoting in part.

28. James, "Merchant Adventurer," p. 79; p. 119, fn. 5 for original sources in GP/C.

29. Ibid., p. 80; p. 119, fn. 9 for original sources in GP/C.

30. Ibid.
31. Miller, "Making of Grace Contract," p. 81.
32. Ibid.
33. Ibid.
34. James, "Merchant Adventurer," p. 80½, from bondholders' proposal, May 1886; p. 119, fn. 11 for original sources in GP/C.
35. Ibid., p. 81, from Edward Eyre to M. P. Grace, July 10, 1886, GP/C.
36. Ibid.
37. Ibid.
38. Ibid., p. 80½; p. 119, fn. 12 for original sources in GP/C.
39. Miller, "Making of Grace Contract," p. 81, quoting from "Memoria del Ministro de Hacienda al Congreso, Agosto de 1887," in Jose Maria Rodriguez, *Anales de la Hacienda Publica del Peru, 1821–1895*, 19 vols. (Lima, 1912–28), 18:268a.
40. Miller, "Making of Grace Contract," p. 82, from *El Comercio*, January 8, 1887.
41. Ibid., p. 83.
42. Basadre, *Historia*, 6:2754.
43. Miller, "Making of Grace Contract," p. 83, citing "Report of the Presidential Commission of Francisco Garcia Calderon, Francisco Rosas, and Aurelio Denegri, 24 November 1886," in Rodriguez, *Anales*, xvii, 407s–23a.
44. Basadre, *Historia*, 6:2754.
45. Ibid., p. 2755.
46. All of above from ibid., pp. 2754–57.
47. James, "Merchant Adventurer," p. 81, from M. P. Grace to Edward Eyre, August 31, 1887, GP/C.
48. Miller, "Making of Grace Contract," p. 83.
49. Basadre, *Historia*, 6:2758.
50. Ibid.
51. Miller, "Making of Grace Contract," p. 84.
52. Robert N. Burr, *By Reason or Force: Chile and the Balancing of Power in South America, 1830–1905* (Berkeley and Los Angeles: University of California Press, 1965), p. 180.
53. Ibid.
54. James, "Merchant Adventurer," p. 81½; p. 119, fn. 19, although that footnote does not contain references to any letters from Eyre to anybody; however, the note is attributed to Eyre in the James text.
55. M. P. Grace to A. A. Caceres, August 31, 1887, GP/C.
56. Miller, "Making of Grace Contract," p. 85.
57. M. P. Grace to Charles Mansfield, September 2, 1887, GP/C.
58. Miller, "Making of Grace Contract," p. 86.
59. Ibid., p. 87.
60. Ibid.
61. Ibid., quoting from the Pauncefote memo.
62. Ivins to Secretary of State, September 29, 1887, GP/C.
63. W. R. Grace to Secretary of State Bayard, December 19, 1887, GP/C.
64. Miller, "Making of Grace Contract," p. 85, quoting from *El Comercio*, October 3, 1887.
65. M. P. Grace to Charles Buckingham, Midway, Ky., December 17, 1887, GP/C.
66. M. P. Grace to W. R. Grace, February 3, 1888, Washington, D.C., GP/C.
67. Ibid.
68. M. P. Grace to Denegri, February 20, 1888, GP/C.
69. Ibid.
70. M. P. Grace to Edward Eyre, March 9, 1888, GP/C.
71. Ibid.
72. M. P. Grace to Edward Eyre, April 10, 1888, GP/C.
73. James, "Merchant Adventurer," p. 82; p. 119, fn. 22.
74. M. P. Grace to J. A. Miro Quesada, February 25, 1888, in GP/C.
75. W. M. Ivins to Edward Eyre, June 26, 1888, GP/C.
76. Ibid.
77. Ibid.
78. W. M. Ivins to M. P. Grace, June 15, 1888, GP/C.

79. Ibid.
80. Ibid.
81. Ibid.
82. Ibid.
83. Ibid.
84. W. M. Ivins to E. Eyre, June 28, 1888, GP/C.
85. Ibid.
86. Ibid.
87. W. M. Ivins to M. P. Grace, June 15, 1888, GP/C.
88. Ibid.
89. Ivins to Edward Eyre, July 9, 1888, GP/C.
90. Ibld., June 29, 1888, GP/C. Ivin writes Eyre that "the sending to me of Zagarra's instructions, which I shall use with utmost discretion, shows me most how far I can go with perfect safety and I think puts him at our mercy—anywhere inside of resort to actual force which, I repeat, is out of the question."
91. Ibid., July 9, 1888, GP/C.
92. Ibid.
93. Ibid.
94. Ibid.
95. Ibid.
96. Grace Brothers, Lima, to Ivins, September 1, 1888, GP/C.
97. Miller, "Making of Grace Contract," p. 93; Basadre, *Historia*, 6:2760–61.
98. Miller, "Making of Grace Contract," pp. 87, 90, quoting from same letter by Charles Watson to Charles Watson Jr., January 25, July 1888, from Watson letters, Meiggs Archive, Peruvian Corporation Archive, Lima.
99. William S. Bollinger, "The Rise of United States Influence in the Peruvian Economy, 1869–1921" (M.A. thesis, University of California at L.A., 1971), p. 125.
100. James, "Merchant Adventurer," p. 83; p. 119, fn. 27 for original sources of GP/C.
101. Miller, "Making of Grace Contract," p. 89; James, "Merchant Adventurer," p. 83; p. 119, fn. 27 for original sources in GP/C.
102. James, "Merchant Adventurer," p. 83; p. 119, fn. 27 for original sources in GP/C.
103. Ibid.
104. Miller, "Making of Grace Contract," p. 89.
105. Federico Blume to G. A. Ollard, January 5, 6, & 8, 1889, GP/C.
106. Basadre, *Historia*, 6:2764–65.
107. Ibid., p. 2767.
108. Ibid., p. 2768.
109. Ibid.
110. Burr, *By Reason or Force*, p. 181.
111. W. R. Grace to M. P. Grace, July 13, 1889, GP/C.
112. Burr, *By Reason or Force*, p. 187.
113. Ibid.
114. W. R. Grace to J. G. Blaine, December 26, 1889, with enclosure, GP/C.
115. Miller, "Making of Grace Contract," p. 91.
116. Burr, *By Reason or Force*, pp. 187–88.
117. Miller, "Making of Grace Contract," p. 97, summarizing Peruvian interpretations to that effect.
118. Basadre, *Historia*, 6:2770.
119. Miller, "Making of Grace Contract," pp. 92–93, 100.
120. Ibid.; according to James, "Merchant Adventurer," p. 84½, the *London Financial News* estimated the worth of that contract to be about £800,000, which was a gross exaggeration, as even James admitted.

Chapter 8

1. Marquis James, "Merchant Adventurer: The Story of W. R. Grace" (ms., 1948), p. 17, p. 114, fn. 5; William S. Bollinger, "The Rise of United States Influence in the

Peruvian Economy, 1869–1921" (M.A. thesis, University of California at Los Angeles, 1971), p. 105.

2. Most of following on chartering extracted from letter by John F. Fowler written in 1920 at the request of the Grace Line. Fowler had served with William Grace as early as the 1870s and in this letter, dated August 1920, he describes the chartering business as he remembered it. In GP/C.

3. Ibid.

4. Ibid.

5. James, "Merchant Adventurer," p. 21; p. 114½, fn. 9 for original sources in GP/C.

6. "The Shipbuilders of Thomaston, Chapman & Flint," *Log Chips: A Periodical Publication of Recent Maritime History* 2, no. 7 (July 1951): 73–76.

7. Ibid.

8. Ibid.

9. The foregoing on *M. P. Grace* and *W. R. Grace* from a mimeo by F. Sands, "Grace Line" (n.d.), W. R. Grace & Co. Archive.

10. "Shipbuilders of Thomaston," p. 76.

11. James, "Merchant Adventurer," p. 66; p. 117½, fn. 14 for original sources in GP/C; the John F. Fowler reminiscence states the line was commenced in 1879, but the weight of the documentation points to 1882.

12. James, "Merchant Adventurer," p. 66; p. 117½, fn. 14 for original sources in GP/C.

13. Most of the following drawn from Rollie Poppino, *Brazil: The Land and the People* (New York and Oxford: Oxford University Press, 1968), pp. 138 ff.; John Melby, "Rubber River: An Account of the Rise and Collapse of the Amazon Boom," *Hispanic American Historical Review* 22 (August 1942): 452–69; D. C. M. Platt, *Latin American and British Trade 1806–1914* (New York: Harper & Row, 1973), pp. 266 ff.

14. James, "Merchant Adventurer," pp. 65½–66; p. 117½, fn. 13 for original sources in GP/C.

15. Ibid., p. 75; p. 118½, fn. 2 for original sources in GP/C.

16. Ibid., p. 118½, fn. 4 for original sources in GP/C.

17. Ibid.; fn. 5 for original sources in GP/C.

18. Charles R. Flint, *Memories of an Active Life: Men, Ships, and Sealing Wax,* (G. P. Putnam's Sons, 1923), pp. 69, 287, 288.

19. James, "Merchant Adventurer," p. 76; p. 118½, fn. 7 for original sources in GP/C.

20. Ibid., p. 75½; p. 118½, fn. 7 for original sources in GP/C.

21. James A. Field, Jr., "American Imperialism: The 'Worst Chapter' in Almost Any Book," *American Historical Review* 83, no. 3 (June 1978), 644–68.

22. Bollinger, "Rise of United States Influence," p. 126.

23. James, "Merchant Adventurer," p. 76; p. 118½, fn. 10 for original sources in GP/C.

24. Ibid.; p. 118½, fn. 12 for original sources in GP/C.

25. Ibid.; fn. 13 for original sources in GP/C.

26. Ibid., p. 76; p. 118½, fn. 15 for original sources in GP/C.

27. Ibid., p. 77; p. 119, fn. 18 for original sources in GP/C.

28. Ibid.; p. 119, fn. 21 for original sources in GP/C.

29. Ibid., pp. 77–77½; p. 119, fn. 22 for original sources in GP/C.

30. Ibid.

31. Ibid., p. 77½; p. 119, fnn. 23, 24 for original sources in GP/C.

32. Melby, "Rubber River," p. 457; Platt, *Latin America and British Trade*, pp. 267–69.

33. John H. Kemble, *The Panama Route, 1848–1869* (Berkeley and Los Angeles: University of California Press, 1943).

34. David McCulloch, *The Path Between the Seas: The Creation of the Panama Canal, 1870–1914* (New York: Simon & Schuster, 1977).

35. All of following from a series of letters dated May 20, 24, June 10, 1884, between W. R. Grace & Co., New York, J. W. Grace & Co., San Francisco, and Furth & Campbell, Panama.

36. Ibid.

37. Ibid.

38. Ibid.

39. Ibid.

40. Ibid.
41. Ibid.
42. Ibid.
43. Ibid.
44. Ibid.
45. Ibid; a letter from W. R. Grace & Co. to Furth & Campbell, January 1885, does exist in the GP/C, indicating that at least a liaison of sorts continued between the two firms: unfortunately, water damage to the letter rendered it mostly illegible.
46. Ivins to M. P. Grace, July 18, 1884, New York, GP/C.
47. This and the following on the navy incident from a series of letters between the Grace houses, December 1884–January 1885; and between W. R. Grace & Co. and the secretary of the navy, William F. Chandler, same dates, GP/C.
48. Ibid.
49. Ibid.
50. Ibid.
51. Ibid.
52. Ibid.
53. Ibid.
54. Ibid.
55. Ibid.
56. Ibid.
57. Ibid.
58. Ibid.
59. Ivins to J. W. Grace, New York, February 20, 1885, GP/C. Ivins was writing to John Grace in Valparaiso to report on a wide range of subjects, the revocation of the order being one item mentioned.
60. Most of following derived from letters, September 10–November 30, 1889, between W. R. Grace & Co. and correspondents in England and South America who will be identified in the following notes, GP/C.
61. Tripler to W. R. Grace & Co., September 20, 1889, Liverpool, GP/C.
62. W. R. Grace & Co., New York, to Greenock Steamship Co., Ltd., October 1, 1889, GP/C.
63. Ibid.
64. Ibid.
65. Ibid.
66. Ibid.
67. Ibid.
68. Ibid.
69. W. R. Grace & Co., New York, to Grace & Co., May 9, 1889, GP/C.
70. Ibid.
71. Ibid.
72. D. MacDougall, Managing Director, Greenock S. S. Co., Greenock, Scotland, to W. R. Grace & Co., October 17, 1889, GP/C.
73. Ibid.
74. Claudio Veliz, *Historia de la marina mercante de Chile* (Santiago: Universidad de Chile, 1961), pp. 213 ff.
75. W. R. Grace & Co. to Heraclio Lyon, October 9, 1889, New York, GP/C.
76. W. R. Grace & Co. to Lyon, November 30, 1889, New York, GP/C.
77. Ibid.
78. Ibid.
79. Ibid.
80. Ibid.
81. Ibid.
82. Ibid.
83. Lyon to W. R. Grace & Co., October 2, 1889, Valparaiso, GP/C; Veliz, *Historia*, pp. 283–84.
84. Veliz, *Historia*, p. 217.
85. W. R. Grace & Co., New York, to Lyon, November 30, 1890, GP/C.
86. Lyon, Valparaiso, to W. R. Grace & Co., October 2, 1889, GP/C.
87. Ibid.

88. John F. Fowler, New York, to E. W. Gombers, August 1930, Rye, GP/C.

89. James, "Merchant Adventurer," p. 101; p. 121, original sources in GP/C. Also, personal communication, William Kooiman to Lawrence A. Clayton, May 9, 1985, Point Reyes, California; I thank Mr. Kooiman for information on the *Bayley,* which was purchased from C.C. Barton, renamed the *Coya,* and sailed for the Graces for the first time from Greenpoint, Brooklyn, on Feb. 7, 1893.

90. W. R. Grace & Co., New York, to Heraclio Lyon, November 30, 1889, GP/C.

91. Joseph P. Grace, New York, to Edward Eyre, January 12, 1907, GP/C.

92. Ibid.

93. Ibid.

94. Ibid.

95. Veliz, *Historia,* pp. 284–86; correspondence touching on the Grace bid, mostly from Joseph P. Grace to John Eyre, then Grace manager in Valparaiso, also exists in the GP/C.

96. Veliz, *Historia,* p. 285.

97. Ibid., p. 287.

Chapter 9

1. Fredrick B. Pike, *Chile and the United States, 1880–1962* (Notre Dame, Ind.: Notre Dame University Press, 1963), pp. 64–65; and Robert N. Burr, *By Reason or Force: Chile and the Balancing of Power in South America, 1839–1905* (Berkeley and Los Angeles: University of California Press, 1965), pp. 188–89.

2. Burr, *By Reason or Force,* p. 189.

3. Pike, p. 64.

4. Ibid., p. 65.

5. Ibid., pp. 64–65.

6. *History and Description of "Casa Grace" Activities in the Republic of Chile* (Santiago, 1953), p. 1. Privately printed by W. R. Grace & Co. in Chile.

7. Ibid.

8. Marquis James, "Merchant Adventurer: The Story of W. R. Grace" (ms., 1948), p. 85; p. 119½, fn. 2, W. R. Grace to Edward Eyre, July 21, 1890, GP/C.

9. William Dale Petersen, "Diplomatic and Commercial Relations Between the United States and Peru," (Ph.D. dissertation, University of Minnesota, 1969), pp. 122–24, and Pike used to re-create the scene above.

10. For the involvement of Great Britain and its subjects in Chilean economic and political affairs during this period, see Harold Blakemore's excellent *British Politics and Chilean Nitrates, 1886–1896: Balmaceda and North* (London: Athlone Press, 1974).

11. James, "Merchant Adventurer," p. 85½; p. 119½, fn. 5 for original sources in GP/C.

12. The following account of Egan, the *Itata* incident, and the *Baltimore* affair, all of which took place between January 1891 and January 1892, is from three major sources: Pike, *Chile and the United States;* Petersen, "Diplomatic and Commercial Relations"; and James, "Merchant Adventurer." All three drew upon original sources, and a comparison and integration of the three accounts have produced, perhaps for the first time, the complete picture of the complicated United States–Chilean relationship and the role W. R. Grace played in its development.

13. Pike, *Chile and the United States,* p. 67.

14. Ibid.

15. Ibid.

16. Ibid., p. 70.

17. Ibid.

18. James, "Merchant Adventurer," p. 86½, fn 8, quoting from Galdames, pp. 342–46; Dana Gardner Munro, *The Latin American Republics: A History* (New York: D. Appleton-Century Co., 1942), pp. 310–11; Henry Clay Evans, Jr., *Chile and Its Relations with the United States* (1927), pp. 136–139.

19. James, "Merchant Adventurer," p. 86½; p. 119½, fn 9, which is Evans, p. 138, and Washington *Post*, May 6, 1891.

20. Various letters between Edward Eyre, W. R. Grace & Co., New York, M. P. Grace and others, 1884–88, dealing with orders for arms, purchases, specifications, etc., GP/C.

21. The account of *Itata* incident is from: Osgood Hardy, "The Itata Incident," *Hispanic American Historical Review* 5 (May 1922): 195–226; Hardy, "Was Patrick Egan a Blundering Minister?" *Hispanic American Historical Review* 8 (February 1928): 65–81; Petersen, "Diplomatic and Commercial Relations," pp. 124–26; W. R. Sherman, *The Diplomatic and Commercial Relations Between the United States and Chile, 1820–1914* (Boston, 1926), pp. 146 ff.; Alice Felt Tyler, *The Foreign Policy of James G. Blaine* (Minneapolis, 1927); and James, "Merchant Adventurer," pp. 87–91½.

22. James, "Merchant Adventurer," p. 87½; p. 119½, fn. 13, *Washington Post*, May 6, 1891; Hardy, "Itata Incident," pp. 204–5.

23. James, "Merchant Adventurer," p. 87; p. 119, fn. 10.

24. *New York Times*, April 21, 1891; Hardy, "Itata Incident," pp. 202–4; *New York Herald*, May 6, 1891.

25. James, "Merchant Adventurer," p. 87½, fn. 15; Hardy, "Itata Incident," pp. 209–13.

26. *New York Commercial Advertiser* May 7, 1891; *New York Times*, May 8, 1891; *New York Herald*, May 8, 1891; *New York Evening Post*, May 9, 1891; *New York Tribune*, May 10, 1891.

27. Petersen, "Diplomatic and Commercial Relations," p. 125.

28. Ibid., p. 126.

29. Ibid., p. 125.

30. Ibid., pp. 125–26.

31. Pike, *Chile and the United States*, pp. 67–68.

32. Ibid.

33. Ibid., p. 68; Petersen, "Diplomatic and Commercial Relations," p. 127.

34. Pike, *Chile and the United States*, p. 68.

35. W. R. Grace to Augusto Matte, September 8, 1891, GP/C.

36. James, "Merchant Adventurer," p. 88½, fn. 25; *New York Herald*, September 22, 1891.

37. *New York Herald*, September 26, 1891.

38. Pike, *Chile and the United States*, pp. 71–72; Petersen, "Diplomatic and Commercial Relations," p. 128.

39. Pike, *Chile and the United States*, p. 72.

40. Ibid., pp. 71–72.

41. *New York Evening World*, September 29, 1891; *New York Journal*, September 29, 1891.

42. Pike, *Chile and the United States*, pp. 73–74.

43. Ibid., pp. 72–73.

44. Ibid.

45. Ibid., p. 75.

46. *New York Times*, October 27, 30, 1891.

47. Pike, *Chile and the United States*, p. 75.

48. James, "Merchant Adventurer," p. 89, fn. 30; Grace & Co., Valparaiso, to W. R. Grace & Co., November 4, 1891, in GP/C.

49. W. R. Grace to M. P. Grace, November 16, 1891, original in GP/C.

50. James, "Merchant Adventurer," p. 89, fn. 31.

51. Ibid.

52. Ibid.

53. W. R. Grace to W. S. Eyre, December 8, 1891, and other letters in GP/C.

54. *New York World*, November 3, 1891.

55. W. R. Grace to M. P. Grace, November 16, 1891, original in GP/C.

56. James, "Merchant Adventurer," p. 89½, fn. 35; *New York Times*, January 10, 1891; W. R. Grace to Pedro Montt, December 9, 1891; Pike, *Chile and the United States*, p. 76.

57. Pike, *Chile and the United States*, p. 76.

58. W. R. Grace to Pedro Montt, December 11, 1891, in GP/C.

59. Pike, *Chile and the United States*, p. 76; James, "Merchant Adventurer," p. 90. Pike

and James differ in some details of how the message reached the United States, but the result is the same.

60. Pike, *Chile and the United States,* p. 76.

61. Ibid., p. 78.

62. *New York World,* December 27, 1891; *New York Herald,* December 27, 1891; *New York Recorder,* December 27, 1891.

63. *Chicago Times,* January 3, 1892.

64. Pike, *Chile and the United States,* p. 77.

65. Petersen, "Diplomatic and Commercial Relations," p. 131; Pike, *Chile and the United States,* p. 79.

66. Petersen, "Diplomatic and Commercial Relations," p. 131.

67. Pike, *Chile and the United States,* p. 77.

68. Ibid.

69. W. R. Grace to M. P. Grace, February 12, 1892, GP/C.

70. Petersen, "Diplomatic and Commercial Relations," p. 132. In fn. 16, Petersen, citing *Foreign Relations,* January 21, 1892, pp. 307–8, observed that "the ultimatum probably was written by Harrison. Blaine was a sick man, and the general thrust of his policy had been that of forbearance toward Chile." The above interpretation struck this author as sound and consistent with the facts.

71. Pike, *Chile and the United States,* p. 79; James, "Merchant Adventurer," p. 91, fn. 45; U. S. Department of State, *Papers Relating to Foreign Relations,* 1891, pp. 307–8.

72. Pike, *Chile and the United States,* p. 79.

73. Petersen, "Diplomatic and Commercial Relations," p. 133; Pike, *Chile and the United States,* p. 79.

74. Pike, *Chile and the United States,* pp. 80–81. Here James erroneously—following traditional United States accounts—ascribes the Chilean response as a complete capitulation, including the offering of an "apology; indemnity; withdrawal of the Note of December 11" (p. 91), based on the Harrison threats. As the text above notes, the basis for mediating the dispute had already been reached by Montt and Blaine earlier.

75. Pike, *Chile and the United States,* p. 80.

76. Ibid.

77. Ibid., p. 81.

78. James, "Merchant Adventurer," p. 90½, fn. 39; original in GP/C.

Chapter 10

1. James A. Field, Jr., "American Imperialism; The 'Worst Chapter' in Almost Any Book," *American Historical Review* 83, no. 3 (June 1978): 644–68.

2. Marquis James, "Merchant Adventurer: The Story of W. R. Grace" (ms. 1948), p. 48½; p. 116½, fn. 29, Morgan S. Grace to W. R. Grace, February 4, 1876, GP/C.

3. Ibid.

4. W. R. Grace to J. W. Grace, August 1, 1884, GP/C.

5. W. R. Grace to "Kathleen," January 15, 1891, GP/C.

6. J. P. Grace to Marquis James, various letters, 1890–98, GP/C.

7. Ibid.

8. W. R. Grace to William E. Holloway, December 4, 1888, GP/C.

9. L. H. Stevens to W. R. Grace, December 27, 1873, GP/C.

10. Elizabeth Hall to William R. Grace, January 13, 1877, GP/C.

11. Mrs. M. E. Weymouth to W. R. Grace, June 18, 1869, GP/C.

12. Ibid.; notation by WRG on letter from Mrs. Weymouth, GP/C.

13. *New York World,* May 22, 1898; *New York Daily News,* March 25, 1897; *Catholic News,* March 28, 1897; W. R. Grace to Eda M. Chapman, April 13, 1897; W. R. Grace to Sister Mary Rose, May 21, 1897, GP/C.

14. James, "Merchant Adventurer," p. 102; p. 121, fn. 17, W. R. Grace to J. F. Fowler, August 2, 1893, GP/C.

15. Lawrence H. Shearman to W. R. Grace, August 13, 1899, GP/C.

16. J. P. Grace, New York, to Shearman, December 4, 1900, GP/C.

17. W. R. Grace to D. S. Lamont, March 10, 1887, GP/C.

18. W. R. Grace to W. R. Roberts, April 1, 1887, GP/C.

19. Ibid., p. 73½; p. 118½, fn. 60, W. R. Grace to Grover Cleveland, July 13, 1888, GP/C.

20. Grover Cleveland to W. R. Grace, July 13, 1888, GP/C.

21. James "Merchant Adventurer," pp. 91½–92; p. 120, fnn. 3–7 for original sources in GP/C.

22. Ibid., p. 91½; p. 120, fn. 1 for original sources in GP/C.

23. Ibid., pp. 92–94; pp. 120–20½, fnn. 1–25 for original sources in GP/C.

24. Ibid., pp. 95–96½; p. 120½, fnn. 42–47 for original sources in GP/C.

25. Ibid., pp. 96½–97; p. 120½, fnn. 43–55 for original sources in GP/C.

26. Ibid., pp. 97½ 98; pp. 120½–21, fnn. 56–60 for original sources in GP/C.

27. Ibid.; pp. 120½–21, fnn. 56–66 for original sources in GP/C.

28. Walter LaFeber, *The New Empire: An Interpretation of American Expansion, 1860–1898* (Ithaca: Cornell University Press, 1963), pp. 112–13.

29. *New York Times*, March 11, 1890.

30. W. R. Grace to J. G. Blaine, March 12, 1890, original sources in GP/C.

31. David McCullough, *The Path Between the Seas: The Creation of the Panama Canal, 1870–1914* (New York: Simon & Schuster, 1977), pp. 28–30.

32. David I. Folkman, Jr., *The Nicaragua Route* (Salt Lake City: University of Utah Press, 1972), p. 7.

33. Ibid., p. 19.

34. Ibid., p. 24.

35. Ibid., p. 35.

36. Jackson Crowell, "The United States and a Central American Canal, 1869–1877," *Hispanic American Historical Review* 49, no. 1 (February 1969): 27–52.

37. James, "Merchant Adventurer," pp. 104½–5; J. S. Zelaya, *Mensaje del Señor Presidente del Estado a la Asamblea Legislative en sus sesiones extraordinarias de 1898* (Managua: Tipografia Nacional, October 1898), p. 1, in GP/C. See also Lawrence A. Clayton, "John Tyler Morgan and the Nicaragua Canal, 1897–1900," *South Eastern Latin Americanist* 27, no. 2 (September 1983): 1–22; and Clayton, "Dreams of Empire: The Nicaragua Canal in the Nineteenth Century" (manuscript delivered as a paper at the 44th International Congress of Americanists, September 1982, Manchester, England), for more complete details on the American attempts to build the Nicaragua canal, including the roles of William R. Grace, Hiram Hitchcock, president of the Maritime Canal Co., and John Tyler Morgan, senator (1877–1906) from Alabama.

38. Description of Morgan from McCullough's *Path Between*, pp. 260–61.

39. Ibid.

40. Ibid., p. 261.

41. Ibid., pp. 252–53; see also Edmund Morris's monumental biography of Roosevelt's career to 1901, *The Rise of Theodore Roosevelt* (New York: Ballantine Books, 1979).

42. McCullough, *Path Between*, pp. 254–55.

43. W. R. Grace to P. W. Webb, July 28, 1898, GP/C.

44. James, "Merchant Adventurer," p. 106. For much of the following account on the maneuvering of Morgan and the Maritime supporters I have drawn from original sources in the John Tyler Morgan Papers, Manuscript Division, Library of Congress. See fn. 37 for articles based partially on this collection.

45. Zelaya, *Mensaje*, p. 1.

46. Thomas L. Karnes, *Failure of Union: Central America, 1824–1960* (Chapel Hill: University of North Carolina Press, 1961).

47. Alexander S. Bacon, San José, Costa Rica, to Edward F. Cragin, September 22, 1898, GP/C.

48. Ibid.

49. Ibid.

50. Ibid.

51. Ibid.

52. Ibid.

53. Ibid.

54. Edward Eyre, Managua, to M. P. Grace, October 16, 1898, GP/C.

55. Ibid.

56. M. P. Grace, New York, to José Santos Zelaya, October 29, 1898, GP/C.
57. Ibid.
58. Zelaya, *Mensaje*, p. 1.
59. Ibid.
60. James, "Merchant Adventurer," pp. 106½–7; p. 121½, fnn. 14–16 for original sources in GP/C.
61. Ibid., p. 106½; p. 121½, fn. 14; and W. R. Grace, New York, to J. S. Zelaya, December 7, 1898, GP/C.
62. W. R. Grace, New York, to Zelaya, December 6, 1898, GP/C.
63. Ibid., December 17, 1898, GP/C.
64. J. R. Whittle, Nashville, to W. R. Grace, November 28, 1898, GP/C.
65. F. C. Smith, Warrington, Fla., to W. R. Grace, November 19, 1898, GP/C.
66. Henry Curtis Spalding, New York, to W. R. Grace, January 4, 1899, GP/C.
67. William H. Orrett, Kingston, Jamaica, to F. G. Fischer, November 15, 1898, GP/C.
68. James, "Merchant Adventurer," pp. 107–7½; p. 121, fn. 18 for original sources in GP/C.
69. McCullough, *Path Between*, p. 264.
70. W. R. Grace, New York, to J. S. Zelaya, January 5, 1899, GP/C.
71. M. P. Grace, London, to W. R. Grace, January 18, 1899, GP/C.
72. Pedro Gonzales, Managua, to Edward Eyre, April 22, 1899, GP/C.
73. Ibid.
74. Contract Between the Government of Nicaragua and Edward Eyre and Edward F. Cragin for the Construction of the Interoceanic Canal, printed in Managua, October 31, 1898, in GP/C.
75. McCulloch, *Path Between*, pp. 256–59.
76. W. R. Grace to J. D. Phelan, May 29, 1900, GP/C.
77. "Replies to Possible Objections," typed notes, undated, with additions in W. R. Grace's handwriting, GP/C.
78. McCulloch, *Path Between*, p. 266.
79. "Analysis of Profit and Loss Account of W. R. Grace & Co., for the year ended December 31, 1891" (ms.), p. 4, GP/C.
80. James, "Merchant Adventurer," p. 101½; p. 121, fn. 16 for original sources in GP/C.
81. "Amazing Grace: The W. R. Grace Corporation," *North American Congress on Latin America, Latin America and Empire Report* 10, no. 3 (March 1976): 5. My thanks also to John R. Talbot, for providing me with invaluable information on the nature of partnerships, especially on the marvelous legalese distinctions between "winding up" and "dissolutions."
82. Joseph P. Grace, New York, to Theodore Roosevelt, March 15, 1898, GP/C.
83. Ibid.
84. J. P. Grace, New York, to John Eyre, February 21, 1900, GP/C.
85. Ibid.
86. Ibid.
87. J. P. Grace, New York, to John Eyre, August 28, 1900, GP/C.
88. J. P. Grace, New York, to J. F. Fowler, April 2, 1901, GP/C.
89. Claudio Veliz, *Historia de la marina mercante de Chile* (Santiago, Universidad de Chile, 1961), pp. 284–86.
90. J. P. Grace, New York, to L. H. Shearman, May 23, 1900, GP/C.
91. Ibid.
92. Ibid.
93. J. P. Grace, New York, to J. F. Fowler, May 23, 1900, GP/C.
94. Ibid., July 17, 1900, GP/C.
95. J. P. Grace, New York, to L. H. Shearman, December 4, 1900, GP/C.
96. J. P. Grace, New York, to J. F. Fowler, April 2, 1901, GP/C.
97. Veliz, *Historia*, p. 285.
98. Ibid., pp. 286–87.
99. T. A. H. Clark, "The Chilean Nitrate Industry," *Grace Log* 1, no. 4 (August 1918): 15–30.
100. Ibid.; "Memorandum for Mr. Vernon H. Brown," February 28, 1898, unsigned, GP/C.

101. J. P. Grace, New York, to L. H. Shearman, February 10, 1898, GP/C.

102. Robert Greenhill, "The Nitrate and Iodine Trades, 1880–1914," in D. C. M. Platt, ed., *Business Imperialism, 1840–1930: An Inquiry Based on British Experience in Latin America* (Oxford: Oxford University Press, 1977), p. 284, table 7.2.

103. Ibid., p. 250.

104. Clark, "Chilean Nitrate," pp. 27–28.

105. "Recommendation No. F, Committee on Appeals and Review, Internal Revenue Service, 1917," in GP/C.

106. Various letters from J. P. Grace to correspondents, 1900–1902.

107. James, "Merchant Adventurer," p. 110–10½; p. 121½, fn. 34 for original sources in GP/C.

108. *New York Evening Telegram,* March 21, 1904; *Brooklyn Eagle,* March 21, 1904; *New York Times,* March 22, 1904; *New York Daily News,* April 3, 1904.

109. Samuel A. Lawrence, *United States Merchant Shipping Policies and Politics* (Washington, D.C.: Brookings Institute, 1966), p. 33.

110. J. E. Saugstad, *Shipping and Shipbuilding Subsidies,* U.S. Department of Commerce, Trade Promotion Series No. 129 (Washington, D.C.: Government Printing Office, 1932), pp. 31 ff.; the above cited in fn. 6 of Lawrence, *U.S. Merchant Shipping,* p. 35.

111. Ibid., p. 40.

112. J. P. Grace, New York, to J. Fowler, July 27, 1898, GP/C.

113. Most of the above and following from three sources; an eleven-page memo by F. Sands about 1950 titled, "Grace Line"; a fourteen-page background memo prepared September 1935 for magazine article "Casa Grace," *Fortune,* December 1935 (title of the background memo is "The Grace Steamship Enterprises"); and, a speech, "Transportation of the West Coasts of South and Central America," given by J. P. Grace at Third Pan-American Commercial Conference, Washington, D.C., May 3, 1927. All are in the GP/C.

114. McCulloch, *Path Between,* p. 609; Panama Company, *Panama Canal Transit and Port Information* (Panama City, 1971), p. 35.

115. Internal company literature claims that the *Santa Clara* made the first commercial passage through the Panama Canal on June 18, 1914, but that cannot be correct, for the first full, ocean-to-ocean transit of the canal was not made until August 3 by the *Cristóbal. Santa Clara,* however, did make a test run of the Pacific locks two months before the canal was opened, but had to turn around in Gatun and make the long haul via Magellan, William Kooiman to L. A. Clayton, May 9, 1985, Point Reyes, Calif.

116. Captain F. S. Blackadar, "The 'Santa Clara' in War Time," *Grace Log* 2, no. 11 (November 1919): 21 ff.

117. Ibid.

118. Ibid.

119. Several other Grace vessels were not as fortunate as the *Santa Clara;* according to one company source, the following Grace ships were lost in this period: the *Concore* and *Cacique* by enemy action; the *Charcas* was sunk by a German submarine; the *Chincha* was turned over to the Italians; and the *Curaca* was lost in the great Halifax explosion.

120. Interview with Allen S. Rupley, New York, December 4, 1979.

121. From a listing and map of the "Grace Organization," *Grace Log* 3, no. 1 (January 1920): 32–33.

Chapter 11

1. Interview with Enrique Gómez-Sánchez, January 19, 1980, Lima.

2. See Susan Ramirez Horton's *The Sugar Estates of the Lambayeque Valley, 1670–1800: A Contribution to Peruvian Agrarian History* (Madison, Wis.: Land Tenure Center, Research Papers, no. 58, 1974).

3. Pablo Macera, *Trabajos de historia,* 4 vols. (Lima: Instituto Nacional de Cultura, 1977), 4:30 ff.

4. Ibid.

5. Peter Klaren, *Modernization, Dislocation, and Aprismo: Origins of the Peruvian Aprista*

Party, 1870–1932 (Austin: University of Texas Press, 1973), p. xx. This book is the most satisfactory history of the sugar industry in the Chicama Valley within the dates of its title.

6. Ibid.

7. Ibid., pp. 7–10, for material for Larco and Gildemeister.

8. Ibid., p. 7. fn. 10, quoting from Rafael Larco Herrera, *Veintisiete años de labor en Chiclín: Reminiscencias y apuntes* (Lima: M. Moral, 1923), p. 171.

9. Marquis James, "Merchant Adventurer, The Story of W. R. Grace" (ms., 1948), p. 42; p. 116, fn. 21, W. R. Grace to M. P. Grace, January 13, 1876, original in GP/C.

10. Details on the life of Alzamora from interview with Enrique Gómez-Sánchez.

11. Actually, the hacienda's proper name from the colonial period was San Francisco de Buenos Aires, alias Cartavio. It acquired the more common modern name from one of its seventeenth-century owners, Don Domingo de Cartavio. Furthermore, the colonial site of the plantation was different from today's location. The old plantation backed up to an ancient Indian mound, or *huaca,* still standing in the midst of field number three of the modern plantation.

12. Guillermo Alzamora to Pablo de la Barrera, April 14, 1875; it reads, "Querido y recordadado Amigo, Por la carta que me ha dirijido Pedro Melchor se que se halla Usted en Chiclin como representante de la casa de Brice Grace Y Cia que su comportamento es digno de mi antiguo amigo. Me felicito de que ya que Dios a querido tenga una persona de la confianza de dha. Cara a mi lado haya caido dha. Comision en manos de una persona tan digna como Usted de lo que me felicito. Espero que pronto tendre el gusto de darle un abrazo i mande. . . ," GP/C.

13. Shearman to M. P. Grace, January 23, 1909, Lima, GP/C; a long letter, it contains a summary of Cartavio's modern history, with emphasis on productivity, improvements, etc.

14. Contract between Guillermo Alzamora and Gabriel Larrieu, May 24, 1879, signed in Lima. The original of this contract was graciously loaned to me in January 1980 by Percy Barclay of Lima.

15. Ibid.

16. See, for example, Klaren, *Modernization,* first published in Spanish as *La formación de las haciendas azucareras y los orígenes del APRA* (Lima, 1970); Joaquin Díaz Ahumada, *Historia de las luchas sindicales en el valle de Chicama* (Trujillo: Editorial "Bolivariana," n.d.); C. D. Scott, "Peasants, Proletarianization and the Articulation of Modes of Production: The Case of Sugar Cane Cutters in Northern Peru, 1940–1969," *Journal of Peasant Studies* 3 (April 1976); Richard W. Patch, "The Role of a Coastal Hacienda in the Hispanization of Andean Indians," *American Universities Field Staff Reports* (March 15, 1959); Solomon Miller, "Hacienda to Plantation in Northern Peru: The Process of Proletarianization of the Tenant Farmer Society," in Julian Steward, ed., *Contemporary Change in Traditional Societies,* vol. 3, *Mexican and Peruvian Communities* (Urbana: University of Illinois Press, 1967); Pablo Macera, *Cayaltí, 1875–1920: organización del trabajo en una plantación azucarera del Perú* (Lima: Instituto Nacional de Cultura, 1975); and the most satisfying and balanced assessment to date, Arnold J. Bauer, "Rural Workers in Spanish America: Problems of Peonage and Oppression," *Hispanic American Historical Review* 59, no. 1 (February 1979): pp. 34–63. Michael J. Gonzales, "Capitalistic Agriculture and Labour Contracting in Northern Peru, 1880–1905," *Journal of Latin American Studies* 12, no. 2 (November 1980): 291–315, argues a position somewhere between Bauer and Klaren, citing instances and trends of both worker independence and planter abuse. Gonzales' article contains a good description of the way *enganche* worked, especially of the relationship between an *enganchador*—often a merchant or sierra landowner of some substance—and a sugar estate.

17. Klaren, *Modernization,* p. 25.

18. Ibid., p. 29.

19. Bauer, "Rural Workers," p. 37.

20. Ibid., p. 38.

21. Ibid., pp. 46–47.

22. Ibid., p. 62.

23. From Grace Brothers, Lima, to W. R. Grace & Co., March 5, 1887, Lima, GP/C.

24. Ibid.

25. Ibid.

26. Ibid.

27. Rosemary Thorpe and Geoffrey Bertram's *Peru, 1890–1977: Growth and Policy in an Open Economy* (New York: Columbia University Press, 1978), p. 28, and their "Industrialization in an Open Economy: A Case-Study of Peru, 1890–1940," in Rory Miller, Clifford T. Smith, and John Fisher, eds., *Social and Economic Change in Modern Peru* (Liverpool: Centre for Latin-American Studies, University of Liverpool, Monograph Series, no. 6, 1976).

28. Grace Brothers, Lima, to W. R. Grace & Co., March 5, 1887, Lima, GP/C.

29. Ibid.

30. Ibid.

31. Ibid.

32. Ibid.

33. Charles D. Hamil, Chairman, Committee on Appeals and Review, to Deputy Commissioner, Head, Income Tax Unit, n.d. (but about April 1924), p. 12, GP/C.

34. J. P. Grace to L. H. Shearman, August 20, 1900, GP/C.

35. Ibid., January 22, 1901, GP/C.

36. Shearman to M. P. Grace, January 23, 1909, GP/C.

37. Hamil to Income Tax Unit, 1924, GP/C.

38. Thorpe and Bertram, *Peru, 1890–1977*, pp. 44–46.

39. Ibid., p. 330.

40. Shearman to M. P. Grace, January 23, 1909, GP/C.

41. Ibid.

42. Ibid.

43. Ibid.

44. Ibid.

45. Thomas F. Sedgwick, *Relating to the Sugar Industry in Peru (with Special Mention of Hacienda Cartavio)* (Lima, 1905).

46. Later on Sedgwick moved on to Argentina, Chile, Uruguay, Colombia, Mexico, and Jamaica before returning to Hawaii to establish "The World's Agricultural and Industrial Exporting Office" in Honolulu, devoted to the sugar industry. Information from a printed flyer advertising the same firm, GP/C.

47. Klaren, *Modernization*, pp. 55–56.

48. MacDougall to Shearman, April 14, 1909, Cartavio, GP/C.

49. J. P. Grace to Shearman, September 22, 1909, Lima, GP/C.

50. Ibid.

51. Klaren, *Modernization*, p. 15; Thorpe and Bertram, *Peru, 1890–1977*, p. 46.

52. Wages had not increased absolutely between 1900 and 1910, but to the planter and owner, labor increased relative to the decline in prices. For wages, see Klaren, *Modernization*, p. 30, who quotes from George Vanderghem et al., *Memorias presentadas al Ministerio de Fomento del Perú sobre diversos viajes emprendidos en varias regiones de la república* (Lima: C. Fabbri, 1902), pp. 58–59: "The peons are paid approximately 50 centavos a day" about 1901; in "Peru's Sugar Industry," *Peru Today* 2, no. 6 (August 1910): 17–20, the daily wages in 1910 were reported at between $0.50 and $0.60.

53. In Grace Papers.

54. Clay to Shearman, April, 26, 1909, Lima, GP/C.

55. Ibid.

56. Ibid.; Clay's "firm" not identified in correspondence.

57. Ibid.

58. Coll MacDougall, "Hacienda Cartavio. Report for the Year 1908 and Prospects for 1909," April 12, 1909, GP/C.

59. Ibid.

60. Ibid.

61. See Thorpe and Bertram, *Peru, 1890–1977*, p. 340, table A. 2.3, for rise in sugar production between 1910 and 1921, tabulated yearly.

62. "La práctica moderna aplicada a la fabricación del azucar," *Grace Log* 4, no. 3 (May–June 1921): 79–84.

63. Interview with Enrique Gómez-Sánchez.

64. William Dale Peterson, "Diplomatic and Commercial Relations Between the United States and Peru from 1883 to 1918" (Ph.D. dissertation, University of Minnesota, 1969), pp. 137–38.

65. Enrique Gómez-Sánchez stated that two estates were purchased by W. R. Grace & Co. in 1917, Infantas and Caudivilla. Most other evidence does not mention Caudivilla. See, for example, *West Coast Leader*, July 10, 1920, p. 1, and letter from D. S. Iglehart to J. P. Grace, December 16, 1920, reporting on the sale of Infantas, with no mention of Caudivilla. It may be that Infantas actually had a double name, Infantas-Caudivilla, and I have so indicated in the text as the only explanation for Gómez-Sánchez's statement.

66. Edward Eyre, "Early Reminiscences of the Grace Organization" (typescript memoir, n.d.—probably authored in 1930s), 34 pp., GP/C.

67. Numerous sources were consulted for the above passages on Michael Grace and his relations with the Peruvian Corporation and the Peruvian government: "Cerro de Pasco Claim, Memorial of Michael P. Grace, April 5, 1911," 44 pp.; M. P. Grace to John Hay, Secretary of State, January 10, 1904; Edward B. Eyre to Charles G. Bennett, June 2, 1904; and others mentioned in chap. 7 on Grace Contract.

68. Edward Eyre to Charles Bennett, June 2, 1904, GP/C.

69. Thorpe and Bertram, *Peru, 1890–1977*, pp. 79 ff.

70. For example, by 1912 the company had $25 million invested in railroads, mines and smelters—Mira Wilkins, *The Emergence of Multinational Enterprise: American Business Abroad from the Colonial Era to 1914* (Cambridge: Harvard University Press, 1970), pp. 183–84.

71. The following from James, "Merchant Adventurer," p. 100½; p. 121, fn. 10, which reads: "The rebuilding and extension of the Oroya Railroad can be traced through the correspondence exchanged among the New York, London, and Lima houses, 1890–93. The sale of the lease by M. P. Grace [writing of the lease to operate the railroad] in 1893 [actually, it was part of the contract of 1890] appears in the records of the Peruvian Corporation at Lima."

72. See Thorpe and Bertram, *Peru, 1890–1977*, pp. 32–36, for rapid diversification of the economy.

73. H. R. Kelley, "The Cotton Mills of Peru," *Grace Log* 2, no. 9 (September 1919): 10–12.

74. Ibid.

75. Thorpe and Bertram, *Peru, 1890–1977*, p. 55.

76. Ibid., pp. 34, 119.

77. William S. Bollinger, "The Rise of U. S. Influence in the Peruvian Economy, 1869–1921" (M.A. thesis, University of California at Los Angeles, 1971), pp. 137–38.

78. W. T. Smithies to L. H. Shearman, December 9, 1909, and Thomas A. Lewis to Messrs. W. R. Grace & Co., Lima, December 15, 1909, GP/C.

79. Bollinger, "Rise of U. S. Influence," p. 41.

80. Interview with Allen S. Rupley, December 4, 1979, New York.

81. Hugh Exton Steele, "Electrical Development in Peru," *Grace Log* 2, no. 5 (May 1919): 13–16.

82. J. David Suárez-Torres, "Clorinda Matto de Turner," *Americas* 31, no. 8 (August 1979): 23–32.

83. Her first novel, *Aves sin nido* (1889), was an attempt "to awaken the slumbering conscience of the government"—Suárez-Torres, "Clorinda Matto," p. 30.

84. Witness today's opposition to the spread of nuclear power; objections are based on the uncertainty of a natural force, now harnessed but still capable of accidents that haunt the imagination.

85. See also *60 anōs de Empresas Eléctricas Asociadas* (Lima: Imprenta Santa Rosa, 1966).

86. Steele, "Electrical Development," p. 16; most of the above on the historical development of the electrical industry is also from the Steele article.

87. Ibid.

88. Anecdotal material on Peru in 1910 from *Peru Today* 1, nos. 11, 12 (January–February 1910).

89. The United States replaced Great Britain as the principal external influence on Peru in the second decade of the century. However, when precisely it occurred is largely a case of selecting determinants—imports, exports, direct foreign investments, loans, etc. All authors agree that the period of World War I, including the few years before and after, marked the transition.

90. James, "Merchant Adventurer," p. 110½.

Chapter 12

1. W. Elliot Brownlee, *Dynamics of Ascent: A History of the American Economy* (New York: Alfred A. Knopf, 1974), pp. 277–79.

2. Mira Wilkins, *The Maturing of Multinational Enterprise: American Business Abroad from 1914 to 1970* (Cambridge: Harvard University Press, 1974), pp. 50–52, 102–3.

3. Ibid.

4. David T. Layman, Jr., New York, to J. P. Grace, May 4, 1923, GP/C; "Casa Grace," *Fortune,* December 1935, p. 99.

5. Iglehart, Valparaiso, to J. P. Grace, January 6, 1921, GP/C.

6. Ibid.

7. A. Barrelet de Ricou, Paris, to J. P. Grace, December 2, 17, 1920, GP/C.

8. Ibid.

9. Ibid.

10. Ibid.

11. J. P. Grace, New York, to Sir William Maxwell, December 11, 1920, GP/C.

12. Ibid.

13. Ibid.

14. Iglehart, S.S. *Santa Cecilia,* to J. P. Grace, December 16, 1920, GP/C.

15. Ibid.

16. Iglehart, S.S. *Santa Louisa,* to J. P. Grace, January 27, 1921, GP/C.

17. Ibid.

18. J. P. Grace, New York, to Major Jos. Benshin, May 22, 1922, GP/C.

19. Farrer, London, to J. P. Grace, January 26, 1921, GP/C.

20. Frederick Lewis Allen, *Only Yesterday* (New York: Harper & Row, 1959), pp. 45–46.

21. Various letters, dated 1924, 1925, 1926, from Joseph P. Grace to J. P. Grace, Jr. and others, GP/C.

22. "Dita" to Janet and JPG, Sr., 1922 or 1923: to "Dearest Old Josie" and coming from Westbury House, Westbury, Long Island.

23. J. P. Grace to W. G. Holloway, January 10, 27, 1922; W. G. Holloway to J. P. Grace, February 6, May 3, 1922.

24. Ibid.

25. Ibid.

26. Ibid.

27. Ibid.

28. Ibid.

29. Ibid.

30. Ibid.

31. Iglehart, New York, to J. P. Grace, February 28, 1928, GP/C.

32. Layman, Jr., New York, to J. P. Grace, May 4, 1923, GP/C.

33. J. P. Grace, New York, to Layman, May 24, 1923, GP/C.

34. Ibid.

35. Ibid.

36. Ibid.

37. J. P. Grace, New York, to Valverde, November 10, 1924, GP/C.

38. Ibid.

39. J. P. Grace, New York, to Valverde, July 5, 1921, GP/C.

40. "Chilean Nitrate," *Grace Log* 3, no. 6 (June 1920): 196–97.

41. John H. Davis, *The Guggenheims: An American Epic* (New York: William Morrow, 1978), p. 193.

42. J. P. Grace, New York, to Wightman, January 17, 1922, GP/C.

43. R. H. Patchin to J. P. Grace, ca. 1922–23.

44. "The Machinery Business of W. R. Grace & Co.," *Grace Log* 2, no. 9 (September 1919): 13–16.

45. Ibid.

46. Interview with William H. Clayton, various dates, 1976–78, Central, S. C. Clayton joined Grace in 1923.

47. Ibid.

48. Ibid.
49. Ibid. In some cases quoting directly.
50. Ibid.
51. Ibid.
52. "Reducing Farm Costs with Chilean Nitrapo," *Grace Log* 6, no. 5 (November–December 1923): 129–31.
53. Clayton interview.
54. Ibid.
55. Ibid.
56. Ibid.
57. J. P. Grace, New York, to Carter, July 22, 1926, GP/C.
58. Clayton interview.
59. Douglas Campbell, Hacienda Cartavio, Peru, to J. P. Grace, July 15, 1922, GP/C.
60. Interview with Douglas Campbell, June 29, 1979, Cos Cob, Conn.
61. Ibid.
62. Ibid.
63. Ibid.
64. Douglas Campbell, "The Eggs" (one-page remembrance); in possession of author.
65. Campbell interview.
66. Douglas Campbell, "Si, Señor" (two-page remembrance); in possession of author.
67. Ibid.
68. Douglas Campbell, Cartavio, to J. P. Grace, July 15, 1922, GP/C.
69. Ibid.
70. In fact, Cartavio's shop and factory workers were the first granted an eight-hour day in the Chicama Valley; see Peter Klaren, *Modernization, Dislocation, and Aprismo: Origins of the Peruvian Aprista Party* (Austin: University of Texas Press, 1973), p. 38.
71. D. Campbell, Cartavio, to J. P. Grace, July 15, 1922.
72. J. P. Grace, New York, to D. Campbell, September 22, 1922, GP/C.
73. Ibid.
74. Ibid.
75. Clayton Sedgwick Cooper, "Peru's Rich Resources," *Grace Log* 5, no. 2 (March–April 1922): 38–42.
76. J. P. Grace, New York, to Russell Grace, March 12, 1924, GP/C.
77. Klaren, *Modernization*, p. 20.
78. Ibid., pp. 45 ff., to re-create the labor scene and the rise of APRA in this period.
79. Redshaw, Lima, to Iglehart, November 9, 1927, GP/C.
80. Ibid.
81. *Grace Log* 2, no. 6 (June 1919): 20.
82. Marquis James, "Merchant Adventurer: The Story of W. R. Grace" (ms., 1948), p. 39; original sources in GP/C.
83. W. C. Hebard, Lima, to Franklin Remington, December 10, 1924, GP/C.
84. Geoffrey Bertram and Rosemary Thorpe, *Peru, 1890–1977: Growth and Policy in an Open Economy* (New York: Columbia University Press, 1978), p. 122.
85. W. C. Hebard, Lima, to F. Remington, December 10, 1924, GP/C.
86. Ibid.
87. Ibid.
88. F. Remington, New York, to J. P. Grace, December 31, 1924, GP/C.
89. J. P. Grace, New York, to F. Remington, January 8, 1925, GP/C.
90. Ibid.
91. Ota, Lima, to J. P. Grace, June 25, 1921; S. Asano, Tokyo, to J. P. Grace, October 2, 1925; J. P. Grace, New York, to Asano, December 11, 1925, GP/C.
92. Ibid.
93. Ibid.
94. Ibid.
95. Ibid.
96. Ibid.
97. Ibid.
98. Ibid.
99. Ibid.
100. Thorpe and Bertram, *Peru, 1890–1977*, p. 378, fn. 37.

101. William S. Bollinger, "The Rise of United States Influence in the Peruvian Economy, 1869–1921" (M.A. thesis, University of California at Los Angeles, 1971), p. 41; "History of W. R. Grace & Co. in Peru" (in-house history in typescript), p. 53; Eugene W. Burgess and Frederick H. Harbison, *United States Business Performance Abroad: The Case Study of Casa Grace in Peru* (National Planning Association, 1954), p. 22.

102. Clayton Sedgwick Cooper, "Trade with Latin America in 1921" *Grace Log* 5, no. 1 (January–February 1922): 1–3.

103. Ibid.

104. "Casa Grace," *Fortune,* December 1935, pp. 94–164.

105. Ibid.

106. *Grace Log* 11, no. 4 (July–August 1928): 80–81.

107. "New Grace Liner 'Santa Clara' Launched," *Grace Log* 12, no. 5 (November–December 1929): 129–31.

108. *Grace Log* 5, no. 1 (January–February 1922): backpage advertisement for Grace Line.

109. Ibid., p. 32.

110. Various *Grace Logs,* 1928–30.

111. Most of foregoing from "The 'Santa Maria's' Maiden Voyage," *Grace Log* 11, no. 4 (July–August 1928): 69–71.

112. *Grace Log* 11, no. 4 (July–August 1928): backflap.

113. Fielding Robinson, "The Grace Line—North Pacific Division," *Grace Log* 3, no. 2 (November 1920): 369.

114. Ibid.

115. F. S. Durie, "The Pacific Mail Flag Around the World," *Grace Log* 3, no. 10 (October 1920): 327–29.

116. *Grace Log* 11, no. 1 (January–February 1928): 28 (advertisement).

117. Ibid., p. 29.

118. Ibid.

119. Iglehart, New York, to J. P. Grace, February 28, 1928, GP/C.

120. J. P. Grace, New York, to Gale H. Carter, July 22, 1926, GP/C.

121. Ibid.

122. Iglehart, New York, to J. P. Grace, August 7, 1930, GP/C.

123. Ibid.

124. J. P. Grace, New York, to G. H. Carter, July 22, 1926, GP/C.

125. Interview with Harold R. Harris, November 5, 1979, Falmouth, Mass.; "Sixty Years of Aviation History: One Man's Remembrance," speech by Harris at Tenth Annual Northeast Historians Meeting, Windsor Locks, Conn., October 12, 1974.

126. Harris interview.

127. Ibid.

128. Ibid.

129. Wesley Phillips Newton, *The Perilous Sky: U. S. Aviation Diplomacy and Latin America, 1919–1931* (Coral Gables, Fla.: University of Miami Press, 1978), pp. 157–70; Richard Daley, *Juan Trippe and His Pan American Empire* (New York, 1980).

130. David Lewis and Wesley Phillips Newton, *Delta: The History of an Airline* (Athens: University of Georgia Press, 1979), pp. 10 ff., for Huff Daland, the forerunner of Delta.

131. Harris interview.

132. Harris, "Sixty Years," p. 16.

133. Newton, *Perilous Sky,* pp. 24–30.

134. Harris interview.

135. Grow had come to Peru as a member of the U. S. Naval Mission and later resigned his commission to accept the position in Leguía's government—Newton, *Perilous Sky,* pp. 180–90.

136. Harris interview.

137. Ibid.

138. Ibid.; Newton, *Perilous Sky,* pp. 191–92.

139. Paper, April 13, 1944, prepared by New School for Social Research, 4 pp., GP/C.

140. Harris interview.

141. Ibid.

142. Newton, *Perilous Sky,* p. 191.

143. Harris interview.

144. Incidentally, the concession Harris obtained from the Ecuadorian government was in his name personally, with the right to transfer the concession to a corporation; thus was the Harris association with Peruvian Airways tactfully avoided. Harris interview.

145. Newton, *Perilous Sky*, pp. 232–33, 241–42.

146. See chap. 9 herein.

147. Newton, *Perilous Sky*, p. 254.

148. "Christening the New Ford Trimotor Plane, 'Santa Rosa' at Lima, Peru," *Grace Log* 12, no. 5 (November–December 1929): 139.

149. Harris interview.

150. "Inauguration of Argentine-United States Air Mail," *Grace Log* 12, no. 5 (November–December 1929): 134–35.

151. Junius B. Wood, "The United States–Argentine Air Mail: A Personal Record of a Flight over the Longest and Fastest Air Mail Route in the World," *Grace Log* 12, no. 5 (November–December 1929): 140–41, reprinted by permission of *Chicago Daily News* in *Grace Log*.

152. Ibid.

153. Interview with John Shannon, August 14, 1979, Greenwich, Conn.

154. Wood, "United States–Argentine Air Mail," p. 141.

155. "Pan American–Grace Extends Service," *Grace Log* 13, no. 3 (January–February 1930): 14.

156. J. P. Grace, New York, to Iglehart, March 5, 1930, GP/C.

157. Ibid.

158. Edward Eyre, London, to J. P. Grace, November 24, 1930, GP/C.

Bibliography

MANUSCRIPT COLLECTION

W. R. Grace & Co. Papers. Rare Book and Manuscript Library, Columbia University, New York. More than 32,000 items make up this collection, the most important body of documents for the nineteenth- and early twentieth-century history of the company.

W. R. Grace & Co. Records and Archives, W. R. Grace & Co., New York City. Housed in various areas, the records date from the 1920s through the contemporary era. Thousands of items constitute the collection, which is constantly being updated through the company's records-retention program.

Early Mayors Papers. Municipal Archives and Records Center, New York City. Valuable for the public life of W. R. Grace as mayor.

John Tyler Morgan Papers. Manuscript Collection, Library of Congress. Much on Nicaragua canal politics at end of century.

UNPUBLISHED MATERIALS

Theses and Dissertations

Bollinger, William S. "The Rise of United States Influence in the Peruvian Economy, 1869–1921." Master's thesis, University of California at Los Angeles, 1971.

Meagher, Arnold J. "The Introduction of Chinese Laborers to Latin America: The Coolie Trade, 1847–1874." Ph.D. dissertation, University of California, Davis, 1975.

Muccigrosso, Robert H. "Tammany Hall and the New York Irish in the 1884 Presidential Election." Master's thesis, Columbia University, 1961.

Nolan, Louis Clinton. "The Diplomatic and Commercial Relations of the United States and Peru, 1826–1875." Ph.D. dissertation, Duke University, 1935. Offers a description of the trade and its importance to the United States market.

Parmet, Robert D. "Cleveland, Blaine, and New York's Irish in the Elections of 1884." Master's thesis, Columbia University, 1961.
Petersen, William Dale. "The Diplomatic and Commercial Relations Between the United States and Peru from 1883 to 1918." Ph.D. dissertation, University of Minnesota, 1969.

Books

Burton, Katherine. "Anchor in Two Continents: The Story of William Russell Grace." Ca. 1939, W. R. Grace & Co. Records and Archives.
James, Marquis. "Merchant Adventurer: The Story of W. R. Grace." 1948. In galleyproof stage. Copyrighted 1980 and owned by W. R. Grace & Co. Magnificent source of biographical material on W. R. Grace by two-time Pulitzer Prize–winning biographer.

Papers, Notes, Miscellaneous

Campbell, Douglas. "The Eggs." Remembrance.
———. "Si Señor." Remembrance.
Eyre, Edward. "Early Reminiscences of the Grace Organization."
Grace, Joseph Peter. "Transportation on the West Coasts of South and Central America." Speech before Third Pan-American Commercial Conference, Washington, D.C., May 3, 1927.
Grace, Lillius. "Reminiscences."
Harris, Harold. "Sixty Years of Aviation History: One Man's Remembrance." Speech made by Harris before Tenth Annual Northeast Historians Meeting, Windsor Locks, Conn., October 12, 1974.
Quiroz Norris, Alfonso W. "Las actividades comercial-financieras de la casa Grace y la Guerra del Pacífico, 1879–1890." 1982. This excellent 27-page essay is one of the first studies based on the W. R. Grace & Co. Papers, Columbia, and adds details of Grace operations—especially financial—in Peru heretofore unknown.
Sands, F. "Grace Line."

INTERVIEWS

With Douglas Campbell, June 29, 1979, Cos Cob, Conn.
With William H. Clayton, various dates, 1976–79, Central, S.C.
With Harold R. Harris, November 5, 1979, Falmouth, Mass.
With Allen S. Rupley, December 4, 1979, New York.
With John Shannon, August 14, 1979, Greenwich, Conn.
With Enrique Gomez-Sander, January 15, 1980, Lima, Peru.

NEWSPAPERS

Brooklyn Eagle, 1880s–1904.
New York Daily News, 1880s–1904.

New York Tribune, 1880s–1890s.
New York Evening Mail, 1880s–1890s.
New York World, 1880s–1890s.
New York Staats-Zeitung, 1880s.
New York Evening Post, 1880s–1890s.
New York Sun, 1880s–1890s.
New York Commercial Advertiser, 1890s.
New York Herald, 1890s.
New York Evening World, 1890s.
New York Journal, 1890s.
New York Evening Telegram, 1880s–1904.
New York Times, 1880s–1904.

ARTICLES

"Amazing Grace: The W. R. Grace Corporation." *North American Congress on Latin America, Latin America and Empire Report* 10, no. 3 (March 1976).
Blackadar, F. S. "The 'Santa Clara' in War Time." *Grace Log* 2, no. 11 (November 1919).
Bonilla, Heraclio. "The War of the Pacific and the National and Colonial Problem in Peru." *Past and Present*, no. 81 (November 1978). A thoughtful, well-documented appraisal of the effects of the War of the Pacific on the society and economics of Peru from a Marxist point of view.
"Casa Grace." *Fortune*, December 1935.
"Chilean Nitrate." *Grace Log* 3, no. 6 (June 1920).
Clayton, Lawrence A. "Chinese Indentured Labour in Peru." *History Today* 30 (June 1980).
Cooper, Clayton Sedgwick. "Peru's Rich Resources." *Grace Log* 5, no. 2 (March–April 22).
———. "Trade with Latin America in 1921." *Grace Log* 5, no. 1 (January–February 1922).
Cortada, James W. "Diplomatic Rivalry Between Spain and the United States over Chile and Peru, 1864–1871." *Inter-American Economic Affairs* 27 (Spring 1974).
Crowell, Jackson. "The United States and a Central American Canal, 1869–1877." *Hispanic American Historical Review* 49, no. 1 (February 1969).
Durie, F. S. "The Pacific Mail Flag Around the World." *Grace Log* 3, no. 10 (October 1920).
Field, James A., Jr. "American Imperialism: The 'Worst Chapter' in Almost Any Book." *American Historical Review* 85, no. 3 (June 1978).
Grace Log 2, no. 6 (June 1919); 5, no. 1 (January–February 1922); 11, no. 1 (January–February 1928).
Greenhill, Robert. "The Nitrate and Iodine Trades, 1880–1914. In *Business Imperialism, 1840–1930: An Inquiry Based on British Experience in Latin America*, edited by D. C. M. Platt. Oxford: Clarendon Press, 1977.
Hardy, Osgood. "The Itata Incident." *Hispanic American Historical Review* 8 (February 1928).
———. "Was Patrick Egan a Blundering Minister?" *Hispanic American Historical Review* 8 (February 1928).
MacDonagh, Oliver. "Irish Emigration to the United States of America and the British Colonies During the Famine." In *The Great Famine: Studies in*

Irish History, 1845–52, edited by R. Dudley Edwards and T. Desmond Williams. Dublin: Browne & Nolan, 1956.

McDowell, R. B. "Ireland on the Eve of the Famine." *The Great Famine.*

"The Machinery Business of W. R. Grace & Co." *Grace Log* (September 1919).

Mathew, W. M. "Foreign Contractors and the Peruvian Government at the Outset of the Guano Trade." *Hispanic American Historical Review* 52, no. 4 (November 1972).

———. "Peru and the British Guano Market, 1840–1870." *Economic History Review*, 2d ser. 23, no. 1 (April 1970).

———. "A Primitive Export Sector: Guano Production in Mid-nineteenth Century Peru." *Journal of Latin American Studies* 9, no. 1 (May 1977).

Melby, John. "Rubber River: An Account of the Rise and Collapse of the Amazon Boom." *Hispanic American Historical Review* 22 (August 1942): 452–69.

Miller, Rory. "The Making of the Grace Contract: British Bondholders and the Peruvian Government, 1885–1890." *Journal of Latin American Studies* 8, no. 1 (May 1976). Article is based largely on the records of the Peruvian Corporation and clearly presents bondholders' acts and points of view. A sound piece of excellent historical research, the piece adds a dimension—the bondholders' acts—to the story of the Grace Contract that has appeared nowhere else. Furthermore, Miller concludes the article with an excellent analysis of the profitability of the Peruvian Corporation, *and* with an assessment of the impact of the railroads on Peru in the post–Grace Contract period. This constitutes the most rigorous and impartial attempt yet to evaluate fully, although largely from an economic viewpoint, the contract's effects on Peru.

"New Grace Liner 'Santa Clara' Launched." *Grace Log* 12, no. 5 (November–December 1929). Also, "Christening of the New Ford Trimotor Plane, 'Santa Rosa,' at Lima, Peru," and "Inauguration of Argentine–United States Air Mail."

O'Brien, Thomas F. "The Antofagasta Company: A Case Study of Peripheral Capitalism." *Hispanic American Historical Review* 60, no. 1 (February 1980). A recent interpretation of economic development in Chile relating foreign capital to domestic capital and postulating a thesis on the ultimate effects of the structure of capitalism in Chile.

"Pan American–Grace Extends Service." *Grace Log* 13, no. 3 (January–February 1930).

Peskin, Allan. "Blaine, Garfield, and Latin America: A New Look." *Americas* 36, no. 1 (July 1979).

Pletcher, David M. "Inter-American Trade in the Early 1970s: A State Department Survey." *Americas* 33, no. 4 (April 1977).

"Reducing Farm Costs with Chilean Nitrapo." *Grace Log* (November–December 1923).

Robinson, Fielding. "The Grace Line–North Pacific Division." *Grace Log* 3, no. 2 (November 1920).

"The Santa Maria's Maiden Voyage." *Grace Log* 11, no. 4 (July–August 1928).

"The Shipbuilders of Thomaston, Chapman and Flint." *Log Chips: A Periodical Publication of Recent Maritime History* 2, no. 7 (July 1951).

Suárez-Torres, David. "Clorinda Matto de Turner." *Americas* 31, no. 8 (August 1979). A view of feminism in nineteenth-century Peru and the emergence of the social conscience.

Wood, Junius B. "The United States–Argentine Air Mail: A Personal Record of a Flight over the Longest and Fastest Air Mail Route in the World." *Grace Log* 15, no. 5 (November–December 1929).

Worcester, Donald E. "Naval Strategy in the War of the Pacific." *Journal of Inter-American Studies* 5 (January 1963).

BOOKS

Allen, Frederick Lewis. *Only Yesterday*. New York: Harper & Row, 1959.
Basadre, Jorge. *Historia de la República del Perú*, vol. 6, 5th ed. 6 vols. Lima: Ediciones "Historia," 1962.
Bernasconi, Edmundo Civati. *Guerra del Pacífico*. Buenos Aires, 1946.
Bertram, Geoffrey, and Thorpe, Rosemary. *Peru–1890–1977: Growth and Policy in an Open Economy*. New York: Columbia University Press, 1978.
Blakemore, Harold. *British Politics and Chilean Nitrates, 1886–1896: Balmaceda and North*. London: Athlone Press, 1974.
Bonilla, Heraclio. *Guano y burguesía en el Perú*. Lima: Instituto de Estudios Peruanos, 1974.
Bowser, Frederick P. *The African Slave in Colonial Peru, 1524–1650*. Stanford: Stanford University Press, 1974. A major study of blacks in the early Peruvian colony.
Breen, Matthew P. *Thirty Years of New York Politics, Up-to-Date*. New York: published by author, 1899.
Brownlee, Elliot W. *Dynamics of Ascent: A History of the American Economy*. New York: Alfred A. Knopf, 1974.
Bulnes, Gonzalo, *Resumen de la Guerra del Pacific*. Santiago: Editorial del Pacífico, 1976.
Burgess, Eugene W., and Harbison, Frederick H. *United States Business Performance Abroad: The Case Study of Casa Grace in Peru*. National Planning Association, 1954.
Burr, Robert N. *By Reason or Force: Chile and the Balancing of Power in South America, 1839–1905*. Berkeley and Los Angeles: University of California Press, 1965.
Caivano, Tommaso. *Historia de la guerra de America entre Chile y Bolivia*. 2 vols. Iquique, 1904.
Castillo, Ernesto Yepes del. *Peru, 1820–1920: Un siglo de desarrollo capitalista*. Lima: Instituto de Estudios Peruanos, 1971.
Crosby, Alfred W. *The Columbian Exchange: Biological and Cultural Consequences of 1492*. Westport, Conn.: Greenwood Press, 1972.
Daley, Richard. *An American Saga: Juan Trippe and his Pan American Empire*. New York: Random House, 1980. It does not have the historical depth about aviation in the 1920s related to Latin America that is contained in the Newton book. I have preferred the latter for its thoroughness in writing parts of chap. 12 related to aviation in Latin America.
Davis, John H. *The Guggenheims: An American Epic*. New York: William Morrow, 1978.
Davis, William C. *The Last Conquistadors: The Spanish Intervention in Peru and Chile, 1863–1866*. Athens: University of Georgia Press, 1950.
Dennis, William Jefferson. *Tacna and Arica: An Account of the Chile-Peru Boundary Dispute and of the Arbitration by the United States*. New Haven: Yale University Press, 1931.
Duffield, A. F. *The Prospects of Peru: The End of the Guano Age and a Description Thereof*. London: Newman & Co., 1881.
Edwards, R. Dudley, and Williams, Desmond T., eds. *The Great Famine: Studies in Irish History, 1845–1852*. New York: Russell & Russell, 1956.

Fisher, Lillian. *The Last Inca Revolt, 1780–1783*. Norman: University of Oklahoma Press, 1966.

Flint, Charles R. *Memories of an Active Life: Men, Ships, and Sealing Wax*. New York: G. P. Putnam's Sons, 1923.

Folkman, David I., Jr. *The Nicaragua Route*. Salt Lake City: University of Utah Press, 1972. Set in the midnineteenth century and a good presentation of the basics of the Nicaragua route.

Gibson, Florence E. *The Attitudes of the New York Irish Toward State and National Affairs, 1848–1892*. New York: Columbia University Press, 1951.

Grace, Morgan S. *A Sketch of the New Zealand War*. London: Horache Marshall & Son, 1899.

Herreshoff, Lewis Francis. *Captain Nat Herreshoff, the Wizard of Bristol: The Life and Achievements of Nathaniel Greene Herreshoff*. New York: Sheridan House, 1953.

Hershkowitz, Leo. *Tweed's New York: Another Look*. Garden City, N.Y.: Doubleday, Anchor Press, 1977.

History and Description of "Casa Grace" Activities in the Republic of Chile. Santiago, 1953. Privately printed by W. R. Grace & Co. in Chile.

History of W. R. Grace & Co. in Peru, 1854–1972. Inhouse history in typescript.

Hobsbawn, E. J. *Industry and Empire: The Making of Modern English Society*. Vol. 2, *1750 to the Present Day*. New York: Pantheon Books, 1968.

Horton, Susan Ramirez. *The Sugar Estates of the Lambayeque Valley, 1670–1800: A Contribution to Peruvian Agrarian History*. Madison, Wis.: Land Tenure Center, 1974. Good introduction to sugar growing in one area of colonial Peru.

Hudson, William C. *Random Recollections*. New York: Cupples & Leon Company, 1911.

Ivins, William. *Machine Politics and Money in New York City*. New York: Harper Brothers, 1887. Ivins' account of his years with William Grace.

Karnes, Thomas L. *Failure of Union: Central America, 1824–1960*. Chapel Hill: University of North Carolina Press, 1961. Best work in English on the subject.

————. *Tropical Enterprise: Standard Fruit and Steamship Company in Latin America*. Baton Rouge: Louisiana State University Press, 1979. Excellent introduction to rise of the banana trade.

Keller, Morton. *Affairs of State: Public Life in Late Nineteenth Century America*. Cambridge: Harvard University Press, Belknap Press, 1977.

Kemble, John H. *The Panama Route, 1848–1869*. Berkeley and Los Angeles: University of California Press, 1943. Best study of Panama Railroad in its early days.

Klaren, Peter. *Modernization, Dislocation, and Aprismo: Origins of the Peruvian Aprista Party, 1870–1932*. Austin: University of Texas Press, 1973.

LaFeber, Walter. *The New Empire: An Interpretation of American Expansion, 1860–1898*. Ithaca: Cornell University Press, 1963.

Lawrence, Samuel A. *United States Merchant Shipping Policies and Politics*. Washington, D.C.: Brookings Institute, 1966.

Levin, Jonathan V. *The Export Economics: Their Pattern of Development in Historical Perspective*. Cambridge: Harvard University Press, 1960.

Lewis, David, and Newton, Wesley Phillips. *Delta: The History of an Airline*. Athens: University of Georgia Press, 1979.

McCulloch, David. *The Path Between the Seas: The Creation of the Panama Canal, 1870–1914*. New York: Simon & Schuster, 1977. Splendid account of Panama Canal, combining best scholarship with storytelling ability.

Macera, Pablo. *Trabajos de Historia*. 4 vols. Lima: Instituto Nacional de Cultura, 1977.

Mandelbaum, Seymour J. *Boss Tweed's New York*. New York: John Wiley & Sons, 1965.

Markham, Clements R. *The War Between Peru and Chile, 1879–1882*. London, 1882.

Millington, Herbert. *American Diplomacy During the War of the Pacific*. New York: Columbia University Press, 1948.

Morgan, H. Wayne. *From Hayes to McKinley: National Party Politics, 1877–1896*. Syracuse, N.Y.: Syracuse University Press, 1969.

Morris, Edmund. *The Rise of Theodore Roosevelt*. New York: Ballantine Books, 1979. Monumental biography of Roosevelt's career to 1901.

Myers, Gustavus. *The History of Tammany Hall*. New York: Boni & Liveright, 1917.

Nevins, Allan. *Grover Cleveland: A Study in Courage*. New York: Dodd, Mead, 1933. Most comprehensive biography of Cleveland.

Newton, Wesley Phillips. *The Perilous Sky: U. S. Aviation Diplomacy and Latin America, 1919–1931*. Coral Gables, Fla.: University of Miami Press, 1978.

Panama Agencies Company. *Panama Canal Transit and Port Information*. Panama City, 1971.

Peck, G. W. *Melbourne and the Chincha Islands, with Sketches of Lima and a Voyage Around the World*. New York: Charles Scribner, 1854.

Phelan, John Leddy. *The People and the King: The Comunero Revolution in Colombia, 1781*. Madison: University of Wisconsin, 1978.

Pike, Fredrick B. *Chile and the United States, 1880–1962*. Notre Dame, Ind.: Notre Dame University Press, 1963.

———. *The United States and the Andean Republics: Peru, Bolivia and Ecuador*. Cambridge: Harvard University Press, 1977.

Platt, D. C. M., ed. *Business Imperialism, 1840–1930: An Inquiry Based on British Experience in Latin America*. Oxford: Oxford University Press, 1977.

———. *Latin America and British Trade, 1806–1914*. London: Adam & Charles Black, 1972; New York: Harper & Row, 1973.

Pletcher, David M. *The Awkward Years: American Foreign Relations Under Garfield and Arthur*. Columbia: University of Missouri Press, 1972.

Poppino, Rollie. *Brazil: The Land and People*. New York and Oxford: Oxford University Press, 1968.

Reyna, Alberto Wagner de. *Las relaciones diplomáticas entre el Perú y Chile durante el conflicto con España, 1864–1867*. Lima: Ediciones del Sol, 1963.

Ritchie, Pedro Espina. *Monitor Huascar*. Santiago: Editorial Andres Bello, 1974.

Robinson, David A. *Peru in Four Dimensions*. Lima: American Studies Press, 1964. Extraordinarily perceptive and detailed fountain of information on Peru.

Saugstad, J. E. *Shipping and Shipbuilding Subsidies*. U. S. Department of Commerce, Trade Promotion Series, no. 129. Washington: Government Printing Office, 1932.

Sherman, William R. *The Diplomatic and Commercial Relations Between the United States and Chile, 1820–1914*. Boston: R. G. Badger, 1926.

Soldan, Mariano Felipe Paz. *Narración histórica de la guerra de Chile contra el Perú y Bolivia*. Buenos Aires: Imprenta de Mayo, 1884.

Stewart, Watt. *Chinese Bondage in Peru: A History of the Chinese Coolie in Peru, 1849–1874*. Durham: Duke University Press, 1951.

———. *Henry Meiggs: Yankee Pizarro*. Durham: Duke University Press, 1946.

———. *Keith and Costa Rica: A Biographical Study of Minor Cooper Keith*. Albuquerque: University of New Mexico Press, 1964.

Summersell, Charles G. *The Journal of George Townley Fullam: Boarding Officer of the Confederate Sea Raider Alabama.* University, Ala.: By the Friends of the Mobile Public Library through the University of Alabama Press, 1973.

Trevelyan, George Macaulay. *British History in the Nineteenth Century and After (1782–1919).* New York: David McKay, 1962.

Tschudi, J. J. von. *Travels in Peru, on the Coast, in the Sierra, Across the Cordilleras and the Andes, into the Primeval Forests.* Translated from German by Thomasina Ross. New York: A. S. Barnes, 1847.

Tyler, Alice Felt. *The Foreign Policy of James G. Blaine.* Minneapolis: University of Minnesota Press, 1927

Valcarcel, Carlos Daniel. *Tupuc Amaru.* Lima, n.d.

Van Aken, Mark. *Pan-Hispanism: Its Origin and Development to 1866.* Berkeley: University of California Press, 1959.

Veliz, Claudio. *Historia de la marina mercante de Chile.* Santiago: Universidad de Chile, 1961.

Vidal, Ramon Menendez. *The Spaniards in Their History.* New York: W. W. Norton, 1950. Short, brilliant, inductive essay on counterpoint in the Spanish character.

Werlich, David. *Peru: A Short History.* Carbondale: University of Southern Illinois Press, 1978.

Whipple, A. B. C. *The Whalers.* Alexandria, Va.: Time-Life Books, 1979.

Wilhelm, Joseph. *The Family of Grace: Pedigrees and Memoirs Collected and Edited.* London: Kegan Paul, Trench, Trubner & Co., 1911. Excellent work that surpasses mere genealogy, as the title may imply; broadly traces Irish history from twelfth century to early twentieth, delineating the family's development.

Wilkins, Mira. *The Maturing of Multinational Enterprise: American Business Abroad from 1914 to 1970.* Cambridge: Harvard University Press, 1974.

Woodward, E. L. *The Age of Reform, 1815–1870.* Oxford: Clarendon Press, 1938.

Woodward, Ralph Lee. *Central America: A Nation Divided,* 2nd Ed. New York: Oxford University Press, 1985. Best general survey of Central American history.

Zelaya, J. S. *Mensaje del Señor Presidente del Estado a la Asamblea Legislative en sus sesiones extraordinarias de 1898.* Managua: Tipografía Nacional, October 1898.

Index